Contemporary Perspectives on European Integration

Recent Titles in
Contributions in Political Science
Series Editor: Bernard K. Johnpoll

The Fall and Rise of the Pentagon: American Defense Policies in the 1970s
Lawrence J. Korb

Calling a Truce to Terror: The American Response to International Terrorism
Ernest Evans

Spain in the Twentieth Century World: Essays on Spanish Diplomacy, 1898–1978
James W. Cortada

From Rationality to Liberation: The Evolution of Feminist Ideology
Judith A. Sabrosky

Truman's Crises: A Political Biography of Harry S. Truman
Harold F. Gosnell

"Bigotry!": Ethnic, Machine, and Sexual Politics in a Senatorial Election
Maria J. Falco

Furious Fancies: American Political Thought in the Post-Liberal Era
Philip Abbott

Politicians, Judges, and the People: A Study in Citizens' Participation
Charles H. Sheldon and Frank P. Weaver

The European Parliament: The Three-Decade Search for a United Europe
Paula Scalingi

Presidential Primaries: Road to the White House
James W. Davis

The Voice of Terror: A Biography of Johann Most
Frederic Trautmann

Presidential Secrecy and Deception: Beyond the Power to Persuade
John M. Orman

The New Red Legions
Richard A. Gabriel

Contemporary Perspectives on European Integration

ATTITUDES, NONGOVERNMENTAL BEHAVIOR, AND COLLECTIVE DECISION MAKING

Edited by Leon Hurwitz

CONTRIBUTIONS IN POLITICAL SCIENCE, NUMBER 45

GREENWOOD PRESS•WESTPORT, CONNECTICUT

Grateful acknowledgment is given for the permission to use:
Figures 6.1 and 6.2 that were taken from *Agropolitics in the European Community: Interest Groups and the Common Agricultural Policy* by William F. Averyt, Jr. Copyright © 1977 by Praeger Publishers, Reprinted by permission of Holt, Rinehart and Winston.

Figure 6.3 that was taken from *Domestic Political Realities and European Integration: A Study of Mass Publics and Elites in the European Community Countries* by Werner J. Feld and John K. Wildgen. Copyright © 1976 by Westview Press. Reprinted by permission of Westview Press.

Library of Congress Cataloging in Publication Data

Main entry under title:

Contemporary perspectives on European integration.

(Contributions in political science; no. 45 ISSN 0147–1066)
Bibliography: p.
Includes index.
1. European Economic Community—Addresses, essays, lectures. 2. Europe—Economic integration—Addresses, essays, lectures. 3. European Parliament—Addresses, essays, lectures. I. Hurwitz, Leon. II. Series.
HC241.2.C683   341.24'2   79–6573
ISBN 0–313–21357–7 lib. bdg.

Library of Congress Catalog Card Number: 79–6573
ISBN: 0–313–21357–7
ISSN: 0147–1066

First published in 1980

Greenwood Press
A division of Congressional Information Service, Inc.
88 Post Road, Westport, Connecticut 06880

Printed in the United States of America

10 9 8 7 6 5 4 3 2 1

To my wife Fran

LH

Contents

Figures   ix

Tables   xi

Preface   xv

Acknowledgments   xix

INTRODUCTORY ESSAY

1. *Leon Hurwitz*, Contemporary Perspectives on EC
   Integration: Attitudes, Nongovernmental Behavior,
   and Collective Decision Making   3

PART I. INTEGRATION AT THE ATTITUDINAL LEVEL

2. *Ronald Inglehart and Jacques-René Rabier*, Europe
   Elects a Parliament: Cognitive Mobilization, Political
   Mobilization, and Pro-European Attitudes as Influences
   on Voter Turnout   27

3. *Elisabeth Noelle-Neumann*, Phantom Europe: Thirty
Years of Survey Research on German Attitudes Toward
European Integration   53

PART II. INTEGRATION AT SOCIETY'S LEVEL: TRANS-
ACTION FLOWS AND NONGOVERNMENTAL
BEHAVIOR

4. *Wilfried Prewo*, Trade, Interdependence, and European
Integration   77

5. *Emil J. Kirchner*, Interest Group Behavior at the
Community Level   95

PART III. INTERNAL EC COLLECTIVE DECISION MAKING
AND ITS DOMESTIC REALITIES

6. *Werner J. Feld*, Two-Tier Policy Making in the EC:
The Common Agricultural Policy   123

7. *Stephen D. Kon*, The Delicate Balance Between Municipal
Law and Community Law in the Application of Articles 85
and 86 of the Treaty of Rome   151

8. *Roger Vaissière and Jean-Marc Mascaro*, Health Policies
in the EC: Attempts at Harmonization   171

9. *Robert J. Lieber*, Energy, Political Economy, and the
Western European Left: Problems of Constraint   189

10. *Donald J. Puchala*, European Fiscal Harmonization:
Politics During the Dutch Interlude   209

PART IV. EXTERNAL EC COLLECTIVE DECISION MAKING
AND ITS INTERNATIONAL REALITIES

11. *Corrado Pirzio-Biroli*, Foreign Policy Formation within
the European Community with Special Regard to
the Developing Countries   225

12. *Harold S. Johnson*, EC-US Relations in the Post-Kissinger
Era   255

Abbreviations   271

Bibliographical Essay   275

Index   279

Figures

2.1 Attitude Toward the Election of the European Parliament   28

4.1 Preference and Language Coefficients and Tariff Elasticities,
     1958–74   90

6.1 Farm Interest Group Strategies   135

6.2 Farm Interest Group Emergency Strategies   136

9.1 Schematic Diagram of Policy Choices for a Leftist Gov-
     ernment: Some Past, Present, and Future Choices   202

Tables

2.1 Rates of Electoral Participation for the Election of the European Parliament and for the Most Recent National Election   29

2.2 Voters Saying They Would "Certainly" Vote in the Election of the European Parliament   30

2.3 Attitude Expected of a Member of the European Parliament, by Level of Cognitive Mobilization   33

2.4 Assessment of Whether Membership in Common Market is Good or Bad, by Level of Cognitive Mobilization   34

2.5 Assessment of Common Market Membership by Cognitive Mobilization, by Nation   35

2.6 Respondents Classified as "Voters" and Actual Turnout in the European Community   36

2.7 Predicted Turnout for European Elections, by Level of Cognitive Mobilization   36

2.8 Awareness of European Elections Among EC Publics, April 1979   37

2.9 Predicted Turnout for European Elections, by Awareness of Elections and Campaign   38

2.10 Diffuse Support for European Unification, by Nation   40

2.11 Utilitarian Assessment of Country's Membership in Common
      Market, by Nation   41

2.12 Voter Turnout, by Assessment of Nation's Membership in
      Common Market   42

2.13 Assessments of Nation's Membership in Common Market
      Among Voters and Nonvoters   43

2.14 Distribution Between the Political Groups of the Members
      of the European Parliament Before and After the Election   45

2.15 Distribution of the Members of the European Parliament, by
      Country and by Political Trend, Before and After the Election   46

2.16 Comparison of the Votes Obtained by the Political Groups
      in the Most Recent National Elections and in the European
      Election   47

2.17 Predicted Turnout by Left-Right Self-Placement   48

2.18 Turnout, by Vote in Last National Election   49

3.1   Attitude Toward Continuation of the EC   54

3.2   Belief in Progress   55

3.3   Attitude Toward a United States of Europe   56

3.4   Attitude Toward the European Parliament   57

3.5   Attitude Toward a European Currency   57

3.6   Attitude Toward a European Government   58

3.7   Attitude Toward a European Olympic Team   58

3.8   Attitude Toward a European Flag   59

3.9   Attitude Toward Closeness of EC Countries   59

3.10 Attitude Toward Membership in the EC   60

3.11 Interest in the Problems of the EC   61

3.12 Extent of Knowledge about the European Parliament   62

3.13 Attitude Toward the Future Form of Europe   63

3.14 Attitude Toward German National Identity   64

3.15 Attitude Toward Language Differences   64

3.16 Attitude Toward Cultural and National Identity   65

3.17 Attitude Toward Rate of European Integration   66

3.18 Attitude Toward Economic Benefits of the EC   67

3.19 Attitude Toward Economic Disadvantages of the EC   68

3.20 Attitude Toward German Membership in the EC   68

3.21 Attitude Toward Future Membership of a United Europe   69

3.22 Attitude Toward Other People's Views on the Future
      Membership of a United Europe   70

3.23 The Railway Test   71

3.24 Attitude Toward the EC as a Step Toward World Government 72

3.25 European Attitude Toward Conservatism   73

4.1   EC Imports from OECD Countries, 1958–74   84

4.2   EFTA Imports from OECD Countries, 1958–72   85

4.3   Estimates for Major Variables, 1958–74   89

5.1   Formation of European Interest Groups   102

5.2   Type of Decision Making Practiced on Policies for
      External Purposes   107

5.3   Extent of Contacts with the EC Institutions   111

6.1   Trend of Revenues from Import Levies and Levies on
      Sugar, 1971–76   127

6.2   Breakdown by Groups of Sectors of Aid Granted,
      1964–76   130

6.3   Functions of Civil Servants and Integration   143

8.1   Some Comparative Figures on Density, Number, and Rate of
      Increase of Physicians in the EC   174

8.2   Approximate Annual Income of Physicians in the EC   182

8.3   Effect of Free Circulation of Physicians in France, 1978 185

9.1   Energy Sources, 1975   191

9.2   EC Energy Consumption: Estimates and Targets   194

Preface

The views and opinions expressed in this book are those of the authors, and they do not necessarily represent the views of the European Commission, any other agency of the European Communities, or of any national government or public institution. The institutional affiliations of the contributors are given for informational purposes only.

The goal of this book is to present in one volume a collection of perspectives on the contemporary nature of European integration. Some of the essays have been contributed by the leading scholars in the field; all are original and were written expressly for this volume. Many of the contributors have had direct experience with the European Community and/or national governmental agencies and, although the disclaimer is offered that the views expressed by the authors do not necessarily represent those of the European Commission or of any national government, these essays do have the advantage of personal experience and information.

The essays reflect a balance among theoretical overviews on the nature of the integrative process, empirical data analyses, and descriptive-narrative case studies. There is also a balance between American and European perspectives since several of the essays have been contributed by my European colleagues: Emil Kirchner is at the University of Essex; Stephen Kon is at the University of Sussex; Elisabeth Noelle-Neumann is at Johannes Gutenberg

University and at the Institut für Demoskopie Allensbach; Corrado Pirzio-Biroli, an Italian national, is currently employed as an economic counselor at the Delegation of the European Commission to the United States in Washington, D.C; Wilfried Prewo is at the Institut für Weltwirtschaft in Kiel; Jacques-René Rabier is currently a special advisor to the EC Commission for Public Opinion; and Roger Vaissière and Jean-Marc Mascaro are French physicans. Other than myself, the American contingent is composed of Werner J. Feld (University of New Orleans); Ronald Inglehart (University of Michigan); Harold Johnson (Michigan State University); Robert J. Lieber (University of California at Davis); and Donald J. Puchala (Columbia University).

The essays also reflect a fair representation of disciplines. Although the editor and a majority of the contributors are political scientists, the services of people from other disciplines have been enlisted to present alternative approaches: law (Kon); economics (Pirzio-Biroli and Prewo); mass communications (Noelle-Neumann); and medicine (Vaissière and Mascaro). Their essays serve as valuable counterbalances to those of the political scientists.

Part I of this collection deals with integration at the attitudinal level and contains two essays. The first, written by Ronald Inglehart and Jacques-René Rabier, analyzes the recent (June 1979) election for the European Parliament. The second essay, written by Elisabeth Noelle-Neumann, deals with German public opinion toward the EC and European integration. Part II deals with integration at society's level and also includes two essays: Wilfried Prewo presents a most rigorous examination of transaction flow analysis applied to recent European trade flow data; Emil Kirchner's essay concerns interest group activity at the Community level.

Part III deals with collective decision making in areas internal to the EC, with "internal" here referring to relations among the nine EC countries. There are essays by Werner J. Feld on the common agricultural policy; Stephen Kon on competition law; Roger Vaissière and Jean-Marc Mascaro on health policies; Robert J. Lieber on the relationship between the EC's energy policy (or lack thereof) and domestic national policies; and Donald J. Puchala on the decision-making process in the Netherlands on the implementation of the tax on value added (VAT). The final section is concerned with external collective decision making, that is, decisions and policies dealing with countries other than the Nine, and there are two essays in Part IV. The first is by Corrado Pirzio-Biroli on the formulation of foreign policy in the EC Commission's Directorate-General for Development, and the final essay, written by Harold Johnson, presents a discussion of the EC's current relationships with the United States.

Some brief comments about the institutional framework of the EC are presented at this point before the general reader begins the essays. The term "European Community" (or "European Communities") is the collective

name of the European Coal and Steel Community (ECSC), the European
Economic Community (EEC or the Common Market), and the European
Atomic Energy Community (Euratom). Prior to July 1, 1967, each of these
three communities had its own executive institutions (the ECSC's Commission was called the "High Authority"). In 1967, these three merged and now
share the same institutions, although each maintains a separate legal character. This merger into the "European Community" has allowed increased
policy coordination in the areas covered by each separate community. A single
Commission and a single Council of Ministers now govern community policy.

The Community's executive is divided: the Commission proposes and
supervises the execution of laws and policies, and the Council of Ministers en-
acts laws and programs, based on Commission proposals. The Commission is
a collegiate body, representing the nine member states. The national governments appoint the members for four-year renewable terms. Although appointed by member states, the Commission is expected to be independent and
to consider the interests of the Community as a whole rather than the specific
interests of any individual state.

The Council of Ministers is the Community's main decision-making unit. It
is composed of one minister from each of the nine members, and it represents
the national viewpoints and interests that are a part of the decision-making process. Ministers with different portfolios attend Council meetings, depending
upon the agenda, but it is usually the nine Foreign Ministers who participate.
The Council can make most decisions by a simple or "weighted" majority vote
but usually tries to achieve unanimity. Some decisions—acceptance of a new
member—must be unanimous.

The other main Community institutions are the European Parliament, the
Court of Justice, the Committee of Permanent Representatives (CPR or
COREPER, following its French title), and the Economic and Social Com-
mittee (ESC).

The European Parliament has undergone some recent changes. Prior to
June 1979, the Parliament consisted of 198 members, appointed from and by
the national legislatures. The appointment procedure was similar to the
method of appointing members to the United States Senate before the Seven-
teenth Amendment was passed. The Parliament's power was limited but, in
June 1979, its members were directly elected by the people in the nine
member states. There are now 410 members who sit together as members of
transnational party federations that have, in varying degrees, worked out joint
political programs. As a democratically elected body, the new European
Parliament possesses a political legitimacy that the former, appointed
Parliament never had. This does not automatically give it a more influential
role in decision making at the European level, but it strengthens the
Parliament's potential to do so.

The Court of Justice (not to be confused with the International Court of Justice at The Hague or with the European Court of Human Rights at Strasbourg) is the Community's "Supreme Court." There is one judge from each member state, judges are appointed by the member states for a term of six years. The decisions of the Court are final and cannot be appealed in national courts. The Court of Justice attempts to maintain law and justice in the interpretation and application of the various treaties and laws passed to execute them. Appeals may be brought to the Court by a member state, the Council of Ministers, the Commission, or any person or company affected by a Community decision.

The Committee of Permanent Representatives is composed of the nine member countries' ambassadors to the Community. This Committee does much of the groundwork for Council meetings by reviewing Commission proposals and indicating areas of agreement among the national viewpoints. The Economic and Social Committee has no power of decision, but it does influence policy making and must be consulted by the Commisson and Council on most major policy proposals. The Committee members are selected from labor, management, agricultural, consumer, professional, and family organizations. The ESC is one of the Community's major avenues for involving the European public in the decision-making process.

Acknowledgments

This book is a collaborative and cooperative effort. I have received aid and comfort from numerous people, and I would like to acknowledge their help. Most important, I am indebted to all the contributors—Werner J. Feld, Ronald Inglehart, Harold Johnson, Emil Kirchner, Stephen Kon, Robert J. Lieber, Jean-Marc Mascaro, Elisabeth Noelle-Neumann, Corrado Pirzio-Biroli, Wilfried Prewo, Donald J. Puchala, Jacques-René Rabier, and Roger Vaissière—for graciously providing the essays and suffering through my editing.

The Department of Political Science at Cleveland State University, especially its chairperson Ev Cataldo, has been most generous in terms of financial assistance and for providing an atmosphere conducive to research. The Office of Provost/Academic Vice-President at Cleveland State University has also been most generous in providing financial support, and I wish to thank John Flower and Melvin Dunn. For most efficient secretarial services, my thanks go to Leslie Bowman, Katy Hanrahan, James Lebovitz, Charles Urbancic, and the Word Processing Center of the College of Arts and Sciences at Cleveland State University.

I also want to thank the editorial and production staff at Greenwood Press for their professional assistance, particularly Bernard K. Johnpoll, series editor for Greenwood's Contributions in Political Science, Margaret M.

Brezicki, and Mildred Vasan. James T. Sabin, Greenwood's editorial vice-president, deserves special mention since this book was really his idea, and his continuous support was most appreciated.

I also want to thank Holt, Rinehart and Winston and Westview Press for granting permission to print some previously copyrighted material.

Several people rendered specific assistance, and each will know what I am thanking them for: Marc and Susan Millius, John Holm, Bob Charlick, Tom Pelsoci, Sidney Kraus, Joseph Caplin, Henry Anna, Ted Wright, Jr., John Nagle, Rodger Govea, Bela Balassa, Benjamin Cohen, Barry Hughes, Edward Morse, Roger Benjamin, and Wolfgang Koschnick.

I want to thank my children, Elise and Jonathan, for suffering (although not in silence) through this project and my wife, Fran, who still shows more interest in and understanding of my writing on political science than I show in her writings on composite materials.

Finally, in this collaborative effort, whatever merit the reader may see in this book rightly belongs to my colleagues who wrote the essays; any shortcomings belong to the editor.

INTRODUCTORY ESSAY

LEON HURWITZ

1

Contemporary Perspectives on EC Integration: Attitudes, Nongovernmental Behavior, and Collective Decision Making

As I have written elsewhere,[1] an important milestone was reached in the European integrative process when Denmark, Ireland, and the United Kingdom formally entered the European Economic Community on January 1, 1973. The six original European Community countries perceived the intracommunity consensus and integration levels to have been of sufficient strength and stability to deal with the problems inherent in the expansion by 50 percent in the number of participants in the decision-making process and in the marked increase in the group's heterogeneity. Decisions that previously had to synthesize six separate (and often quite diverse) views must now, in the post-1973 period, reconcile nine national interests and positions.

The short-term result of this increase in numbers and cultural heterogeneity may very well be less decisional output or, and this is the more likely alternative, output that is more limited in scope or applicability. With nine participants, a decision-making process utilizing either the lowest common denominator or splitting the difference will result in a lower level of output than the same process in a group of six. Only with the upgrading of common interests will the countries of the EC continue with what appears to be a most remarkable performance in international integration and community building.

Regardless of the alleged dysfunctional, short-term results injected into the decision-making process, it nonetheless appears that the original six felt secure enough among themselves so that the three additional participants would not unravel the accomplishments achieved prior to 1973. Indeed, some recent EC decisions question this assertion of lower or more limited decisional output. The 1975 Council of Ministers' Directive giving "European" status to EC physicians and thus permitting them "free circulation" entered into force in December 1976; the European Monetary System [EMS], an attempt to control fluctuations in exchange rates, began operation in March 1979; the first direct election for the European Parliament took place in 1979; and the 1980s will probably witness the entry of Spain, Portugal, and Greece into the EC. These actions do present evidence of concrete policies at a rather high level of scope and applicability.

The literature is not in total agreement, of course, that levels of consensus and integration are increasing along all the variables comprising the integration process. Several studies have demonstrated in quite a systematic fashion that, along specific dimensions, consensus and integration within the EC were not appreciably higher even ten or fifteen years after the Rome Treaty. Donald J. Puchala shows, for example, that Franco-German integration levels moved in different directions for different variables between 1955 and 1965. Puchala writes that several of the political amalgamation indices reflected "disintegration in process," whereas community formation (bonds of confidence, amity, and interdependence) increased during the same period.[2] More recently, Charles G. Nelson, employing a modified version of the Savage-Deutsch RA [relative acceptance] model on international trade data, concluded that EC members' preferences for one another have increased only modestly since the establishment of the EC and that other groups of Western industrial countries have shown a greater rise in intragroup trade preference in the same period than has the EC. Nelson's study suggests that only a little integration has actually occurred among the EC along the variable of international trade.[3]

But whether the literature posits increasing, stagnant, or decreasing levels of integration, a review of the literature on the theoretical aspects of international integration and community building as well as the literature specific to the EC produces three major categories or perceptual approaches to the study of integration. These three conceptual approaches or levels of analysis are seen to be: integration at the individual's (or groups of individuals) attitudinal level; integration at society's level; and integration at the level of formal governmental behavior and collective decision making.

It is necessary to comment at the outset that, as Leon Lindberg has written,[4] international integration is a multifaceted societal attribute requiring multivariate measurement. The above three categories are not offered as monomeasures; they are only convenient analytical devices with which to organize the voluminous and rapidly expanding literature on the EC. Practically all the writings on the theoretical aspects of supranational integration agree that "integration" is indeed a multidimensional concept which transcends any one individual attribute.[5]

The first general category or approach to the study of EC integration is seen to be integration at the attitudinal level of the individual or of groups of individuals, and, briefly stated, this approach seeks to identify and examine what *people* think about the process of integration and their views on the current status of such integration. Studies here have dealt with mass public opinion; attitudes of the business, political, social, and military elites; and the views of the mass media, especially the international elite press.[6]

The second level of analysis is seen to be integration at the societal or nongovernmental level. Two general approaches are taken at this level: transaction flow analysis and the linkages of nongovernmental organizations. Transaction flow analysis (and there are several empirical procedures or models employed) involves the exchange of goods, services, people, ideas—virtually any transferable commodity—in order to measure the degree of integration or integration potential between or among sets of countries.[7] Transaction flow analyses on the EC have dealt with tourist traffic, labor flows, capital markets, "foreign" students, information flow (mail, book translations, telephone calls), trade and other economic transactions, business collaboration, and cultural exchanges.[8]

Transaction flow analysis is not, however, the only methodology utilized at this level. The activities and linkages of nongovernmental organizations, such as trade unions, interest groups, and political parties, are often employed to note the nature of the integrative process at society's level.[9] These studies are usually descriptive-narrative and, although not cast in the quantitative mold of transaction flow analyses, they present a rich and valuable contribution to the literature.

The last analytical level concerns integration at the governmental level and the formal structural processes of integration. This perspective is not concerned primarily with what people think about integration or the degree to which societies may or may not be linked; rather, this approach deals with formal intergovernmental contacts, common participation in international organizations and institutions, and collective decision making with common policies applicable to all members of the group. Formal collective decision making can be approached both in terms of "internal" collective decision making—policies that are common or harmonized in relation to the members of the group[10]—and "external" collective decision making—the extent to which the group can coordinate their external (foreign) behavior and form a consensus on foreign policy questions.[11]

As mentioned above, the process of integration in general, and EC integration in particular, is a combination of these three perceptual approaches or levels of analysis, and there have been several admirable studies examining the temporal and correlative links among the three dimensions.[12] The essays introduced in the following section approach the analysis of EC integration along the lines of these analytical devices: attitudes, societal behavior, and formal governmental collective decision making. Part I deals with integration at the attitudinal level, and there are two essays in this section. The first is by Ronald Inglehart, a political scientist at the University of Michigan, and Jacques-René Rabier, a former EC Director-General and currently a special advisor to the EC Commission for Public Opinion, on "Europe Elects a Parliament." The second essay is by Elisabeth Noelle-Neumann, director of the Institut für Demoskopie Allensbach (West Germany), on "Phantom Europe: Thirty Years of Survey Research on German Attitudes toward European Integration."

In "Europe Elects a Parliament: Cognitive Mobilization, Political Mobilization, and Pro-European Attitudes as Influences on Voter Turnout," Inglehart and Rabier employ data from the Eurobarometers and the actual electoral results in order to interpret the meaning of the first European-wide election for a European Parliament. The authors suggest that individual awareness of the elections had a major impact on whether or not one voted in the European elections. This factor is examined from two perspectives: cognitive mobilization and political mobilization. Cognitive mobilization, an individual-level characteristic, is seen as the possession of cognitive skills that facilitate processing information about remote political objects, one's inner predisposition to attend to politics. Political mobilization is seen as external factors, such as political parties or electoral campaigns, that can inform and motivate the individual to act politically regardless of his educational level or skills. Related to these two factors was a third: the strength of pro-European attitudes.

Through a rigorous examination of survey data and electoral statistics, Inglehart and Rabier clearly show that the above factors were strongly related to turnout in the European elections. Their essay shows that those high on the cognitive mobilization factor were most likely to vote and that turnout was highest in countries where a relatively strong information campaign (political mobilization) was conducted. In addition, those respondents who were relatively pro-European were most likely to vote, and the publics of the original six EC countries were most favorably oriented toward the European institutions and, therefore, most likely to vote. The nonvoters are not seen as "anti-European," but rather, as relatively uninformed. Inglehart and Rabier write that, in a certain sense, the European election was a referendum on European integration. In some countries, it was very poorly publicized; in others, no clear alternatives were presented. But in those countries where a relatively clear set of alternatives did exist, the pro-European parties won.

In the final section of their essay, Inglehart and Rabier effectively put to rest the preliminary journalistic notion about a swing to the Right across Europe. Only in Great Britain, where the Labour party put on a dismal show, is there any ground for such an interpretation. The swing to the Right across Europe is anything but evident when the composition of the newly elected European Parliament is compared to that of the old assembly and when the votes cast in the European election are compared to those in the most recent national elections. The swing was very limited in a geographical sense (the UK). A far more pervasive pattern was a tendency for the relatively pro-European parties to gain ground since, although the Right was not disproportionately likely to turn out and vote, the pro-Europeans were.

In "Phantom Europe: Thirty Years of Survey Research on German Attitudes toward European Integration," Professor Elisabeth Noelle-Neumann presents a most rigorous analysis of German public opinion toward the European Community and the process of European integration. Employing data generated by her own Institut für Demoskopie Allensbach and from the EC Commission-sponsored "Eurobarometers," she traces the German mood from the late 1940s to its contemporary status.

Some early surveys from the late 1940s and early 1950s showed a high (2 to 1) degree of willingness among the German respondents to yield national sovereignty to "Europe" by transferring decision-making power on important questions to a European Parliament. Professor Noelle-Neumann writes that, after the horrors of the Hitler period and the 1945 collapse, the European idea was something like a refuge for many Germans, a compensation for their own lost national consciousness. The assumption thus grew that the Germans were prepared to accept a "supranational" structure of European political organs. But this assumption is questionable today, for between 1974 and 1977, the Germans' confidence in the supranational course for the EC was shaken.

Although the Germans' "noncommittal benevolence" toward Europe remained high and although support was high, the data indicate that the willingness to go supranational decreases as soon as it becomes imaginable and phrased in everyday terms (a "European" flag or a "European" Olympic team). There is thus the recent tendency among the Germans to dissociate themselves from Europe even though there is a pro-European stance on the surface. There are various causes for this: hope they once entertained in connection with the EC may have dwindled, or the Germans may have become conscious of dangers previously unnoticed. The underlying variables are identified by Professor Noelle-Neumann as being the economy and the possibility of increased Communist influence.

The German population assesses the EC's economic consequences differently now than in the past. Surveys done in 1977 and 1978 show that German membership in the EC was perceived as presenting more of a disadvantage than an advantage, and the diminished readiness to introduce a "European" currency in place of the deutschmark most clearly depicts the core of economic uneasiness. Professor Noelle-Neumann writes that, given the trauma of the great inflation after the First World War and the currency collapse after the Second World War, the Germans react more sensitively to rising inflation than do other peoples. Germany was able to halve its inflation rate between 1972 and 1978; France and Italy, for example, have had steadily increasing inflation rates. The idea that the Germans' successful effort in combating inflation might have been in vain—a European currency might have exported higher inflation rates into Germany—makes a future European currency and, by extension, future efforts at increased EC integration, appear less attractive.

The second critical issue, Europe's future relationship to Communist ideology, is more complex than the economic issue, but it supports the tendency to withdraw from the concept of the European Community. The author writes that staving off Eurocommunism has a completely different urgency for a large segment of the German population than has the uniting of Europe, and there is an obvious concern that, via the European Parliament and a coalition of Social Democrats and Communists, communism might acquire an influence it has up to now been unable to gain directly in land or federal elections.

Professor Noelle-Neumann concludes her essay with a discussion of the relatively high level of support given to a concept of Europe that includes both East and West, although the general mood of the German Left is not easy to discern. She writes that the adherents of the idea of a united Europe including East and West form a considerable potential to set public opinion in motion. This process, however, might only get underway after the European Parliament has convened and demonstrated the different camps' political strength and the manner in which coalitions will be formed.

Part II concerns integration at the societal level approached from transaction flow analysis and nongovernmental behavior. There are two essays in this section: "Trade, Interdependence, and European Integration" by Wilfried Prewo, a German economist at the Institut für Weltwirtschaft (Kiel); and "Interest Group Behavior at the Community Level" by Emil Kirchner, a political scientist at the University of Essex and a consultant to the EC's Economic and Social Committee.

In "Trade, Interdependence, and European Integration," Prewo analyzes, via a transaction flow model, international trade flows among eighteen OECD (Organization for Economic Cooperation and Development) countries from 1958 to 1974, in order to reveal the trade effects of European integration. His empirical results, generated after a rigorous methodological examination, concern the changes over time in the roles of the major determinants of the equilibrium trade pattern, particularly variations in the effects of the trade-resistance factors (tariffs, preference orderings, and language barriers). Prewo comments that, although tariff changes did not play a major role in increasing trade among European countries after about 1965, membership in a preferential trade group (the EC) and language barriers continue to be important trade-promoting (preference orderings) or trade-impeding (language barriers) factors. He concludes that further reductions in nontariff and language-related barriers provide a rich source for future integration effects.

It is quite difficult, however, to offer a precise empirical evaluation of the degree of EC integration in the late 1970s–early 1980s, based upon the transaction flow model applied to international trade. There are several reasons for this difficulty. First, there seems to be general agreement among economists that free movement of goods (free trade) was not only achieved *de jure* but also *de facto* by the late 1960s–early 1970s (tariffs had been eliminated by 1968). This agreement is based partly upon empirical evidence—and partly upon the lack of contradicting evidence—that trade adjusts fairly quickly to permanent tariff changes. Whatever linkage trading patterns might have had with the EC thus concentrated in the years 1958 to about 1972.

A second reason is that even if one believes that there *were* integration effects on trade after 1972–74, it is virtually impossible to measure them because of the political and economic turbulence in the mid-to-late 1970s. The 1960s were relatively serene as far as recession, inflation, currency changes, and "external" shocks via oil prices and the energy crisis were concerned. Just about the only major thing that did happen in the 1960s was integration, and thus, at least in principle, it was possible to separate out integration effects from nonintegration effects: such a separation would be impossible for the 1970s. The trade data cannot be distilled in such a manner as to identify the effects on trade due to integration from those effects caused by recession, inflation, the energy crisis, and so forth.

In other words, the EC did *not* exert trade-increasing effects of late in its totality, but it *might* have if the integration factors could be set off from the other relevant factors. Prewo's transaction flow model (and other such models) cannot make this separation, and, solely in terms of the data, one cannot conclude that the EC is any "more" integrated along this nongovernmental societal characteristic (international trade) in the late 1970s—early 1980s than it was in the 1960s. One could look at factor markets, perhaps, where *de jure* free movement of capital and labor has been achieved and there have been some studies on movement of unskilled labor. But the evidence on capital movements (foreign investments in particular) and on the mobility of skilled labor and professionals is just too thin at this time.

There is, moreover, a general feeling among economists that the EC itself recently has inhibited or distorted trade flows more than it has promoted them. One reason is the Common Agricultural Policy and other attempts within the EC Commission to "organize" agriculture and "rationalize" trade in steel and chemicals. National—as opposed to EC—policies also continue to affect the pattern of trade: national subsidies (steel, shipbuilding, textiles) have become more and more fashionable. These subsidies are in most cases not harmonized at the EC level and, consequently, they distort the trade pattern. Finally, the imposition of national quotas on imports from nonmember countries and the reluctance to open up bidding on governmental contracts to nondomestic concerns also have "disintegrating" effects.

In conclusion, it is very doubtful that further economic-trading integration has been achieved within the EC in the 1970s compared to the 1960s. But this is a speculative opinion without any real empirical evidence, and until the methodology of transaction flow analysis is able to provide such evidence, Prewo's essay, for valid and compelling reasons, does not treat this question.

In "Interest Group Behavior at the Community Level," Emil Kirchner also deals with integration at the nongovernmental societal level but not through a transaction flow model. Rather, he presents a careful consideration of the twenty-one largest European interest groups. Professor Kirchner first reviews the literature that previously attempted to explain the behavior of interest groups in the EC in order to generate a framework for his own analysis. The three distinct analytical approaches considered are: the neofunctionalist theory (Mitrany, Haas, Lindberg, Schmitter); the structural-functional approach (Caporaso's application of Almond's functional analysis to a revised neofunctionalist interpretation of integration); and aspects of group theory (Beer, La Palombara, Averyt).

Drawing from the group theorists, Kirchner constructs a number of typologies of European interest groups on the basis of their structural characteristics, including the date of establishment and the groups' aims and objectives. From this, an analysis is then made of the similarities and differences among European interest groups regarding their development and structure and the factors that have contributed to or initiated the groups' activities. Typologies are also constructed along the lines suggested by the neofunctionalists on the style of decision making and the mechanisms for resolving internal conflicts. Finally, characteristics of the structural-functional approach are adopted when the author considers the interest groups in terms of the functions they perform in the Community system.

Kirchner's essay also involves consideration of the groups' activities and their access to, or targets of influence on, Community institutions: the Council of Ministers, the Commission, the European Parliament, and consultative committees such as the Economic and Social Committee. Some insight is thus gained into the relationship between the types of interest groups and the types of issues they promote, the channels of influence they utilize, and the impact of their actions on Community-level policy. He also indicates the degree of autonomy these twenty-one groups exercise vis-à-vis their national counterparts and most important, given the scheme of this collection, the level of integration achieved by these transnational interest groups.

Kirchner maintains that, in general, there is a linkage between the extent to which "Community" policies exist in a given sector and the degree of cooperation and integration reached by European interest groups of that sector. Further, as the EC moves toward more specific policies, the European interest groups have reacted with specific parallel suggestions or demands. There is also a linkage between the extent of Community activity and the number of opinions or observations prepared by the groups. The author illustrates these linkages with a detailed discussion of one such interest group, the COPA (Committee of Professional Agricultural Organizations in the European Community). Conversely, the lack of progress at the Community level or the actions of individual national governments in the fields of interest to these groups perpetuates some groups' national orientations, and thus stifles a more "European" outlook. Such groups find it less necessary to introduce highly cohesive or integrative structures and processes, and they remain a loose confederation of "national" groups rather than a cohesive *European* institutional structure.

Kirchner concludes his essay with some speculation on how direct elections to the European Parliament might affect the behavior of the European interest groups, particularly if direct elections lead to the Parliament having greater authority over the Council of Ministers. He comments that, under such conditions, one will probably see a rapid escalation in the activities of the interest groups as they attempt to utilize fully the Community's legislature. One might also see the transnational European political parties jockeying for support among the interest groups and the groups then using whatever electoral strength they may have to bargain for desired policies. This may then alter the nature of interest groups and provide a more balanced representation of interests. Up to now, the strongest groupings have been those of the producers and employers; a realignment will see the trade unions, social, consumer, and environmental interest groups with a stronger voice at the Community level.

Part III of this book approaches integration at the third general level, collective governmental decision making, and the essays here deal with collective decision making in areas internal to the EC. In our terms, "internal" refers to relations among the nine and the impact, if any, such decisions may have upon domestic politics. There are five essays in Part III: "Two-Tier Policy Making in the EC: The Common Agricultural Policy" by Werner Feld, a political scientist at the University of New Orleans; "The Delicate Balance Between Municipal Law and Community Law in the Application of Articles 85 and 86 of the Treaty of Rome," by Stephen Kon, an English attorney on the faculty of the University of Sussex; "Health Policies in the EC: Attempts at Harmonization," by Roger Vaissière and Jean-Marc Mascaro, two French physicians in private group practice in Grenoble; "Energy, Political Economy, and the Western European Left: Problems of Constraint," by Robert J. Lieber, a political scientist at the University of California at Davis; and the last essay in Part III, by Donald J. Puchala, a political scientist at Columbia University, on "European Fiscal Harmonization: Politics During the Dutch Interlude."

In "Two-Tier Policy Making in the EC: The Common Agricultural Policy," Werner Feld examines the CAP in rich detail. His contribution is partly based on some recent interview data obtained in extensive conversations with a number of officials in the Commission's Directorate-General VI in Brussels.

Professor Feld discusses the history and evolution of the CAP, its decision-making process, and the impact of domestic policies. He also offers some speculation on the CAP's future prospects.

The broad outline of the CAP took shape in the early 1960s, and, in general, its goals were to raise farm incomes in the Community member states and to improve agricultural production efficiency through structural changes in those farms in certain regions of the Community that have traditionally been cost-inefficient. A uniform Community-wide system governing the marketing of agricultural products within the EC and international trade with nonmember states was established. In addition, in order to assure a satisfactory and stable farm income, a system of target and support prices was introduced: the Community and national authorities must intervene in the market if prices threaten to fall below the established support levels.

In order to furnish the financial resources to administer the CAP, a European Agricultural Guidance and Guarantee Fund (EAGGF) was established. The EAGGF's main functions are: to provide funds for the purchase of farm products whose prices have reached or broken through the intervention price levels; to furnish money for structural improvements and reforms in regions of the Community where individual farms are very small or inefficient; and to subsidize exports of surplus farm products which, because of the CAP's steadily higher fixed prices, have been priced out of world market competition. Feld gives a few examples of these inflated prices: in 1977, EC wheat was 204 percent of the world market price, butter was 401 percent, skimmed milk powder 511 percent, and beef and white sugar 192 percent.

Many Europeans hailed the CAP in the 1960s as an essential ingredient for successful economic and eventual political integration of the EC. But considerable doubts have arisen in the 1970s about the survival of the CAP as originally designed. Vast surpluses have accumulated in several products, and the cost of the CAP is fast approaching $10 billion per year. There is a valid fear that the CAP may disintegrate into nine national policies instead of the one common policy.

Feld's essay examines the reasons for the problems encountered by the CAP; specifically, the related problems of the high cost of implementing the policy, the surpluses of various commodities, and the breakdown of the unified market and price concepts. One underlying general cause offered by Feld for not obtaining the major objectives of the CAP has been the loss of momentum in the forward movement toward political integration of the EC as reflected in the shift of power from the Commission to the Council of Ministers and the Committee of Permanent Representatives (CPR or COREPER). As a consequence, the national interests of the member states and the special interests of the agricultural sector interest groups, often at variance with the Community interest, can impede basic goal attainment and contribute to policy failures. A second general cause for the CAP's problems is the behavior of national civil servants and their desire to retain positions of individual and institutional power. Bureaucratic perceptions often reinforce undesirable policy outcomes.

Feld also identifies several specific causes of the CAP's shortcomings. One is the increased national control over prices, which has provided opportunities for the governments to give special advantages to their own farmers. Second, price policies to counter surpluses in various areas have not been applied very vigorously for fear of domestic political repercussions from powerful farm pressure groups. Another cause of failure is seen to be the slow progress of structural improvements of farms due to the absence of national matching funds and to fears of increased unemployment.

Professor Feld concludes that, from a purist point of view, the CAP does exhibit various failings in relation to its professed goals, but its policy implementation has adapted itself to the prevailing political and economic realities. The CAP is likely to survive, although its basic nature will probably be much different than originally conceived, especially with the entry of Greece, Portugal, and Spain into the EC. The farm products of the new three will compete with similar French and Italian products, and this will require adjustments and safeguard measures. At the same time, the new three are characterized by traditional agricultural structures, which will certainly increase the demands on the monies available for structural improvements.

In "The Delicate Balance Between Municipal Law and Community Law in the Application of Articles 85 and 86 of the Treaty of Rome," Stephen Kon examines the antitrust and competition policy of the EC through an analysis of leading decisions of several national courts and the European Court of Justice. Kon writes that the very idea of a common market—free movement of people and capital, freedom to provide services, and the right of establishment—makes the antitrust policy not an end in itself but rather a means by which the goals of the common market could be attained. There would be very little value in suppressing economic barriers among member states if private enterprises could erect private barriers having as their objective or effect the repartitioning of the EC.

The fundamental objectives of the Community's antitrust and competition policy are pursued along two avenues, both of which have as their origin the idea that competition must be effective if it is to fulfill its role as an integrating factor. First is the protection of the competitive system against interference arising from the agreement or concerted practices of enterprises. The second is the protection against corporate structures and monopolies generated by economic and commercial growth. Kon emphasizes from the outset that, notwithstanding the general wording of Articles 85 and 86 (the general prohibitions relative to trust behavior and competition), the Articles are all-embracing in their effects, containing absolute prohibitions against restrictive practices and abuses of dominant positions. The system established is an impregnable one; it cannot be evaded, avoided, or circumvented.

Kon writes that the essential problem with which both the European Court of Justice and the Commission have had to deal involved the establishment of a common European antitrust policy out of and compatible with the individual needs of, and legislation in force in, each of the member states, while at the same time maintaining the essential supremacy of Community objectives. In examining the manner in which the Court and the Commission have reconciled the individual national competition laws with the evolving Community antitrust policy, the essay considers both the procedural balance between the EC and state authorities as well as the substantive law developed regarding the EC and state competition rules.

The essay concludes by stating that in both conflicts of resolution and conflicts of law between the two authorities (the European Court and the national courts), whatever problems generated by this overlapping of legal systems have been resolved by making the Commission and "European" law prevail over their respective national counterparts. The result has been a competition policy in which the Commission can act without fear of its work being diluted or interfered with by national antitrust authorities, although the latter may themselves enforce the Community rules, subject to the supervision of the European Court of Justice in their interpretation of Community law. The national antitrust jurisdictions may equally enforce their own national rules, provided such national rules do not prevent the Community rules from being applied accurately and in their entirety. One can thus see, at least in antitrust and competition matters, a truly "European" policy which strengthens the integrative nature of the EC.

In "Health Policies in the EC: Attempts at Harmonization," Drs. Roger Vaissière and Jean-Marc Mascaro present an overview of the current status and future prospects of the European health community. They discuss the legislative history and impact of some of the more relevant documents, the instruments of Community action, and the differing health care systems in effect and conclude with a discussion of some of the obstacles to be overcome before a complete harmonization of health policies in the EC can be effected.

Drs. Vaissière and Mascaro discuss several important documents. These include the 1967 Nuremberg Charter (reaffirming the major principles of European medical ethics), the 1967 Hospital Physicians Charter (containing certain guarantees that European hospital physicians have a right to expect from their status), and two 1975 EC Directives (dealing with the mutual recognition of diplomas and the right to establish a practice and with the regulatory and administrative oversight of the physician's activities). The most important document in terms of immediate impact is the 1975 Council of Ministers Directive on the "free circulation" of EC physicians. This Directive entered into force in December 1976, and gave "European" status to EC physicians by providing (with certain limitations) free circulation and the right of establishment in the nine countries of the EC.

Although the Council of Ministers and the Commission constitute the essential decision-making units, the real work in health care policies, including the free circulation decision, is performed by three advisory bodies: the Permanent Committee of Physicians of the EC, the Consultative Committee for Medical Education, and the Committee of Public Health Officials. The Permanent Committee was established in 1959, the component parts now being the nationally recognized medical delegation from each of the Nine. The Consultative Committee is composed of representatives from the medical profession, the universities, and the national administrations, in equal strength. The Committee of Public Health Officials is composed of high-level administrative officials in the Nine who have direct responsibilities in the area of public health care. All three are consultative to the Council of Ministers and to the Commission in the latter two's decision-making function.

This essay also contains an in-depth discussion of the different health care systems within the EC. The health care systems in all the EC countries have the state as a principal actor through their health insurance schemes, but this governmental intervention has different forms in each country. Two polar types exist: (1) "private" medicine, wherein medical practice takes place without governmental intervention, be it in terms of the financing and structures of health care or in terms of the actual delivery of medical care itself, and (2) "nationalized" medicine, wherein medical personnel are public employees paid by the state and all equipment and facilities are state property. These are, however, only polar types for, in reality, a compromise position exists in most European countries in the form of a health insurance fund (the *caisse*). Drs. Vaissière and Mascaro comment that the diversity in the operation of the caisses across the EC represent a major problem in the eventual integration of the European health care systems.

In the section titled "Some Current Problems and Possible Solutions," Drs. Vaissière and Mascaro discuss several problems perceived to be a barrier to a complete harmonization of health care systems: language, medical education, mode of remuneration of physicians, and physician access to insured patients. The authors regard the language barrier as a false problem, for it is inconceivable to them that a physician, whose civil and criminal liabilities are tremendous, would treat patients without being able to understand their complaints and thus risk severe malpractice suits. The diversity of general practice and specialist training across the EC and the resulting diversity in diplomas must also be reduced in the harmonization process.

The differing methods in the EC for physician remuneration and the wide variation in incomes also present some difficult obstacles. The lure of a (substantially) higher income may possibly become an important factor in the free circulation of physicians, and certain areas in Europe may have their medical shortages exacerbated. The complexities of the finanical and administrative relationships between the physician and the social security organizations also need to be made more coherent throughout the EC.

Drs. Vaissière and Mascaro argue that there must be a uniform and standard policy of access to insured patients throughout the EC before the free circulation decision can have any real meaning. The migrating physician, of course, has the option of *not* joining the host country's health insurance system, indeed, participation is not required in any country, but the migrating physician would have very few patients if he were *denied* access to the insurance system. Private practice may be a risky venture for the migrating physician and access to insured patients is seen as a necessity in any future European health care system. Drs. Vaissière and Mascaro comment that to allow a physician to establish a practice in the host country but then to deny or delay his access to 95 percent of the population does very little in the integrative process.

The effects of the free circulation decision are also discussed although, due to the short time that the decision has been in force, all comments are only tentative. Preliminary figures show only 0.1 percent of all EC physicians taking advantage of the free circulation decision, and it appears that the level of physician remuneration, as well as the level of physician density, has had very little influence in determining the choice of host country. Trends to the contrary may surface when more data is available, but EC physicians are not yet chasing the money or the patients (one may see a future migration to Europe's "sunbelt," especially if Greece, Portugal, and Spain enter the EC). Drs. Vaissière and Mascaro conclude their essay with a discussion of the need of a "European" health system, and the authors themselves would prefer a *European* system rather than the nine different systems that currently exist.

Robert J. Lieber's essay, "Energy, Political Economy, and the Western European Left: Problems of Constraint," discusses the international energy crisis and the EC's energy policy (or lack thereof) in terms of domestic European political realities for both existing governments and possible future governments. Professor Lieber writes that, unlike much of the Community's previous experience with energy matters, the crises (first the security of oil supplies and then rising energy costs) led to serious failures of response within the EC. The crises' impact also affected the member states in ways that continue to burden their internal politics, economics, and industrial structures as well as their ability to cooperate among themselves.

The EC failed to cohere in face of the crisis: while paying lip service to common policy, most governments of the Nine reacted in ways that reemphasized national priorities or else moved beyond the EC level toward multilateral cooperation with the Americans, Japanese, and other OECD countries. Some (France in particular, but also Britain and Italy) sought to placate the Arabs by adopting more or less pro-Arab positions on the Middle East conflict. They then sought to insure the security of their imported oil supplies by negotiating bilateral deals with individual oil-producing states, often via the sale of massive amounts of industrial goods, weapons, or development projects.

Other EC member states sought, unsuccessfully, to rally the Nine to common energy policies or to cooperate at the OECD level in order to cope with the effects of what would become both a resource and economic crisis.

The EC's own energy policy is limited in scope, and there are many obstacles preventing a coherent and common policy. These obstacles include the very different energy situations of member states: some, the UK for example, are potential energy exporters, while others, such as France and Italy, remain dependent on energy imports. There is also a general reluctance to increase the Community's energy budget, and there are differing views about the limits of common EC action compared with the retention of national sovereignty. The consequences of the EC's inability to create a rational energy policy and attain a major reduction in dependence on imported energy affect the internal politics and economies of the Nine (balance-of-payments problems, inflation, economic stagnation, and unemployment).

Professor Lieber then notes that the problems of coping with supply and price consequences of the energy crisis are difficult enough for conservative and centrist regimes, or even a status quo-oriented social democratic government; but for a leftist government wishing to enact ambitious and costly programs of domestic change, the constraints generated by the energy crisis would be quite troublesome. The essay examines how such leftist governments may cope with the supply and price aspects of the energy crisis.

Four possible options are presented in a 2 x 2 matrix of policy choices for some past, present, and future governments: domestic policies may involve either continuation of the status quo in some form or efforts at substantial reform or even radical change; international policies are represented as openness to continued participation in a liberal economic order or a move toward protectionism and a more closed orientation. An extended discussion is then presented of the policy options available to the United Kingdom (the Wilson and Callaghan governments) and to France (a Mitterrand government).

Professor Lieber concludes his essay with a discussion of the policy options available to the United States in its dealings with the EC and the individual national governments in the context of the energy crisis. He warns that the facts of European energy and security dependence and the nature of international political and economic interdependence confine and restrict the degree to which any government, status quo or leftist, in Europe is likely to drift apart from the United States unless it is left with no other choice. U.S. policy should be flexible enough to maintain relationships in a way that minimizes tendencies toward mutually harmful economic chaos or political collapse.

In "European Fiscal Harmonization: Politics During the Dutch Interlude," Donald J. Puchala presents a case study of Dutch behavior during the EC's institution of the tax on value added (VAT), the first step toward community-wide fiscal harmonization. The essay is concerned with political "reverberation," that is, how, when, why, and with what result are issues transferred from the national arenas to the European one. Professor Puchala writes that to conceive of EC processes as moving in "fits and starts," with short periods of feverish activity interspersed among long lapses into immobility, is usually inaccurate. Once started by the Commission, Community activity in particular issue areas is normally continuous, and what appear to be intervals of inaction are really transfers of activity to the national arenas. The new national stance is then reinjected into the European area to stimulate a new round of political play in Brussels.

The chronology of events surrounding the design, promulgation, and implementation of the VAT is crucial to the analysis because it reveals patterns of political reverberation. It took the member states of the EC fourteen years to move from treaty commitment to community-wide implementation of the VAT—three years of expert study and analysis (1959–62), five years of national and international deliberation (1962–67), and six years to complete implementation (1967–73). What is most revealing about the fourteen years of the VAT episode is that activity toward bringing the new regime into existence was continuous but it shifted (reverberated) several times between the "European" arena and the various national ones.

The Dutch interlude in the political chronology of the VAT was significant for it casts an interesting light on political reverberation in the EC. The Dutch interlude was between 1964 and 1967, and Professor Puchala writes that the source of stagnation at Brussels was no mystery: the Dutch government would not accept the directives on the new VAT, and this opposition from The Hague was preventing closure in the Council of Ministers where unanimity was required. A rich and well-documented study is presented on the Dutch behavior, especially the attitudes and obstructionist maneuvering by some senior Dutch civil servants in the Finance Ministry. The finance officials eventually lost in the intrabureaucratic contest in The Hague, and the long play of VAT politics in the Dutch arena drew to a close.

Professor Puchala writes that it is obvious from the case study that fiscal movement at the "European" level was stalled between 1964 and 1967 because the Dutch government was incapable of changing its position on the proposed VAT. The incapacity stemmed from both the opposition of the Finance Ministry and its fiscal experts and the political-structural difficulty of circumventing or overriding these elements of resistance. Therefore, "Europe" could not move until the Dutch government moved, and the Dutch government would not move until its Finance Ministry moved. Whatever the degree of anyone's good will toward European unity in this situation, the fact was that the system was politically stalled because the Dutch could not change their policy.

This essay concludes with the view that longer delays and more political interludes in national arenas are to be expected, all compounded by an increased number of national arenas after the next enlargement. Professor Puchala writes that, even though progress has been at a snail's pace, the final outcomes are still likely to be integrative and that political reverberation has been functional to progress toward greater European unity because it has been the EC's circuitous, but ultimately dependable, pathway to international consensus.

The final section of this collection, Part IV, also deals with collective decision making, but here we are concerned with "external" decision making: decisions and policies that relate to countries other than the nine EC members. There are two essays in this concluding section: "Foreign Policy Formation within the EC with Special Regard to the Developing Countries," by Corrado Pirzio-Biroli, an Italian developmental economist currently employed as an economic counselor at the Delegation of the European Commission to the United States in Washington, D.C., and "EC-U.S. Relations in the Post-Kissinger Era," by Harold Johnson, a political scientist at Michigan State University.

In "Foreign Policy Formation within the EC with Special Regard to the Developing Countries," Dr. Pirzio-Biroli presents an inside view of foreign policy formation within one of the EC Commission's Directorate-Generals. He argues that the EC's foreign policy toward the Third World and the less developed countries (LDCs) is a policy of a defense of interests. He writes that the Community's interest is to promote a world system in which it can prove its independence from superpower politics by securing a fair share of influence in world affairs. This depends on its success in helping to build a world where it can assert and maintain its character as a civilian society. The way the Community shapes its international economic relationships is therefore a highly political issue.

In this context, the Community was capable of demonstrating an ability to innovate in the field of north-south relations and the relationship of mutual support with the LDCs became a cornerstone of its foreign policy. The positive response the Community found to its offers of development cooperation was due not only to the LDCs' perceived interest but also to the belief that the socialist inclination of most European countries allowed them to understand, better than other powers, the LDC's requests that the principles of resource allocation and income distribution presently applied in progressive Western democracies be applied to the international economy as well.

Dr. Pirzio-Biroli writes that the Community approach has world relevance insofar as it acts as a pilot scheme for the extension of new cooperation policies worldwide and insofar as it remains outward-looking. No LDCs are excluded from joint Community action, and the member states do not inhibit the EC from making improvements in its policies toward the Third World. The "multi-laterization" of EC action—placing all LDCs on the same footing—does not exclude the modulation of action to meet the special needs of single LDCs. Moreover, the privileged position of the closest partners can always be reestablished through additional concessions. The author believes that, despite its internal divisions, the EC has become the only place where there is a promise of dynamism and cooperation with the Third World.

Dr. Pirzio-Biroli then describes the EC's policy formulation process in three separate case studies: the Lomé Convention, the agreements with the Southern Mediterranean, and the Euro-Arab Dialogue (EAD). These case studies are unusually rich in detail and present excellent examples of EC external collective decision making in terms of both the process as well as the substance of such policies.

The essay concludes with the view that the Community's development policy formation process has shown that coordination among as well as within national bureaucracies is an antagonistic process, particularly when it involves a perceived transfer of power, which may in fact be a net addition of power. This may be aggravated by the lack of flexibility of individual negotiators who may fight to one step beyond what their respective country or institution could have been ready to accept. Member states' reluctance to extend Community responsibility to new areas has often resulted—as in the three case studies—in refined legal debates on the Commission's international negotiating capacity and on Community representation on specific issues.

Future prospects are uncertain and depend very much on EC domestic policies. There are internal social costs involved with the liberalization of the EC's external trade, and, in order to reduce these social costs, the member states are tempted to resort to the use of national instruments of protection which are still in their own hands (subsidies, taxes, credits). These instruments of protection are often used in an uncoordinated way and in contradiction to the Community's (or indeed their own) foreign policies. Dr. Pirzio-Biroli thus sees a need for a closer link between the EC's development policy and internal EC common policies.

The concluding essay is by Harold Johnson on "EC-U.S. Relations in the Post-Kissinger Era." Professor Johnson writes that, in the two decades following the Second World War, the United States conceived of its relationship with Western Europe as a partnership—a partnership in the context of an Atlantic Alliance within which the U.S. would remain the senior partner. U.S. security was linked to that of Western Europe, and the U.S. assumed the primary initiative for organizing this defense. The commitments toward this defense eventually contributed to the United States' position of being economically overextended and the balance-of-payments problem. Since the early 1970s, however, the two partners have bargained from positions of varying strength.

There evolved an ambivalence as to what the U.S. expected from Europe. The Nixon Doctrine, as defined and applied by Henry Kissinger, projected the development of a five-power, multipolar system, with a unified Western Europe as one of the poles. When the U.S. balance-of-payments deficit soared in 1971, the Nixon administration expected its European creditors to share the burden and responsibility. The U.S. adopted policies requiring a retooling of the international monetary system aimed, in part, at realigning Western currencies as a means for boosting U.S. exports. Negotiations within GATT (General Agreement on Tariffs and Trade) began to focus on nontariff barriers, particularly those which limited access of American agricultural products to the EC market and limited the ability of U.S. firms to bid on EC member governments' contracts.

Nixon's "New Economic Policy" was directed toward a redress in the balance of power in international economic relations. While critical of the protectionism of the CAP, the U.S. adopted policies of its own that protected its home market. At the same time, however, within Western Europe, the EC became the largest trading bloc in the world and began to challenge the status of the U.S. dollar.

Professor Johnson comments, however, that the relative positions of the EC and the U.S. began to shift around 1973. The EC itself is under new (and severe) internal pressures with its monetary system after a series of competitive devaluations, although the 1979 EMS (European Monetary System) decision should help counter some of these effects. The rise of petroleum prices has left serious deficits in their balance of payments, resulting in the formation of the International Energy Agency under U.S. leadership. Pressures from Japanese competition has placed the U.S. in a position as a go-between for the EC and Japan. President Carter's Trilateral Policies have generated an awareness of an interdependency among the three developed areas: North America, Western Europe, and Japan.

Carter's Trilateralism is described by Professor Johnson as defining the relationship between the U.S. and the principle democratic, industrialized, and market-economy countries. The term was generated by the Trilateral Commission, and among its objectives were the formation of joint policy-making institutions in order to coordinate relations among themselves as well as with the Third World and the Communist bloc nations. Trilateralism was seen by some as a reaction to the former U.S. Treasury Secretary John Connally-dominated economic policy of the Nixon administration, a policy which was based upon the assumption that Western Europe and Japan had prospered at American expense and that the dynamism of their economies had come because of U.S. leadership.

Professor Johnson comments that Trilateralism is an uncertain basis upon which to restructure relations, particularly with Western Europe. It could very well represent a shared leadership role for the three points of the triangle; it could also represent a way for the U.S. to recapture its status of first among equals. The major problem seen by Professor Johnson here is that, at least until now, the EC has not functioned as a single entity in its dealings with the U.S. In fact, it was not until the London Summit (May 1977) that the EC was directly represented in the discussions among the Western industrialized countries. Professor Johnson concludes his essay by noting that the EC requires a much more integrated foreign economic policy before it will be able to negotiate with the United States as a unit and be seen as a true equal partner.

Notes

1. Leon Hurwitz, "The EEC in the United Nations: The Voting Behaviour of Eight Countries, 1948–1973," *Journal of Common Market Studies* 13, no. 3 (March 1975): 224–43.

2. Donald J. Puchala, "Integration and Disintegration in Franco-German Relations, 1954–1965," *International Organization* 24, no. 2 (Spring 1970): 183–208.

3. Charles G. Nelson, "European Integration: Trade Data and Measurement Problems," *International Organization* 28, no. 3 (Summer 1974): 399–433.

4. Leon N. Lindberg, "Political Integration as a Multidimensional Phenomenon Requiring Multivariate Measurement," *International Organization* 24, no. 4 (Fall 1970): 649–731.

5. There is a large body of literature on the theoretical aspects of international integration, and the following represents only a small portion of the literature: Karl W. Deutsch et al., *Political Community in the North Atlantic Area: International Organization in the Light of Historical Experience* (Princeton, N.J.: Princeton University Press. 1957): Ernst B. Haas, *The Uniting of Europe* (Stanford, Calif.: Stanford University Press, 1958); Haas, *Beyond the Nation-State* (Stanford, Calif.: Stanford University Press, 1964): Haas, "International Integration: The European Process and the Universal," *International Organization* 15, no. 3 (Summer 1961): 366–92; *International Political Communities: An Anthology* (Garden City, N.Y.: Doubleday and Co., 1966); Lindberg, "Political Integration as a Multidimensional Phenomenon"; Leon N. Lindberg and Stuart Scheingold, *Europe's Would-Be Polity* (Englewood Cliffs, N.J.: Prentice-Hall, 1970); Lindberg and Scheingold, eds., *Regional Integration: Theory and Research* (Cambridge, Mass: Harvard University Press, 1971); and Joseph S. Nye, Jr., "Comparative Regional Integration: Concept and Measurement," *International Organization* 22, no. 4 (Fall 1968): 855–80.

6. *See*, for example, Karl W. Deutsch *et al., France, Germany and the Western Alliance: A Study of Elite Attitudes on European Integration and World Politics* (New York: Charles Scribner's Sons, 1967); Werner J. Feld and John K. Wildgen, *Domestic Political Realities and European Integration: A Study of Mass Publics and Elites in the European Community Countries* (Boulder, Colo.: Westview Press, 1976); Ronald Inglehart, "Public Opinion and Regional Integration," *International Organization* 24, no. 4 (Fall 1970): 764–95; Ronald Inglehart and Jacques-René Rabier, "Economic Uncertainty and European Solidarity: Public Opinion Trends in the Europe of the Nine" (Paper presented at the Annual Meeting of the American Political Science Association, New York, August 30–September 3, 1978); Daniel Lerner and Morton Gorden, *Euratlantica: Changing Perspectives of the European Elite* (Cambridge: MIT Press, 1969); Robert J. Lieber, "European Elite Attitudes Revisited: The Future of the European Community and European-American Relations," *British Journal of Political Science* 5, no. 3 (July 1975): 323–40; Donald J. Puchala, "The Common Market and Political Federation in Western European Public Opinion," *International Studies Quarterly* 14, no. 1 (March 1970): 32–59; and Glenda G. Rosenthal, *The Men Behind the Decisions* (Lexington, Mass.: D.C. Heath and Co., 1975).

7. For a discussion of the various transaction analysis methodologies, see the following: Steven J. Brams, "Transaction Flows in the International System," *American Political Science Review* 60, no. 4 (December 1966): 880–98; Michael P. Gehlen, "The Integrative Process in East Europe: A Theoretical Framework," *Journal of Politics* 30, no. 1 (February 1968): 90–113; Barry B. Hughes, "Transaction Analysis: The Impact of Operationalization," *International Organization* 25, no. 1 (Winter 1971): 132–39; Donald J. Puchala, "International Transactions and Regional Integration," *International Organization* 24, no. 4 (Fall 1970): 732–63; I. Richard Savage and Karl W. Deutsch, "A Statistical Model of the Gross Analysis of Transaction Flows,"

Econometrica 28, no. 3 (July 1960): 551–72; and Ingo Walter, *The European Common Market: Growth and Patterns of Trade and Production* (New York: Frederick A. Praeger, 1967).

8. For some transaction analyses specific to the EC, see: Theodore Caplow and Kurt Finster-busch, "France and Other Countries: A Study of International Interaction," *Journal of Conflict Resolution* 12, no. 1 (March 1968): 1–15; Werner J. Feld, "Political Aspects of Transnational Business Collaboration in the Common Market," *International Organization* 24, no. 2 (Spring 1970): 209–38; Helen S. Feldstein, "A Study of Transaction and Political Integration: Trans-national Labour Flow within the European Economic Community," *Journal of Common Market Studies* 2, no. 3 (March 1964): 251–62; Nelson, "European Integration: Trade Data and Measurement Problems"; and Hans O. Schmitt, "Capital Markets and the Unification of Europe," *World Politics* 20, no. 2 (January 1968): 228–44.

9. Some of the best work in this area has dealt with trade unions. See Emil J. Kirchner, *Trade Unions as a Pressure Group in the European Community* (Farnborough, Hants: Saxon House, 1977); and Norris Willatt, *Multinational Unions* (London: Financial Times, 1974).

10. *See,* for example, William F. Averyt, Jr., *Agropolitics in the European Community* (New York: Praeger, 1977); Donald J. Puchala, "Domestic Politics and Regional Harmonization in the European Communities," *World Politics* 27, no. 4 (July 1975): 496–520; Carole Webb, "Mr. Cube versus Monsieur Beet: The Politics of Sugar in the European Communities," in *Policy-Making in the European Communities*, ed. Helene Wallace, William Wallace, and Carole Webb (London: John Wiley and Sons, 1977), pp. 197–226; and Roger Williams, *European Technology: The Politics of Collaboration* (New York: John Wiley and Sons, 1973).

11. For an overview of external collective decision making in the EC, see Frans A.M. Alting von Geusau, ed., *The External Relations of the European Community* (Westmead, England: D.C. Heath/Saxon House, 1974); Ph. P. Everts, ed., *The European Community in the World: The External Relations of the Enlarged European Community* (Rotterdam: Rotterdam University Press, 1972); Werner J. Feld, *The European Community in World Affairs: Economic Power and Political Influence* (Port Washington, N.Y.: Alfred, 1976), especially chapter 2, "The Competences, Structures, and Procedures for External Policy Formulation and Implementation," pp. 17–62; Leon Hurwitz, "The EEC and Decolonization: The Voting Behaviour of the Nine in the UN General Assembly," *Political Studies* 24, no. 4 (December 1976): 435–47; and Ievan John, ed., *EEC Policy Toward Eastern Europe* (Westmead, England: D.C. Heath/Saxon House, 1975).

12. *See* Mario Barrera and Ernst B. Haas, "The Operationalization of Some Variables Related to Regional Integration: A Research Note," *International Organization* 23, no. 1 (Winter 1969): 150–60; James A. Caporaso and Alan L. Pelowski, "Economic and Political Integration in Europe: A Time-Series Quasi-Experimental Analysis," *American Political Science Review* 65, no. 2 (June 1971): 418–33; Barry B. Hughes and John E. Schwarz, "Dimensions of Political Integration and the Experience of the European Community," *International Studies Quarterly* 16, no. 3 (September 1972): 263–94; Lindberg, "Political Integration as a Multidimensional Phenomenon"; Puchala, "Integration and Disintegration in Franco-German Relations"; and Donald J. Puchala, "Patterns in West European Integration," *Journal of Common Market Studies* 9, no. 2 (December 1970): 117–42.

INTEGRATION AT THE ATTITUDINAL LEVEL

Part I

RONALD INGLEHART
AND
JACQUES-RENÉ RABIER

2

Europe Elects a Parliament: Cognitive Mobilization, Political Mobilization, and Pro-European Attitudes as Influences on Voter Turnout

In June 1979, 112,000,000 citizens of the nine European Community countries voted to select representatives to the European Parliament—the first directly elected supranational parliament in history. Representatives from nine nations sit together as members of transnational party federations that have, in varying degrees, worked out joint political programs. As a democratically elected body, the new European Parliament possesses a political legitimacy that the former, appointed Parliament never had. By itself, this does not automatically give it a more influential role in decision making at the European level, but it certainly strengthens the Parliament's potential to do so. The election of Simone Veil as president of the new Parliament reflects that body's enhanced prestige. A prominent and extremely popular member of the French cabinet, she resigned her post in order to devote full time to the European Parliament.

Rising public support for a directly elected parliament is manifest in responses to the following question, asked in national surveys since 1973:

... The citizens of countries belonging to the European Community, including (your nationality) will be asked to vote to elect members of the European Parliament.... Are you, yourself, for or against this particular election?"[1]

Figure 2.1 shows the pattern of responses over time. The changes are particularly marked among the publics of the three nations that entered the Community in 1973. Originally reluctant to accept a directly elected parliament, support rose steadily among these three publics. By 1977, absolute majorities of the Danish, Irish, and British publics supported the idea together with absolute majorities in the six original member nations.

The election of the European Parliament was not an unmixed success, however. Voter turnout varied widely from nation to nation, ranging from a low of 33 percent in the United Kingdom, (32.6 in Great Britain and 57.0 in Northern Ireland), to a high of 91 percent in Belgium; for the Community as a whole, 62 percent of the electorate took part. A respectable turnout by American standards, it was a disappointing performance for these countries, in which about 85 percent of the electorate normally votes in national elections.

Table 2.1 compares the rates of electoral participation in the most recent national election for each country and in the European election. For those familiar with the results of public opinion surveys published during the months preceding the election, the low turnout came as no surprise. The old Parliament was virtually powerless. As long as this remains true, there is little reason for a citizen to go out and vote: nothing is at stake. Accordingly, the publics of most countries attached only modest importance to these elections.[2] The fact that 111 million citizens *did* turn out to vote for the European Parliament

Figure 2.1   Attitude Toward the Election of the European Parliament

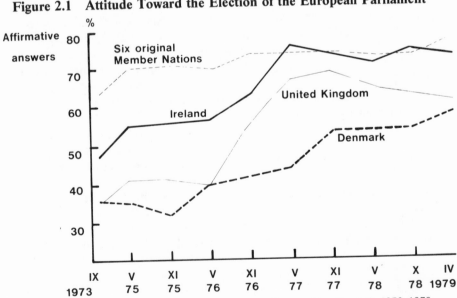

Source: Eurobarometers, Commission of the European Communities, Brussels, 1973–1979.

Table 2.1   Rates of Electoral Participation for the Election of the European Parliament and for the Most Recent National Election[a]

(percentage)

	Most Recent National Election		Election of European Parliament	Difference
Belgium[b]	94.6	(1977)	91.4	− 3.2
Denmark	88.9	(1977)	47.8	−41.1
Germany	90.7	(1976)	65.7	−25.0
France	82.8	(1978)	60.7	−22.1
Ireland	76.9	(1977)	63.6	−13.3
Italy	89.9	(1979)	85.5	− 4.4
Luxembourg[b]	90.1	(1979)	88.9	− 1.2
Netherlands	87.5	(1977)	57.8	−29.7
United Kingdom	76.0	(1979)	32.6	−43.4
European Community[c]	85.1		62.2	−22.9

Source: European Parliament

Notes:

[a]Number of voters compared with registered voters.

[b]In these countries voting is compulsory. In Luxembourg, the two elections took place the same day.

[c]Average weighted by voters registered in each country.

seems to reflect the influence of a sense of civic duty, together with hopes or expectations that the new European Parliament will play a more significant role than the old. Moreover, public awareness of the forthcoming election was low in most countries, and this was reflected in a correspondingly low level of intention to vote. Table 2.2 shows the rates of voting intention reported in five successive Eurobarometer surveys carried out from Spring 1977 to Spring 1979. The proportion saying that they would "certainly" vote foreshadowed the actual results rather closely for most countries.

Commenting on the low overall turnout, *Pravda* asserted that it was due to a growing disaffection with the European Community among the working class.[3] This analysis seems a trifle hasty. Electoral participation unquestionably *was* low among British workers. But it is difficult to reconcile *Pravda's* interpretation with the fact that the Italian and French Communist parties made major—and effective—efforts to mobilize their voters. Survey evidence indicates that 74 percent of the French Communist electorate, and 89 percent of the Italian Communist electorate, voted in the European elections. In the Community as a whole, the Communists showed the *highest* rate of turnout

Table 2.2   Voters Saying They Would "Certainly" Vote in the Election of the European Parliament
(percentage)

	Denmark	Germany	France	Ireland	Italy	Nether-lands	United Kingdom
April–May 1977	44.0	28.0	52.0	55.0	67.0	61.0	48.0
October–November 1977	55.0	35.0	61.0	57.0	67.0	64.0	49.0
May–June 1978	50.0	35.0	62.0	53.0	67.0	70.0	46.0
October–November 1978	53.0	31.0	65.0	60.0	69.0	66.0	46.0
April 1979	52.0	34.0*	65.0	56.0	85.0	60.0	32.0
Actual Turnout	47.8	66.7	60.7	63.6	85.5	57.8	32.6

Source: The *Eurobarometers* (Brussels: Commission of the EC, 1977–79). National representative samples of the population aged fifteen years and more, revised to take only those eligible to vote into consideration; that is, those aged eighteen years and more. Belgium and Luxembourg, where voting is compulsory, are not included.

*By adding the percentage of the replies "will probably go and vote," the total becomes 34 + 36 = 70 percent.

among the six major groupings in the European Parliament.[4] Furthermore, whether or not one intended to vote was only weakly related to social class indicators, such as income, occupation, or education. Far more important than one's social class affiliation was, quite simply, whether or not one was aware that a European election was taking place.

Cognitive and Political Mobilization

To a quite astonishing degree, the publics of given countries were not aware of the elections. The extreme case is that of Great Britain. Six weeks before the election, only 55 percent of the British electorate said that they had recently read or heard anything about the European Parliament. Among those who had, less than half (25 percent of the total sample) were able to mention the European elections when asked what they had heard. One week before the election, the British public had become somewhat better informed; instead of 25 percent, 42 percent were well enough informed to mention the European elections.[5] Viewed in this context, it is hardly surprising that only 33 percent of the British electorate voted: this figure represents 79 percent of those who were aware of them one week before they took place. The Italian public, by contrast, was far better informed. Six weeks before the elections, the vast majority had read or heard something about the European Parliament, and 60 percent could specify that elections were about to occur. By the time of the elections themselves, public awareness had risen still higher: 86 percent of those eligible voted.

In short, we suggest, public awareness of the elections had a major impact on whether or not one voted in the European elections. We propose to examine this factor from two perspectives: (1) One's inner predisposition to attend to politics. We refer to this individual-level characteristic as "cognitive mobilization": the possession of cognitive skills that facilitate processing information about remote political objects;[6] and (2) External factors, such as political parties or electoral campaigns, that can inform and motivate the individual to act politically, regardless of his educational level or skills. We refer to this factor as "political mobilization."

Both factors are important. On one hand, the possession of skills in dealing with political abstractions enhances the likelihood that one takes on a cosmopolitan, rather than a parochial, political outlook. Thus, those with high levels of political information and awareness are relatively apt to identify with Europe as a whole, rather than the province or nation in which they live.[7] Other things being equal, those with a cosmopolitan outlook tend to be relatively supportive of European integration. At the same time, those skilled in dealing with political abstraction are more apt to participate in politics.[8] The implications for European politics are significant. Insofar as cognitive mobilization is linked with *both* a tendency to support European integration and high rates of political participation, pro-Europeans are inherently more apt to vote than anti-Europeans.

This does not guarantee automatic victories for pro-European forces under all circumstances, of course. Norway's rejection of EC membership in their 1972 referendum is proof enough of that. But it does imply that unless anti-European parties or movements make relatively strong efforts to mobilize their supporters, they are apt to fall short of their potential.

"Political mobilization" is thus a crucial complement to "cognitive mobilization." An inner predisposition to participate does not, by itself, produce political action. It is also necessary that one's external setting provide information and stimulation to act. A sufficiently strong organizational network can mobilize even those who would normally be least involved, diminishing or multiplying the impact of individual-level differences. In the European elections, the effectiveness of the electoral campaign varied widely from nation to nation and from party to party. To a considerable extent, this explains the varying rates of turnout. The fact that the British Labour party failed to conduct any campaign worth mentioning has more to do with the low rate of British turnout than does disaffection among the working class. It also helps explain why the results were an electoral catastrophe for the Labour party, which won less than a third as many seats as the Conservatives and seriously weakened the position of the entire Socialist group in the European Parliament.

For further evidence of this point, let us examine the impact of cognitive mobilization and political mobilization more closely, using data from the European Community's nine-nation public opinion survey conducted in April 1979. It is more difficult to measure skills than attitudes in a public opinion survey. For practical reasons, our measures of cognitive level are indirect. The cognitive mobilization indicator used here is based on responses to two questions that have become standard items in the European Community surveys. They are:

When you get together with your friends, would you say that you discuss political matters frequently, occasionally, or never?

When you, yourself, hold a strong opinion, do you ever find yourself persuading your friends, relatives or fellow workers to share your views? (if yes): Does this happen often, from time to time, or rarely?

Our reasoning in using these items as indicator of *skills* (which, clearly, they do not measure directly) is that those who know and understand something about political life are most likely to discuss it, and those most skilled in argumentation are most apt to attempt to persuade others to adopt their opinions. Needless to say, this is not always true. But overall, the "mobilized" responses to these items show strong positive correlations with one's level of political information, sense of political competence, and education.[9]

On the basis of responses to these items, we constructed an index of cognitive mobilization.[10] Are those who rank high on this index relatively European in their outlook? In general, the answer is yes. One illustration of the overall tendency for those with relatively high political skills to have a more cosmopolitan outlook has a direct bearing on the role that the members of the new European Parliament will be expected to play. Our respondents were asked:

Which of the following attitudes would you expect a member of the European Parliament from (your country) to have?

1. He should support things that are good for the European Community as a whole, even if they are not always good for (my country) at the time.
2. He should support the interests of (my country) all the time whether or not they are good for the European Community as a whole.

Across the nine nations taken together, responses were almost equally divided between the two options, with emphasis on the interests of the respondent's own nation prevailing in the three new member nations, and emphasis on the interests of the Community as a whole tending to prevail among the publics of the six original member nations. But the responses differ rather strikingly when analyzed according to the respondent's cognitive mobilization level, as Table 2.3 demonstrates.

Among those coded as "low" on this variable, only 29 percent emphasize the interests of the European Community as a whole, while 47 percent opt for the interests of their own nation. Among those coded "high" on cognitive

Table 2.3   Attitude Expected of a Member of the European Parliament, by Level of Cognitive Mobilization
(percentage)

Respondent's Level of Cognitive Mobilization	A Member of the European Parliament from My Country Should Support:			
	Interests of European Community as a Whole	*Don't Know*	*Interests of My Country*	*Number*
Low	29	24	47	(1,993)
Medium low	38	15	47	(2,951)
Medium high	51	9	40	(2,846)
High	57	8	35	(1,142)

Source: European Community Survey, *Eurobarometer*, no. 11 (April 1979).

The figures reported are weighted by population.

mobilization, an absolute majority (57 percent) emphasizes the interests of the Community as a whole, while only 35 percent expect their representative to support the interests of their own country at all times.

Another question shifts the focus from one's preference for a European or national frame of reference to one's assessment of membership in the Common Market. Our respondents were asked:

Generally speaking, do you think that (your country's) membership in the Common Market is a good thing, a bad thing, or neither good nor bad?

Table 2.4 shows the results for the European Community as a whole. A perception that membership in the Common Market has had good effects is definitely more prevalent among those ranking high on cognitive mobilization than among those ranking low. But there is little difference, overall, in the prevalence of *negative* assessments; instead, we find the assessment that membership has been "neither good nor bad" to be twice as widespread among those "low" on cognitive mobilization as among those who rank "high." To a considerable extent, the former group has not developed any clear opinion on the subject—hardly a surprising finding, but entirely in keeping with our expectation of differential rates of turnout.

Responses to this question are discussed in more detail below. It seems to tap a relatively concrete assessment of the costs and benefits of the Common Market for one's own country and not simply one's positive or negative feelings toward the Community. As such, responses are more situation-

Table 2.4   Assessment of Whether Membership in Common Market is Good or Bad, by Level of Cognitive Mobilization
(percentage)

Respondent's Level of Cognitive Mobilization	Membership in Common Market Is:			
	Good	*Neither*	*Bad*	*Number*
Low	54	30	16	(1,690)
Medium low	62	25	13	(2,536)
Medium high	70	20	10	(2,558)
High	69	15	16	(996)

Source: European Community Survey, *Eurobarometer*, no. 11 (April 1979).

The figures reported are weighted by population.

specific than with many other items, reflecting perceived conditions at a given time and place. In France and Denmark those ranking high on cognitive mobilization were substantially more apt to attribute *negative* effects to membership than were those who ranked low in April 1979. This may reflect the impact of the relatively strong and well-organized "antimarket" campaigns conducted in those two countries: their impact was greatest among those most attentive to politics, although in both cases, favorable assessments outweighed unfavorable ones among those "high" on cognitive mobilization. Table 2.5 shows the pattern in each of the nine nations. In every country but France, those high on cognitive mobilization were relatively apt to perceive beneficial effects.

As we have just seen, cognitive mobilization is linked with a pro-European outlook, though the relationship seems stronger with affective orientations than with utilitarian assessments. What about our second hypothesis: were those who rank high on cognitive mobilization more likely to vote in the European elections? The answer is clear "yes." Our analysis of turnout is based on voting intention as ascertained in the April 1979 Eurobarometer survey, using the following item:

On June 7th the citizens of countries belonging to the European Community, including (your nationality) will be asked to vote to elect members of the European Parliament. Everybody will be entitled to vote. How likely is it that you will go and vote? Certainly, probably, probably not, or certainly not?

For most of the nations surveyed, the percentage saying they would "certainly" vote provides a close approximation of the actual turnout. Germany is an interesting exception: for that country, we obtain a rather close approxi-

Table 2.5   Assessment of Common Market Membership by Cognitive Mobilization, by Nation
(percentage)

Respondent's Level of Cognitive Mobilization	Belgium		Denmark		Germany		France		Ireland	
	Good	*Bad*	*Good*	*Bad*	*Good*	*Bad*	*Good*	*Bad*	*Good*	*Bad*
Low	63	3	37	24	61	6	60	8	50	21
Medium low	73	2	43	24	72	5	63	6	57	17
Medium high	82	4	45	27	76	3	64	8	65	10
High	83	4	46	42	75	11	54	18	68	18

	Italy		Luxembourg		Netherlands		United Kingdom		EC	
	Good	*Bad*	*Good*	*Bad*	*Good*	*Bad*	*Good*	*Bad*	*Good*	*Bad*
Low	81	4	75	6	73	2	19	48	54	16
Medium low	82	3	83	2	83	1	32	40	62	13
Medium high	84	1	92	1	89	2	44	30	70	10
High	85	3	91	5	93	3	46	32	69	16

Source: European Community Survey, *Eurobarometer*, no. 11 (April 1979).

mation of the actual vote if we take the percentage saying they will "certainly" vote together with the percentage saying they will "probably" do so.[11] Table 2.6 compares the percentages of our samples that were classified as "voters" on this basis with the actual turnout.[12] We cannot, of course, be sure that all those who said they would "certainly" vote actually did so; but it seems extremely likely that they were more apt to do so than those who said they wouldn't. Given the close correspondence between predicted turnout, as operationalized here, and actual turnout, we will use this as an indicator in subsequent analysis.[13]

Now let us examine the relationship between cognitive mobilization and turnout. Table 2.7 shows the pattern that prevailed in the seven nations for which we have data on predicted turnout. Insofar as declared voting intentions are a guide, those who rank "high" were markedly more apt to vote than were other respondents, and the pattern is uniform across nations. When we analyze results for each of the seven countries, we find a margin of at least 14 percentage points between the turnout rates of the "high" and "low" groups. The largest gap (30 points) is found in Denmark, which had the second lowest rate of turnout. The smallest margin exists in Italy (where turnout was relatively high even among the least politicized group). As was suggested earlier, effective political mobilization can minimize the importance of one's internal predisposition to participate in politics.

Let us attempt to assess the impact of political mobilization. We have no quantitative measure of the amount of effort expended on the campaign for the

Table 2.6   Respondents Classified as "Voters" and Actual Turnout in the European Community
(percentage)

	"Voters" in Sample	Actual Turnout
United Kingdom	32	33
Denmark	52	48
Netherlands	60	58
France	65	61
Ireland	56	64
Germany	70	66
Luxembourg	*	89
Italy	85	86
Belgium	*	91

Source: European Community Survey, *Eurobarometer*, no. 11 (April 1979).

*The question about voting intention was not asked in Belgium and Luxembourg, where voting is required by law.

European elections. We do have various measures of the extent to which various electorates *perceived* the campaign, however, and the results vary markedly from country to country. Our respondents were asked:

"Have you recently seen or heard in the papers or on the radio or TV, anything about the European Parliament?" Those who responded "yes" were asked:

"Can you remember what it was you heard then?"

Table 2.7   Predicted Turnout for European Elections by Level of Cognitive Mobilization*

Respondent's Level of Cognitive Mobilization	Percentage Classified as "Voters"	Number
Low	52	(1,616)
Medium low	61	(2,315)
Medium high	66	(2,341)
High	74	(896)

Source: European Community Survey, *Eurobarometer*, no. 11 (April 1979).

*Based on all EC nations except Belgium and Luxembourg, where the question about voting intention was not asked.

Table 2.8 shows the percentages who had read or heard something and were able to mention the forthcoming elections. It also shows the percentages answering "yes" to another question (asked ten minutes later):

"Over the last few months have you noticed a publicity campaign about the European elections?"

On both indicators of awareness, the Italian public stands at or near the top, and on both indicators the British public falls below all of the other nationalities by a wide margin.

Fieldwork for these surveys was completed about six weeks before the elections themselves. It seems highly probable that public awareness of the elections increased during the remaining weeks preceding the elections. In the case of Great Britain, we *know* this was the case but, as mentioned earlier, only to a limited extent. During the week preceding the elections, only 42 percent of the British public could spontaneously mention the European elections; only 48 percent said that they had noticed a publicity campaign. Their awareness of the elections remained below the levels that had existed in the other European Community countries six weeks earlier!

Within Britain, the information level of Labour party supporters was about

Table 2.8   Awareness of European Elections Among European Community Publics, April 1979

	Percentage Able to Mention Spontaneously the European Elections	Percentage Saying They Had Noticed a Publicity Campaign for the European Elections
Italy	60	72
Luxembourg	57	63
Netherlands	53	75
Denmark	51	57
Ireland	48	70
Belgium	47	44
Germany	46	50
France	38	47
United Kingdom	25	29
European Community	43*	51*

Source: European Community Survey, *Eurobarometer*, no. 11 (April 1979).

*Percentages weighted according to population.

ten points lower than that of Liberals and Conservatives, probably a reflection of the fact that the latter parties made an effort to mobilize their electorate, while Labour conducted virtually no campaign at all. One would expect that the almost incredibly low information level prevailing among the British public limited electoral turnout in that country. The expectation is well founded. Those who were least aware of the elections and campaign had markedly lower levels of voting intention than those who were aware of them. Table 2.9 shows predicted turnout rates from the seven nations for which we have the relevant data. The pattern is consistent cross-nationally. For the seven nations as a whole, expected turnout was 44 percent among those who hadn't read or heard anything about the European Parliament as compared with 80 percent among those aware of the elections and campaign. To a significant extent, high or low turnout rates reflect whether or not the public was aware of the elections.

Cognitive and political mobilization do not tell the whole story, however, for

**Table 2.9   Predicted Turnout for European Elections,
by Awareness of Elections and Campaign**
(percentage)

	Denmark	Germany	France	Ireland	Italy	Nether-lands	United Kingdom	European Community[a]
Able to Mention Elections and Noticed Campaign (33%)[b]	66	89	73	62	89	69	47	80
Able to Mention Elections but Hadn't Noticed Campaign (11%)[b]	51	82	66	63	83	68	40	66
Had Read or Heard Something about European Parliament but Couldn't Specify Elections (22%)[b]	48	68	69	59	89	64	38	63
Hadn't Read or Heard Anything about European Parliament (33%)[b]	27	51	45	44	70	46	21	44

Source: European Community Survey, *Eurobarometer*, no. 11 (April 1979).

[a]Based on combined results from seven nations, weighted according to population.

[b]Figures in parentheses show the weighted percentage falling into each category, across the seven nations.

there is some truth in *Pravda*'s interpretation of the elections as a referendum on the European Community: those who were more favorable to European integration were more likely to vote than those who opposed it. In part, this follows from the fact that those ranking high on cognitive mobilization are relatively pro-European *and* relatively active politically, but it goes beyond this: pro-Europeans are relatively apt to vote even when we control for cognitive mobilization.

This phenomenon has two distinct components: First, reflecting *cross-national differences*, the publics of the six nations that have been members of the European Community since 1952 are distinctly more pro-European than the publics of the three nations that joined in 1973. This seems to reflect the gradual emergence of a sense of European identity among the publics of the six original members, an outlook that has developed less fully in the three new member nations: Second, reflecting *individual-level differences* within given nations, pro-Europeans were relatively likely to vote, even controlling for cognitive and political mobilization. This differential turnout of pro-Europeans seems consistent with the hypothesis that many of those who voted did so out of hopes or expectations that the new parliament would take on a more important role.

Thus, four related factors show particularly strong relationships with turnout in the European elections: (1) *individual-level awareness of the elections*: those high on cognitive mobilization were most likely to vote; (2) *national-level awareness of the elections*: turnout was highest in countries where a relatively strong information campaign was carried out; (3) *individual-level evaluation of the European Community*: relatively pro-European respondents were most apt to vote; and (4) *national-level evaluation of the European Community*: the publics of the original six member nations were most favorably oriented toward the European institutions and hence most likely to vote.

These factors are interrelated. Cognitive mobilization predisposes one to be pro-European *and* to attend to an electoral campaign. In addition, the publics of the six original member nations are relatively pro-European; partly for this reason, relatively energetic and effective campaigns tended to be waged in those countries.

Support for European Integration and Voter Turnout

Let us glance back at Table 2.6, which shows the turnout rates for each nation. Perhaps the most striking feature of this table is the fact that voter turnout tended to be higher in the six original member nations than in the three new ones. To be sure, Irish turnout was substantially higher than would be predicted on the basis of length of membership alone; but on the whole, when we compare turnout in the three new member nations with that in the six original members, we find that 35.5 percent of the electorate in the three new members voted, as compared with 71.2 percent of the electorate in the six original members, exactly twice as high. Is this pure coincidence? Apparently not. In the first place, it corresponds to a long-term difference in the degree to which the respective publics have taken on a pro-European outlook. This difference was apparent from the time the three new nations entered and persisted in 1979; it apparently reflects the fact that the development of a pro-European consensus requires a relatively long period of positive, shared experiences.[14] The contrast between the the attitudes of the old and new member publics is reflected in responses to a variety of questions.

We will provide two examples. The following question seems to tap a relatively diffuse attitude of affective support for European integration:

"In general, are you for or against the efforts being made to unify Western Europe?"

Table 2.10 shows the responses of the respective publics in April 1979. Among the publics of the Six, attitudes are overwhelmingly favorable, with a preponderance of at least ten to one in favor of unification. In the United Kingdom and Denmark, one encounters substantial opposition, though even in Denmark support clearly outweighs opposition.

Another question seems to tap a more concrete utilitarian assessment of the advantages and disadvantages of one's own country's membership in the European Community. It is:

"Generally speaking, do you think that (your country's) membership of the Common Market is a good thing, a bad thing, or neither good nor bad?"

Table 2.10   Diffuse Support for European Unification, by Nation (ranked according to ratio of support to opposition) (percentage)

	"For" or "Strongly For"	"Against" or "Strongly Against"
Italy	87	4*
Luxembourg	89	6
Germany	82	7
Netherlands	84	8
Belgium	71	7
France	72	10
Ireland	64	7
United Kingdom	61	20
Denmark	49	31

Source: European Community Survey, *Eurobarometer*, no. 11 (April 1979).

*The row percentages do not add up to 100 because nonresponse is not reported directly.

Table 2.11 shows the responses of the nine publics in April 1979. Favorable attitudes are less overwhelming here than in response to the previous question, but support outweighs opposition in eight of the nine countries. 60 percent consider membership "good" while only 12 percent consider it "bad" in the European Community as a whole. The one exception is the United Kingdom, where opinion is evenly divided. This fact is not entirely surprising. It seems to reflect Britain's present economic difficulties, coupled with the fact that Britain is currently contributing a heavily disproportionate share of the EC budget as a result of the common agricultural policy. This fact apparently is perceived as an inequity—though an inequity which may change. When asked whether they think their country's membership will prove to be a good or a bad thing ten or fifteen years from now, the British figures shift to 41 percent "good" and 25 percent "bad." We find a somewhat similar pattern in the other country that pays a relatively heavy share of the costs of the Community, the German Federal Republic. Though the Germans rank near the top in affective support, their utilitarian assessment of the advantages and disadvantages of membership is noticeably less positive. Conversely, the Irish—strongly advantaged by the common agricultural policy—show a relatively high level of utilitarian support (and of affective support as well).

In sum, comparisons at the national level support the hypothesis that turnout was highest in the original six member nations because their publics had developed a relatively pro-European outlook. But the problems of ecological inference are well known. Is it also true that within given countries those individuals with pro-European attitudes were relatively likely to vote? The answer is an unequivocal "yes."

Table 2.11   Utilitarian Assessment of Country's Membership in Common Market, by Nation
(ranked according to ratio of positive to negative assessments)
(percentage)

	Respondent's Nation's Membership in Common Market Is:	
	A Good Thing	*A Bad Thing*
Netherlands	84	2
Italy	78	2
Belgium	65	2
Luxembourg	83	3
Germany	66	5
France	56	8
Ireland	54	14
Denmark	37	25
United Kingdom	33	34

Source: European Community Survey, *Eurobarometer*, no. 11 (April 1979).

Table 2.12 shows the relationship between our indicator of utilitarian support and voter turnout for the seven nations from which relevant data are available and for the seven nations together weighted according to population. For the Community as a whole, (more precisely, for the 96 percent of its population represented in this table) those with a favorable assessment of their country's membership were twice as likely to vote as those with an unfavorable one. But the cross-national differences are significant.

In Italy, on one hand, there is very little difference between the turnout rates of those who made favorable and unfavorable assessments because of the excellent overall turnout: all shades of opinions were represented because nearly everyone voted. In Belgium and Luxembourg, where voting is compulsory, the pattern would probably resemble that of Italy.

In Denmark, on the other hand, the difference in turnout between pro-Europeans was relatively modest because a well-organized anti-European movement presented a clear alternative, campaigning against membership in the Common Market and mobilizing an appreciable share of the public. The anti-European movement won several seats at the expense of the Social Democrats, who took no clear position, but the final result resembled that of the 1972 referendum in Denmark: anti-Market candidates won only a third of the Danish seats in the European Parliament—partly because anti-Europeans were somewhat less likely to vote, but more basically, because favorable attitudes toward membership outweighed unfavorable ones among the Danish public.

The situation in France was somewhat more complex. All four of the major parties claimed to be "for" European unification (a rational strategy, in view of the overwhelming support it held among the French public); nevertheless, there were perceptible differences between the Socialists and the Giscardians (who took a relatively favorable stance toward the European institutions), on one hand, and the Gaullists and Communists, whose campaign consisted

Table 2.12   Voter Turnout, by Assessment of Nation's Membership in Common Market[a]

(percentage)

Respondent Feels that Membership is:	Denmark	Germany	France	Ireland	Italy	Netherlands	United Kingdom	European Community[b]
"A Good Thing"	65	83	69	66	89	66	48	76
"A Bad Thing"	53	43	59	49	85	50	24	36

Source: European Community Survey, *Eurobarometer*, no. 11 (April 1979).

[a]Percentage defined as "voters."

[b]Weighted according to population, with Belgium and Luxembourg excluded.

largely of warning against the dangers of increased powers for the European
Parliament, alleged to be dominated by the Germans, on the other. The results
were mixed. On the Left, the Communists not only held their own, but made
modest gains in relation to the Socialists. In view of the exceptionally strong
organizational network and disciplined electorate which the French Communist party possesses, this result is not entirely surprising in a situation of relatively low voter turnout. On the Center and Right, the election was disastrous
for the Gaullists, whose share of the vote plummeted from 22.6 percent in the
1978 national elections, to 16.2 percent in the European elections. Conversely, it was a major victory for the Giscardians, who emerged as the strongest
party in France, having ranked third in 1978.

Ironically, in Britain—where utilitarian assessments of membership in the
Community were least positive—the results were more one-sided than anywhere else. Deeply divided on the European issue, the Labour party waged virtually no campaign at all, leaving the field to the relatively pro-European
Conservatives. The difference in turnout rates of pro-Europeans and anti-
Europeans was far larger there than in any other country, contributing to the
result that the Conservatives won sixty seats, and Labour seventeen (excluding Northern Ireland).

On the whole, those with positive assessments of the European Community
were substantially more likely to vote than those with negative assessments.
Does this mean that the nonvoters were predominantly anti-European? No. As
Table 2.13 indicates, in the seven nations for which we have relevant data,
those who presumably voted were far likelier to have favorable attitudes than
those who didn't. But even among those we have identified as nonvoters, favorable assessments of membership were almost twice as prevalent as unfavorable ones.

The largest single group among the presumed nonvoters, however, consists

**Table 2.13   Assessments of Nation's Membership in Common Market,
Among Voters and Nonvoters***

(percentage)

Respondent Feels that Membership Is:	"Voters"		"Nonvoters"	
"A good thing"	72	(2,909)	38	(869)
"Neither" or "don't know"	21	(481)	41	(918)
"A bad thing"	7	(336)	21	(548)

Source: European Community Survey, *Eurobarometer*, no. 11 (April 1979).

*Based on combined results from the seven nations for which relevant data are available, weighted
according to population.

of those who had no clear conviction that membership was either good or bad, or expressed no opinion. In large measure, the nonvoters seem to have been relatively uniformed. Even in Britain, where utilitarian assessments were least favorable, nonvoting cannot be equated with opposition to membership. Among British nonvoters, 39 percent felt that British membership was "a bad thing"; an almost equal proportion (36 percent) felt it was neither good nor bad, or had no opinion; and 25 percent said it was "a good thing." In a certain sense, the European election was a referendum on European integration, albeit in some countries a very poorly publicized one and in others one presenting no clear alternatives. But in those countries where a relatively clear set of alternatives did exist, the pro-European parties won.

A Swing to the Right?

A lot has been said in the press about a swing to the Right in the new assembly as compared to the old. It is true that the raw results—and in particular the British results—have given some grounds for this interpretation.

Among the political groups that are generally considered as being on the Left, the Communists and their allies have slightly improved their position and occupy approximately 10 percent of the seats, while the Socialist group has lost 5 points, dropping from 33 percent to 28 percent of the seats. In the Center, one notes little change, apart from a slight decrease affecting in particular the European Progressive Democrats' group, made up for the most part of the "Gaullists" of Messrs. Jacques Chirac and Michel Debré. On the Right, the European Conservative group, most of whose members are British, has progressed by 6 points, moving from 9.1 percent to 15.6 percent. Last, the group of the "others," that is to say, parliamentarians whose label does not correspond to any of the six organized groups, has increased by approximately 3 points. Table 2.14 retraces this development, which appears to be limited principally to a transfer of seats from Labour to Conservative in Britain.

A more detailed examination, taking into account the increase in the total number of parliamentarians, the modification in the number of seats given to each member nation, and the results of the election, enables us to specify precisely the relative weight of each "fraction of delegation," defined jointly by its nationality and political label. These results, given in Table 2.15, show clearly that the only swing of any importance, from one assembly to another, is that affecting the British representation: Labour fell from 9.09 percent to 4.39 percent of the total number of seats, and the Conservatives moved up from 8.08 percent to 14.88 percent. If there is a swing to the Right, it is very limited geographically.

It is not sufficient, of course, to examine the distribution of seats between the political groups and its development from one assembly to another in order to

Table 2.14   Distribution Between the Political Groups of the Members of the European Parliament Before and After the Election

	Seats			Percentage of Total		
	Before	*After*	*Difference*	*Before*	*After*	*Difference*
Communist and Allies Group	18	44	+ 26	9.09	10.73	+1.64
Socialist Group[a]	66	113	+ 47	33.33	27.56	−5.77
Liberal and Democratic Group[b]	23	40	+ 17	11.62	9.76	−1.86
Christian Democratic Group[b]	53	107	+ 54	26.77	26.10	−0.67
Group of European Progressive Democrats[c]	16	22	+ 6	8.08	5.37	−2.71
European Conservative Group[d]	18	64	+ 46	9.09	15.61	+6.52
Others	4	20	+ 16	2.02	4.88	+2.86
Total	198	410	+212	100.00	100.00	—

Source: European Parliament.

[a]Including one Danish representative of the Siumut party (Greenland).

[b]As far as France is concerned, eight elected of the Veil list of twenty-five have decided to sit with the Christian Democrats. This group has decided to call themselves European People's party.

[c]Including, after the election, Mrs. Ewing, elected for the Scottish National party, who formerly had a seat among those who were not registered.

[d]This group has decided to call themselves "Group of European Democrats."

measure the swing to the Right which has been the subject of so much commentary. It is also necessary to study the distribution of the votes and its development, since the composition of an elected assembly is never rigorously representative of the votes cast.[15]

We will therefore compare, for each of the major political families, the percentage of votes obtained in the election of the European Parliament and in the most recent election for the national parliament. The general impression that emerges from Table 2.16 is one of great stability, which is not really surprising since the different possible variables in each country are likely to cancel one another out at the level of the Community as a whole.

The only variations equal to or greater than 3 percentage points are the following: (1) an increase in the percentage of votes given to the Christian Democrats, who advance slightly in five countries, going from 24.6 percent to 29.9 percent of the total votes; (2) a decrease in the votes given to the Socialists (-3.0 points), who regress principally in Denmark (-15.1 points) and in the United Kingdom (-4.3 points), while advancing in Ireland (+2.9 points) and in Italy (+1.7 points); and (3) a decrease—however surprising that may appear—in the votes given to the Conservatives, although their percentages rise

Table 2.15 Distribution of the Members of the European Parliament, by Country and by Political Trend, Before and After the Election
(percentage of total number of seats)

	Belgium	Denmark	Germany	France	Ireland	Italy	Luxembourg	Netherlands	United Kingdom	Total
Former Parliament										
Communists and Their Allies	0	0.51	0	2.53	0	6.06	0	0	0	9.09
Socialists	2.53	2.02	7.58	5.05	0.51	2.53	1.01	3.03	9.09	33.33
Liberals and Democrats	1.01	0.51	1.52	4.55	0	1.01	1.01	1.52	0.51	11.62
Christian Democrats	3.54	0	9.09	1.52	1.52	7.58	1.01	2.53	0	26.77
European Progressive Democrats	0	0.51	0	4.55	3.03	0	0	0	0	8.08
European Conservatives	0	1.01	0	0	0	0	0	0	8.08	9.09
Not registered	0	0.51	0	0	0	1.01	0	0	0.51	2.02
Total	7.07	5.05	18.18	18.18	5.05	18.18	3.03	7.07	18.18	100.00
New Parliament										
Communists and Their Allies	0	0.24	0	4.63	0	5.85	0	0	0	10.73
Socialists	1.71	0.98	8.54	5.36	0.98	3.17	0.24	2.20	4.39	27.56
Liberals and Democrats	0.98	0.73	0.98	4.15	0.24	1.22	0.49	0.98	0	9.76
Christian Democrats	2.44	0	10.24	1.95	0.98	7.32	0.73	2.44	0	26.10
European Progressive Democrats	0	0.24	0	3.66	1.22	0	0	0	0.24	5.37
European Conservatives	0	0.73	0	0	0	0	0	0	14.88	15.61
Others	0.73	0.98	0	0	0.24	2.20	0	0.49	0.24	4.88
Total	5.85	3.90	19.76	19.76	3.66	19.76	1.46	6.10	19.76	100.00

Source: European Parliament.

Table 2.16   Comparison of the Votes Obtained by the Political Groups in the Most Recent National Elections and in the European Election[a]

(percentage of expressed votes)

	National Election	European Election	Difference
Communists and Their Allies	11.4	13.5	+2.1
Socialists	29.6	26.6	−3.0
Liberals and Democrats	11.0	10.2	−0.8
Christian Democrats[b]	24.6	29.9	+5.3
European Progressive Democrats	5.2	3.7	−1.5
European Conservatives[c]	10.2	6.3	−3.9
Miscellaneous[d]	3.9	5.2	+1.3
Others[d]	4.1	4.6	+0.5
Number of votes expressed (thousands)	152,746	111,998	−40,748

Source: The main sources for the national elections are Thomas T. Mackie, "Elections in the European Community Countries, 1945–1978," *Studies in Public Policy* , Glasgow: University of Strathclyde, 1979, no. 29, and for the European election, figures released by the Directorate General for Information and Public Relations of the European Parliament, based on results as of July 17, 1979. This table can only have an indicative value, especially as far as the details per country are concerned.

[a]The political groups are those existing in the European Parliament before the election of June 1979.

[b]Have decided to call themselves, in the European Parliament, Group of the European People's party.

[c]Have decided to call themselves "European Democrats."

[d]The category of "miscellaneous" corresponds to political parties having obtained at least one seat in the European Parliament and "others" to unrepresented lists and candidates.

in the two countries where they are represented: Denmark (+5.3 points) and in the United Kingdom (+4.5); this decrease of their relative share in the Community as a whole is explained by the fact that the total of votes cast in the nine countries dropped by 27 percent, while that cast in Britain and Denmark fell by more than 50 percent.[16]

As we have just seen, as regards both the composition of the newly elected European Parliament compared to that of the old assembly and the development of the votes cast in comparison with the most recent national elections, the so-called swing to the Right is anything but evident. In the new Parliament, the Communists and Socialists combined have a slightly *higher* percentage of the seats than they had in the old (provided we momentarily exclude Britain from consideration). When we include the British results, of course, we have a different picture: the Labour party's setback was so severe that it weakened the entire Socialist group, which now holds about 20 fewer seats than it might normally expect. But there was *no* Europe-wide swing to the Right.

Survey data provide additional evidence on this point. The respondents in the April 1979 survey were asked to place themselves on a Left-Right scale, according to their political views. There was no significant change in the percentages placing themselves on the Left or Right portion of the scale, by comparison with other recent Eurobarometer surveys asking the same question. Nor was there an overall tendency for those who placed themselves on the Right to show a higher turnout rate in the European elections than those who placed themselves on the Left (though this did take place in the British Isles).

Table 2.17 shows the relationship between Left-Right self-placement and predicted turnout rate for our seven-nation sample. For the combined sample, turnout was lowest among those placing themselves at the Center and highest at the two extremes, with the Left showing a slightly higher turnout than the Right. These results are consistent with results from an analysis according to the respondent's reported vote in the last national election (as contained in Table 2.18). One cannot speak of an overall swing to the Right; a far more pervasive pattern was a tendency for the relatively pro-European parties to gain ground. Though the Right was not disproportionately likely to turn out and vote, the pro-Europeans *were*.

By far and away the strongest influences on voter turnout were whether one had a favorable or unfavorable attitude toward European integration and

Table 2.17   Predicted Turnout by Left-Right Self-Placement*

Respondent Placed Self on the:	Percentage "Voters" (Number)	
Far Left (1, 2)	76	(481)
Left (3, 4)	65	(1,427)
Center (5, 6)	61	(2,688)
Right (7, 8)	63	(1,297)
Far Right (9, 10)	72	(487)

Source: Eurobarometer, no. 11 (April 1979).

*The Left-Right scale contained ten cells with the word "Left" at the left end and the word "Right" at the right end. We have collapsed the ten categories into five groups here.

Table 2.18 Turnout, by Vote in Last National Election*
(grouped according to party affiliation in European Parliament)

Respondent Voted for:	Turnout Percentage (Number)	
Communists	83	(391)
Christian Democrats	78	(1,043)
European Progressive Democrats	76	(204)
Liberals	66	(650)
Socialists	63	(1,667)
Conservatives	44	(399)
Didn't Vote	40	(1,684)

Source: European Omnibus Survey, Brussels.

*Based on data from Denmark, Germany, France, Italy, the Netherlands and Great Britain; percentages are weighted according to population. Vote in last national election was not asked in Ireland.

whether one was aware of the elections and publicity campaign. Whether one was ideologically on the Left or the Right had a relatively weak—and curvilinear—relationship with electoral turnout. Consequently, for the EC as a whole, pro-European parties (regardless of whether they were on the Left or Right) won more than their usual share of the vote. Conversely, those parties perceived as relatively anti-European (or took no clear stand) lost ground.

Notes

1. This question underwent minor changes in wording, connected with the fact that the elections were originally scheduled for Spring 1978, and were finally held in June 1979.
2. *See Eurobarometer*, no. 10 (January 1979): 35–39. The European Commission has been carrying out, since 1974, in the spring and autumn of each year, sample surveys representative of the population of each of the nine Community countries. The results of these surveys are published in the six Community languages in the *Eurobarometer*. The corresponding data are accessible to all researchers, without restriction.
3. Cited in an AFP dispatch from Moscow, June 12, 1979.
4. *See* Table 2.18 below.
5. Based on results from a British Gallup Poll survey conducted from May 30 to June 3, 1979.
6. For a fuller discussion of "cognitive mobilization," *see* Ronald Inglehart, *The Silent Revolution: Changing Values and Political Skills among Western Publics* (Princeton, N.J.: Princeton University Press, 1977), chapters 11 and 12.
7. Ibid., chapter 12.
8. *See* Samuel H. Barnes, *et al.*, *Political Action: Mass Participation in Five Nations* (Beverly Hills, Calif.: Sage, 1979), chapters 9 and 10.
9. See Inglehart, *The Silent Revolution*, chapter 12.
10. Our cognitive mobilization index was constructed as follows:

		Persuade Others:			
Discuss Politics:	Often	Time to Time	Rarely	Never	Don't know
Frequently	++	++	+	+	+
Occasionally	+	+	−	−	−
Never	−	−	−−	−−	−−
Don't know	−	−	−−	−−	−−

The "++" group is labeled as "high," the "+" group as "medium high," the "−" group as "medium low" and the "−−" group as "low" for present purposes.

11. Two possible explanations suggest themselves: either Germans are inherently more modest in describing the likelihood that they will vote than are other nationalities or the campaign was exceptionally effective in Germany during its last six weeks. We do not at present have adequate information to choose between these alternatives.

12. The question about voting intention was not asked in Belgium or Luxembourg, where voting is required by law. Accordingly, these two nations (with 4 percent of the Community's population) are excluded from survey-based analysis of turnout in this chapter. In Italy, voting is considered a civic duty but is not required by law.

13. Surveys carried out *after* the European election— in France by SOFRES (Société française d'Etudes pour Sondages) and in Great Britain by GALLUP—provide us with an additional argument: the percentages of the responses to the question on the voting *intention* are, in these two countries, nearer to the effective turnout than the responses to a question asked *after* the event about votes or abstention. In other words, and for the present case, the responses from people interviewed before the election seem to be more reliable than those interviewed afterward.

	France	Great Britain
Said they would go and vote	65 percent	32 percent
Actual turnout	61	33
Say they actually went to vote	79	44

Source: For France, Jacques Juillard, "Les transfuges et les deserteurs du 10 juin," *Le Nouvel Observateur* (July 23, 1979). For Great Britain, "European Elections," Gallup Report, (London: International Institute of Communications, June 1979).

14. See Ronald Inglehart and Jacques-René Rabier, "Economic Uncertainty and European Solidarity: Public Opinion Trends," *Annals* 440 (November 1973): 66–97.

15. The electoral system in force in Great Britain is a well-known example of nonproportional representation. All of the other member nations used a system of proportional representation, for the election of the European Parliament, but some of these systems deliberately avoided strict proportionality, in particular in France and Germany. In accordance with Article 7 of the Act of September 20, 1976, it falls to the European Parliament to draw up a draft uniform electoral system. No easy task!

16. Bearing in mind the numbers involved, it is obviously the massive abstention of British voters which is the dominant variable in this development.

	Votes Cast in the United Kingdom (millions)	
	National Elections (3/5/79)	*European Elections (7/6/79)*
Labour party	11.5	4.4
Conservative party	13.9	6.6
Liberal party	4.3	1.7
Others	1.6	0.7
Total	31.3	13.4

ELISABETH
NOELLE-NEUMANN*

3

Phantom Europe: Thirty Years of Survey Research on German Attitudes Toward European Integration

Future historians will be better informed about the general mood of how the people of Western Europe awaited the emergence of the European Community than they have been about any other era in which a new political community was taking shape. The European Community has been the subject of representative surveys since the late 1940s, and since the early 1970s there have even been uniformly designed surveys, first in the six and then in the nine member countries. These latter surveys, called "Eurobarometers," have been conducted semiannually since 1973 upon the initiative of the EC Commission.[1]

Nevertheless, it would be wrong to contend that the structure of public opinion in the six original EC countries, and in the three who joined in 1973, can be described reliably. To be sure, the attitudes reflected in the surveys are pro-European, but they have not been tested for no one yet to make any recognizable sacrifices. Up to the present, the subject of "Europe" has not held any potential of risk: no courage has been required to profess one view or another; the subject has not been controversial; it had no partisan contours.

*Author's Note: I wish to acknowledge that Wolfgang J. Koschnick translated this essay into English from the original German.

This lack of partisan contours can be illustrated by some recent data from the Federal Republic of Germany. Table 3.1 contains the responses given in a 1978 survey to the question:

"Suppose you were told that the EC were to be dissolved. How would you take this news?"

Although the responses are "pro-European" (approximately 64 percent answered very or quite regrettable), there is very little difference among political parties. The CDU/CSU (Christian Democratic Union/Christian Social Union), SPD (Social Democratic Party), and FDP (Free Democratic Party) all show roughly the same distribution of responses, and, indeed, the subject is nonpartisan.

There are quite a few cases where opinions change unpredictably under the pressure of a vote, say, when the rival camps match forces or, more generally, under circumstances when the subject becomes a matter of topical controversy. During the Austrian referendum on the nuclear energy plant at Zwentendorf in the fall of 1978, for example, those opposed to nuclear energy were able to shatter a climate of opinion that was originally favorable.[2] Could the innocuously genial climate of opinion toward the EC likewise be destroyed? Could the opinion climate shift to become a dangerous public opinion? Public opinion is always dangerous. In the words of Ferdinand Tönnies, it demands, if not the consent, at least the silence of dissidents.[3] We are referring here to a definition of public opinion taken from its historical roots: opinions one *must* express in public in order to avoid isolation or, wherever controversies arise, opinions one *can* express in public without

Table 3.1   Attitude Toward Continuation of the European Community (percentage)

QUESTION: "Suppose you were told that the EC were to be dissolved. How would you take this news?"

	Federal Republic of Germany April 1978			
	Total popula- tion over 16 number = 2,006	*Christian Democrats number = 787*	*Social Democrats number = 715*	*Liberals number = 158*
Would be very regrettable	33	33	33	35
Quite regrettable	31	31	31	35
Wouldn't matter to me	16	15	15	8
Would rather be an advantage	7	8	8	11
Don't know	13	13	13	11
	100	100	100	100

Source: Allensbach Archives, IfD (Institut für Demoskopie) Survey, no. 3056.

danger of isolating oneself. Currently, the subject of the EC lacks the potential to isolate.[4] Any view can be expressed without encountering lively interest or debate, determined approval or disapproval, but one does not know how long this will remain true.

The probable future accession of Greece, Spain, and Portugal to the EC and the real progress toward greater integration with the directly elected European Parliament will both demand sacrifices. The German population, however, is little prepared to make such sacrifices. There are no signs of real enthusiasm for the European idea, and people do not appear to be captivated by the historical moment. For many years, the people of Europe have shared a fundamental belief in progress, a belief that life will improve and that the individual can contribute to this development. But, as Table 3.2 shows, there has been a breach in the belief in progress, especially among the younger generation, and we are only beginning to understand its social and psychological significance.

As Table 3.3 indicates, there is a historical pathos in the wording of the question with which, some twenty five years ago, a survey explored the reality of the European idea in Germany:

"Do you think that you will live to see the day when the Western European countries join together to form the United States of Europe?"

In 1953, a plurality of 41 percent expected to witness this event, 29 percent said no, while slightly less than one-third were undecided. In 1974, after almost an entire generation, only 29 percent expected to witness a United States of Europe, and 51 percent now said that they will not live to see the

Table 3.2   Belief in Progress
          (percentage)

QUESTION: "Do you believe in progress—a belief that mankind is heading for a better future?"

	Total Population					Age Group 16–29				
	1967	*1972*	*1975*	*1977*	*1978*	*1967*	*1972*	*1975*	*1977*	*1978*
Believe in progress	56	60	48	39	34	66	72	55	38	37
Don't believe	26	19	30	35	40	19	13	26	35	38
Undecided/no reply	18	21	22	26	26	15	15	19	27	25
Total	100	100	100	100	100	100	100	100	100	100
Total number	1,979	2,018	2,031	1,026	987	543	516	521	257	255

Source: Allensbach Archives, IfD Survey nos. 2030, 2086, 3017, 3050, 3062.

Table 3.3   Attitude Toward a United States of Europe
(percentage)

QUESTION: "Do you think that you will live to see the day when the Western European countries join together to form the United States of Europe?"

	1953	1956	1961	1967	1969	1974
Yes, I do	41	34	36	34	38	29
No, I don't	29	36	30	39	42	51
Undecided	30	30	34	27	20	20
Total	100	100	100	100	100	100

Source: Allensbach Archives, IfD Surveys, nos. 059, 1001, 1059, 2028, 2052, 3002.

event. No wonder the German mass media have dealt with the subject of the EC with the greatest reservation—a journalist can hardly think of anything more thankless than immobility or decreasing salience.

After the horrors of the Hitler period and the 1945 collapse, the European idea was something like a refuge for many Germans, a compensation for their own lost national consciousness. A 1947 survey question ("If a vote were held in Europe, would you vote for or against the creation of a United States of Europe? Or would the whole matter not concern you?") was posed to a representative cross section of 100 students at the Universities of Tübingen and Freiburg. A full 70 percent of the students said they would vote for and only 12 percent said they would vote against the proposal.[5] Similarly, as Table 3.4 shows, a 1953 question on the willingness to yield national sovereignty to Europe resulted in a more than two to one response rate in favor of transferring the decision-making power on important questions to the European Parliament.

It was assumed, then, that the Germans were prepared to accept a supranational structure of European political organs. But this assumption is questionable today, for between 1974 and 1977, the Germans' confidence in the supranational course for the European Community was shaken. Four test questions indicated this change (Tables 3.5 through 3.8), and due to the dates, it appears that the break must have occurred after 1974. The first question (Table 3.5) concerned a common European currency, an idea that was approved by a majority of the German population in 1970 but disapproved by a majority in 1977, although this opposition could not yet be discerned in 1974. Likewise, the number supporting a supranational form of government for Europe (Table 3.6) did not decrease between 1970 and 1974. However, two other questions of symbolic significance—a European Olympic team (Table 3.7) and a European flag (Table 3.8)—show decisive changes similar to that which occured with the question about the deutschmark.

Table 3.4   Attitude Toward the European Parliament
(percentage)

QUESTION: "Who should have the last say on all important questions of the future, the European Parliament or the parliaments of the individual countries?"

	February 1953		
	Total Population	Men	Women
The European Parliament	37	46	30
The parliaments of the individual countries	14	18	11
It depends	5	7	3
Don't know	44	29	56
Total	100	100	100

Source: Elisabeth Noelle-Neumann and Erich Neumann, eds., *Jahrbuch der öffentlichen Meinung, 1974–1955* (Allensbach am Bodensee: Verlag für Demoskopie, 1956), p. 340.

A very peculiar insight is revealed here. People benevolently, if noncommittally, approve of the European Community, as discussed earlier, but on the surface everything appears almost motionless. A 1963 survey indicated that 28 percent of the respondents named "the union of the Western European countries into a united Europe" as one of their three greatest wishes; in 1977, fourteen years later, 27 percent also listed a united Europe as a wish.[6] As Table 3.9 shows, the same percentage of the respondents (43 percent) in 1974 and 1977

Table 3.5   Attitude Toward a European Currency
(percentage)

QUESTION: "Would you be in favor of or against a single European currency in place of the deutschmark?"

	1970	1974	1977
Would be in favor	52	57	35
Would be against	26	22	49
Makes no difference	14	13	11
Undecided	8	8	5
Total	100	100	100
Total number	2,039	991	1,013

Source: Allensbach Archives, IfD Survey, nos. 2060, 3002, 3046.

Table 3.6 Attitude Toward a European Government
(percentage)

QUESTION: "Would you be willing to accept, over and above the federal government a European government responsible for a common policy in foreign affairs, defense, and the economy?"

	1970	1974
Willing	56	55
Not willing	20	21
Undecided/no reply	24	24
Total	100	100
Total number	2,042	1,004

Source: Allensbach Archives, IfD Survey, nos. 2059, 3002.

thought that the countries of the EC had come closer to each other. An occasional tremor seems to disturb this noncommittal benevolence toward Europe, although it remains at a high level among the population of both the Federal Republic and of France (Table 3.10). Although the data indicate *support*, there is the paradox that *interest* in the EC has steadily decreased as the first direct election for the European Parliament approached. As Table 3.11 shows, interest shown in the problems of the EC had decreased in both France and Germany between 1973 and 1978.

A 1977 survey reveals, however, how grossly boring the European machinery—that intricate system of cross-national linkages and institutions—

Table 3.7 Attitude Toward a European Olympic Team
(percentage)

QUESTION: "Would you approve or disapprove if, instead of a German team going to the next Olympics, there were only a European team, representing all European countries?"

	1970	1977
Approve	25	19
Disapprove	51	64
Wouldn't care	13	13
Don't know	11	4
Total	100	100
Total number	2,039	1,013

Source: Allensbach Archives, IfD Survey, nos. 2060, 3046.

Table 3.8   Attitude Toward a European Flag
(percentage)

QUESTION: "Would you approve or disapprove if the German flag were no longer raised at major official ceremonies but a European flag instead?"

	1970	1977
Approve	35	21
Disapprove	41	60
Wouldn't care	18	14
Undecided	6	5
Total	100	100
Total number	2,039	1,013

Source: Allensbach Archives, IfD Survey, nos. 2060, 3046.

must be for the German population. There may be reasonable levels of internalized support and somewhat lower levels of interest, but the level of knowledge is low. The survey posed the following question (Table 3.12):

"Do you happen to know whether there is a European Parliament?"

A full 63 percent of the German respondents answered either "no" or "don't know"; only 37 percent replied with the correct answer. But when these 37 per-

Table 3.9   Attitude Toward Closeness of European Community Countries
(percentage)

QUESTION: "Do you think that the countries of the European Community have come closer to each other in recent years?"

	Federal Republic of Germany and West Berlin Population 16 and Over	
	March 1974	*August 1977*
The EC countries		
have come closer	43	43
have not come closer	37	33
Undecided	20	24
Total	100	100

Source: Allensbach Archives, IfD Survey, nos. 3002, 3046.

Table 3.10   Attitude Toward Membership in the European Community
(percentage)

QUESTION: "Generally speaking, is the membership (of your country) in the European Community a good thing or a bad thing?"

	Federal Republic of Germany Fall of Every Year			
	1973	*1975*	*1977*	*1978*
Good thing	63	61	59	63
Bad thing	4	6	7	4
Neither good nor bad	22	27	24	21
Undecided	11	6	10	12
Total	100	100	100	100

	France Fall of Every Year			
	1973	*1975*	*1977*	*1978*
Good thing	61	67	57	59
Bad thing	5	4	9	7
Neither good nor bad	22	24	28	26
Undecided	12	5	6	8
Total	100	100	100	100

Source: Commission of The European Community, *Eurobarometer*, no. 10 (January 1979), excerpt from table 3, appendix A 20.

cent were then asked a follow-up question ("Who elects or appoints the German representatives to the European Parliament?"), only about 16 percent of this group could correctly identify the Bundestag as the appointing agency for the German members of the European Parliament. In other words, only 6 percent of the more than 1,000 people questioned knew the correct answer, and 63 percent were not even aware of the existence of the European Parliament in Strasbourg. But lack of precise knowledge rarely hinders the expression of opinions, and, as demonstrated in Table 3.13, German ideas about the supranational character of the future European Community have remained relatively stable in the 1970s.

Although nothing seems to change on the surface, the preparedness to go supranational decreases as soon as it becomes imaginable and phrased in everyday terms. As Tables 3.7 and 3.8 showed, the percentage of those rejecting the idea of a European team going to the Olympics instead of a German team increased from 51 percent in 1970 to 64 percent in 1977, and the use of a

Table 3.11 Interest in the Problems of the European Community
(percentage)

QUESTION: "Are you interested in the problems of the European Community?"

	Federal Republic of Germany Fall of Every Year			
	1973	*1975*	*1976*	*1978*
Very much so	31	23	23	16
A little	48	51	50	53
Not at all	16	23	24	25
No reply	5	3	3	6
Total	100	100	100	100

	France Fall of Every Year			
	1973	*1975*	*1976*	*1978*
Very much so	20	23	18	14
A little	45	54	57	54
Not at all	33	22	24	30
No reply	2	1	1	2
Total	100	100	100	100

Source: EC, *Eurobarometer*, no. 10 (January 1979): 16–17, excerpt from table 7.

European flag instead of a German flag at official ceremonies was opposed by 41 percent in 1970 and by 60 percent in 1977. What is happening below the surface? One might immediately suspect signs of a new nationalism or a strengthened self-assurance to be behind this. But the survey data do not show an increased nationalism to an extent that might explain the change in attitudes on the Olympic team or the German flag. Nor do the data show concern about a loss of national identity: Tables 3.14, 3.15, and 3.16 show that German national identity is not threatened by the idea of the European Community.

The questions that diagnose this growing German weariness with "Europe"—the questions about the flag and Olympic team but not the one about the European currency—have been confirmed by surveys conducted in Germany by other members of the European Community. In response to a question first posed in 1973 (Table 3.17: "Should the union of the European Community be sped up, slowed down, or continued at the same pace?"), only in the Federal Republic of Germany did the answer "speed up" decrease in comparison to 1973.

The more recent tendency of the Germans to dissociate themselves from

Table 3.12   Extent of Knowledge about the European Parliament
(percentage)

QUESTION: "Do you happen to know whether there is a European Parliament?"

Federal Republic of Germany and West Berlin
Population 16 and over
August 1977

	Total Population	Education Elementary	Secondary
Yes, there is	37	32	48
No, there isn't	24	21	32
Don't know	39	47	20
Total	100	100	100

Follow-up question to persons who know that the European Parliament exists: "And could you tell me how the representatives of the Federal Republic come to be in the European Parliament, who appoints or elects them?"

	Total Population	Education Elementary	Secondary
The Bundestag (federal parliament)	6	4	10
The government	5	3	6
The political parties	3	3	5
Elected by the people	2	2	3
Other reply	1	1	1
Don't know, no (concrete) answer	20	19	23
Respondents not given the question	63	68	52
Total	100	100	100
Total number	1,013	695	317

Source: Allensbach Archives, IfD Survey, no. 3046.

Europe, observed under the surface of a pro-European stance, could have various causes: hope they once entertained in connection with the EC may have dwindled, or the Germans may have become conscious of dangers previously unnoticed. These developments could not have arisen until after 1974, for no symptoms of dissociation could be ascertained to 1974. The underlying

Table 3.13   Attitude Toward the Future Form of Europe
(percentage)

QUESTION: "What should a United Europe look like—in which form would you imagine it? Could you please answer with the help of this list?"

	Federal Republic of Germany and West Berlin Population 16 and over	
	February/March 1970	*August 1977*
There is only one single European government, the national governments having been abolished. All tasks hitherto fulfilled by the national government are taken over by the European government	15	12
There is a superordinate European government fulfilling certain tasks. But each country still has a government of its own to fulfill special government tasks of the country	52	53
There is no European government. The governments of the individual countries meet regularly to make decisions on their common policies	16	21
None of these	4	4
No reply	13	10
Total	100	100
Total number	2,021	2,058

Source: Allensbach Archives, IfD Surveys, nos. 2060, 3046.

variables involved here are the economy and the possibility of increased Communist influence.

In a 1978 speech, the EC Commissioner for Energy and Research, Guido Brunner, declared, "The fact is that our European Community is predominantly regarded as an economic affair by the people in Europe."[7] Economic hopes were certainly a central motive in 1970, when a survey investigated in some detail what expectations the population placed in the EC. The 1970 data (Tables 3.18 and 3.19) show that 59 percent of the respondents felt the EC would generate economic advantages. The questions of 1970 have not yet

Table 3.14   Attitude Toward German National Identity
(percentage)

QUESTION: "If someone said, 'I am proud of being a German,' would you agree?"

	Federal Republic of Germany and West Berlin	
	1970	1977
Agree absolutely	38	36
Largely agree	33	41
Rather not	14	12
Not at all	9	6
Undecided	6	5
Total	100	100
Total number	2,039	1,045

Source: Allensbach Archives, IfD Surveys, nos. 2060, 3046.

been repeated, but, nevertheless, one must recognize that the German population now assesses the EC's economic consequences differently. As shown in Table 3.20, the prevailing answers in 1977 and 1978 surveys were that German membership in the EC presented more of a disadvantage than an advantage compared to the prevailing answer in 1975, when membership was seen as advantageous.

Table 3.15   Attitude Toward Language Differences
(percentage)

QUESTION: "If someone said, 'It is impossible to unite Europe because we all speak different languages,' would you agree?"

	Federal Republic of Germany and West Berlin	
	1970	1977
Agree absolutely	5	4
Largely agree	15	13
Rather not	25	28
Not at all	44	34
Undecided	11	21
Total	100	100
Total number	2,039	1,045

Source: Allensbach Archives, IfD Surveys, nos. 2060, 3046.

Table 3.16   Attitude Toward Cultural and National Identity
(percentage)

QUESTION: "If someone said, 'In a United States of Europe there is a danger that the different peoples will lose their cultural and national identities,' would you agree?"

	Federal Republic of Germany and West Berlin	
	1970	1977
Agree absolutely	9	3
Largely agree	20	14
Rather not	29	30
Not at all	26	29
Undecided	16	24
Total	100	100
Total number	2,039	1,045

Source: Allensbach Archives, IfD Surveys, nos. 2060, 3046.

Diminished readiness to introduce a European currency in place of the deutschmark most clearly depicts the core of economic uneasiness. One must remember Germany's special situation here—the trauma of the great inflation after the First World War and the currency collapse after the Second World War. In the 1960s, survey research showed that the Germans react more sensitively to rising inflation than do other peoples.[8] It will suffice to compare two sets of figures to explain the attitude change of the Germans toward a European currency: in 1972, the inflation rate in the Federal Republic was 5.5 percent, in France 6.2 percent, in Italy 5.7 percent; in 1978, the figures were 2.6 percent, 9.5 percent, and 12 percent, respectively. The problem of inflation which the Germans considered to be highly alarming in the early 1970s was combatted successfully. The idea that this effort might have been in vain, that is, that a European currency might have exported higher inflation rates into Germany, makes a future European currency appear less attractive.

The second critical area—Europe's future relationship to socialist ideology—is substantially more complex. Here, two trends overlap: one is clearly visible, the other almost invisible. Both support the tendency to withdraw from the concept of the European Community.

There is an obvious concern that, via the European Parliament and a coalition of Social Democrats and Communists, Communism might acquire an influence it has up to now been unable to gain directly in land or federal elections. Staving off Eurocommunism has a completely different urgency for the German population than has the uniting of Europe. Approximately 24 percent of the German population answered, "There will be a United States of

Table 3.17   **Attitude Toward Rate of European Integration**
(percentage)

QUESTION: "At what speed should the development toward a united Europe continue—should it speed up, slow down, or go on as in the past?"

	Federal Republic of Germany Fall of Each Year			
	1973	*1975*	*1976*	*1978*
Speed up	49	47	41	38
Slow down	4	6	9	7
Same as in the past	34	36	37	34
Undecided	13	11	13	21
Total	100	100	100	100

	France Fall of Each Year			
	1973	*1975*	*1976*	*1978*
Speed up	36	45	42	40
Slow down	3	6	10	5
Same as in the past	40	36	35	37
Undecided	21	13	13	18
Total	100	100	100	100

Source: EC, *Eurobarometer*, no. 9 (July 1978); 10; *Eurobarometer*, 10 (January 1979); 13 [excerpts].

Europe," to a question about how the world will look in five or ten years, but twice as many, 52 percent, said, "The Communists will be in power in some countries of Western Europe." In addition, when asked which of some thirty political concerns were especially important to them, the Germans placed "to prevent Communist influences from advancing in Europe" in tenth place; "the union of European states" was rated twentieth.[9]

The "Left" maintains a totally different ambivalence to these issues. The question of which coalition will eventually gain ground in the European Parliament remains undecided. If a conservative majority were to emerge, an anti-socialist power bloc would be formed and the rapprochement between Western and Eastern Europe—a goal of the Left—would be severely affected. For this reason, the present idea of the European Community does not hold a real attraction for the Left. Their attention is focused on the East, for "Europe" is there as well, and it is vital for the Left to strengthen these bonds.

The general mood of the Left is not easy to discern, but with the aid of instru-

Table 3.18   Attitude Toward Economic Benefits of the European Community
(percentage)

QUESTION: "If someone said, 'In a United States of Europe, those people who have thus far been suffering the most economically would, above all others, have chances for a better life,' would you agree?"

	Federal Republic of Germany Adult Population 16 and Over		
	1970		
Agree absolutely	23	}	59
Largely agree	36		
Rather not	14	}	21
Not at all	7		
Undecided	20		
Total	100		
Total number	2,039		

Source: Allensbach Archives, IfD Survey, no. 2060.

ments that have been developed for observing the processes of public opinion the symptoms can be seen.[10] Three observations can be made about this general mood of the German Left. First, approximately 34 percent of the Federal Republic population sixteen years old and over—a remarkably high number—do not want to see the future of Europe limited to the countries of Western Europe. On the contrary, they wish it to include the countries of Eastern Europe and the Soviet Union (no matter how utopian this may seem to be). Among the Social Democrats, as shown in Table 3.21, the proponents of a Europe encompassing West and East (41 percent) are as strong as the adherents of the Western conception (40 percent).

The second observation concerns the important role that the environment plays in the process of public opinion. Someone who feels that his own conviction is widespread will speak openly and self-assuredly for it in public. But someone who thinks that he is in the minority will tend to remain silent in order to avoid isolation through his deviant opinion. In the case of most questions, the number of a specific view's proponents clearly relates to the number of individuals believing this view to be prevalent in the environment.[11] When a view's popularity is highly overrated, the false impression can usually be traced back to the emphasis the mass media place on it. When it is grossly underrated, one can conversely assume that the topic is no longer a matter of public concern, either in the mass media (sometimes because it is purposively suppressed) or in conversation in broader circles. For example, as Table 3.22

Table 3.19   Attitude Toward Economic Disadvantages of the European Community
(percentage)

QUESTION: "If someone said, 'In a united Europe, the cost of living would be higher and the danger of unemployment greater,' would you agree?"

	Federal Republic of Germany Adult Population 16 and Over
	1970
Agree absolutely	6 } 20
Largely agree	14
Rather not	31 } 59
Not at all	28
Undecided	21
Total	100
Total number	2,039

Source: Allensbach Archives, IfD Survey, no. 2060.

Table 3.20   Attitude Toward German Membership in the European Community
(percentage)

QUESTION (1975): "If you were to take stock of developments today, what would you say: has our membership in the European Community been advantageous to our national interest or disadvantageous?"

QUESTION (1977): "Does the Federal Republic draw more advantages or more disadvantages from its membership in the European Community, or would you say that the advantages and disadvantages balance out?"

QUESTION (1978): "All things considered, would you say that we have more advantages or less advantages than the other member countries in the European Community?"

	1975	1977	1978
EC an advantage	34	15	20
EC a disadvantage	17	25	31
Neither	26	46	32
Undecided	23	14	17
Total	100	100	100
Total number	1,011	1,045	n.a.

Source: Allensbach Archives, IfD Surveys, nos. 3020, 3046; EC, *Eurobarometer*, no. 10 (January 1979): 102, table 54.

Table 3.21   Attitude Toward Future Membership of a United Europe
(percentage)

QUESTION: "How should a united Europe look in your view? Should only the countries of Western Europe belong to it, or should a united Europe also include Russia and the Eastern European countries?"

	Fall 1978			
	Population of the Federal Republic 16 Years and Over	*Christian Democrats*	*Social Democrats*	*Liberals*
Only the countries of Western Europe	47	56	40	57
Also the Soviet Union and Eastern Europe	34	28	41	26
Undecided	19	16	19	17
Total	100	100	100	100
Total number	2,002	814	667	103

Source: Allensbach Archives, IfD Survey, no. 3060.

shows, the present number of proponents of a Europe encompassing West and East is distinctly underestimated, and this underestimation indicates that the process of winning public opinion for this idea is not yet underway.

The third observation relates to the situation when, if the adherents of a united Europe including West and East feel they have public support, they can be activated immediately (as shown by the so-called railway test). This test was developed to measure the willingness of respondents to speak or to remain silent in public—public in the sense that, in principle, all people have access to the situation and that the individual is among people whose names and convictions he does not know. The text of the question describes a five-hour railway journey. Someone in the compartment begins to talk about a subject—in one-half of the interviews he speaks out *in favor* of this subject, in the other half he speaks out *against* it. The decisive part of the question reads:

"Would you like to enter into a discussion with this traveling companion, or would you prefer not to do so?"

The adherents of a Europe encompassing both East and West are reticent as long as the traveling companion advocates a united Europe consisting of the Western European countries only; that is, as long as their perception that the climate of opinion in the railway compartment runs counter to their own individual view. But the respondents behave quite differently when they feel their convictions find support: all of a sudden, 70 percent of them are willing to enter

Table 3.22   Attitude Toward Other People's Views on the Future Membership of a United Europe
(percentage)

QUESTION: "Apart from your own opinion, what, do you believe, do most people in the Federal Republic think: are most for a united Europe including Russia and the Eastern European countries, or are most for a European unification of the Western countries alone?"

	Fall 1978			
	Population of the Federal Republic 16 Years and Over	*Christian Democrats*	*Social Democrats*	*Liberals*
Most are for a united Europe including Eastern Europe and the Soviet Union	8	8	10	5
Most only want a Europe of the Western European countries	59	61	61	65
Undecided	11	10	10	15
Impossible to say	22	21	19	15
Total	100	100	100	100
Total number	2,002	814	667	103

Source: Allensbach Archives, IfD Survey, no. 3060.

into the conversation (Table 3.23). The adherents of the idea of a united Europe including East and West thus form a considerable potential to set public opinion in motion. This process might only get underway after the European Parliament has convened and demonstrated the different camps' political strength and the manner in which coalitions will be formed. These events, however, are beyond the scope of this essay.

In 1970, a survey conducted by the Institut für Demoskopie investigated the motives supporting the European idea, and the results showed the hope for more security to form a sort of second pillar beside the hope for a European market (Table 3.24). When read today, however, the question of 1970 sounds naive. Today, one would associate the European Community and NATO (North Atlantic Treaty Organization) close together as an integral economic, political, and military concept. This sense of the security nature of the EC was underscored by Christoph Bertram, Director of the International Institute for Strategic Studies in London, when he remarked that the European common policy remained—and even more so in the 1980s—a security policy.[12]

We do not yet know how much the countries of the European Community really have in common with respect to history, tradition, and geography. Is

Table 3.23 The Railway Test
(percentage)

QUESTION: "Suppose you were on a five-hour railway journey, and the people in your compartment were discussing this subject. Someone says that he favors a European union of the *Western countries alone*. Would you like to enter.into a discussion with this person, or would you prefer not to join the conversation?"

In every second interview, the question read: ". . . Someone says that he favors a united Europe that *includes Russia and the Eastern European countries. . . .*"

Those Who Under the Condition that the Traveling Companion Advocates a Europe of the West:	Persons Who Favor a United Europe of the West Themselves	Persons Who Favor a United Europe of the East and West Themselves
Want to join the discussion	49	43
Prefer not to join the conversation	41	44
Don't know	10	13
Total	100	100
Total number	350	438

Those Who Under the Condition that the Traveling Companion Advocates a Europe Consisting of West and East:	Persons Who Favor a United Europe of the West Themselves	Persons Who Favor a United Europe of the East and West Themselves
Want to join the discussion	40	70
Prefer not to join the conversation	45	22
Don't know	15	8
Total	100	100
Total number	501	321

Source: Allensbach Archives, IfD Survey, no. 3060 (September–October 1978).

there a common denominator—a groundswell—that moves the continent as a whole? Perhaps one could think of an exhibition that was shown in Paris in 1978, "Paris-Berlin: 1900 to 1933." It was surprising for many people to see how many similarities had apparently developed unintentionally between the two cities. An EC Eurobarometer survey contains a question that appears to show this groundswell. The question concerns a fundamental feeling that is common to every epoch: the demand for change or for preservation. The question reads:

"On this list are three basic points concerning the society we live in. Which of the three expresses what you tend to think?"

The points listed were: the whole social order has to be changed radically by a revolution; our society has to be improved step by step through reforms; our existing society has to be defended courageously against all revolutionary forces.

As Table 3.25 indicates, there was a rise of conservatism in all Western European countries in the 1970s, with Germany showing the greater increase. But Table 3.25 also shows, between the spring and fall of 1978, a decrease of the conservative mood everywhere as if it were coordinated. The observation of such regularities across Europe will be a new area of research in the study of European integration.

As discussed at the beginning of this essay, the subject of the EC lacks real conflict potential since one can voice any opinion in public and not be isolated. But this in itself may indicate some potential for future conflict. In the event that the process of EC integration is speeded up, bringing with it partisan contours and real consequences for the individual, it is possible that people may long for the time when European integration was a slow-paced affair, with the mass media finding the entire subject so uninteresting that they reported only what was absolutely necessary.

But there remains one more fact, a fact which is more a question for the future than a comment on the present: the younger generation is no more enthusiastic about Europe than the older generation. An enthusiasm for the European Community from the under-thirty-year-olds which surpasses that from the over-thirty-year-olds cannot be registered by means of any question. One should expect that an idea embodying the future would have inspiration for the younger generation, but this is not the case. This lack of any more

Table 3.24   Attitude Toward the European Community as a Step Toward World Government
(percentage)

QUESTION: "If someone said that the United States of Europe were a first step toward a world government that would prevent wars, would you agree or not agree?"

	Federal Republic of Germany Adult Population 16 and Over
	1970
Agree absolutely	40 ⎫ 66
Largely agree	26 ⎭
Rather not	13 ⎫ 21
Not at all	8 ⎭
Undecided	13
Total	100
Total number	2,039

Source: Allensbach Archives, IfD Survey, no. 2060.

Table 3.25   European Attitude Toward Conservatism (percentage)

QUESTION: "On this list are three basic points concerning the society we live in. Which of the three expresses what you tend to think?"

	Belgium	Denmark	Germany	France	Ireland	Italy	England	Netherlands
Favoring – "Our existing society has to be defended courageously against all revolutionary forces"								
Spring 1970	14	—*	20	12	—*	11	—*	15
Fall 1976	19	38	39	18	23	18	25	32
Spring 1977	18	39	48	19	26	28	26	32
Fall 1977	19	40	50	22	26	27	28	37
Spring 1978	21	42	50	20	24	31	31	35
Fall 1978	15	29	44	13	20	24	25	25

*Not asked in 1970.

Source: EC, Eurobarometer, no. 9 (July 1978): 10; Eurobarometer, 10 (January 1979): 13 [excerpts].

support among the young does not augur well for the future of the European Community.

Notes

1. This paper takes these reports into account. The most recent report considered is no. 10, "Eurobarometer: Public Opinion in the European Community: (January 1979), based on a survey conducted on November 15–21, 1978, with 8,702 interviews.

2. See Institut für Demoskopie [IfD] Allensbach/IMAS, Survey, no. 4625.

3. Ferdinand Tönnies, Kritik der öffentlichen Meinung (Berlin: J. Springer, 1922), p. 138.

4. Elisabeth Noelle-Neumann, "The Spiral of Silence: A Theory of Public Opinion," Journal of Communication 24, no. 2 (Spring 1974): 43–51; and "Turbulences in the Climate of Opinion: Methodological Applications of the Spiral of Silence Theory," Public Opinion Quarterly 41, no. 2 (Summer 1977): 143–58.

5. Jahrbuch der öffentichen Meinung, 1947–1955 (Allensbach am Bodensee: Verlag für Demoskopie, 1956), p. 339.

6. Allensbach Archives, IfD Survey nos. 1073 and 3039; Elisabeth Noelle-Neumann, ed. Jahrbuch der Demoskopie, 1977, Institut für Demoskopie Allensbach (Vienna, Munich, Zurich and Innsbruck: Verlag Fritz Moldeu, 1977), p. 92.

7. Guido Brunner, cited in Das Parlament, no. 14 (April 8, 1978): 13.

8. Elisabeth Noelle-Neumann, "Geldwert und öffentliche Meinung: Anmerkungen zur Psychologie der Inflation," in Geldtheorie und Geldpolitik. Gunter Schmölders zum 65. Geburtstag, ed. C. A. Andreae, K. H. Hansmeyer, and G. Scherhorn (Berlin: Duncker und Humbolt, 1969).

9. Elisabeth Noelle-Neumann, "Die Europawahl und die Medien," in In der Diskussion Unsere Zukunft: Europa, Heft 4/77, Europa-Kongress der CDU, Landesverband Rheinland-Pfalz am 25./26. November, 1977 (Mainz: herausgegeben von der Stimme der Union Rheinland-Pfalz, 1977).

10. Elisabeth Noelle-Neumann, "The Spiral of Silence," and "Turbulences in the Climate of Opinion."

11. Elisabeth Noelle-Neumann, "Turbulences in the Climate of Opinion."

12. Christoph Bertram, "Was anders sein wird in den 80er Jahren," *Frankfurter Allgemeine Zeitung*, no. 282 (December 12, 1977): 10.

INTEGRATION AT SOCIETY'S LEVEL: TRANSACTION FLOWS AND NONGOVERNMENTAL BEHAVIOR

Part II

WILFRIED PREWO

4

Trade, Interdependence, and European Integration

This essay examines the use and appropriateness of models to explain the interdependence of bilateral trade flows in a multicountry trade network. Special attention is paid to an empirical specification which among political scientists has become known as the analysis of transaction flows, following the approach suggested by Savage and Deutsch.[1] This essay discusses the application of related models developed by economists and applies such a model to international trade flow among eighteen OECD countries in order to reveal the trade effects of European integration from 1958 to 1974.

In the social sciences, empirical models of transaction flows were first developed by noneconomists. Sociologists, geographers, psychologists, and political scientists have applied models of transaction flows to a wide spectrum of social phenomena.[2] Common to these analyses of interactions and interdependences among social "agents" (individuals, households, groups, regions, nations) is an empirical specification which relates interactions positively to properties of these social agents and negatively to impediments, which usually are taken to be exogenous to the agents themselves.[3] Some examples for properties that influence interactions positively are: population sizes of cities in studies of telephone communications; income differences in studies of migration; and bonds among family members (father-son) in studies of occupational choice. Impediments which may restrict interactions are factors such as distance, costs of communication, and transportation.[4]

The question an economist might be asked is this: Why have these models, which carry such intuitive appeal, played only a minor role in explaining economic transactions, especially in international trade where flows and their economic determinants are measurable? One reason is that models of transaction flows are empirical hypotheses which have not been explicitly derived from economic theory. But this is not a satisfactory explanation, since "measurement without theory," though proclaimed a cardinal sin in economics, is widely practiced. The more important explanation for the minor role of multicountry trade flow models is that trade theory itself (and hence the testable hypotheses derived from it) has usually been restricted to the two-country sphere (for example, the "home country" vs. the "rest of the world") and has been concerned with departures from the equilibrium trading pattern as a result of changes in economic variables (such as price changes). Consequently, empirical studies have addressed dynamic disequilibrium features of trade, and they usually have been demand-oriented on the assumption that the supply to satisfy the import demand of the (small) home country would always be forthcoming from the (large) rest of the world at given world prices. Differentiation of total imports by countries of origin has been rare.[5]

The traditional two-dimensional (home vs. foreign country) approach is a simple but powerful tool for analyzing effects specific to the home country or the rest of the world. Examples are the effects of exchange rate changes, changes in world prices, changes in domestic income, or tariff changes on home-country trade. However, when the focus is on multifaceted interdependence relations, the usefulness of the demand-oriented approach is limited. In a multicountry world we can no longer assume that the supply of exports of any country is infinitely elastic at given prices (that any country is large enough to export unlimited quantities at given prices). Therefore, supply conditions have to be incorporated in a multicountry analysis. In addition, natural trade barriers due to location, which have been neglected in the two-dimensional framework, now become important, since the effects of location (transportation cost being one major aspect) will discriminate against distant in favor of nearby countries. Furthermore, artificial trade barriers (tariffs, quotas, and so forth), if not applied uniformly, also have to be considered. In sum, three groups of factors have to be incorporated in studies of trade interdependence: demand, supply, and artificial as well as natural trade resistance factors.

The analysis of economic integration among European countries calls for a multicountry approach in which all of these three factors are prominent. Not only demand but also supply conditions and locational factors have been crucial determinants of the effects of integration, especially in Europe; and a discriminatory (or preferential) application of tariffs and other artificial trade barriers has been the essential trade aspect of integration. Therefore, any analysis of integration that does not take into account all three elements of inter-dependence would be incomplete.

Theoretical Background and Empirical Model

This study starts from the premise that supply and demand conditions, as well as trade resistance factors, are the major determinants of the bilateral trade pattern in a multicountry trade network. Ideally, a structural model incorporating all of these aspects should be derived from Walrasian general equilibrium considerations. Such a general model could start with the specification of bilateral demand and supply equations, containing activity variables (such as real output and income) and price variables. The prices entering this model would be bilateral prices, since a general export (import) price which is equal across all receiving (supplying) countries does not exist in reality owing to differences in the commodity composition of aggregate trade and demand differences which may leave scope for monopolistic discrimination. A further complication is introduced by trade resistance factors (tariffs, transport costs, and so on), which will drive a wedge between the bilateral export and import prices of identical goods. Disregarding resistance factors would be a serious omission, since it would reduce the set of trade policy questions that can be addressed. In general form, the bilateral import demand and export supply equations can be expressed as follows:

(1) $X_{ij}^d = f(D_j; P_{11}, P_{12}, \ldots, P_{1m}; P_{21}, P_{22}, \ldots, P_{2m}; \ldots;$
$P_{m1}, P_{m2}, \ldots, P_{mm})$

(2) $X_{ij}^s = g(S_i; \pi_{11}, \pi_{12}, \ldots, \pi_{1m}; \pi_{21}, \pi_{22}, \ldots, \pi_{2m}; \ldots;$
$\pi_{m1}, \pi_{m2}, \ldots, \pi_{mm})$

where d indicates demand; s indicates supply; i is the exporting country index $(i=1, \ldots, m)$; j is the importing country index $(j=1, \ldots, m)$; ;m is the number of countries; X_{ij} is the quantity of trade flows from i to j; D_j is the activity variable on the demand side, for example, income; S_i is the activity variable on the supply side, for example, real output or productive capacity; and P_{ij}, π_{ij} are bilateral demand and supply prices. P_{ij} and π_{ij} differ by trade resistance factors (tariffs, transport costs, and so on).

If the trading world consists of m = 18 countries (as in the empirical part of this study), there would be 306 (17 x 18) bilateral demand and an equal number of bilateral supply equations, each containing 324 (18 x 18) price terms. It is a hopeless task to determine bilateral demand and supply from equations (1) and (2) and to estimate all the output, income, bilateral price, and substitution elasticities. Even if the difficulties in specifying a full structural model are overcome, data requirements and computational difficulties may render it impractical for estimation of the trade pattern in a multicountry network as large as the one in this study.

This makes it necessary to introduce simplifying assumptions in order to arrive at a practical model. Three alternative specifications have been proposed in the trade literature. From the theoretical point of view the most appealing avenue is to follow the approach suggested by Armington,[6] who presented a theory of demand for products distinguished by country of production. He provided a theory-based allocation scheme which distributes predetermined total import demand among supplying countries. The Armington approach has so far been restricted to the demand side on the assumption that supply is infinitely elastic at the given prices. While this simplifies the analysis to a single demand equation, it is a strong assumption.

In the second category belong so-called constant-market share models, which incorporate supply elements but disregard the full effects of relative price changes by virtue of the constant-share assumption. The constant-market share approach also results in a single-equation model, but again at the cost of a strong assumption, which also precludes many policy questions. In addition to the mentioned restrictions, the Armington and constant-market share models also have abstracted from factors that impede or promote trade, such as transport costs, tariffs, quotas, subsidies, and trade preferences.[7] This specifications omission reduces the set of policy questions that can be addressed.

The third alternative is to follow the approach of trade interdependence (or transaction flow) models.[8] Rather than attempting the task of specifying a full structural model, these studies concentrate on the equilibrium pattern of bilateral trade flows. This is achieved by specifying a reduced form equation for the equilibrium trade pattern which is conceived on (not derived from) general equilibrium notions. The enormous advantage of this specification is the joint inclusion of demand, supply, and trade resistance factors. Its drawback is the restriction to an analysis of the equilibrium pattern of trade. It thus disregards disequilibrium aspects and precludes an analysis of the dynamic aspects of the trade pattern. It is an empirical question whether this imposes a severe limitation, that is, whether the dynamic disequilibrium features of bilateral trade interdependence turn out to be more important than the static equilibrium characteristics. The empirical evidence in the trade literature is not sufficient for a definitive answer to this question.[9]

The theory underlying the trade interdependence models can be outlined as follows. It is assumed that equilibrium bilateral trade flows are determined within a competitive supply and demand system, such as equations (1) and (2) above. Import demand is a function of domestic real income, domestic and foreign goods prices, and factor prices. The latter are assumed to be determined exogenously by the country's resource endowment, capital, labor, and technological factors. Analogously, export supply depends on the exporting country's final output, domestic and foreign goods prices, and factor prices. With prices constant, changes in real income will change the country's demand for imports. On the supply side, changes in the country's productive resources or in their degree of utilization change final output and in turn change that country's supply of exportables. Within a competitive supply and demand framework, world price ratios will be equalized in terms of the exporter's valuation (which is before the incidence of international transport-related charges and tariffs). In the equilibrium trade framework, export price variables may thus be eliminated because they merely adjust to equate supply and demand.[10] Yet prices paid for identical commodities will diverge in different countries because of the differential impact of natural and artificial trade barriers. Whether and to what extent two countries i and j trade depends then, not only on demand and supply conditions, but also on the trade resistance factors between i and j. These may reduce and even nullify comparative advantage reflected in producer price comparisons.

In equilibrium, the following empirical equation for the bilateral trade flow from country i to j can be written:

(3) $X_{ij} = f(Y_i, Y_j, R_{ij})$ $(i \neq j = 1, \ldots ,m)$ where

$$\delta f/ \delta Y_i \gtreqless 0, \quad \delta f/ \delta Y_j \gtreqless 0, \quad \delta f/ \delta R_{ij} < 0.[11]$$

In (3) the variables are defined as follows: X_{ij} is the aggregate value of exports (f.o.b.) from i to j; $Y_{i(j)}$ is Gross Domestic Product of country i (j) representing final output and domestic real income, respectively; and R_{ij} is a vector of trade resistance factors for exports from i to j.

While X_{ij}, Y_i and Y_j are measured directly, the resistance variables in R_{ij} are not. The trade resistance factors include all tariff and nontariff barriers to trade. Given the multitude of trade barriers, we limit ourselves to a few crucial barriers. The resistance factor R_{ij} has both quantitative and qualitative components. First, three qualitative variables are used to characterize R_{ij}. These are:

$G_{ij} = \begin{cases} 1 \text{ if trading partners i and j are members} \\ \quad \text{of the same preferential trading group (EC, European Free Trade} \\ \quad \text{Association [EFTA], British Commonwealth),} \\ 0 \text{ if not.} \end{cases}$

$L_{ij} = \begin{cases} 1 \text{ if trading partners i and j have common language} \\ 0 \text{ if not.} \end{cases}$

$B_{ij} = \begin{cases} 1 \text{ if trading partners i and j are neighbors,} \\ 0 \text{ if not.} \end{cases}$

Second, R_{ij} has two quantitative components. The first quantitative component is the nominal tariff rate of country j on imports from country i, Z_{ij}. This rate will not be uniform over all exporters to j in the presence of discriminatory tariff arrangements. The second quantitative component is the ratio of true c.i.f. (cost, insurance, and freight) value to true f.o.b. (free on board) value, T_{ij}, called the transport cost factor. In principle, the differences between c.i.f. and f.o.b. trade values represent the costs of freight and insurance.[12]

For estimation purposes we express the bilateral trade flow equation as linear in logarithms:

$$(4) \quad X'_{ij} = \overset{a}{0} + {}^{a}_{1}Y'_i + {}^{a}_{2}Y'_j + {}^{a}_{3}Z_{ij} + {}^{a}_{4}G_{ij} + {}^{a}_{5}L_{ij}$$
$$+ {}^{a}_{6}B_{ij} + {}^{a}_{7}T_{ij} + \mu_{ij}$$

where the " ' " denotes the logarithm and μ is assumed to be a classical stochastic disturbance term.[13] This specification's major departure from other studies is the explicit treatment of transport costs and tariffs. The incorporation of transport costs has posed major problems in earlier studies of this type since there are no precise measures of transport costs. This difficulty has been resolved in a recent work, however.[14]

The inclusion of both qualitative and quantitative components, for example, the joint inclusion of a tariff variable and an indicator for membership in a customs union such as the EC, does not amount to double-counting. Our hypothesis in this regard is that economic integration is a process whose effect on trade cannot be attributed to tariff changes alone. The presumption is that psychological barriers (such as "buy domestic products" preferences) and communication barriers are reduced as well by the integration process. As far as transport costs are concerned, it is sometimes asserted that, irrespective of actual transport costs, adjacent countries will enjoy more intensive trade than country pairs without common border areas. Since the model includes both qualitative and quantitative trade impediments, it allows for a test of the hypothesis that these qualitative indicators exert effects on trade flows above and beyond the quantitative trade barriers.

Equation (4) is a model rich in empirically testable hypotheses about the effects of demand, supply, and various bilateral resistance or preference factors on the equilibrium level of trade flows at a specific point in time. Since it is an equilibrium specification by virtue of the elimination of prices, its major drawback is that it precludes an analysis of the disequilibrium aspects of trade interdependence. However, this does not rule out comparisons of the determinants of the trade pattern at various points in time. If the trade structure is stable in the short run but undergoes systematic changes in the long run (through changes in tastes, technological conditions, trade barriers, integration), then it is appropriate for an intertemporal analysis of the trade pattern to estimate a cross section such as equation (4) at different times. The specification chosen here is suitable for such a comparative analysis of static equilibria, and the estimation of this model with cross-section data for different times serves to indicate any systematic changes in the roles of the major economic determinants of the equilibrium trade pattern.[15]

The Development of Trade in the EC and EFTA

Before discussing the empirical results, it is useful to provide some descriptive statistics on trade within the EC and EFTA and between these two trading blocs and the other Western industrial countries belonging to the OECD. Although this study's primary focus is on the EC, the now defunct EFTA has played a major role in shaping the trading pattern during the 1960s. In this study, "EC" refers to the original six member countries and excludes the three new member countries.[16] Since the latter countries joined the EC on January 1, 1973, it is too early for a full evaluation of the trade impact due to EC enlargement.[17]

The economic backbone of integration in the Common Market has been the creation of a customs union characterized by the elimination of tariffs between member states and the setting up of a common external tariff on imports from nonmember countries.[18] The discriminatory (or preferential) elimination of internal tariffs, which had also been achieved by EFTA, has two distinct trade effects: lower-cost imports from partner countries will be substituted for higher-cost domestic products (trade creation), and higher-cost imports from partners will be substituted for lower-cost imports from nonmember countries (trade diversion).[19] Trade diversion will take place in those cases where the preferential customs treatment that partners receive will allow them to sell their products, despite higher costs of production, below the price (cost + duty) of imports from nonmember sources. Trade diversion will generally decrease welfare, whereas trade creation increases welfare.

The summary statistics provided in Tables 4.1 and 4.2 highlight the changes in the trade pattern that have occurred since the creation of the two trading blocs. The tables show the total values of imports of the individual member countries of the EC and EFTA together with average annual growth rates. The imports are broken down by exporting area into imports received from member countries of the respective trade blocs and imports from external OECD sources. The shares of imports from external and internal sources in total OECD imports are also provided below the respective value figures.

Total imports by both the EC and EFTA have increased rather strongly, reflecting both integration effects as well as the general increase in world trade, which was aided by the tariff reductions due to the outcomes of the Dillon (1962) and Kennedy Round (1968–72) negotiations. But, on an average yearly basis, EC imports from 1958 to 1972 grew 3 percent faster than EFTA

Table 4.1 EC Imports from OECD Countries, 1958-74*

Importing Country	OECD Value f.o.b. (millions of dollars) 1958	OECD Value f.o.b. (millions of dollars) 1974	OECD Average growth rate (%)	EC Value f.o.b. (millions of dollars) 1958	EC Value f.o.b. (millions of dollars) 1974	EC Average growth rate (%)	Other OECD Value f.o.b. (millions of dollars) 1958	Other OECD Value f.o.b. (millions of dollars) 1974	Other OECD Average growth rate (%)
Belgium-Luxembourg (Shares %)	2,382	24,069	14.6	1,449 / 60.8	17,332 / 72.0	15.7	934 / 39.2	6,737 / 28.0	12.3
France	2,590	33,461	16.2	1,282 / 49.5	23,276 / 69.6	18.6	1,308 / 50.5	10,185 / 30.4	12.8
Germany	4,820	46,857	14.3	1,862 / 38.6	29,441 / 62.8	17.6	2,958 / 61.4	17,416 / 37.2	11.0
Italy	2,029	23,760	15.6	772 / 38.0	15,571 / 65.5	19.3	1,257 / 62.0	8,189 / 34.5	10.2
Netherlands	2,683	27,917	14.8	1,501 / 55.9	17,753 / 63.6	15.6	1,182 / 44.1	10,165 / 36.4	13.5
EC	14,505	156,065	15.0	6,866 / 47.3	103,374 / 66.2	17.3	7,639 / 52.7	52,691 / 33.8	12.0

Source: OECD, Overall Trade by Countries, series A, various issues.

*EC refers to the original five EC member countries listed in the table (Belgium-Luxembourg is considered as one country). OECD refers to the eighteen OECD listed in the paper. Other OECD refers to the thirteen OECD countries not members to the original EC.

Table 4.2 EFTA Imports from OECD Countries, 1958–72*

Importing County	OECD Value f.o.b. (millions of dollars) 1958	OECD 1972	OECD Average growth rate (%)	EFTA Value f.o.b. (millions of dollars) 1958	EFTA 1972	EFTA Average growth rate (%)	Other OECD Value f.o.b. (millions of dollars) 1958	Other OECD 1972	Other OECD Average growth rate (%)
Austria (Shares %)	799	4,351	12.0	120 / 15.0	1,056 / 24.3	15.6	680 / 85.0	3,296 / 75.7	11.1
Denmark	1,027	4,066	9.6	454 / 44.2	1,986 / 48.8	10.3	573 / 55.8	2,080 / 51.2	9.0
Finland	437	2,267	11.6	191 / 43.7	1,225 / 54.0	13.2	246 / 56.3	1,042 / 46.0	10.1
Norway	1,077	3,618	8.4	499 / 46.3	1,898 / 52.5	9.3	578 / 53.7	1,720 / 47.5	7.5
Portugal	335	1,662	11.3	145 / 43.2	531 / 32.0	9.1	190 / 56.8	1,131 / 68.0	12.6
Sweden	1,727	6,642	9.4	567 / 32.8	3,181 / 47.9	12.2	1,160 / 67.2	3,461 / 52.1	7.6
Switzerland	1,479	8,385	12.3	200 / 13.5	1,862 / 22.2	16.0	1,279 / 86.5	6,524 / 77.8	11.5
UK	4,927	16,718	8.5	1,151 / 23.4	4,463 / 26.7	9.5	3,776 / 76.6	12,256 / 73.3	8.2
EFTA	11,808	47,710	9.8	3,325 / 33.4	16,201 / 34.0	11.1	8,482 / 66.6	31,509 / 66.0	9.1

Source: OECD, *Overall Trade by Countries*, series A, various issues.

*OECD refers to the eighteen OECD countries listed in the paper. Other OECD refers to the eleven other OECD countries that are not EFTA members. Data for the EFTA countries cover only the period prior to 1972, the date Denmark and the UK left EFTA.

Imp.   G·N·P· Per capita   'Imports\ exports   England.
Ireland.
Denmark.

86   INTEGRATION AT SOCIETY'S LEVEL

imports.[20] The average growth rates for the individual Common Market countries are very similar, while there is more variance in EFTA import increases. This is a reflection of the more heterogenous character of the EFTA economies in contrast to the EC.

In all EC countries, partner imports grew more rapidly than imports from external sources. Italy and France had the highest tariffs at the beginning of the EC, and it could therefore be expected that intra-EC imports would grow strongly in these countries owing to both trade creation and trade diversion. This is borne out by the shares and growth rates shown in Table 4.1. On the other hand, the Benelux countries already had low protective barriers at the time of the establishment of the EC, and the potential for trade increases due to integration was therefore smaller. This is again shown by the figures in Table 4.1, which indicate a high Benelux dependence on EC imports already in 1958 (over 50 percent) and correspondingly smaller growth rates on intra-EC imports after 1958.

The development of the trade shares from 1958 to 1974 illustrates a major point. Divergencies in the intra-EC shares, which were quite large in 1958 (38 to 61 percent), have become much smaller by 1974 (63 to 72 percent), while the average has risen very strongly from 47 to 66 percent. Differences in interdependence have been reduced while the level of interdependence has risen remarkably to the point that two-thirds of total OECD imports in the EC are supplied by partner countries. The mirror image of this is the development in the shares of imports from nonmember countries. While non-EC exporters to the Common Market have not suffered absolute losses, their market shares in the EC have declined from more than 50 percent to 34 percent over the seventeen-year period from 1958 to 1974.

The development of internal and external EFTA imports reflects the heterogenous character of the EFTA countries. On the average, external and internal EFTA imports grew at a more even pace than in the EC. This suggests that trade-creating and diverting forces were weaker in the EFTA than in the EC. Another reason is the lower degree of homogeneity among EFTA countries and some special trade linkages. The relatively low intra-EFTA trade of Switzerland reflects her strong ties with France and Germany, and the special relationships among Scandinavian nations (all members of EFTA) have influenced the trade shares for these countries. While the structural and external trade shares have, on average, remained constant at one-third and two-thirds, respectively, the variance between individual EFTA countries' shares has not been reduced as much as in the EC. Trade interdependence among EFTA countries has remained low compared with the EC.

Trade creation and diversion have usually been attributed to the tariff changes implemented by the EC and EFTA. Tariff changes alone, however, fail to provide a full explanation of the large magnitude and the incidence over time of trade creation. For the EC, for example, it has been found that trade creation after 1965 was substantial, that is, after a reduction of intra-EC tariffs by roughly two-thirds.[21] And the trade-creating momentum of the EC appears not to have lost all force right after the complete elimination of internal tariffs (July 1968). What other phenomena could therefore have been responsible for trade share increase in the Common Market? The establishment of one large (common) market has allowed firms to exploit the benefits of economies of scale; and there is convincing evidence that this, in conjuction with increased competition, has resulted in substantial intra-industry specialization.[22]

Apart from consideration of these cost and demand-oriented aspects, few studies have searched for non-price-related causes of integration.[23] The EEC Treaty contains many provisions which have not affected trade directly through the price mechanism, as in the case of tariff changes, but indirectly through changes in social, political, and psychological barriers as well as reductions of nontariff barriers. This calls for a consideration of such impacts in a study of integration and trade. The major difficulty for such a broad study is to find quantifiable measures or proxies for these essentially qualitative phenomena. The incorporation in this study of dummy variables for common language, neighboring countries, and membership in the EC and EFTA is an attempt in this direction. Since the quantitative trade barriers (tariffs and transport costs) are included as well, the coefficients on the qualitative variables (G, L, B in equation 4) serve to indicate the separate influences of these characteristics on bilateral trade.

Empirical Results

The trade interdependence model specified above has been estimated for seventeen yearly cross sections of aggregate bilateral trade flows among eighteen OECD countries for the years 1958 to 1974. The number of bilateral trade flows is therefore 18 x 17 = 306 for each yearly cross section. These yearly samples encompass a substantial portion of total world trade. The eighteen countries in the sample are Canada, the United States, Japan, Australia, Austria, Belgium, Denmark, Finland, France, West Germany, Italy, the Netherlands, Norway, Portugal, Spain, Sweden, Switzerland, and the United Kingdom. The estimates for the major variables are shown in Table 4.3, and all the estimates included are significant except where noted.

The elasticities on Gross Domestic Product (GDP) show remarkable stability over the seventeen-year period, and their values conform to previous studies for different country groups and time periods. These elasticities on GDP are interesting in two respects. First, the sum of the two elasticities is always greater than one, implying that the intensity of bilateral trade is proportionately higher (as measured by level of GDP) among large trading partners than among small ones. In a dynamic context this would imply that bilateral trade grows more rapidly than world production, which is consistent with historical experience. Second, supply conditions in the exporting country exert a stronger influence on trade flows than demand conditions in the importing nation. This result is not immediately obvious, since it implies that the level of output affects the trade balance, in particular, that large countries will become net exporters vis à vis small countries. In the dynamic context this second result on the GDP elasticities implies that rapidly growing countries will become net exporters (Japan and Germany are examples). This is consistent with the observation that faster growing countries will become exporters to markets where they had not sold before, on the basis of economies of scale or technological innovation.

Besides the relative magnitude of the GDP coefficients, the constancy of the elasticities over the entire period is remarkable. This constancy gives confidence that GDP is a proper proxy for the basic underlying forces: tastes and income on the demand side; factor endowments, technological conditions, and production capacity on the supply side. Given their constancy, the elasticities are apparently not influenced by transitional factors. This result is important, since it would otherwise be improper to draw long-run dynamic inferences from these cross-sectional results.

The elasticities of trade flows on the ad valorem transport cost rates are provided in Column 3 of Table 4.3.[24] The transport cost rate elasticities are consistently above unity over the entire period, with a typical value of -1.5. This result contrasts with the elasticities on distance, which would be in the neighborhood of -.6,[25] and thus demonstrates that distance is an improper proxy variable for transport costs.

The estimates for the elasticity of bilateral trade flows with respect to tariff rates are also shown in Table 4.3 (Column 5). Both the tariff rates and the coefficient on Z_{ij}, and therefore also the tariff rate elasticities, have persistently fallen over the seventeen-year period. Reductions in tariff rates have been brought about by the GATT negotiations and the elimination of tariffs within the EC and EFTA. In the framework of GATT, tariffs on manufactured goods have been reduced by about 20 percent in 1962 as a result of the Dillon Round and by about 40 percent as a result of the Kennedy Round. The latter reduction was applied over a five-year period from 1968 to 1972. The tariffs within the EC and EFTA had been gradually eliminated by 1968 and 1967, respectively. The tariff rate elasticity became insignificant in 1972, which coincided with the completion of the Kennedy Round reductions. But the tariff rate elasticities for the second half of the 1960s are already at such low magnitudes that the major trade effects of integration experienced after 1965 cannot be attributed to tariff reductions. As a corollary, this suggests that the major sources of integration effects on trade of an enlargement of the EC might not be caused by tariff reductions but by the reduction of other (nontariff) barriers to trade.

Such nontariff effects of preferential trade arrangements are reflected in the coefficients on membership in a preferential trade group (shown in Column 7

Table 4.3   Estimates for Major Variables, 1958–74

Year	GDP-Elasticities Exporting Y_i	GDP-Elasticities Importing Y_j	Transport Cost Elasticities (e)	Transport Cost Rate^a (t) in %	Tariff Elasticity $(\bar{Z}a_3)$	Tariff Rate $(\bar{Z})$ in %	Coefficients on Preference G_{ij}	Coefficients on Language L_{ij}
1958	.796	.677	−1.83	8.0	−.57	12.9	.191	.490
1959	.808	.706	−1.41	8.4	−.60	12.7	.250	.529
1960	.833	.696	−1.86	7.0	−.52	12.1	.291	.437
1961	.824	.677	−0.98	7.9	−.41	11.9	.307	.522
1962	.817	.674	−1.96	9.1	−.44	11.2	.207	.528
1963	.826	.677	−1.52	11.4	−.30	9.5	.303	.567
1964	.811	.672	−1.63	8.5	−.35	9.2	.260	.537
1965	.820	.652	−1.26	8.9	−.27	9.0	.304	.561
1966	.825	.668	−1.29	10.8	−.20	8.8	.396	.535
1967	.812	.679	−1.65	9.7	−.20	8.2	.441	.533
1968	.828	.717	−1.51	9.6	−.20	7.5	.478	.519
1969	.822	.712	−1.27	8.5	−.15	6.8	.580	.494
1970	.846	.700	−1.58	11.3	−.13	6.2	.635	.479
1971	.847	.705	−1.48	11.1	−.12	5.5	.679	.428
1972	.852	.729	−1.07	7.7	−.08^b	4.9	.698	.380
1973	.849	.747	−1.66	7.8	−.05^b	4.6	.701	.380
1974	.873	.749	−1.38	11.6	−.03^b	4.5	.643	.338
Overall Average	.829	.696	−1.49	9.3	−.27	8.6	.433	.486

Source: Table is based on data given by Wilfried Prewo, "Determinants of the Trade Pattern among OECD Countries from 1958 to 1974," *Jahrbücher für Nationalökonomie und Statistik,* vol. 193 (1978), pp. 341–58.

^{a}The yearly transport cost rate averages are based on observed (unadjusted) c.i.f. and f.o.b. values, where t = (c.i.f. − f.o.b.)/f.o.b.
^{b}Based on insignificant regression coefficient.

of Table 4.3). These preference coefficients exclusively indicate the nontariff effects of integration, since by incorporation of tariffs the model attempts to control on tariff changes. Comparison of the tariff and preference coefficients indicates that nontariff effects of membership in the EC or EFTA appear to have a far greater expansionary impact on trade than the mere reduction of tariffs. The importance of nontariff effects is amplified by the increase in the preference effect after 1967 and 1968, that is, after the complete elimination of internal tariffs among EFTA and EC countries, respectively. This result is consistent with the finding of other studies that trade expansion due mainly to trade creation and partly to trade diversion has considerably exceeded expectations formed on the basis of tariff reductions at the start of EC and EFTA.

The coefficients on L_{ij} (Column 8 of Table 4.3) show that common language has exerted an important and fairly steady impact on bilateral trade flows during the 1960s. Since the mid-1960s, however, its importance has fallen contemporaneously with the further rise in the preference effect. In the 1970s, membership in a preference group has become about twice as important for bilateral trade than the absence of language barriers. The coefficient for neighboring countries (B_{ij}), on the other hand, is insignificant throughout the period from 1958 to 1972.

The coefficients on the language and preference effects are illustrated in Figure 4.1 together with the tariff rate elasticities. Figure 4.1 shows the time-varying impacts of these variables. While the tariff elasticities have monotoni-

Figure 4.1   Preference and Language Coefficients and Tariff Elasticities, 1958–74

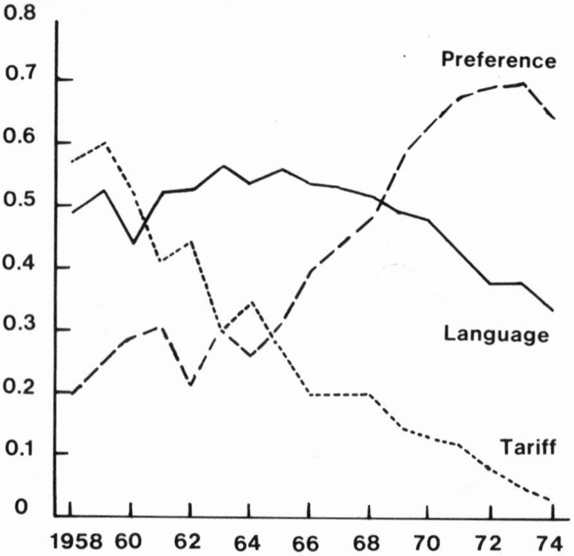

Source: Based on estimate results from Equation 4, in chapter 4.

cally declined, the preference effect has increased in near-monotonic fashion. The language effect remained steady at first and declined gradually after 1965. The opposite movements of preference and tariff effects have already been discussed, but the opposite movements of preference and language coefficients point to an important non-price source of integration effects. Beyond the removal of internal tariff barriers, the EC and EFTA have promoted trade among member countries by setting international standards and specifications, facilitating the flows of information and communication, and reducing nontariff barriers to trade. All of these components have reduced the transaction costs commonly associated with language barriers. Progress toward the reduction of such barriers has initially been slow, which explains the hesitant increase in the preference coefficient in the early 1960s and the initial constancy of the language coefficient. The dramatic changes in these qualitative coefficients after the elimination of tariff barriers suggest that policies aimed at a further reduction of nontariff barriers provide a major source of future integration effects.[26]

Summary and Conclusions

This chapter has examined the use and appropriateness of models aimed at explaining the interdependence of bilateral trade flows in a multicountry framework. The theoretical specification of such a model should include supply and demand conditions together with trade resistance factors as determinants of bilateral trade flows. To capture the general equilibrium nature of trade interdependence, the ideal empirical model should be a structural model, but in practice it would be difficult to develop such a model. The practical alternative followed here is the specification of a reduced form equation for the equilibrium trade pattern, which is conceived on the basis of general equilibrium notions. Such models are known as trade interdependence or transaction flow models.

Since trade interdependence models incorporate the major economic factors shaping the equilibrium pattern of bilateral trade, they appear well suited for an empirical analysis of bilateral trade flows in a multicountry framework. Their disadvantage is that they neglect dynamic disequilibrium aspects of trade. But their important advantage is the incorporation and separate consideration of many empirically relevant variables, which makes them attractive for an analysis of the importance of integration effects.

The experience of integration has revealed major changes in the trading pattern that cannot be explained solely on the basis of tariff changes. Consequently, a complete analysis of integration requires an approach allowing for the identification of other (nontariff) causes of integration effects. The empirical specification of the chosen trade interdependence model includes various qualitative indicators of integration-related variables, in addition to demand and supply conditions and the more traditional trade resistance factors, tariffs and transport costs. This model has been applied to seventeen yearly (1958–74) cross-sectional data panels on bilateral trade flows among eighteen OECD countries. The eighteen countries encompass all the EC and EFTA countries as well as their major trading partners. The empirical results highlight the changes over time in the roles of the major determinants of the equilibrium trade pattern.

The empirical results show interesting variations over time in the effects of trade resistance factors, in particular tariffs, preference effects, and language barriers. While tariff changes have not played a major role in increasing trade among European countries after about 1965, membership in a preferential trade group (such as the EC) and language barriers continue to be important trade-promoting or trade-impeding forces, respectively. The results suggest that further reductions in nontariff and language-related barriers provide a rich source for future integration effects. The diversity among trade-impeding and trade-promoting factors and their time-varying impacts warrant separate and careful consideration in studies of integration.

Notes

1. I. R. Savage and K. W. Deutsch, "A Statistical Model of the Gross Analysis of Transaction Flows," *Econometrica* 28 (July 1960): 551–72.

2. *See*, for example, S. A. Stouffer, "Intervening Opportunities: A Theory Relating Mobility and Distance," *American Sociological Review* (December 1940): 845–67; and S.- C. Dodd, "The Interactance Hypothesis: A Gravity Model Fitting Physical Masses and Human Groups," *American Sociological Review* 15 (1950): 245–56.

3. Impediments, or factors with negative influences on interaction levels, are not always specified explicitly. Their influence may be recognized implicitly in a residual approach by attributing the difference between "hypothetical" (or "predicted," or "normal") and actually observed transaction levels to the impact of impediments. This approach is especially appealing when impediments are difficult to measure or to identify.

4. The range of possible applications was so wide that some social scientists could not resist showing a correspondence between "laws" of social interaction and laws in the natural sciences, especially the law of gravity and the law of Coulomb. *See* Dodd, "The Interactance Hypothsis."

5. For a survey of several multicountry pure demand studies, *see* R. M. Stern, J. Francis, and B. Schumacher, *Price Elasticities in International Trade and Finance: An Annotated Bibliography* (Toronto: Macmillan, 1976), esp. pt. 2, pp. 22–69. For a survey of two-region supply and demand studies, *see* S. P. Magee, "Prices, Incomes and Foreign Trade," in *International Trade and Finance: Frontiers for Research*, ed., P. B. Kenen, (Cambridge, England: Cambridge University Press, 1975), pp. 175–252, esp. 181–84.

6. P. S. Armington, "A Theory of Demand for Products Distinguished by Place of Production," *International Monetary Fund Staff Papers* 16 (March 1969): 159–78.

7. An exception is J. D. Richardson, "On Improving the Estimate of the Export Elasticity of Substitution," *Canadian Journal of Economics* 5 (August 1972): 349–57. For a discussion of such factors, *see* B. Balassa, *The Theory of Economic Integration* (Homewood, Ill.: Richard D. Irwin, 1961).

8. In this category belong the studies by J. Tinbergen, *Shaping the World Economy* (New York: Twentieth Century Fund, 1962), esp. pp. 262–93; P. Pöyhönen, "A Tentative Model for the Volume of Trade between Countries," *Weltwirtschaftliches Archiv*, vol. 90, no. 1 (1963): 92–99, and "Towards a General Theory of International Trade," *Ekonomiska Samfundet Tidskrift*, no. 2 (1963): 69–77; K. Pulliainen, "A World Trade Study: An Econometric Model of the Pattern of Commodity Flows in International Trade in 1948–1960," *Ekonomiska Samfundet Tidskrift*, no. 2 (1963): 78–91; H. Linnemann, *An Econometric Study of International Trade Flows* (Amsterdam: North-Holland, 1966); and V. J. Geraci and W. Prewo, "Bilateral Trade Flows and Transport Costs," *The Review of Economics and Statistics* 59 (February 1977): 67–74.

9. On the issue of lags and adjustment speeds, *see* Magee, "Prices, Incomes and Foreign Trade"; and H. B. Junz and R. R. Rhomberg, "Price Competitiveness in Export Trade among Industrial Countries," *Division of International Finance Discussion Paper*, no. 22 (Washington, D. C.: Board of Governors of the Federal Reserve System, 1973).

10. E. Leamer and R. M. Stern, *Quantitative International Economics* (Boston: Allyn and Bacon, 1970), p. 146.

11. Pure theory allows negative income and output responses, but the empirical expection is $\delta f/\delta Y > 0$ and $\delta f/\delta Y > 0$. Other studies [Linnemann, *An Econometric Study of International Trade Flows* and N. D. Aitken, "The Effect of the EEC and EFTA on European Trade: A Temporal Cross-Section Analysis," *American Economic Review* 53 (December 1973): 881–92] have also included the total population of exporting and importing countries as determinants of market size. On the export side they argued that a larger population, by implying the larger market size, would afford domestic producers economies of scale. A large domestic market would allow them to produce efficiently without reliance on foreign markets. The potential export supply should thus decrease with increased population. The analogous argument is advanced for the importing country (Linnemann, *An Econometric Study*, pp. 11–24, and Aitken, "The Effect of the EEC," p. 882). However, from standard trade theory and profit maximization analysis, producers benefiting from economies of scale should take advantage of this by exporting. Indeed, in studies of the commodity composition of trade, this hypothesis has been supported. Lacking a convincing theoretical rationale for including *total* population as a determinant of *aggregate* bilateral exports or imports, this variable is not included in Eq. (3).

12. F.o.b. (free on board) value excludes international transport and insurance changes, which are included in the importer's c.i.f. (cost, insurance, and freight) valuation.

13. The disturbances have zero means, constant variance, and are uncorrelated with each other. The tariff variable Z_{ij} has not been entered in log form, since it will be zero if countries i and j belong to EEC or EFTA and have eliminated tariffs between them.

14. Geraci and Prewo, "Bilateral Trade Flows and Transport Costs."

15. Pulliainen, "A World Trade Study," and Aitken, "The Effect of the EEC," also provided estimates for a series of cross-sectional data. But these studies suffered from the choice of distance as a proxy for transport costs, and they did not include tariffs.

16. Due to data limitations, Belgium-Luxembourg will be considered as a single country.

17. It would also be hazardous to apply the methodology of this study to trade data on the most recent years, since the trading pattern for these years cannot be assumed to be in equilibrium, and it has not yet fully adjusted to the major shocks due to oil price increases, recession, and major currency changes, as evidenced by balance-of-payments disequilibria.

18. *See* Part Two, Title I of the Treaty establishing the European Community. The other major aspect of the EC has been the adoption of a Common Agricultural Policy. While there is agreement that the creation of the customs union has increased trade in manufactured goods and welfare during the 1960s, there is considerable fear that the highly protective effects of the agricultural policy continue to result in trade diversion and negative welfare effects.

19. The distinction between trade creation and trade diversion was drawn by J. Viner, *The Customs Union Issue* (New York: Carnegie Endowment for International Peace, 1950).

20. For 1972, total EC imports were $85.5 billion; this implies an average growth rate of 12.9 percent from 1958 to 1972.

21. W. Prewo, "Integration Effects in the EEC: An Attempt at Quantification in a General Equilibrium Framework, *European Economic Review* 5 (1974): 379–405.

22. B. Balassa, "Trade Creation and Trade Diversion in the European Common Market: An Appraisal of the Evidence," *Manchester School of Economic and Social Studies* 42, no. 2 (June 1974): 93–135.

23. An exception is Aitken, "The Effect of the EEC." His model is related to the approach used here but suffers from the exclusion of tariffs and the choice of distance as a proxy for transport costs. This misspecification is critical in analyzing the trade effects of the EC and EFTA. While transportation costs have, on the whole, not decreased, Aitken's estimates (p. 885) for the impact of distance are systematically declining during the integration period. This is evidence that distance is a proxy not only for transport costs but also for phenomena that have been affected by integration, such as psychological barriers, language barriers, and so on. Aitken's omission of a tariff variable raises further doubts about the conclusions drawn from his estimation results.

24. The coefficient on T_{ij}, the transport cost factor, is the elasticity of trade flows with respect to the ratio of c.i.f. to f.o.b. value. These elasticity values have the expected signs, and the standard errors are relatively small. The elasticities on T_{ij} can be interpreted with reference to an ad valorem transport cost rate, t_{ij}, defined as the ratio of true transport costs (the difference between true c.i.f. and true f.o.b. value) to true f.o.b. value, that is, $t_{ij} = T_{ij} - 1$. Thus, the elasticity of bilateral trade with respect to the transport cost rate, e, is estimated by $e = a_7 (t/(t + 1))$. This is a variable elasticity which rises with the transport cost rate. In lieu of true transport cost rates, which are unobserved, Table 4.3 gives the simple averages of the observed transport cost rates (t) for each year's 306 bilateral trade flows, together with the associated elasticities. In light of the measurement errors contained in these data, it should be noted that the rates in Table 4.3 are not the true transport cost rates, although averaging has removed certain offsetting measurement errors. Over the seventeen-year period the average transport cost rates vary from 7 percent to 11.6 percent, with an overall average of 9.3. The year-to-year variations are certainly plausible given the fluctuations—around a generally rising trend—of freight rates. Their absolute levels are also in conformity with other information. For further discussion, see W. Prewo, "Determinants of the Trade Pattern Among OECD Countries from 1958 to 1974," *Jahrbücher für Nationalökonomie und Statistik*, vol. 193 (1978): 341–58.

25. This distance elasticity conforms to the results of the studies which used distance as a proxy for transport costs. This misspecification casts doubt on the results obtained in simulation studies such as Aitken, "The Effects of the EEC," where it was assumed, without proof, that trade liberalization reduces the distance elasticity.

26. B. Balassa, "Trade Creation and Trade Diversion," points out that the maintenance of border formalities poses a psychological barrier and that governmental institutions and public enterprises continue to favor domestic over partner sources in their purchases of industrial products.

EMIL J. KIRCHNER

5

Interest Group Behavior at the Community Level

Toward a Framework for Analysis

Although interest groups are recognized as important actors in the process of European integration, particularly by neofunctionalists such as Haas and Lindberg,[1] little systematic analysis has been conducted on the behavior of European interest groups. A majority of writers concern themselves with the structure and organization of individual interest groups at the European level or restrict their analysis to consideration of the impact of individual interest groups on the passage of particular Community policy.[2] Given these limitations, a more careful consideration of the formation and development of interest groups at the European level, together with a detailed look at the structural characteristics of these groups, their relationship to the Community institutions, and the diverse ways in which they attempt to influence Community-level decision making, would help to clarify the strengths, weaknesses, and potential of these groups in the decision-making process of the EC. This study is based upon information gathered from a detailed examination of the structure, development, activity, and effectiveness of the twenty-one largest European interest groups.[3]

One of the main problems with a study of interest groups is the perennial problem of definition. Numerous meanings are attached to the terms "interest" and "group," and this lack of specificity ultimately presents difficulties when one attempts to construct typologies of groups or indeed to categorize the channels they utilize in order to influence decision makers. For the purpose of this study, the definition of "interest group" is based on Robert J. Lieber's application of the term.[4] It designates those organizations which are occupied, at any time, in trying to influence the policy of public bodies in their own chosen direction. European interest groups, otherwise referred to as umbrella organizations, are centrally organized associations of interest groups and essentially of a confederal type, each of which represents either a number of similar national groupings or both national groupings and European industry committee groupings.[5] Among the umbrella organizations examined are (UNICE) Union of Industries of the European Community for industry, (COPA) Committee of Professional Agricultural Organizations in the European Community for agriculture, and (ETUC) European Trade Union Confederation for trade unions.

It is first necessary to construct a framework for analyzing these groups and their activities at the Community level. Hence, although our aim is not to develop a theory of European interest groups, it will be useful to take a look at several approaches that seek to explain the behavior of interest groups in the EC in order to establish in what ways, if at all, these approaches could serve as a framework for this study. The three distinct analytical approaches considered are: the neofunctionalist theory; Caporaso's structural-functionalist approach to European integration; and aspects of group theory.

The Neofunctionalist Theory

The neofunctionalist school can be traced from the work of Mitrany[6] to that of Haas, Lindberg, and Schmitter. Although there are certain differences among these writers' interpretations of the process of European integration, they maintain similar definitions and hypotheses, one of which is to recognize the central role that interest groups play as political actors in the integrative process. The neofunctionalists emphasize the pluralistic nature of society; competing elites and interest groups who perceive advantages in regional groupings rather than simple national ones and change their values, loyalties, and orientations in this direction as a means of satisfying wants. This is an inherent part of the "expansive logic of integration" applied by the concept of "spillover."[7] It is seen as a process whereby cooperation in one functional sphere flows into another or others. Moreover, as seen by Lindberg, the changing values and orientations of interest groups in the process of integration take two forms: demand and support. The interest groups will maintain a political system because they support it and expect it to satisfy their wants, to which end they will make certain demands on the system.

In accordance with the neofunctionalist thesis, Meynaud and Sidjanski found in their study on European pressure groups that many of these groupings established themselves at the Community level in response to the formation of a new center of decision making and as a result of advantages expected from Community action. As Sidjanski has pointed out, some of these groups

came into being the moment the institutions of the EEC were formed; others . . . were set up at the same time as and according as the regulatory powers of the EEC began to take effect and influence various interests. Sometimes the formation of these organs was spontaneous. Sometimes it was prompted by an invitation or even by some pressure from the Commission.[8]

Yet another reason was the perception of the potential threat that one existing, centrally organized interest group poses to another. On a different occasion I have argued that this largely explains the formation of the European trade union interest group organizations.[9]

However, since the late 1950s and early 1960s, the Community's socioeconomic and political environment has changed. Hence, many of the assumptions upon which the neofunctionalists developed their theory no longer hold. The decline of ideology has been replaced by an emerging consciousness among the electorate of the need for greater participation in decision making. The increasing bureaucratization of politics that prevailed in the 1950s and 1960s has also been declining since the mid-1970s, as the decision makers have become subject to demands for greater "accountability" and "legitimacy." Thus, the rationale of economic incrementalism that was thought to determine the actions of the decision makers has been undermined by other considerations relating to these changed environmental factors. On the other hand, some developments correspond to neofunctionalist thinking. The evident popular concern with welfare has escalated to the extent that there has been a marked increase in social policy demands and an emergence of platforms for environmental and consumer protection.

Possibly the most significant shortcoming of the neofunctionalist thesis is its focus upon private industry and, hence, upon the direction of interests from employers and unions in the private sector toward Community-level decision making. The past ten years have witnessed an increasing number of Social Democratic governments in Western Europe which have implemented, to a varying extent, nationalization programs. The consequences of this for the reorientation of "loyalties, expectations, and political activities" to Community institutions have been great. The nationalization of industries effects a strengthening of the coalition of employers, unions, and the national governments, thereby undermining the incentive to find new centers of decision toward which they can direct their interests and upon which they can focus their attention. Thus the take-off point for integration in certain sectors has been delayed or, once initiated, has not been succeeded by the harmonization of policies, largely because these events counteract the assumptions upon which the neofunctionalists conceived of the spillover mechanism as operating.

Philippe Schmitter's refined approach to the role of European interest groups, which is based on the neofunctionalist tradition, is now considered. Schmitter defines "integration" as

the process of transferring exclusive expectations of benefits from the nation-state to some larger entity. It encompasses the process by virtue of which national actors of all sorts (government officials, interest group spokesmen, politicians, as well as ordinary people) cease to identify themselves and their future welfare entirely with their own national governments and its policies.[10]

It is the emphasis in the final line of the quotation that is of greatest significance. Hitherto, definitions of "integration" have related to the complete transference of actors' expectations, loyalties, and beliefs to a new center of decision making.[11] Schmitter's definition dilutes this emphasis and thereby allows for individuals to hold "divided loyalties." Indeed, it enables him to cope with a problem that the early neofunctionalists could not contend with, the need to explain why political actors seek to pursue their interests at both the European and national levels. Although Schmitter does not focus directly upon the role of interest groups in the EC, his model allows a study of the activities of these particular political actors to be conducted, which could produce a much closer consideration of their role than is possible on the basis of the early neofunctionalist theory. However, the model could have the drawback of being too complex and, indeed, too abstract a view of the role of political actors, such as interest groups, in the formation and development of a regional political community, to allow for it to be readily operationalized.

The Structural-Functionalist Approach

James Caporaso's *The Structure and Function of European Integration*[12] is distinguished by the application of Almond's functional analysis of interest groups to a revised neofunctionalist interpretation of integration. Thus, Caporaso attempts to analyze the role of interest groups in the EC through a comparison with the functions that interest groups perform at national level. He focuses on two functions, interest articulation and interest aggregation, and he considers the roles of both institutional interest groups (the Commission and the individual member states of the EC) and associational interest groups (such as employers' associations and trade unions).[13]

According to Caporaso, the activities of associational interest groups act as mechanisms for the compensation of certain defects in the Community system. For example, the Community has no structured, institutionalized, or differentiated organs for the provision of informed opinion or statistical data relating to the numerous topics on which it can legislate; hence, the interest groups with their professional personnel provide the required technical facilities in the drafting of proposals. A second compensatory role of associational interest groups is the communication of Community affairs to the member organizations and thus to the masses. Without the normal channels of contact between decision makers and the masses, that is to say, elections, the Community has had to rely heavily upon these groups to act as intermediaries.

However, while the actions of the interest groups have a reinforcing effect upon the structural limitations of the Community system, they simultaneously dilute the capability of the groups themselves in their attempts to represent their members' interests faithfully. Hence, a conflict arises between their duties to their members and their Community role as a mechanism whereby compromise is reached among the various national positions on a given policy proposal. This conflict does have its benefits, however. In view of the limited powers of the European Parliament, the Economic and Social Committee, and the Consultative Committee of the EC, the interest groups are forced to focus their attention upon the Council of Ministers and the Commission. Further, the elusive nature of the Council, its reluctance to deal with interest groups directly, and the national orientation of its officials, render the Commission the most popular channel of influence.

If interest groups are limited in their access to the EC institutional channels, they also face an intrinsic problem of their own. Their very nature limits their effectiveness, primarily because the harmonization and coordination of common interests among the member organizations is impeded by the heterogeneity of the sociopolitical systems they represent. Furthermore, the lack of autonomy from their national counterparts exacerbates this problem, together with the lack of formal structures within the EC for the performance of the function of interest aggregation.

From this evidence, Caporaso concludes that associational interest groups are greatly restricted in their activities and, therefore, in their effectiveness at the Community level. Indeed, he argues that interest group activity is consequently directed toward both the national and Community levels in order to influence Community policy.[14] Caporaso has shown that the structural-functionalist approach has a lot to offer for a study of the role of interest groups in the EC, particularly through the value of employing typologies of interest groups and their functions. Moreover, this particular analysis highlights many of the ways in which European interest groups differ in their activities (interest articulation and interest aggregation) from interest groups at the national level. Finally, Caporaso's concern with the intrinsic nature of the groups themselves, together with the characteristics of the political system of the EC, is useful in the search for explanatory variables relating to the phenomena of European interest groups and their formation and development.

However, there are certain limitations with this approach. Caporaso assumes that Almond's typologies of interest groups, which were developed in the context of national political systems, apply to European interest groups. He does not consider the possibility that these groups might include among them other functions that are peculiar to the European or, indeed, to the supranational context. Finally, he does not consider the effect of any factors other than the nature of the groups and the Community system upon his findings. The content of Community policy proposals, the strength of interest groups associated with national counterparts, and international events, together with many other factors, might also be influential factors.

Aspects of Group Theory

While we cannot expect group theory to provide the solutions to all these problems, the concepts and hypotheses developed by some writers in this tradition might have a contribution to make to a study of the behavior of interest groups in the EC. Samuel Beer has proposed that British and American interest groups have the opportunity to influence decision makers at four distinct phases in the policy-making process.[15] These are during elections, in the legislature, in the administration and through political parties. However, in the Community, influence is largely restricted to the administration, that is, the Commission and the Council of Ministers.[16] An exception to this is COPA, one of the most structurally developed of the European interest groups.

In his study of the role of interest groups in Italian politics, Joseph La Palombara distinguished two broad, analytically separate types of access and influence.[17] The first he termed "*clientela*," which refers to the clientelistic relationship between interest groups and the bureaucracy. The second he called "*parentela*," which involves a process of group interaction with the bureaucracy through the intermediaries of political parties and which is thus based essentially on political kinship. Averyt has applied this classification (agency and group variables)[18] in his examination of the relationship between the EC and the national administration, on one hand, and the EC and national interest groups, on the other. Although he does not focus on the European interest groups, he suggests that the extent of national *clientela* will determine both the development of Community-level interest groups and the strength of EC-national linkages. This point could have far-reaching implications for our analysis, as it proposes that, through a more detailed study of not only the activity of interest groups at the EC level but also the conditions under which they operate at the national level, we could gain a clearer understanding of the formation and development of European interest groups.

Each of these three approaches has a contribution to make to an understanding of the behavior of interest groups in the EC. However, a review of their limitations shows that none of them can provide a comprehensive analysis of the topic. Hence, it might be useful to consider ways in which the defects of one approach can be supplemented by aspects of another. For this we attempt to construct a framework for analysis that seeks to: increase and enlarge the existing knowledge regarding the formation and development of European interest groups; elaborate and refine the existing conceptual models; and assess the usefulness of this framework for a study of interest group behavior in the EC.

Drawing from the group theories example, this essay attempts to construct a number of typologies of European interest groups on the basis of their structural characteristics, including the date of establishment and the groups' aims and objectives. From this information, an analysis is made of the similarities and differences between European interest groups with regard to their development and structure and to the factors that have contributed to or initiated the activities of the groups. Typologies will also be constructed along the lines suggested by the neofunctionalists on the style of decision making and the mechanism for resolving internal conflicts. Finally, characteristics of the structural-functionalist approach will be adopted by considering the topic in terms of the functions the groups perform in the Community system. This analysis involves consideration of the groups' activities and their access to or targets of influence on Community institutions: the Council of Ministers, Commission, European Parliament, Economic and Social Committee and other consultative committees. In this way greater insight is gained into the relationship between the types of interest groups and the types of issues they promote, the channels of influence they utilize, and the impact of their actions on Community policy. These findings should also provide an indication of the degree of autonomy they exercise from their national counterparts and the level of integration achieved by these interest groups.[19]

Evolution of the European Interest Groups

In the following examination of the twenty-one European interest organizations, a distinction will be drawn between sectional interest groups and promotional interest groups.[20] Sectional interest groups include organizations that seek to represent the interest of a particular section or functional category of society and are based on their members' occupational roles or professions; economic producer groups, trade unions, organizations in agriculture, and the various professional organizations. Sectional interest group organizations are listed under categories A, B, C, and D. These categories stand, respectively, for occupational roles relating to: industry, banking, and insurance; agriculture; trade unions; and liberal and social professions. The categorization used here pays heed to the perception of interest held by those representing the various European interest groups, that is, whether they thought that the interests of their group were shared by or similar to other existing European interest groups.[21] As a consequence the four categories emerged. Promotional interests cover organizations that seek to promote specific causes or values whose group of reference in principle is constituted by either the whole population or a large section thereof, for example, environmentalists, consumers, and families.

As shown in Table 5.1, some general information characteristics of the twenty one interest group organizations examined can be derived. Four of the organizations were founded either before or after the establishment of the

Table 5.1   Formation of European Interest Groups*

	1951-1956			1957/1958			1959-1967		
	Estab-lished	*Organi-zation*	*Sector*	*Estab-lished*	*Organi-zation*	*Sector*	*Estab-lished*	*Organi-zation*	*Sector*
GROUP A: Industry Banking Insurance	1951 1953	FIPMEC CEA	Trade & crafts Insurance	1957 1958 1958 1958	COCCEE UNICE PC UACEE	Trade & commerce Industry Chambers of com- merce Craft industries	1960 1965	BFEC CEEP	Banking Public enter- prises
GROUP B: Agriculture				1958	COPA	Agricul- ture			
GROUP C: Trade Unions	1951 1955	CIC CIF	Trade union for executive workers Trade union for public service employees	1958 1958	European Secretariat ICFTU European Secretariat WCL	Trade unions (socialist/ social democratic Trade unions (Christian)	1967	Liaison Committee (CGIL/ CGT)	Communist trade unions of Italy & France
GROUP D: Liberal, Intellectual, & Social Pro- fessions									
GROUP Z: Promotional Interest Organiza- tions				1957	EUROCOOP	Coopera- tives	1963	GCECEE	Savings Banks
Total	4 organizations			7 organizations 2 European secretariats			3 organizations 1 liaison committee		

*See list of abbreviations at the back of the book for the full titles of organizations cited herein.

Note: The two 1958-established trade union secretariats of the ICFTU and WCL became two independent trade union organizations (ECFTU and EO/WCL) by 1969. The ECFTU members, together with other European ICFTU members formed the ETUC in 1973 and by 1974 all members of the EO/WCL joined the ETUC, thus dissolving the EO/WCL. The 1967 established

Table 5.1 Continued

1968/1969			1970-1973			1974-1978			Total
Estab-lished	Organi-zation	Sector	Estab-lished	Organi-zation	Sector	Estab-lished	Organi-zation	Sector	
			1972	EUROPMI	Small & medium-sized under-takings				10
			1973	LC/IRU	Trans-port				
									1
	CGIL →		1974 ⟶						5
1969	ECFTU →		1973	ETUC					
1969	EO/WCL →		1974						
						1975	SEPLIS	Liberal Intellec-tual & social professions	1
1969	COFACE	Family	1971	Associa-tion of sav-ing and credit co-operatives		1974	EEB	Environ-mentalists	6
			1973	BEUC	Consumers				
3 organizations			4 organizations 1 liaison committee			2 organizations 1 European secretariat			23

Liaison Committee of the CGT/CGIL ceased to exist when in 1974 the GCIL decided to become a member of the ETUC. The arrows thus mark the continuous flow or gradual strengthening of the trade union movement from being organized in several secretariats to the all-encompassing European trade union organization of the ETUC.

Source: Assessment (by author) of written records (1973–78) and interviews with representatives of the 21 European interest groups between July 1977 and August 1978.

European Coal and Steel Community in 1952. The establishment of six organizations coincided largely with the start of the EC in 1958. The eight years
marking the period between 1959 and 1967 witnessed the establishment of
only three organizations, but within a year of the achievement of the Customs
Union and the free movement of labor in mid-1968, three further organizations emerged. The period between 1970 and 1973, highlighted by two important summit meetings of the EC (The Hague in December 1969, and Paris
in October 1972), and the enlargement of the EC from six to nine member
states, saw the arrival of five more organizations. Finally, the period between
1974 and 1978, marked by the energy and subsequent economic crises of the
EC, bore two organizations.

As can be seen from Table 5.1, sectional groups outnumber promotional
groups by two to one. They are also generally established over a much longer
period than the promotional groups. It is an indication that up until the late
1960s, economic interests prevailed more than, for example, social or environmental ones. In general terms, five formation periods dominate for the individual groups. For Group A (industry, banking, and insurance), 1957–65;
Group B (agriculture), 1958; Group C (trade unions), 1969–73, Group D
(liberal, intellectual, and social professions), 1975; and Group Z (promotional
groups), 1969–74.

In response to their relatively late arrival at the European level, representatives of EUROPMI (Liaison Committee for Small and Medium-Sized Industrial Enterprises in the EEC) pointed out that most of their business was home-
market-based, and transactions across borders had played only a secondary
role However, since 1970, according to these representatives, two important
developments have taken place necessitating a response in the form of a European organization. First, since 1970, the EC alone, mainly through the Commission, has been able to conclude external trade agreements with third world
countries. With the EC adopting liberal external trade policies, especially towards the less developed countries, an increasing number of products were imported by the EC that were in competition with the products produced by small
and medium-sized undertakings.

The second development related to Commission proposals of June 1970
and 1972 (Fifth Directive) for a Statute for a European Company, which
stipulated requirements concerning minimum capital. Since small and medium-sized undertakings could not meet the requirements of the proposed
European company legislation, they pressed for a form to suit their size by
calling for a European group of cooperation and promotion for the harmonization of small and medium-sized company structures. Developments surrounding Commission proposals on European company legislation were also
mentioned by the Association of Cooperative Savings and Credit for the establishment of their organization in 1971. The delay in founding this organization might be largely explained by the different legal provisions of the

member states covering bank cooperatives, which relate specifically to tax privileges, as well as by the absence of either provisions in the Treaty of Rome or proposals from the Commission for a Community legal framework for cooperatives.

With regard to a permanent office, the Liaison Committee for Professional Road Transport is the last European organization to arrive in Group A. Yet, while there is a parallel between the nonexistence of a European organization in this sector and the lack of progress in establishing a Community transport policy, the latter has not improved since the founding of the LC/IRU in 1973.

Concerning trade unions, it must be pointed out that the International Confederation of Executive Staff (CIC) and International Organization of National and International Public Service Unions (CIF) are "international" in character, whereas the European Trade Union Confederation (ETUC) is a more genuine European interest organization in that it purposely denotes the word "European" in its title. The international equivalent of the ETUC, the International Confederation of Free Trade Unions (ICFTU) has existed even longer than either the CIC or the CIF. Trade union organizational structures representing the broad bulk of employees commenced only cautiously and gradually due to some existing ideological divisions in the international trade union movement.[22] Only two European secretariats of the three existing international trade union organizations had been established by 1958, namely those of the ICFTU (Socialist or Social Democratic) and the World Confederation of Labor (WCL) [Christian]. It was not until 1969 that two independent trade union organizations European Confederation of Free Trade Unions (ECFTU) and European Organization of the World Confederation of Labor (EO/WCL) were established. This gestation process then culminated in the establishment of the ETUC in 1973 and the subsequent joining of the member organizations of the EO/WCL, the Italian communist trade union (Confederazione Generale Italiana del Lavoro) CGIL and some other national trade unions to the ETUC. With the exception of the French Confédération Générale du Travail (CGT) [Communist], all major trade unions in Europe are now aligned to the ETUC, representing thirty one member organizations from eighteen European countries and approximately 40 million individual trade union members.[23]

Three main factors can be singled out which appear to have favorably influenced the formation of the ECFTU and EO/WCL and the establishment and expansion of the ETUC from mid-1968 onward: (1) the mergers (encouraged by the operation of the Customs Union) between corporations within individual countries and among several countries of the EC; (2) Community policies in the free movement of labor (accomplished in mid-1960); and (3) the strength of the employers' organizations, which had developed at the European level in pursuit of their interests and the operation of multinational corporations.[24] To some extent, one can observe a parallel between (COFACE)

Committee of Family Organizations in the European Community and the two trade union organizations, ECFTU and EO/WCL, in their responses to the free movement of labor. The concerns of the family organizations with the latter centered especially on the disruptive impact the migration of workers had on family life and the education of the children of migrants.

In contrast to most other European interest groups (SEPLIS) European Secretariat of the Liberal, Intellectual, and Social Professions, the last sectional group, is a relative newcomer at the European level, although a large number of specialized branch committees in the liberal, intellectual, and social professions had existed prior to that date. The fact that different qualifications were required by the member states for nearly all the professions until 1975— and still are to a large extent—seemed to have discouraged the liberal, intellectual, and social professions from organizing themselves centrally at the European level. This is in spite of the fact that the Treaty of Rome contains provisions for the free movement of persons. The guidelines adopted at the Paris Summit Meeting in October 1972 in the field of consumer and environmental affairs[25] can be considered an important stepping stone for the establishment of (BEUC) European Bureau of Consumers Association and the (EEB) European Bureau of the Environment in 1973 and 1974, respectively. In addition, according to representatives of the EEB, the pessimistic predictions put forward by the Club of Rome also made it clearer to the environmental organizations that a European umbrella grouping was necessary for protecting and promoting environmental issues at the EC level.[26]

Decision-Making Style

The organizational characteristics, such as style of decision making, size, and membership composition are now considered. This will provide some information about consensus building or conflict resolution within these organizations. From the written records examined and the interviews conducted, the decision-making style of the twenty-one European interest groups with respect to policies for external purposes can be classified (as in Table 5.2) into five categories ranging from organizations that make decisions on the basis of unanimity to organizations that feature majority decision making.

The organizations examined might be related, in general terms, to the three modes of decision making outlined by Haas: accommodation on the basis of the lowest common denominator; accommodation by "splitting the difference"; and accommodation on the basis of deliberately or inadvertently upgrading the parties' common interests.[27] Applying Haas in a slightly modified form, we can relate his suggested accommodation types to the existence or nonexistence of majority voting within European interest groups.

Generally, it would appear that decision making based strictly on unanimity without allowing majority views comes closest to practicing accommodation by a lowest common denominator. Three of our twenty-one Euro-

Table 5.2   Type of Decision Making Practiced on Policies for External Purposes*

	Strictly or mostly unanimity:	Mostly unanimity, but allowing minority views.	Mostly or usually unanimity, with occasional or some majority decision making; however, minority views are stipulated.	Mostly or usually unanimity, with occasional or some majority decision making, *without* allowing minority views.	Regular majority decision making by *qualified* majority.	Regular majority decision making by simple majority.
Group A	UACEE	BFEC CEA UNICE	LC/IRU PC	CEEP EUROPMI[a]		COCCEE (since 1977)
Group B					COPA (since 1973)	FIPMEC
Group C	CIC[a]				ETUC[b]	CIF
Group D					SEPLIS[b]	
Group Z	COFACE		GCECEE[a]	EUROCOOP EEB	Association[b]	BEUC[b]

Source: Assessment (by author) of written records (1973–78) and interviews with representatives of the 21 European interest groups between July 1977 and August 1978.

[a]The International Confederation of Executive Staffs, Liaison Committee for Small and Medium-Sized Industrial Enterprises in the EEC, and the Savings Bank Group of the EEC make reference to majority decision making on policy decisions but consider it more an aim to achieve than a practice to implement at the present time.

[b]The European Bureau of Consumer's Association, Association of Cooperative Savings and Credit Institutions of the EEC, European Trade Union Confederation, and the European Secretariat of the Liberal, Intellectual, and Social Professions have adopted majority decision making since their establishment.

*See the list of abbreviations at the back of the book for the full titles of the organizations cited herein.

pean interest groups bear a resemblance to such a classification. The practice of unanimity often encourages prolonged discussions and negotiations before a common policy can be formulated.

A situation in which differences are split appears to be practiced by most of the twenty-one European interest groups; from the organizations working generally under unanimity but occasionally allowing either minority views or majority decision making outcomes to those practicing majority decision making quite regularly, either by qualified or simple majority. This means that decisions do not have to be by the lowest common denominator. Instead, they are made by splitting the difference. So, in seeking to achieve their objectives, they do not have to dilute proposals or amendments until everyone agrees, that is, until unanimity is reached. This shows that individual member organizations are willing to put wider European interests before individual interests.

One of the reasons why accommodation on the basis of upgrading the common interest does not prevail among European interest groups (with the possible exception of COPA) is the absence of a reasonably strong independent mediating role by the secretariats of these groups. This again relates in part to the insufficient competencies, resources, and status assigned to these secretariats. It also relates to structural features, such as the number and type ("full" or "associate") of affiliates and the geographic areas from which they are drawn. The nature and salience of the issue involved are also important.

The European interest groups examined use four types of member affiliations: full members, associate members, corresponding members, and liaison members. These affiliations can also be divided into two structures: a horizontal structure, consisting of the national confederations, national industry committees, and national public enterprises; and a vertical structure, comprising European or international federations, known also as industry committees or branch organizations. In some cases, combinations of the two occur. Member affiliations can also be differentiated according to the countries or geographic areas in which they are based; EC countries, European (but non-EC) and non-European countries. Finally, the number of affiliates with voting rights in a given European interest group can affect decision making.

The distinction between full members and other types of members is important from the standpoint of decision making. Full members alone can vote in the administrative bodies, but other types only have a consultative status. For organizations that draw their full members entirely from EC countries, the different type of member affiliation ensures that the content of decisions relates primarily to questions concerning the EC. It allows these organizations to concentrate their organizational efforts more effectively on EC affairs.

Eighteen of the twenty-one European interest groups, including all of Group Z, recruit their affiliates with "full" member status solely or predominantly from EC countries and are, therefore, able to center on EC activities, with the exceptions of (FIPMEC) International Federation of Small and Medium-Sized Enterprises, (CEA) European Insurance Committee, and the ETUC.[28] In other words, thirteen of these eighteen organizations which practice unanimity draw their full members either entirely or predominantly from EC countries. Five other organizations with the same recruitment pattern have the added advantage of practicing majority decision making.

In contrast, the CEA faces not only the task of reconciling interests relating both to EC countries and non-EC countries but also has to deal with a relatively large number of "full" affiliates. It requires agreement of eighteen affiliates before important policy decisions can be adopted in the CEA's administrative bodies. Thus, since both affiliates of EC and non-EC countries are involved in decisions of the administrative bodies of the CEA, the insufficient use of majority decision making (sometimes minority views are issued) might hinder the formulation of common policies, especially when they involve purely EC matters.

For FIPMEC, decision making of a simple majority should, in theory, lead to speedy decisions. However, most of the affiliates come from countries other than the EC and thus not only manage simple majorities but also qualified majorities up to two-thirds, causing perhaps some discomfort to the member affiliates from the EC countries on policy decisions addressed to the EC institutions. The ETUC practices majority voting in its administrative bodies and recruits its affiliates from the EC and other European countries. Fourteen of the thirty-one member affiliates of the ETUC come from non-EC countries, comprising thirteen out of the thirty-three maximum votes. Member affiliates from the EC countries are thus short by two votes in comprising the necessary two-thirds for majority decisions.[29] Seven European interest groups allow participation by industry committees in their administrative bodies, but in various forms. For example, in both UNICE (Union of Industries of the European Communities) and COPA (Committee of Professional Agricultural Organizations in the European Communities), they have only a consultative voice in some of their administrative bodies, whereas in the ETUC, (COCCEE) Committee of Commercial Organizations of the EEC, CIC, and SEPLIS they also have the right to vote.

The relevance of working groups and publications deserves some explanation. The existence of an elaborate structure of working groups helps regular examination of how best to protect and coordinate the interests of a given European interest group. Besides the meetings of the administrative bodies, like the Executive Committees, the discussions in the working groups provide an important forum for both the link between a central European organization and its affiliates and for the exchange of information among members of this central organization. One of the major tasks of the working groups is to prepare the formulation of opinions. Regularly published information reports, pamphlets, and studies maintain a steady flow of communication between a central European organization and its affiliates.

Aims and Objectives

As seen by officials of the secretariats, there are two main tasks for the European interest organizations: to foster and promote the exchange of information and try to find common denominators (consolidate strength); and to coordinate and exert pressure for adopted policies through the European organization and the national affiliations on both the EC and the national government (utilize strength effectively). Of the activities performed by the twenty-one European interest organizations, most fall into the first category. Only COPA and UNICE pursue activities in both categories with the same rigor.

Phase one is aimed primarily at promoting those objectives on which the European interest group affiliates can most readily reach a consensus or, depending on the organizations involved, on which they will not have to abandon ideological principles. At this stage, European interest groups are chiefly attempting to show how problems of common concern to all affiliates can be delt with more efficiently and effectively. Through the holding of information days, seminars, and conferences, European interest organizations try to inform and advise their members on developments in their sectors of interest, in various countries from which the affiliates are drawn, on EC activities, and on other issues of interest. By doing this, they also help to instill a spirit of co-operation and cohesion into their affiliates.

The use of strength and exertion of influence by European interest groups depends on a number of factors, some of which relate to the European interest group itself, such as the ability to formulate specific demands and implement on the national level what has been decided in the central European organization. Other factors concern the collaborative or opposing attitudes of other European interest groups regarding both the EC institutional access of a certain European interest group and the presentation of demands. In addition, the extent to which Community policies are either foreseen in the Treaty of Rome or prevail in practice are factors which might affect their strength and influence.

Channels of Influence

So far, a picture has been presented of how the European interest groups have developed structurally and organizationally. Next, the extent to which they can use certain channels for exerting influence and factors affecting EC institutional access will be considered. The data provided in Table 5.3 reflect the extent of contacts or relations with the EC institutions and not the extent to which European interest groups thought they were successful or effective in influencing these institutions. The data should also not be interpreted as denoting degrees of importance European interest groups attribute to the respective EC institutions. None of the twenty-one organizations had any contacts with the EC's Court of Justice.

Mostly depending on the stage of legislation of a particular issue or policy (preparation and initiation by the Commission; consultation and deliberation in the Economic and Social Committee or European Parliament; deliberation and execution by the Council of Ministers; or implementation and administration by the Commission), the European interest groups will concentrate "more" on one or two channels (institution) than on others. Because of its involvement in the various stages of legislation, however, the Commission, as seen in Table 5.3, is one of the most frequently used channels. The Council of Ministers is seen as the second most important target by COPA (on the annual agricultural price review), UNICE, and the ETUC. The ETUC was particularly interested in a strengthening of its contacts with the Council of Ministers through the Tripartite Conferences on Employment and Social Questions.[30]

FIPMEC, CIC, and CIF share similar characteristics. Although they lack a permanent secretariat in Brussels, they have, through their affiliates, repre-

Table 5.3   Extent of Contacts with the EC Institutions*
(percentage)

	Commission	ESC	European Parliament	Council of Ministers
FIPMEC	35	55	10	0
COCCEE	40	25	15	20
UACEE ELCª	40	25	15	20
CEA	60	0	15	20
UNICE	40	20	15	25
BFEC	45	25	15	15
CEEP	40	25	15	20
EUROPMI	45	25	15	15
IRU	45	25	15	15
PC	45	25	15	15
COPA				
on annual				
agricultural prices	35	10	27	28
other instances	40	20	20	20
SEPLIS	45	30	15	10
CIC	35	45	10	10
CIF	30	50	10	10
ETUC	40	20	15	25
BEUC	40	20	20	20
EUROCOOP CCCᵇ	40	20	20	20
COFACE	40	25	25	10
EEB	55	0	30	15
ASSOCIATION	60	0	25	15
GCECEE	60	0	25	15

Source: Assessment (by author) of written records (1973–78) and interviews with representatives of the 21 European interest groups between July 1977 and August 1978.

ªThe Employers' Liaison Committee (only dealing with social and employment questions).

ᵇThe Consumer Consultative Committee.

*See the list of abbreviations in the back of the book for the full titles of the organizations cited herein.

sentatives in the Economic and Social Committee with whom they maintain much closer contacts than with the Commission. This factor also seems to account largely for the relatively low percentage of their contacts with the Council of Ministers and the European Parliament.

Relations between the European interest groups and the Commission and Council of Ministers are both formal and informal, with a greater emphasis on the latter. The formal contacts, sometimes referred to as institutionalized contacts,[31] consist of participation in one or several of the approximately fifty Advisory Committees established to aid the work of the Commission or Council. The informal contacts with the Commission involve periodic consultation meetings of the European interest groups organized by the Commission or one of its Directorates-General in a certain field. There are also frequent encounters between representatives of the secretariats of the European interest organizations and officials of the Commission. Informal contacts with the Council of Ministers were few. Even though, according to these groups, the scope of concertation and consultation has expanded, many complained that they had not been sufficiently consulted by either the Commission or the Council or Ministers. This complaint centered more on the latter.[32]

The importance of the European Parliament as a target of influence is noteworthy. Caporaso's argument clearly shows that the activity of European interest groups is restricted to the administrative phase of policy making because the Community has no elections, the Parliament is essentially a weak body, and political parties have consequently not developed to any significant degree at the Community level. COPA, however, has begun to exert more influence than the other organizations through the European Parliament, particularly since the Parliament gained greater budgetary controls relating to the annual fixing of agricultural prices. Nearly all the organizations examined indicated that direct elections to the European Parliament would probably bring a new dimension to the EC institutional decision-making process along with a progressive extension of the Parliament's responsibilities. They indicated, especially the promotional interest groups,[33] that efforts were being made to increase and strengthen relations with the European Parliament.

Impact on EC Legislative and Executive Action

In considering the impact of European interest groups on the legislative and executive actions of the EC, this essay is interested less in a verification of the successes or failures than in how progress, setbacks, or stalemates in Community development in one or several related sectors might affect the cooperation or integration of European interest groups. Besides, the former, even if attempted, might prove too difficult to achieve, mainly due to the problem of locating a particular cause, that is, isolating the impact of a *single* interest group vis à vis the others.[34]

The approach here is guided by the general types of policies the European interest groups were interested in safeguarding and promoting and the broad lines of legislative and executive actions adopted by the Council of Ministers in certain policy sectors. It also centers on the views held by the European interest groups on their success in wielding influence. First to be considered is the exertion of influence attempted by the consumer organization, BEUC, and the agricultural organization, COPA, on the common agricultural prices of 1978–79.

With regard to the common agricultural prices for the 1978-79 period, BEUC had specifically demanded that there be no increases on those agricultural products where there were surpluses (milk, beef, veal, sugar, wine, and cereals other than maize). The concerted campaign launched by BEUC in favor of a price freeze for certain agricultural products between Autumn 1977 and 1978 involved lobbying by BEUC on the EC institutions, including the Council of Ministers, and by the affiliates on their national governments. In addition, BEUC effectively collaborated with the other members of the Consumers' Consultative Committee (EUROCOOP, COFACE, and ETUC) for this cause. However, BEUC's campaign was not successful in the end, according to officials of the BEUC secretariat, because of "the counter strength put forward by COPA," although BEUC could take courage from the fact that the common agricultural prices adopted by the Council of Ministers for 1978-79 were the lowest ever.

In spite of regional, national, and sectoral differences, together with the differences between the interests of "small" and "large" farm holders, COPA more than any other European interest organization examined is able to utilize strength and exert influence effectively with respect to the EC institutions. This is evident in the willingness of member affiliates to implement COPA decisions at the national level[35]: the common position the organization presents on the annual agricultural price review and the fact that COPA presents a "united front" to the Community institutions. Underlying these "demonstrative powers" are such factors as: (1) Agriculture is the most integrated sector of the EC and both the securing and promoting of agricultural interests by national organizations require a strong European organization; (2) All affiliated national federations, and the intermediary organizations and specialized sections with which COPA is connected, while formally advised, in practice are requested to channel their demands through the central organization; (3) Decision making in the administrative bodies allows for majority decisions, thus leading to speedy decisions; (4) Member affiliates come solely from the EC countries and, as mentioned earlier, this enables more uniform aims among affiliates; and (5) It possesses relatively well-developed organizational characteristics (resources and working groups).

However, some of the developments emanating from the economic crisis of the Community (1974 to 1976) and the subsequent lack of progress in the alignment of the monetary sector, have also affected COPA. According to COPA officials, the continued application of different "green currencies" by the member states of the EC, coupled with the agricultural price policy of the EC, are progressively affecting the coherence and effectiveness of COPA as an organization. UNICE, (CEEP) European Center of Public Enterprises, (COCCEE) Committee of Commercial Organizations of the EEC, the PC (Permanent Conference of Chambers of Commerce and Industry of the EEC), (BFEC) Banking Federation of the EEC and CEA appear to have lost the momentum of advancing their demands successfully with respect to the EC institutions which they seemed to have around the time the Customs Union came into being and when plans were stipulated for an Economic and Monetary Union (roughly from 1968 to 1972).

While recognizing that progress had been made in a number of areas of interest to them, they also indicated that the insufficient progress in these areas and the setbacks and lack of progress in others had negatively affected their organizational effectiveness and, thus, the spirit of cooperation within each of the individual organizations. They felt that the enlargement of the EC in 1973, economic difficulties (inflation and unemployment), and structural problems encountered in certain industries between 1974 and 1976, accompanied by governmental interventions in some countries in the economic, monetary, or fiscal fields or in the form of nationalization measures for certain industry sectors had largely prevented the execution of policies for the establishment of a common industrial and transport policy at the Community level, harmonization of company law, and tax policies. Representatives of the LC/IRU shared the feelings of these organizations.

For SEPLIS, recent decisions by the Council of Ministers providing for the mutual recognition of diplomas and the right of establishment for certain liberal, intellectual, and social professions are encouraging signs that the mobility of these professions is at least being promoted. There are overlapping interests between the three trade union organizations and the promotional interest groups on Community policies in the social, consumer, environmental, and educational fields. All are relatively new areas of concern, appearing generally in the period between 1973 and the end of 1976. Although initiated with different degrees of emphasis, each of these four sectors has witnessed Community action in one form or another since 1973. The more far-reaching and concrete actions have been taken in the field of social policy,[36] followed by that of consumer questions and again, to a lesser extent, by actions in the environmental and educational fields.

However, while recognizing that some encouraging attempts have been made by the Council of Ministers in recent years on social, consumer, environmental, and educational matters, both the trade unions and the promotional interest groups felt that it was still an unsatisfactory situation. Most displeasing to the consumers' organizations was the Council of Ministers' policy on high agricultural prices.

The results of the EC economic crisis appear, however, to have had different effects on the cooperative efforts of the ETUC than on those of the promotional interest organizations. Whereas the economic recession has tended to make many of the ETUC affiliates look inward, toward national governmental channels, the affiliates of the promotional interest organizations, especially BEUC, COFACE, and the EEB, appear to have become more committed and involved in their respective European organization.

Generally, we can see at the Community level for the first time a form of confrontation between the interests of consumer organizations and those of agricultural and employers' associations. In the not too distant future one can also expect a similar contest over interests between the agricultural and employers' organizations and the European Environmental Bureau (EEB). It adds a new dimension to the pattern, which began belatedly in the late 1960s, between the two principal interest adversaries at the Community level, namely, the employers' organizations and the trade unions. To some extent, of course, this new dimension will also reinforce the negotiating strength of the trade union organizations with respect to that of the employers because of the affinity of interests trade unions have with consumer and environmental issues.

Conclusions

This essay applied some of the empirical themes on interest groups stipulated by the neofunctionalists, structural-functionalists, and group theorists to an examination of interest group behavior at the EC level. One of the main aims was to explain generally why specific European interest groups act as they do: the differences they encounter in organizing, coordinating national positions, and obtaining effective levels of influence within the EC institutional structures.

The data shows that there is a linkage between the extent to which Community policies exist in a given sector and the degree of cooperation and integration reached by European interest groups of that sector.[37] Further, parallel to EC moves toward more specific policies, European interest groups have adapted with specific suggestions or demands. There is also a linkage between the extent of Community activity and the number of opinions or observations prepared by the groups. COPA is a good example of these linkages. The lack of progress at the Community level or of individual government actions in those fields of interest to the European interest groups perpetuates the national orientation of their members, often making it less necessary to introduce highly cohesive or integrative structures. As above, some sectional groups, such as UNICE, PC, and COCCEE, have been affected differently by the developments of Community policy in their respective sectors than have some of the promotional interest groups.

From an examination of the structural and organizational features of the twenty-one European interest groups, three levels of development can be distinguished: well-developed; moderately well-developed; and less well-developed. In relation to the other seventeen organizations, the well-developed interest groups were COPA, UNICE, ETUC, and GCECEE. However, this has to be seen within a margin where COPA takes top honors and the GCECEE occupies fourth place; the high degree of common interest found in COPA is matched, in descending order, by UNICE, ETUC, and GCECEE. Also unparallelled is COPA's authority in dealing with the EC institutions and its reliance on the backing of its affiliates.

While equal in organizational resources, the other three differ slightly from

COPA in terms of either their decision-making style (UNICE and GCECEE) or competences with respect to their affiliates and industry commitees. By considering the organizational features and prospects of Community policies in the relevant sectors of interest, more integrative efforts can be expected in these four organizations in the short to medium-term.

Taking a position between the well-developed and the less well-developed interest groups, were organizations manifesting moderate integrative traits. These were five sectional interest groups (CEA, COCCEE, CEEP, BFEC, and PC) and three promotional interest groups (Association for Savings and Credit, BEUC, and EUROCOOP). Indications are that, except for CEEP, they will continue in a gradual way to adapt more cooperative and integrative traits in response to further EC actions in the monetary and external trade sectors. In contrast to EUROCOOP, the Association for Savings and Credit and BEUC have, in a relatively short time, adapted a moderately high level of cooperation and integration. Moreover, all three promotional interest groups appear to have good prospects for increasing cooperation and integration.

There were nine interest groups with less well-developed organizations. Seven of these might be separated from the the the rest for their international rather than European characteristics (CIC, CIF, FIPMEC) or because they signify some dependency on their international interest group (LC/IRU, SEPLIS, EUROPMI, UACEE).[38] It would seem that the degree of cooperation and integration within these organizations is inhibited by inadequate organizational resources of decision-making procedures and statutory limitations. With meager prospects for Community policies in their respective sectors, one cannot foresee that they will, with the possible exception of SEPLIS, adopt more well-developed structural or organizational features in the near future.

While different from the seven interest groups treated above, cooperation and integration in COFACE and the EEB also appear to be restricted by inadequate organizational resources and unanimous decision-making procedures. However, both COFACE and the EEB might receive a boost for cooperation and integration in their respective organizations from the attempts made by the EC in social, consumer, and environmental policies in recent years.

It is interesting to speculate how the advent of direct elections to the European Parliament might affect the behavior of European interest groups, particularly if this leads to the Parliament's increased authority over the Council of Ministers. Under these new conditions we might see a rapid escalation in the activities of the community interest groups as they attempt to utilize fully the Community legislature, as well as the Council and Commission, in their efforts to influence Community policy. In addition, we may also see the transnational European parties jockeying for support among the interest groups and the groups using their electoral weight to bargain for changes they want. A more balanced representation of interests might then be secured. As noted above, until the late 1960s, the strongest groupings were those of the producers and employers. However, since this period, trade unions, consumer, and environmental groups have established themselves and increased their voice in the process of EC decision making, particularly with regard to social, consumer, environmental, and agricultural (price) policies.

Notes

1. Ernest B. Haas, *The Uniting of Europe* (Stanford, Calif: Stanford University Press, 1958), *Beyond the Nation State* (Stanford, Calif: Stanford University Press, 1964), "Turbulent Fields and the Theory of Regional Integration," *International Organization* 30, no. 2 (Spring 1976): 173–212; Leon N. Lindberg and Stuart A. Scheingold, eds., *Regional Integration: Theory and Research* (Cambridge, Mass: Harvard University Press, 1971).

2. This is with the exception of Fritz Fischer, *Die Institutionalisierte Vertretung der Verbände in der europäischen Wirtschaftsgemeinshaft* (Hamburg: Hansischer Gildenverlag, 1965); Dusan Sidjanski, "Pressure Groups and the EEC," in *New International Actors: The United Nations and the EEC*, ed. Carol Ann Cosgrave and Kenneth Twitchett (London: Macmillan, 1970), pp. 222–36; and William Averyt, "Eurogroups, Clientela, and the European Community," *International Organization* 29, no. 4 (Autumn 1975): 949–72.

3. These interest groups are as follows: Association Savings and Credit (Association of Cooperative Savings and Credit Institutions of the EEC), BEUC (European Bureau of Consumer's Association), BFEC (Banking Federation of the EEC), CEA (European Insurance Committee), CEEP (European Center of Public Enterprises), CIC (International Confederation of Executive Staffs), CIF (International Organization of National and International Public Service Unions), COCCEE (Committee of Commercial Organizations of the EEC), COFACE (Committee of Family Organizations in the European Communities), COPA (Committee of Professional Agricultural Organizations in the European Communities), EEB (European Bureau of the Environment), ETUC (European Trade Union Confederation), EUROCOOP (European Community of Consumer's Cooperatives), EUROPMI (Liaison Committee for Small and Medium-Sized Industrial Enterprises in the EEC), FIPMEC (International Federation of Small and Medium-Sized Enterprises), GCECEE (Savings Banks Group of the EEC), LC/IRU (Liaison Committee of Professional Road Transport of the European Communities), PC (Permanent Conference of Chambers of Commerce and Industry of the EEC), SEPLIS (European Secretariat of the Liberal, Intellectual, and Social Professions), UACEE (Union of Craft Industries and Trades of the EEC), and UNICE (Union of Industries of the European Communities).

4. Robert J. Lieber, "Interest Groups and Political Integration: British Entry into Europe," in *Pressure Groups in Britain*, ed. Richard Kimber and J. J. Richardson (London: J. M. Dent and Sons, 1974), p. 28.

5. European industry committees can be of two types: intermediary or inter-professional associations or specialized branch associations. An example of the former is the Committee of Textile Industries, and, of the latter, the Committee of Cotton Industries. The equivalents of these two types exist at the national level, although in a much more refined form. See Emil J. Kirchner, *Trade Unions as a Pressure Group in the European Community* (Farnborough, Hants: Saxon House, 1977), p. 17.

6. David Mitrany, "The Functional Approach to World Organizations," in *New International Actors*, ed. Cosgrave and Twitchett, pp. 65–75 and "The Prospect of Integration: Federal or Functional?" *Journal of Common Market Studies* 4 (1965): 119–49.

7. Haas describes spillover as "the accretion of new powers and tasks to a central institutional structure, based on changing demands and expectations on the part of such political actors as interest groups, political parties, and bureaucracies. It refers to the specific process which origi-

nates in one functional context initially separated from other political concerns, and then expands into related activities or it becomes clear to the chief political actors that the achievement of the initial aims cannot take place without such expansion." Ernst Haas, "Regional Integration," in *International Encyclopaedia of the Social Sciences*, ed. David Shills (New York: Macmillan, 1968), vol. 7, p. 523.

8. Sidjanski, "Pressure Groups and the EEC," p. 402.

9. Kirchner, *Trade Unions as a Pressure Group in the EC*, p. 28.

10. Philippe C. Schmitter, "A Revised Theory of Regional Integration," in *Regional Integration*, ed. Lindberg and Scheingold, p. 238.

11. Haas, *The Uniting of Europe*, p. 16.

12. James Caporaso, *The Structure and Function of European Integration* (Pacific Palisades, Calif.: Goodyear, 1974).

13. Caporaso defines associational interest groups as functionally specific groups employing full-time, trained experts. Institutional interest groups are formally organized bodies set up to perform another function but which, nevertheless, express an interest of their own or act as vehicles for the expression of other interests. Ibid., pp. 45–46.

14. Ibid.

15. Samuel Beer, "Group Representation in Britain and the United States," in *Group Politics: A New Emphasis*, ed. Edward S. Malecki and H. R. Mahood (New York: Charles Scribner and Sons, 1972), pp. 221–33.

16. *See* David Coombes, *Politics and Bureaucracy in the European Community* (London: George Allen and Unwin, 1970).

17. Joseph La Palombara, "Interest Groups in Italian Politics," in *Group Politics*, ed. Malecki and Mahood, pp. 253–72.

18. William Averyt, "Eurogroups, Clientela, and the European Community."

19. Complementing the written records, forty interviews, primarily with the Secretaries General, their deputies, or both, of the twenty-one European interest groups were conducted between July 1977 and August 1978.

20. In distinguishing between sectional and promotional interests, we are following Jacob A. Buksti and Lars Norby Johansen, who made a similar distinction in "The Danish System of Interest Organization" (Paper prepared for the ECPR Workshop on Corporatism in Liberal Democracies, Grenoble, April 6–12, 1978), pp. 6–7.

21. For example, among the membership criteria specified by SEPLIS is that the applicant organizations represent professions whose activity is mainly intellectual and whose education and discipline requirements are particularly high. SEPLIS also stressed that it has no part in professions dependent on industry, trade, craftmanship, or agriculture.

22. See Norris Willatt, *Multinational Unions* (London: Financial Times, 1974); Rudolf Steiert, "Die Entwicklung transnationaler Strukturen der Gewerkschaftsbewegung in der Europäischen Gemeinschaft," *Zeitschrift für Parlaments Fragen* (Herausgegeben von der Deutschen Vereingung für Parlamentsfragen, Westdeutscher Verlag 2, June 1978), pp. 215–32; and Kirchner, *Trade Unions*, pp. 28–33.

23. Kirchner, *Trade Unions*, pp. 22–25.

24. Ibid.

25. This program was to aim, among other things, at improving working and living conditions and at strengthening and coordinating measures of consumer protection.

26. Interview with Mr. David, Secretary-General of the European Environmental Bureau (September 7, 1977).

27. Ernst Haas, "International Integration: The European and the Universal Process," in *European Integration*, ed. Michael Hodge, (Middlesex, England: Penguin Books, 1972), pp. 93–97.

28. In COCCEE, CIF, CIC, and SEPLIS, most of the affiliated members of the industry committees are located in the EC countries.

29. See Kirchner, *Trade Unions*, p. 49.

30. Officials of the ETUC Secretariat stressed the need to seek influence at the level where decisions are made. They also thought the "courage" of the Commission to initiate legislation had diminished, thus requiring the increased use of other channels.

31. See Fischer, *Die Institutionalisierte Vertretung der Verbände.*

32. For a similar point regarding the ETUC, see Kirchner, *Trade Unions*, pp. 102–07.

33. Promotional interest groups explained that their increased contacts with the European Parliament were in response to this institution's interest and activities in the field of social, consumer, educational, and environmental issues over the last several years.

34. For example, besides UNICE, other employers' organizations, such as COCCEE, CEEP, BFEC, CEA, or the PC, might also seek to influence the outcome of a certain decision by the Council of Ministers. These other organizations may either reinforce the impact of UNICE, if agreement can be reached among them, or diminish it if disagreements prevail.

35. These findings are in contrast to those of Averyt, who believes that COPA is usually unsuccessful in this respect. See Averyt, "Eurogroups, Clientela, and the European Community," p. 970.

36. This involved, among others, a greater application of the European Social Fund, legislation concerning equal pay and equal working conditions for men and women, the principle of a fourty-hour week, four weeks' annual vacation, and provisions covering the dismissal of workers. It left untouched, however, the harmonization of social security systems in general or a common vocational training policy.

37. Slightly deviating from this rule is the development of the savings banks (GCECEE), which have largely increased their cooperation and integration independently of the existence of a reasonably well-developed community policy in the savings and credit sector. However, the GCECEE is interested in a wider spectrum of Community policies, such as consumer and regional policies, and has perhaps found stimulation from developments in these sectors.

38. The titles of both the LC/IRU and SEPLIS denote that they are a Liaison Committee and a European Secretariat, respectively. In the case of EUROPMI and UACEE this is not so clearly shown but the conditions under which they operate resemble those of the IC/IRU and SEPLIS. These four act in some ways as the "extended arm" of their international organizations and are subject, although in different ways, to certain controls concerning their budgets and functions.

INTERNAL EC COLLECTIVE DECISION MAKING AND ITS DOMESTIC REALITIES

Part III

WERNER J. FELD*

6

Two-Tier Policy Making in the EC: The Common Agricultural Policy

Perhaps nothing demonstrates better the changing fortunes of European integration and the fragility of the neofunctionalist logic than the growth and problems of the Community's Common Agricultural Policy (CAP). At the same time, an appraisal of the CAP offers interesting insights into the Community's complex two-tier decision-making process involving governmental and nongovernmental actions on both the "European" and the national levels. Indeed, as far as the Federal Republic of Germany is concerned, it is appropriate to talk of a three-tier process since the state governments (*Laender*) may have a significant impact on the elaboration of certain Community policies and their implementation.

During the second half of the 1960s, most students of Western European integration looked upon the agricultural program of the European Community as "a story of action and success,"[1] and many Europeans hailed the CAP as an essential ingredient for successful economic and eventual political integration

*Author's Note: I would like to express my appreciation to the Commission of the European Communities for financial support for a visit to Brussels that enabled me to have extensive conversations with a number of officials in Directorate-General VI. I would like to emphasize, however, that the views contained in this essay are my own and do not necessarily represent those of the EC Commission or anyone in Directorate-General VI.

of the EC member states. However, only a few years later, considerable doubts have arisen about the survival of the CAP as originally designed. Tremendous surpluses have accumulated in butter, milk powder, beef, sugar, wine, olive oil, and some cereals as the result of ever higher fixed prices; and the cost of the CAP, approaching $10 billion in 1979, has exceeded most projections, no matter how pessimistic.[2] Although there is no dearth of reform proposals, fears have been expressed that regardless of the merit of these proposals the CAP may disintegrate into nine national policies of the Community's member countries.[3] A careful study by a German economist, Ulrich Koester, suggests that the CAP as constituted at present carries within itself the seed for self-destruction and requires new conceptualizations if it is to serve effectively the welfare of all of the people in the Community.[4]

What have been the reasons for the problems encountered by the CAP? Do some of the causes for the unforeseen deficiencies in policy outcomes lie in the complex decision-making procedures? To what extent were governmental and nongovernmental actors and events outside the Community framework responsible for the enormous surpluses and the ever-escalating cost of policy implementation?

In order to gain a greater insight into some of these problems, this essay will focus on various aspects of the CAP policy-making and implementation process. We will begin with a brief survey of the evolution of the CAP. This will be followed by an examination of the two-tier decision-making process in the Community system, especially as far as CAP implementation is concerned. Next will come an assessment of the impact which domestic politics in the member states may have on the progress of the CAP and perhaps on its disintegration, taking into consideration the effect of the devaluation and revaluation of member-state currencies that have occurred again and again since 1968. Finally, we will seek to evaluate the influence of national civil servants in the agricultural ministries of the member governments on the policy formulation and implementation processes. These national officials not only carry out the agricultural regulations emanating from Community authorities but also play a major role in shaping them.

The Evolution of the CAP

For the intent of the CAP we must look at Articles 38 to 47 of the Treaty establishing the European Economic Community. In particular, Article 39 states:

1. The common agricultural policy shall have as its objectives:
   (a) to increase agricultural productivity by developing technical progress and by ensuring the rational development of agricultural production and the optimum utilization of the factors of production, particularly labor;

(b) to ensure thereby a fair standard of living for the agricultural population, par-
    ticularly by the increasing of the individual earnings of persons engaged in
    agriculture;
(c) to stabilize markets;
(d) to guarantee regular supplies; and
(e) to ensure the reasonable prices in supplies to consumers.

In Article 40 we find that:

2. . . . a common organization of agricultural markets shall be effected. This organization shall take one of the following forms according to the products concerned:
   (a) common rules concerning competition;
   (b) compulsory coordination of the various national market organizations; or
   (c) a European market organization.
3. The common organization in one of the forms mentioned in paragraph 2 may
   comprise all measures necessary to achieve the objective set out in Article 39, in
   particular, price controls, subsidies as to the production and marketing of various
   products, arrangements for stock-piling and carry-forward, and common machinery for stabilizing importation or exportation. . . .
   A common price policy, if any, shall be based on common criteria and on uniform methods of calculation.
4. In order to enable the common organization referred to in paragraph 2 to achieve
   its objectives, one or more agricultural orientation and guarantee funds may be
   established.

In general, then, the goals are, first, to raise farm incomes in the Community
member states and, second, to improve agricultural production efficiency
through structural changes in those farms that in certain regions of the Community traditionally have been small in size or cost-inefficient for other reasons. Examples of this are some farms in Germany and the hill farmers of Italy.

The broad outline of the CAP took shape during the early 1960s. A uniform
Community system governing the marketing of agricultural products within
the EC countries and international trade with nonmember states was set up
that included grains, rice, poultry, eggs, pork, dairy products, wine, fruits,
vegetables, and certain fishery products and now covers more than 90 percent
of total agricultural production. Products not falling under this system are, for
example, olive oil and durum wheat. For these latter products "deficiency payments" are made to producers directly.[5] To assure satisfactory stable farm income, a system of "target" prices and support or "intervention" prices were introduced. The target prices for wholesale trade are set from year to year, and
actual market prices move somewhere between the two levels, which have a
spread from 5 to 10 percent. The Community and national authorities must intervene in the market if prices threaten to fall below intervention levels. Intervention may be carried through purchases of surplus products, payment of the
difference between the buying-in price and the selling price of the goods in the

intervention process, and payments of the interest charges on the value of the products stored.[6] Although the Community does not guarantee limitless purchases, so far all intervention costs have been paid.

This system of interlocking target and intervention prices is secured by fixed import prices called "threshold" or "sluice gate" prices. They are set in such a way that, considering the expense of shipping from the port of entry to the interior markets, the cost of farm commodities imported from nonmember states is roughly equal to or slightly higher than the price of farm products raised within the Community. The difference between any c.i.f. (cost, insurance, and freight) import purchase price of a target-price commodity and the threshold price is imposed on the former as an import levy, and to the extent that the prices at which import shipments are offered at the Community frontier vary, the levy also varies. This means that the variable import levy has replaced the usual system of customs duties and quotas for target-price farm commodities.[7]

In the early stages of the CAP the levels of target, intervention, and threshold prices varied from one member state to another. Although a uniform community-wide price level was the ultimate objective, the process of price equalization was highly political and therefore very difficult. It meant relinquishing national control by the member governments over price levels and trade flows, which they were reluctant to do despite their treaty commitment to accept this in a gradual manner.

Nevertheless, in December 1964 the EC Council of Ministers agreed to adopt, as a first step, a common price for grains effective July 1, 1967. This first step was particularly significant because the price of feed grains is a major ingredient for the price of pork, eggs, and poultry, and all four commodities taken together constitute one-third of the value of total Community agricultural production. Additional agreements reached in the Council during 1966 pertained to milk and dairy products, beef and veal, fats and oils, sugar, and rice and thereby substantially extended the Community agricultural market with common price levels.[8]

In order to furnish the financial resources to administer the CAP, a European Agricultural Guidance and Guarantee Fund (EAGGF) was established. The main functions are: (1) to provide funds for the purchase of farm products whose prices have reached or broken through the intervention price levels; (2) to furnish money for structural improvements and reforms in regions of the Community where individual farms are very small or inefficient; and (3) to subsidize exports of surplus farm products which, because of the CAP's steadily higher fixed prices, have been priced out of world market competition. For example, in 1977, wheat was 204 percent of the world price, butter was 401 percent, skimmed milk powder 511 percent, beef 192 percent, and white sugar 192 percent.[9]

Until 1970, 45 percent of EAGGF financing was derived from levies collected on agricultural imports and the remainder from direct budgetary allo-cations from the member governments. Since that year the EAGGF has been given authority to finance all its operations from its "own resources" com-prised of agricultural import levies, customs duties, sugar levies, and an appro-priate part of the value-added tax (VAT) collected by the member govern-ments. However, up to 1978 this last source of revenue had not been forth-coming, and therefore, the share of "own resources" to cover total expendi-tures was only 66.9 percent, with the remainder to be covered by GNP-based contributions from the member governments.[10]

One of the reasons that the Community's own resources are not sufficient to cover expenditures is the tremendous increase in agricultural costs which have nearly tripled between 1974 and 1978, amounting to almost three-quarters of the total budget.[11] Moreover, Table 6.1 shows that the percentage of "own re-sources" contributing to the total expenditures of the Community has de-clined sharply from 1971 to 1974 and remained in 1976 less than half what it was in 1971, although beginning in 1975 this percentage has been rising again. Clearly, the rising cost of intervention purchases and subsidizing exports (the main tasks of the EAGGF Guarantee Section) were responsible for this trend.

Green Rates and MCAs (Monetary Compensatory Amounts).

In addition to the rapidly rising cost of the CAP, brought about by the large surpluses of several commodities, which in turn were caused by the guaranteed high price levels, changes and fluctuations among the member countries' cur-rencies have also generated a major cost factor that amounted to nearly $2 billion in 1976. As we have noted earlier, the aim of the CAP has been to set up

Table 6.1   Trend of Revenues from Import Levies and Levies on Sugar, 1971–76[a]
(units of account)

Year	Total Expenditure of the EC Budget	Resources from Import Levies and Levies on Sugar		Expenditure of the EAGGF Guarantee Section	
		Total	%[b]	Total	%[b]
1971	2,289.4	715.8	31.2	1,514.0	66.1
1972	3,074.4	799.5	26.0	2,094.0	68.1
1973	4,641.0	510.3	11.0	3,912.1	84.3
1974	5,036.7	330.1	6.5	3,097.9	61.5
1975	6,213.6	590.1	9.5	4,718.7	75.9
1976	7,872.9	1,163.7	14.8	5,570.0	70.7

Source: Adapted from EC Commission, Commission of EC, *EAGGF: Importance and Func-tioning* (Brussels, 1978), p. 41.

[a]One unit of account equals approximately $1.30.

[b]Percentage in relation to total expenditure of the Budget of the EC.

common farm prices throughout the Community. This was definitely the case between 1967 and 1969. But when in 1968 France devalued the franc by 11 percent, its government did not want to raise consumer prices as a result of more costly farm imports from other member states. At the same time, it wanted EC target and intervention prices to stay at the same level. When, later that year, the Germans upvalued the deutschmark in relation to other currencies of the EC states, the target and support prices should have been reduced. But such action would have impaired the incomes of German farmers and therefore was politically undesirable. What thus happened was the introduction of an artificial, so-called green rate of exchange, which was a political expedient and somewhat maintained the fiction of "common CAP prices." However, since the "green rate" of exchange differed from the "real world" exchange rate prevailing among EC member states, financial adjustments had to be made in order to protect the farm producers in upvalued countries from imports originating in states with devalued currencies. The result was a system of border levies and subsidies set up within the Community that is operated through so-called Monetary Compensatory Amounts (MCAs). The MCAs, as well as the various price categories, are figured in agricultural units of account (AUAs), which initially were based on the value of the U.S. dollar that prevailed prior to August 1971 (the first devaluation date) but now have their own value fixed currently at about 25 percent above the dollar. Farm exports from high-value currency countries such as Germany into low-value currency countries such as Great Britain receive subsidies to lower their cost (positive MCAs), and exports from low-value countries, France, for example, to high-value states are subject to border levies (negative MCAs). It is the EAGGF guarantee section that provides the funds for the MCAs and receives the border levies.

These developments have resulted in complicated exchange rates. First, the AUA is used for the annual fixing of "common" agricultural and target and intervention prices. In addition, the artificial "green rate" was introduced by the member states when currency devaluations and revaluations were initiated in order to absorb the economic and political shock of monetary fluctuations. Last, the actual monetary rate of the member-state currencies is used for all "real world" market transactions. For these "market" rates some of the member states (Germany, Denmark, and the Benelux countries) have adopted a currency coordination mechanism, a "snake," which keeps their currencies within a maximum spread of 2.25 percent. Others (France, Ireland, Italy, and the United Kingdom) let their currencies float.

With respect to the "snake" countries, the calculation of the MCAs, that is, the difference between the "green" and "market" rates, is based on central market rates since their currencies do not fluctuate much. In these cases, MCAs remain unchanged over long periods of time unless prices are changed. For countries with floating currencies outside the snake, the MCAs are variable and are recalculated every week. It should be noted that MCAs are not only used for intra-Community trade but also for trade with nonmember countries.[12]

The introduction of the green rates and MCAs have had two significant effects. In real currency terms, they have destroyed the common price concept; for example, intervention prices in Germany were 40 percent higher than in Britain. Also, they tend to favor farmers of higher priced products, as in Germany and the Netherlands, and encourage food production in and shift resources to areas which, in terms of unit cost, rank low.[13] As a result, German farmers received 7.5 percent higher prices than the average Community price, which only applies to Denmark. Moreover, operating costs for items such as fertilizer and seed for German farmers have risen at a slower rate than in other EC countries. When such costs are related to food production, a German farmer has to produce 46.7 tons of wheat to buy a tractor, while his French counterpart has to harvest 85 tons.[14]

In terms of gross added value of Community agriculture between 1970 and 1976, Germany's share increased from 10.7 to 19.5 percent, and that of the Netherlands from 6.3 to 7.6 percent, while their share decreased in France from 30.1 to 28.5 percent, in Belgium from 3.1 to 2.7 percent, and in the UK from 8.4 to 8 percent. The shares in Italy, Luxembourg, and Ireland remained more or less stable.[15] Although intra-Community shipments of agricultural and food products rose in all member states, Germany recorded the highest increase (+80 percent) and France the lowest (+40 percent), while the increase of the remainder of the member states was between the two poles.

The existing agrimonetary system has also given rise to discrimination among consumers in the EC. It had an adverse effect on consumers in countries whose market currencies have appreciated and a beneficial effect where currencies have been devalued. For example, in October 1977, one kilogram of butter cost 141 Belgian francs (FB) in Bonn (about $4.20), FB 129 in Paris ($3.90), and FB 72 ($2.40) in London (including special British consumption subsidies).[16] These national aids to producers have been used not only in the UK, but also occasionally in other member states.

The MCAs have brought on an additional administrative burden to the management of the Guarantee Section of the EAGGF, and their total cost in 1977 amounted to 14 percent of the Fund's Guarantee Section.[17] The MCA system has been exploited fraudulently and has thus added to the expenditure of the EAGGF.

The Guidance Section of the EAGGF

Although the disbursements of the Guidance Section represent only between 5 and 7 percent of the total annual expenditures of the EAGGF, they are significant instruments for implementation of the CAP. They aim at the improvement of production and marketing functions of the agricultural structures. The number and type of projects undertaken between 1964 and 1976 and the financial support provided can be seen from Table 6.2.

It should be noted that initially in 1964, the emphasis was placed on individual projects and that generally the financial aid given by the Community was limited to 25 percent of total project costs. Only for projects to improve production methods in the less developed regions of the Community were grants given up to 45 percent of total cost. The remainder of costs had to be borne by the beneficiary (between 25 and 65 percent) and by the member state.[18]

Beginning in 1970, the Community authorities made efforts to focus more sharply on the implementation of structure improvement policies by formulating national and subnational regional programs for each agricultural product or group of products. At the same time, the financing of individual projects was to be phased out. For this purpose, a number of "common measures" were introduced providing limited financial support for irrigation schemes, land reparcelling, and other farm development measures. In addition, the ces-

Table 6.2   Breakdown by Groups of Sectors of Aid Granted, 1964–76

Sectors Improved	Total Number of Projects	Projects Given Aid	% of Funded Aid Projects
Production structures	3,230	871	50.0
Land reallocation		(226)	(13.0)
Hydraulic and irrigation works		(184)	(10.6)
Afforestation		(45)	(2.6)
Miscellaneous[a]		(416)	(23.8)
Marketing structures	2,729	762	43.5
Cereals		(44)	(2.5)
Milk products		(208)	(12.0)
Meat		(139)	(8.0)
Fruit and vegetables		(114)	(6.5)
Wine		(118)	(6.8)
Miscellaneous[b]		(139)	(7.7)
Combined production/ marketing structures	305	108	6.5
Total	6,264	1,741	100.0

Source: Adapted from EC, *EAGGF: Importance and Functioning* (1978), p. 48.

[a]Includes projects involving the building of fishing vessels and meat production centers, programs for the supply of drinking water and for providing farms with electricity, and equipment for research and vocational training.

[b]Includes projects involving the building or improvement of centers for processing various agricultural products, plants for processing fishery products, and cooperative oil mills.

sation of farming was encouraged when the utilized agricultural area could be reallocated to another farm for purposes of structural improvement. Farmers and farm workers aged 55–65 could be given an annuity if affected by the cessation of farming.[19]

The member states have been slow to submit national and regional development plans for these programs for several reasons. First, the agricultural problems are complex; second, member states have already undertaken national measures to solve some of these problems; third, in view of the general rise in unemployment, farmers leaving their land will add to the number of the unemployed; and, fourth, some member states may not want to use their limited financial resources for the necessary matching funds for the EC directives. Indeed, only Germany, Denmark, and the Netherlands have submitted extensive development plans, many of which were approved. Italy and Ireland have not submitted any plans at all.[20]

A later "common measure" promulgated in 1975 may be more attractive to all member states. It provides financial support to regions where productivity is impaired by natural causes such as mountainous areas, small islands, or "areas in danger of depopulation."[21] All these areas represent over 25 percent of the Community's agricultural area and contain more than a million farms but account for only about 10 percent of production.

Financing Procedures

The procedures for finanacing Guidance Section projects and national programs are cumbersome and drag on over years with voluminous dossiers collected in each case. While during the initial years payments for individual projects were often sent directly to the benefiting farm owner, it is politically significant that now the member states make the grant to the farmers and transfer the funds to the beneficiary. Reimbursement by the Community takes place on presentation to the Commission of supporting documents.[22] Aid from the EAGGF may be paid in several installments as the work progresses.

As for the payments by the Guarantee Section of the Fund, the principle of reimbursement of the member states for eligible expenditures prevailed from 1962 to 1970. However, beginning in that year a system of Community advances to the member states was instituted with the member states central government allocating the funds received to the various national agencies which pay to the agricultural producers the necessary amount for intervention purchases and other costs as well as export subsidies. The central government of the member state thus plays the role of intermediary between the Community, to which it applies for and from which it receives the advances, and the paying departments and agencies, to which it allocates the needed funds. The Commission has the power to inspect the paying departments and agencies in order to ascertain the validity of expenditures effected by the member states on behalf of the Community. All this requires that close cooperation and coordination be established among the member governments, their subordinate departments and agencies functioning as payers of the Community funds, the Commission, and a special EAGGF Committee made up of national civil servants representing the member states and of Community officials concerned with the operation of the Fund.

Forty-three paying departments and agencies have been established by the member states to date. They constitute the basic administrative units responsible for the payments relating to intervention activities and subsidies. They are the custodians of the detailed dossiers containing the farmers' and exporters' rights. Their organizational structure varies from one member country to another, but generally they have a certain degree of financial autonomy. Moreover, in many cases interest group representatives participate to a varying extent in their operations. From the Community's point of view, the large number of departments and agencies playing some kind of a role in the finances of the Community and the various influences exerted by nongovernmental actors may well appear to be disadvantageous for its own administration. But for the national civil servants this organizational framework is attractive inasmuch as it permits them to retain maximum control over agricultural decisions in their countries and maintains their pivotal position in the relations with their clientele.

The Community Decision-Making Process and the CAP

The discussion of the EAGGF and especially of the financing procedures have given an initial insight into the complicated framework of the Community decision-making process. Indeed, some of the objectionable outcomes of the CAP, such as the enormous surpluses, high cost, and slow implementation of the structural improvement goals, are the direct or indirect result of opportunities for different governmental and nongovernmental actors to impose their will through the astute exploitation of the complex EC decision-making process that has emerged over the years. On paper, the distribution of functions among the Commission and the Council for decision initiation and approval as laid out by the EEC Treaty appears to be clear-cut. In practice, however, this process involves multilevel interaction and interpenetration among the various Community institutions, national governments and administrations, and interest groups. The goals pursued by national economic groups in the member countries, the domestic politics of each member state, and the interstate politics within the Community play significant roles in the making of specific EC decisions.

Governmental Actions on the Community Level

While the treaties have attempted to draw a careful balance of power between the Commission and the Council of Ministers which would force them to cooperate in governing the affairs of the Community, in practice there is considerable imbalance, weighing heavily in favor of the Council. Moreover, a third organ, the Committee of Permanent Representatives (CPR or COREPER, following the French title), has contributed to the Commission's loss of power. The CPR has the duty of preparing the sessions and decisions of the Council (which usually meets only a few days each month) and of carrying out any tasks assigned to it by the Council. In order to accomplish these missions, the CPR, composed of the ambassadors from the nine member states and their staffs, totaling more than four hundred civil servants, has established a number of working groups, subcommittees, and special ad hoc committees patterned after the administrative structure of the Commission. The staff of the CPR is frequently consulted informally by the Commission before it submits a formal proposal to the Council. But while the staff of the Permanent Representatives usually includes an agricultural councillor, the CPR committees rarely deal with farm problems; these are mostly channeled to a separate body, the Special Committee on Agriculture, which is composed of senior officials of the national ministries and which has jealously guarded its autonomy.[23]

The advice of this Special Committee is usually sought through meetings with national officials who possess expert knowledge on agricultural matters. But perhaps the most significant impact for CAP implementing regulations comes from the twenty-nine agricultural management and legislative committees.

These committees bring together officials of the Commission and the member governments and their purposes are, first, to ensure close cooperation between the Commission and the member states to achieve maximum efficiency in the common organization of markets and, second, to relieve the Council of involvement in the myriad details of the approximately two thousand regulations issued each year by the Community that are necessary to administer the CAP. The Committee sessions are chaired by a senior Commission Representative (without vote) who seeks to win majority or unanimous support by the Committee members for the Commission's draft proposal, which is sometimes amended during the debates to satisfy the delegates of the member governments or may be withdrawn completely. As a consequence, the text of a regulation eventually adopted by the Commission may have undergone considerable changes from the plan originally proposed.[24]

A favorable opinion for adoption of a Commission draft proposal requires a majority of 41 out of 58 votes, with each member state having the same kind of weighted vote as is implied for Council decisions (Article 148, paragraph 2). If 41 votes do not support the Commission's proposal and the 58 votes are split, there is assumed to be "no opinion." If there is a negative majority vote (41 votes) and the Commission still wants to adopt the proposed measure, it can do so provisionally but must communicate it to the Council which, within one month, can confirm, reject, or amend it. In the event that the Council does not rule at all, the Commission's proposal is considered adopted.[25]

The procedure for legislative committees, which are used mainly for customs matters and the harmonization for agricultural legislation among the member states, is somewhat different. The Commission cannot adopt its proposals provisionally, and the Council has three months in which to reach a decision. Approximately five hundred committee meetings were held during 1977, and most of the opinions delivered were favorable to either the original or amended Commission proposals. Of course, one must keep in mind that most of these proposals were prepared by the Commission only after extensive consultation with national experts. In some cases special or ad hoc advisory committees of farm organizations may have been consulted as well or direct contacts with the leadership of these organizations on the national or European level may have been useful.

Interest Group Influence

Farm interest group influence is pervasive in all phases of Community agricultural policy making and is reflected in strong advocacy measures for whatever policy goals or implementation objectives are pursued. In addition to COPA (Committee of Professional Agricultural Organizations in the European Communities), the most powerful Community-level umbrella group which basically supports the CAP, there is another farm umbrella organization, COMEPRA (European Committee for Agricultural Progress), which opposes many aspects of the CAP. COMEPRA represents a number of small farm groups, such as the National Alliance of Italian Farmers, the Action Committee of Walloon Peasants, the Democratic Farmers' Action of Germany, and the National League of Family Farmers of Ireland.[26] A more specialized Community-level umbrella organization is the Confederation of European Sugar Beet Producers (CIBE) which only represents a specific farm sector.

National farm organizations also seek to influence the policy-making and implementation process in the Community. Some are comprehensive in scope, covering all agricultural sectors, such as the German Farmers' Union (DBV, or Deutsche Bauern Verband) and the British National Farmers' Union. Others confine themselves to one sector; an example is the National Federation of Milk Producers in France (FNPL, or Fédération Nationale des Producteurs de Lait). In order to be effective, these groups must have easy access to the national governments and in particular to the Ministry of Agriculture. By working through national authorities, they are able to bring pressure to bear on the EC Council of Ministers in the pursuit of their objectives. But they may also want to deal directly with the Commission. Although the Commission mostly prefers to work with COPA and have the national farm groups channel their demands through that organization, not all farm groups belong to COPA, and even if they do it is sometimes quite difficult to come to an agreement on a particular issue to be presented to the Commission. Moreover, the Commission may at times want to build a constituency for new programs, and for these reasons direct contact with national farm organizations are regarded as useful from time to time outside of the advisory committees mentioned above.

The normal strategies used by European-level and national farm groups to influence CAP formulation or implementation are shown in Figure 6.1. Considering that on major policy issues the Council of Ministers is the final arbiter, national organizations have two channels to pursue their objectives, with channels 4 and 5 likely to be the most potent paths to success. William Averyt, Jr. has outlined special conditions of an emergency nature when instead of the normal strategy a special channeling of demands needs to be used to obtain desired results (as shown in Figure 6.2). In order for this strategy to be effective, the following conditions must prevail:

1. The Commission must initially refuse a COPA request that seems fairly reasonable to most political elites involved in EC affairs.
2. The COPA position must retain member support when the coordinated approaches are made to the national ministers.
3. The national ministers must be persuaded that the farmers' demands are reasonable and merit overriding the Commission's reluctance to act. The institutional balance in the Community has shifted against the Commission sufficiently so that the Council has little hesitation in doing this.
4. The ministers must be able to convince the Commission to reverse its previous refusal to come forth with an emergency proposal. Whether the Council is successful depends in large part on the desire of commissioners, especially the agricultural commissioner, to defy Council wishes. Legally, the Council cannot force the Commission to put forward a specific kind of proposal.[27]

Interpenetration of National and Community Politics

In order to systematize the interaction pattern among Community officials, national civil servants, and nongovernmental groups in the EC decision-making processes, Glenda Rosenthal has developed three conceptual schemes:

Figure 6.1   Farm Interest Group Strategies

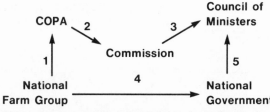

Source: From William F. Averyt, Jr., *Agropolitics in the European Community: Interest Groups and the Common Agricultural Policy* (New York: Praeger, 1977), p. 102. Copyright © 1977 by Praeger Publishers. Reprinted by permission of Holt, Rinehart and Winston.

Figure 6.2   Farm Interest Group Emergency Strategies

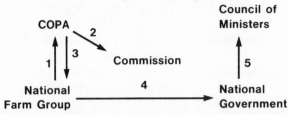

Source: William F. Averyt, Jr., *Agropolitics in the European Community: Interest Groups and the Common Agricultural Policy* (New York: Praeger, 1977), p. 104. Copyright © by Praeger Publishers. Reprinted by permission of Holt, Rinehart, and Winston.

1. *Intergovernmental Politics*: The actors in this scheme are small groups of officials, usually the Foreign Ministers of the EC member states, but other members of the government as well, especially the economics, finance, and agriculture ministers and their top staff. The decision-making arena may be the EC Council of Ministers or miltilateral or bilateral negotiations outside the Community framework, including the EC summit meetings (now called European Council meetings) in which EC Commission officials participate. The main concern of national officials is the enhancement of their country's position.[28]

2. *Grass-Roots, Interest Group, and Parliamentary Pressures*: Decision making in this scheme is the outcome of effective public pressures exercised directly by the public or articulated through interest groups or parliamentary representations. The decision-making arena extends from local, national, and Community umbrella groups to members of national parliaments and administrative staffs of national ministries and finally to civil servants in the Commission structure and the CPR, as well as to members of the European Parliament and the EC Economic and Social Council. Interactions may include "a quiet lobbying visit by an individual representative of one interest group with a member of the EEC Commission or a massive demonstration by 80,000 rioting farmers in the streets of Brussels."[29]

3. *Elite Networks*: In this scheme the actors are small groups of influential persons. These groups may be composed of one outstanding personality surrounded by a small number of loyal personal aides, or it may be a kind of "good old boy" network, individuals brought together by the same interests, background, or training.

The process in the elite networks scheme is usually one of subtle, behind-the-scenes lobbying and elaborate committee work (often behind closed doors or over dinner, drinks, etc.). Much of the preparatory work takes place over the telephone. There is none of the publicity of the intergovernmental negotiations of the Council of Ministers meeting except in the rare case where an outstanding individual rallies around him a staff of loyal and competent aides. Then the process is highly individual and freewheeling, and it depends a great deal on how the person concerned pursues his cause. It may be through subtle pressures and persuasion of his colleagues. On the other hand, he may engage in a headline-making, public relations speaking campaign.[30]

In the implementation of the CAP policy actions all three conceptualizations apply, as has been demonstrated by Rosenthal, Averyt, and others.[31]

The Impact of Domestic Policies

Our discussion of the Community decision-making process makes it obvious that domestic policies in the EC member states can play a significant role in CAP implementation. Political ambitions of members of the national legislatures in the Community and perhaps of the political parties in general may make it essential to promote strongly the interests of their farm constituents when it comes to the various aspects of implementing the broad goals of the CAP.

An interesting example of how domestic political conditions have combined to make a minister of agriculture a most powerful champion of farm interests with respect to his ministerial colleagues is the story of Joseph Ertl, the Minister of Agriculture in the Federal Republic of Germany, who has held his position since 1969, and whose political strength stems from the fact that the farm vote can swing elections. Although Ertl, a member of the Free Democrats (FDP), may not control more than 7 percent of the farm vote, under the combined single-member district-proportional representation list system of the Federal Republic of Germany, the Free Democrats have received many of the list votes from Christian Social Union (CSU) and Christian Democratic Union (CDU) farmers, enough to account for four seats in the Bundestag (Federal Diet), or 10 percent of the total of thirty-nine FDP seats. As a consequence, Mr. Ertl, one of four FDP ministers in Chancellor Helmut Schmidt's cabinet, has been able to secure continually rising farm prices despite the strong oppositon of the German finance, economics, and foreign ministers and even Chancellor Schmidt.[32] Of course, most other governments also have basically supported increases in farm prices during the annual price-fixing sessions, usually in April or May, and for similar domestic political reasons. But for industrialized Germany, often complaining of being the "paymaster" of the Community, resistance to any farm price rise would seem to be the rational policy stand.

We should note that the annual price rise is not uniform across the board, again reflecting differing influence effectiveness of individual farm sector groups and varying responsiveness by political and governmental actors in the member states and by the Commission. For example, as a result of the 1978 price-fixing bargaining sessions the average increase was 2.5 percent AUAs, but the individual increases ranged from 1 percent for rye to 2 percent for rice,

sugar, wine, dairy products, and pork, to 3 percent for maize. Moreover, to reduce powdered milk and butter surpluses, no aids were to be given for these
commodities, but mechanisms existing in some member states for subsidizing
school milk and butter prices to increase consumption are continued.[33] Thus
we can see that CAP implementation with respect to prices is highly differentiated according to products and that some effort is made to correct the
policy failures reflected by the surpluses generated in certain agricultural commodities through previous excessive price increases.

MCAs and "Common Prices"

The annual negotiations for fixing prices of various farm product categories
do not provide a true measure for the income of farmers in the individual
member states. The reason is that, as noted earlier, the prices fixed are no
longer "common," although common prices remain a major, though elusive
CPA goal. With the introduction of the "green rates" and the MCAs as an adjustment mechanism for changes in the market currency rates, the member
governments have been able to control national prices and subsidies and
thereby have weakened the power of the Community institutions and especially the Commission to pursue truly common agricultural policies. Indeed, the
"green rate" and MCA changes by and for individual member states are part of
the annual agricultural price bargaining game but, as we have seen, the decisions taken affect farmers in the various states differently. The practical result has been the restoration of the member governments' ability to determine a
good part of their farm policies. The fact that farmers from different member
states have gathered in Brussels for recurring demonstrations to obtain higher
prices for their products should not be seen as evidence of ideological support
for political unification or as the desire to give greater decision-making latitude
to the Commission, but pure and simply as a pocketbook issue. Brussels is a
convenient target to dramatize the need for higher farm income for all Community farmers, a target to be supported by every farm group in the member
states. But the size of benefits for the different functional categories of farmers
varies from country to country, and national farm groups often are pleased to
have details worked out on the national level.

"Green rate" changes have become part of the annual price-fixing rituals in
the spring. In turn, the MCAs are also modified.[34] But the member governments can also request and get Community approval for changes in the "green
rate" at any time. Great Britain's devaluation of the "green pound" in March
1978 resulted in a 10.6 percent decrease in MCAs. France has announced a
further devaluation of 3.6 percent of "green francs" for the 1979-80 marketing
year, with a further corresponding reduction of MCAs.

Clearly, the MCAs constitute a policy expedient that threatens the general
goals of the *Common* Agricultural Policy. Following the 1978 farm price compromise, the COPA presidium issued a statement noting, "It is becoming in-

creasingly more difficult to ensure the satisfactory operation of the CAP." The statement went on to say:

In the absence of concrete progress regarding the coordination and harmonization of economic and monetary policies in the Community, there is a considerable danger of a renationalization of the agricultural policy. For that reason, COPA is launching a firm appeal to the governments of the member states . . . in order to make progress on the road to economic and monetary union.[35]

While the COPA presidium expressed its strong support for the Commission's efforts to dismantle the MCA system, it deplored "the very unsatisfactory increase in agricultural prices expressed in units of account" because of the adverse effects on the income and purchasing power of farmers in the Community.

In terms of CAP politics the COPA statement is intriguing. It suggests commitment to greater political integration by advocacy of economic and monetary union in the Community, but only at the cost of higher farm prices fulfilling maximally the expectations of its agricultural clientele and serving their special interests. It hardly reflects an ideological commitment of COPA to a united Europe. Indeed, the urging to return to a uniform CAP with "common" prices could well spring from organizational and tactical motivations. COPA's utility as an organization may suffer if the trend toward renationalization of agricultural policies cannot be reversed. Tactically, it makes good sense to support Commission goals and thereby retain this organ's optimum good will; it also serves the purpose of weakening whatever relations the Commission might maintain with competing umbrella and national farm organizations.

No matter what the motivations of the COPA statement may be, there is spreading recognition that the instability of national currencies and the distortions created by the "green rate" and MCA system are jeopardizing the proper implementation of the CAP and perhaps the future of the policy itself. This recognition has provided renewed impetus to the longstanding Commission goal of setting up a European Monetary Union (EMU). During the European Council meeting ("summit") in Bremen in July 1978, France and Germany proposed stabilizing the exchange rates of the member states by gradually introducing a European Currency Unit backed up by a European Monetary Fund of perhaps $50 billion. However, the British so far have been reluctant to commit themselves fully to this plan, and some of the other member governments also seem to have reservations. The reason for their reluctance was, as always, the primacy of national interests. Britain wanted Germany to accept a higher rate of inflation to help British exports, and some of the weaker EC countries such as Italy wanted more economic aid before tying their currencies into such a fund.[36]

Marketing Problems

An important objective of the CAP as originally conceived has been the free movement of agricultural products within the Community with production located in accordance with the principles of optimum allocation of resources and the need for specialization of effort. In other words, there should be a division of labor reflecting the comparative advantages of the widely differing soil and social conditions throughout the Community territory.

Although the rate of increase in intracommunity trade in agricultural products from 1963 on has been higher (409 percent) than that in trade of all goods (335 percent), the instruments used for the implementation of the above CAP objective have been only partially successful. Several causes accounting for this lack of success can be identified. The most serious obstacle to the unity of the common agricultural market is the existence of the MCA system discussed earlier. A second cause of implementation failure is distortion of competition, which results from actions by the national governments of the member states as well as by private enterprise. National governments have from time to time affected the competitive position of farms by influencing the cost factors through the adoption of laws, regulations, and administrative measures, and these actions have varied considerably from country to country.[37]

A third cause of failure has been the interference with the free movement of goods through technical barriers, such as the imposition of overly perfectionist health or administrative standards. At times the principle of free intracommunity movement has been violated by national governments for purely protectionist reasons. An example was the closing of the French borders to the import of low-priced Italian wine, an action which later was rescinded. This problem is in the process of being solved by the introduction of a temporary floor price for certain categories of table wine and by structural improvements of production and marketing procedures under the Guidance Section of the EAGGF in the most affected French wine-growing area, the Languedoc-Roussilon region.[38] Of course, the EAGGF solution will take time to be effective. In the meantime, the impending accession of Greece, Portugal, and Spain to the Community, expected to come in to force in the early 1980s, will create many new marketing problems for many agricultural products grown in Italy and southern France. Special Mediterranean agricultural policy instruments are being negotiated to deal with these problems.

Finally, the implementation of the principle of division of labor in Community agriculture is impeded by the CAP's price guarantee and protection system. Particular crops in a particular area benefit substantially from the effectiveness of this system although, in terms of comparative advantage, the location is only marginal or perhaps poor. Hence, it is the CAP's implementation instrument itself that constitutes an obstacle to the process of specialization.

National Civil Servants and the CAP

As demonstrated earlier, the participation of national civil servants in the shaping of CAP implementation instruments is extensive. Moreover, they are the primary executors of these instruments. Hence, it is interesting and useful to gain a perception as to how the national civil servants, especially in the agricultural ministries of the member states, look upon the integration process in general and its effect on the CAP in particular. Interviews conducted in 1973 by this author with eighty two national officials have shed some light on their attitudes toward these subjects, although only a small number of the interviewees were employed in the agricultural ministries.

The interviews reveal[39] that a major source of concern for the officials employed in the various ministries in the EC member states is the transfer of competence from the national to the European Community level. At the time the Communities were established, many national civil servants were attracted to Luxembourg and Brussels by higher salaries, easier promotions, and an expected new and superior level of government in Europe. Undoubtedly, ideological commitment to a united Europe also played a role in wanting to participate in this novel experiment in political integration. Although the earlier expectations of European unification have not been fulfilled and regional integration seems to have reached a plateau, additional transfers of competence continue to be advocated in the rhetoric of some governmental leaders in the member states. Therefore, apprehension is likely to linger in the minds of national civil servants that they will be faced eventually with a reduction of their powers and authority and increasingly be exposed to the control of Eurocrats.

Bureaucratic Experience and Motivations

Being human, civil servants act at least partially in their own interests and perceive their institutional environment as a factor influencing the pursuit of those interests. As a consequence, their attitudes and behavior are motivated by considerations of power, prestige, income, and security. Although the desire to serve the public interest and pride in proficiency are important motives, they can easily coexist with and in fact may enhance the pursuit of self-interest.[40] Self-interest usually includes the maintenance of the institutions in which appointed officials serve, so changes in these institutions are not likely to be advocated unless the probable rewards from the changes, by contributing to the attainment of the basic goals of power and prestige, outweigh the possible cost flowing from the changes.

Material benefits and other tangible advantages derived from regional integration may be the kind of inducements to prompt individual civil servants to see advantages in progress toward political union. However, only 32 percent of our respondents stated that they had received such benefits, and an even smaller number (7 percent) expected to have integration-related benefits and advantages in the future.

Another factor producing pro-union attitudes may be the assignment for a limited period to the European civil service, assignment to a member country mission of the Permanent Representatives in Brussels, or rubbing elbows with European civil servants in one of the numerous expert working groups set up by the EC Commission or within the Committee of Permanent Representatives. Very few of our respondents had experiences as members of the European civil service or as staff on their country's diplomatic missions to the EC (6 and 5 percent respectively), but a larger number, 32 percent, participated in expert working groups.

Apparently, getting to know integration is not the same thing as getting to love it—at least in the political form. If we can think of experience with expert working groups as a socialization exercise, then in the case of "political" integration it was counterproductive. On the other hand, expert working group experience does seem somewhat productive for attitudes supportive of continued economic integration. This set of findings is largely consistent with trends in the literature on European integration downgrading expectations for spillover effects. The mere fact of having to work together does not unidirectionally impel integrative attitudes.

The Bureaucratic Environment and Integration Support

In order to probe further into the career and personal concerns of the civil servant respondents that might affect their behavior with regard to policy choices and policy development in the Community system, they were asked several clusters of searching questions. First they were asked whether they did indeed consider political integration a threat to their positions inasmuch as it could reduce their chances for promotion. As can be seen from Table 6.3, only 28 percent answered in the affirmative. At the same time, 44 percent felt that participation in interministerial committees, the normal mechanism for evolving consensus within national governments with regard to EC issues, would broaden their responsibilities. About the same percentage thought that ministries furnishing members for such committees would gain in importance in the overall structure. Many national civil servants are apprehensive that as a result of increasing integration the functions they presently perform may be reduced. Although a substantial majority of them do not regard such a reduction as serious—many national officials may not give the political integration process much chance of succeeding in the near furture—they would like to be in posts where functions are likely to be expanded. The feeling of threat to their positions was most acute among officials in the Foreign and Social Affairs Ministries and those of the Economics and Finance Ministries least, with the Agricultural Ministries at the lower end of the scale.

Closely related to a civil servant's job satisfaction is his relationship with the

Table 6.3 Functions of Civil Servants and Integration
(percentage)

	Yes	No	No Opinion
Do you consider political integration a threat to your position?	28	71	1
Does participation in interministerial committees broaden your responsibilities?	43	4	52
Do ministries furnishing members to such committees gain importance?	44	4	52

N = 82

Source: Werner J. Feld and John K. Wildgen, *Domestic Political Realities and European Unification* (Boulder, Colo.: Westview Press, 1976), p. 125. Copyright © 1976 by Westview Press. Reprinted by permission of Westview Press.

ministry's clientele, because it places him in authority with regard to groups and individuals dealing with the ministry and thereby contributes to his position of power and prestige. Moreover, clientele relations may generate constituencies which would oppose the reduction of functions of individual organizations or their complete liquidation. Of course, not all ministries serve a clientele, but the Agriculture Ministries obviously perform such functions to a large extent.

To determine the respondent's perceptions of the influence of political integration on the clientele relationship, two questions were asked: how important did they think political integration was for their clientele; and how might it affect their relationship to their clientele. Three-fourths of those interviewed answered the first question in the affirmative and about half the second. Understandably, for officials in the Ministry of Agriculture (78 percent) the clientele relations were especially important, and it was felt that these relations were likely to suffer if, in the event of political union, Community officials were to make the salient decisions and interest groups were to shift their main contacts to Brussels.

Considering that the relations between officials and their clientele are reasonably close, the question was asked whether they were exposed to pressures from their clientele, especially interest groups, to either maintain or change their attitudes toward political integration and European Community affairs. Such pressures were reported by only a minority.

It is obvious that any reduction in powers caused by the transfer of competences to Brussels is worrisome, but there were differences in judgment as to when political integration would progress to the point that national governmental functions were actually diminished. Without doubt, the transfer of competences has advanced furthest in the agricultural field, and some of the officials in the Agriculture Ministries of Denmark, Germany, Ireland, and the Netherlands felt that the EAGGF funds should be dispersed by them rather than from Brussels and that some of the competences lost should be returned to them. As we have seen, this has actually happened in the disbursement of the Guidance Section and in the payments of the Guarantee Section, the payers of the advances received by the national governments from the Community are indeed national agencies and departments.

During the interviews an Irish agricultural official stated that he considered the farm groups as allies in obtaining maximum benefits for Irish agriculture through the EC Council of Ministers and therefore encouraged them to have direct contacts in Brussels. He also said that unfortunately most Irish farm groups are too poor to have permanent representatives in Brussels. One French official in the *Caisse Agricole* thought that the ideology of his department and that of the Ministry of Agriculture is determined by a strong group of upper-level civil servants who want to hold on to their positions of power. An official of the Danish Ministry of Agriculture stated that membership in the Community had caused a division among the employees in the ministry between those engaged in external functions and those dealing primarily with internal problems. Many tensions have been created as a consequence.

In order to obtain a more direct behavioral cue from the respondents, a few questions were included to determine their reactions when faced with the implementation of Community decisions considered disadvantageous to their country. One question inquired about organizational pressures *not* to comply with such decisions. Fifty-two percent affirmed such pressures were especially strong in the Agricultural Ministries, since the Community Agricultural Policy has already transferred many formerly national competences to Brussels. Usually, attempts are made first to have repugnant decisions modified through top-level appeals to the Council of Ministers. If these appeals fail, other strategies are attempted, including ignoring the decision.

Conclusions and Prospects

If we attempt to assess the reasons for the unintended outcomes of the CAP, such as the high cost of implementing the policy, the surpluses of various commodities, and the breakdown of the unified market and price concept, some general and several specific causes can be identified.

General Causes

An underlying cause for not attaining the major objectives of the CAP has been the loss of momentum in the forward movement toward political integration of the EC, as reflected in the shift of power from the Commission to the Council of Ministers and the CPR. The two-tier system of interaction between Commission and national government officials is especially tilted toward the effective exercise of influence by the latter in the CAP policy-making and implementation area. As a consequence, the national interests of the member states, often divergent, and the special interests of the farm clientele, sometimes differing from group to group and sometimes at variance with the Community interest, can have significant effects on the formulation and execution of policy measures impeding basic goal attainment and contributing to policy failures. Satisfying the expectations of particular farm groups and the aspirations of national political leadership groups for political rewards cannot but disappoint the top layer of the Eurocratic hierarchy seeking to promote first and foremost the Community interest in the proper functioning of the CAP. With the CPR playing a key role in all decisions and the autonomy of the national governments maintained, the desired division of labor in agricultural production, a major goal of the CAP planners, has remained elusive.

A second general cause for problems weakening the attainment potential of the CAP goals as originally envisioned has been the concern of national civil servants involved in the implementation process to retain their positions of individual and institutional power. The greater the likelihood of additional transfer of authority from national governments to the Community institutions, the greater will be the fears of national bureaucrats for their prerogatives. These are normal bureaucratic attitudes often translated into corresponding behavior. Although, as noted earlier, the strength of these attitudes and their anti-integration implications are not quite clear, it is reasonable to assume that bureaucractic perceptions about the direction and intensity of the CAP implementation process are frequently colored by these attitudes and that, therefore, the pursuit of the real Community interest may suffer from time to time. As a result, trends toward undesirable policy outcomes may well be reinforced rather than counteracted by national civil servants engaged in agricultural functions.

Specific Causes

Undoubtedly, the single most disruptive factor in agricultural market and price unity has been the system of "green rates" and MCAs. It has brought back increasing national control over prices in different EC member states and provided opportunities for the government to give special advantage to its farmers. Unfortunately, it has also opened the door to fraudulent manipulation by dishonest farmers and dealers in agricultural products. Only the dismantling of the MCA system could return to the CAP the market and price unity that had been one of its major objectives. But this would require a complete stabilization and assured harmony among the national currencies which, as pointed out earlier, may be a slow process in spite of renewed efforts by some member governments toward this end.

Meanwhile, the MCA system, which was intended to counteract the effects of revaluations and devaluations upon the CAP, continues to distort the benefits to the target group, the farmers in the EC member states. Those in the countries whose currencies have been devalued are penalized, while those in the countries with revalued currencies benefit from the advantages of this revaluation through reduced production costs, notably for imported fertilizers and machinery and lower interest rates. Moreover, member countries, which should have become stronger importers of agricultural products from other member states because of revalued currencies, have become exporters to countries that traditionally were extensive producers of farm commodities. Italy has been the principal victim of these perverse effects and Germany the main beneficiary.[41]

Second, price policies to counter surpluses in the dairy and other fields have not been applied vigorously for fear of domestic political repercussions caused by powerful farm group pressures. The Commission has attempted to use the CAP price policy more energetically to adapt it more closely to market trends, but while the Council has adopted some minor proposed measures, the overall political ambitions have prevented fully effective adjustments.[42]

The third cause of implementation failure is the slow progress of structural improvement of farms. As we have seen, the Guidance Section is allocated only a rather small share of the EAGGF, but even if it received a larger share the chief problem may well be the need for matching funds, which a few countries, such as Italy, may either not have or not want to make available. Other reasons may be the fear of increased unemployment if owners of inefficient farms or farm labor were pushed out of their present occupation. Political and institutional reasons may also be responsible for governmental reluctance to apply for guidance aid and make matching funds available for improvement projects.

Without doubt, the need for profound structural reorganization remains if eventually economies of scale are to be applied in the agricultural sector and a proper division of labor is to be instituted to make agriculture as effective an economic sector as others are in the European Community. The basic philosophy of the agricultural provisions in the EEC Treaty has always been to achieve full and complete integration of the agricultural sector in the economy as a whole. To attain these objectives the Community should perhaps provide funds for the total cost of structural improvements while continuing to leave to the national administrators the task of determining and supervising the projects undertaken. Moreover, social policy instruments should be devised in close cooperation with the national member governments to solve social and economic problems caused by structural improvement projects in the agricultural sector.

The accession of Greece, Portugal, and Spain to the EC within the next few years will bring particularly difficult challenges in the agricultural sector of the economy. Obviously the farm products of the three new member states will compete vigorously with similar Italian and French products requiring manifold adjustments and perhaps safeguard measures. At the same time, the new member states are characterized by traditional agricultural structures, many of them quite small, and therefore the demands on the Guidance Section of the EAGGF will rise considerably.[43] It is obvious, then, that the CAP planners must have responses to these challenges, and problems and proper policy evaluation procedures and measures will ease this task.

The question of renationalization of agricultural policies in the EC is a serious matter because if such a development were to occur it might deal a mortal blow to integration prospects and, worse, might lead to a gradual unravelling of the present integration structure. Despite the fact that most action regarding CAP policy instruments is initiated in Brussels, a slight trend toward renationalization has existed since the late 1960s, and the potential of this trend was strengthened with the introduction of the MCA system. However, to put this trend in perspective, we must keep in mind that CAP formulation and implementation have always been responsive to the explicit or implicit preferences of national actors, governmental as well as nongovernmental, and although cast in the form of EC regulations their content is in fact the result of "intergovernmental" negotiations within the complicated two-tier decision-making process. But this does not mean that this trend will inevitably culminate in the CAP's disintegration; the Brussels forum offers the national political leadership a convenient scapegoat and alibi mechanism when it becomes realistically impossible to meet excessive and specialized demands of farm interest groups. While from a purist point of view the CAP does indeed exhibit various failings in relation to its professed goals, policy implementation has adapted itself to the prevailing political and economic realities. As a result of past, present, and probably future adaptability, the CAP is likely to serve as best as it can the many conflicting farm and other interests articulated and pressed in the polities of the member states. Thus, it most probably will survive, although its basic nature may be quite different from that conceived by the framers of the original policy. At the same time, remedying some of the implementation problems will improve policy performance and spread benefits more evenly.

Meanwhile, demands for reform of the CAP are likely to receive an increasingly sympathetic hearing. Great Britain has been in the forefront of this movement, which the British government considers necessary in the fight against inflation. Britain and other member governments have also been calling for a budgetary limit on spending for 1980 and future years for the CAP, which continues to receive the lion's share of the EC budget ($10 billion, or about 70 percent of total expenditures in 1979).[44] A properly reformed CAP could again become a major energizer for progress toward political unification.

Notes

1. Leon N. Lindberg and Stuart A. Scheingold, *Europe's Would-Be Polity* (Englewood Cliffs, N. J.: Prentice-Hall, 1970), p. 41.

2. *The Economist* (April 1, 1978); 60–62.

3. Ibid., p. 62.

4. Ulrich Koester, *EG-Agrapolitik in der Sackgasse* (Baden-Baden: Nomos Verlagsgesellschaft, 1977).

5. See Supplement 2/75 to Bulletin of the European Communities, *Stocktaking of the Common Agricultural Policy* (February 25, 1975).

6. For details, see Commission of the European Communities (EC), *EAGGF: Importance and Functioning* (1978), pp. 20–21.

7. Ibid.

8. Lindberg and Scheingold, *Europe's Would-Be Polity*, pp. 147–48.

9. *The Economist* (April 1, 1978); 60.

10. EC, *Eleventh General Report* (1977), pp. 49–52.

11. Ibid., table 2, p. 47; and EC, *Seventh General Report* (1973), p. 82.

12. For details, see EC, *Economic Effects of the Agri-Monetary System* (February 10, 1978).

13. *The Economist* (April 1, 1978); 62.

14. *Die Zeit*, April 21, 1978.

15. EC, *Economic Effects of the Agri-Monetary System*, p. 13.

16. Ibid., p. 12.

17. Ibid., p. 13.

18. EC, *EAGGF*, pp. 45–46, 53.

19. See EEC Directives 72/159, 72/160, and 72/161, April 17, 1972.

20. EC, *EAGGF*, p. 55.

21. EEC Directive, 75/268, April 28, 1975.

22. Ibid., pp. 50–53.

23. Roy Pryce, *The Politics of the European Community* (London: Butterworths, 1973), p. 68.

24. See Giancarlo Olmi, "The Role of Community and National Institutions in the Implementation of the Common Agricultural Policy," in *European Integration*, ed. Michael Hodges (Harmodsworth, UK: Penguin Books, 1972), pp. 241–64.

25. See EC, *Commission Note* VI/3044/77 (November 8, 1977).

26. See William F. Averyt, Jr., *Agropolitics in the European Community* (New York: Praeger, 1977), pp. 86–88.

27. Ibid., pp. 103–04.

28. Glenda G. Rosenthal, *The Men Behind the Decisions* (Lexington, Mass.: D. C. Heath, 1975), p. 3.

29. Ibid., p. 5.

30. Ibid., p. 6.

31. Ibid., pp. 3–6; Averyt, *Agropolitics in the European Community*; and Lindberg and Scheingold, *Europe's Would-Be Polity*, pp. 155–63.

32. For details, see *The Economist* (November 5, 1977); 54–55. Ertl's pivotal position may be seriously compromised if the FDP losses in recent state elections, where it was unable to obtain the necessary 5 percent of the vote to elect deputies, should spill over into the next federal elections in 1980.

33. *Agence Europe Bulletin*, May 12, 1978.

34. Ibid., May 13, 18, 1978.

35. Ibid., May 16, 17, 1978.

36. *International Herald Tribune*, July 8–9, 1978; and *The Economist* (May 27, 1978); 55–56.

37. *Stocktaking of the Common Agricultural Policy*, pp.14, 29.

38. *Agence Europe Bulletin*, May 12, 13, 1978.

39. See Werner J. Feld and John K. Wildgen, *Domestic Political Realities and European Integration* (Boulder, Colo.: Westview Press, 1976), pp. 119–37.

40. For a full discussion of officials' motives and goals, *see* Anthony Downs, *Inside Bureaucracy* (Boston: Little, Brown, 1967), pp. 79–81.

41. *Agence Europe Bulletin*, May 22–23, 1978 (editorial).

42. EC, *Stocktaking of the Common Agricultural Policy*, pp. 34–35.

43. *See* EC, *General Considerations on the Problems of Enlargement* (April 24, 1978), COM (78) 120 Final.

44. *International Herald Tribune*, July 19, 27, 1978.

STEPHEN D. KON

7

The Delicate Balance Between Municipal Law and Community Law in the Application of Articles 85 and 86 of the Treaty of Rome

The antitrust policy of the European Community does not contain a notion of competition as an end in itself. It treats competition as a means of achieving certain objectives as set down in Article 2 of the Treaty, notably:

By establishing a Common Market and progressively approximating the economic policies of Member States to promote throughout the Community a harmonious development of economic activities, a continuous and balanced expansion, an increase in stability, an accelerated standard of living and closer relations between states belonging to it.

These objectives are to be achieved partially by the creation of a customs union, in which there is created a regime for the free movement of goods and the elimination of quantitative restrictions and also guaranteed is the free movement of workers and capital, the freedom to supply services and the right of private individuals and companies to "establish" themselves for the purposes of carrying out professions, trade, or business in the member states. The creation of these freedoms together with the development of common policies in agriculture, transport, and economic and social matters, are aimed at achieving these objectives.

This general structure to the Common Market was described by the European Court of Justice in the following terms:

While the Treaty's primary object is to eliminate . . . the obstacles to the free movement of goods within the common market and to confirm and safeguard the unity of that market, it also permits the community authorities to carry out certain positive, though indirect actions with a view to promoting a harmonious development of economic activities within the whole community in accordance with Article 2.[1]

However, it was recognized that within such a framework there must be created a structure whereby producers were free to make their offers and negotiate freely with their customers and consumers were able to choose freely between goods or services according to their quality and prices and according to the fluctuations within a free market economy of supply and demand. Thus, Article 3(f) includes among the objectives of the Community "the establishment of a system ensuring that competition in the Common Market is not distorted." There was little value in suppressing economic barriers among member states if private enterprises could resurrect private barriers having as their object or effect the partitioning of the Common Market. The fundamental objective of Article 3(f) of the Treaty is pursued along two avenues, both of which have as their origin the idea that competition must be effective if it is to fulfill its role as an integrating factor: first, the protection of the competitive system against interference arising from the agreement or concerted practice and, second, its protection against corporate structures generated by economic and commercial growth. It must be emphasized from the outset that notwithstanding the generality of the wording of Articles 85 and 86 they are both all-embracing in their effects, containing absolute prohibitions against restrictive practices and abuses of dominant positions. The system established is impregnable; it cannot be evaded, avoided, or circumvented.

The Treaty of Rome expresses these two general prohibitions in the following terms:

Article 85
(1)The following shall be prohibited as incompatible with the Common Market: all agreements between undertakings, decisions by associations of undertakings, and concerted practices which may affect trade between Member States and which have as their object or effect the prevention, restriction, or distortion of competition within the Common Market, and in particular those which: (a) directly or indirectly fix purchase or selling prices or any other trading conditions; (b) limit or control production, markets, technical development, or investment; (c) share markets or sources of supply; (d) apply dissimilar conditions to equivalent transactions with other trading parties thereby placing them at a competitive disadvantage; (e) make the conclusion of contracts subject to acceptance by the other parties of supplementary obligations which, by their nature or according to commercial usage, have no connection with the subject of such contracts.

Article 86
Any abuse by one or more undertakings of a dominant position within the Common Market or in a substantial part of it shall be prohibited as incompatible with the Common Market insofar as it may affect trade between Member States. Such abuse may, in particular, consist in: (a) directly or indirectly imposing unfair purchase or selling prices or other unfair trading conditions; (b) limiting production, markets, or technical developments to the prejudice of consumers; (c) applying dissimilar conditions to equivalent transactions with other trading parties, thereby placing them at a competitive disadvantage; (d) making the conclusion of contracts subject to acceptance by the other parties of supplementary obligations which, by their nature or according to commercial usage, have no connection with the subject of such contracts.

The detailed application and implementation of these provisions is left to subsequent Community legislation and to the general supervision of the European Commission. The European Court of Justice is given (Article 164) the task of ensuring that the law is observed in the interpretation and application of the Treaty. In exercising this function, the Court has from its earliest days stressed the importance of the unity of the Community legal order and of the fact that the Community legal order in all its spheres is a separate and distinct system from those of the member states. Thus, in one of its early judgments, the Court stated, "The Community constitutes a new legal order of international law for the benefit of which the states have limited their sovereign rights, albeit within limited fields, and the subjects of which comprise not only member states but also their nationals."[2] Similarly, the Court has always stressed the fundamental importance of the rules of competition in the attainment of the Community's general objectives. In 1966 it stated:

Article 85 as a whole should be read in the context of the provisions of the preamble to the Treaty which clarify it and reference should be made to those relating to "the elimination of barriers" and to "fair competition," both of which are necessary for bringing about a single market.[3]

The essential problem with which both the court and the Commission have had to deal in the general system of Articles 85 and 86 was to evolve from a tabula rasa a common European antitrust policy compatible with the individual needs and legislation in force in each of the member states, while retaining the essential supremacy[4] of community objectives in the establishment of a Common Market. In examining the manner in which the Court and the Commission have reconciled the individual competition laws of member states with the evolving EC antitrust policy, this essay briefly considers both the procedural balance established between Community and state authorities and certain aspects of the substantive law developed regarding the relationship between Community competition rules and the municipal competition rules of the nine member states.[5] The aim of this essay is to demonstrate how the competition policy developed is a progressive and effective force in the achievement of the objectives laid down in Article 2 by virtue of the procedural and substantive balance established between Community law and the municipal laws of member states.

In order for a European antitrust policy to be effective in all member states of the Community, it is essential that any rules in force in those states be incapable of impeding the full and uniform application of the Community rules. Robert Lecourt, former president of the Court, aptly summarizes the rationale behind such a principle:

What is the Community if not an autonomous and supreme authority, imposed simultaneously and uniformly over and above national boundaries? The existence of common rules is the foundation stone of any community. To want a common market and to deny the common character of the rules which create it would be contradictory. There is no unity within the market without there being only one overriding law having the same authority and value everywhere. Without this the Community would break up into a simple juxtaposition of independent entities, brought together by the force of recommendations.[6]

Clearly, for Articles 85 and 86 to have an identical value throughout the Community, the overlap in the fields of application of Community rules and national rules, from both the territorial and the substantive points of view, has to be strictly regulated. Although Treaty Article 87-2(e) requires that regulations or directives be passed to determine the relationship between national competition laws and Community competition laws, no such regulations or directives have yet been passed. Until such legislative action is undertaken, national antitrust rules will continue to apply in parallel with EC antitrust rules, providing such parallel application does not give rise to conflict. Hence, in principle, there is nothing in the Community system to prevent two different sets of antitrust rules being applied at the same time to identical economic circumstances.

The problem of a potential conflict between the two systems poses two related but nonetheless distinctive questions. The first question is essentially procedural or jurisdictional in nature and concerns which authority is to enforce and which authority is to be supreme in the application of the Community rules. The second question is essentially substantive and relates to how the two sets of rules, national and Community, relate to one another.

Conflicts of Resolution

Essentially, three different organs are competent to adjudicate upon Articles 85 and 86. First, there is the European Commission, which exercises such powers generally as custodian of the Treaty (Article 155) and by virtue of specific competence granted to it in competition matters by Articles 87 and 88. Next, the individual courts and tribunals of member states have competence by virtue of the direct effect of Articles 85 and 86 in their territory[7] and also by certain provisions in Articles 87 and 88. Finally, there is the European Court of Justice, which has the overall responsibility for the control of legality and the interpretation of Community law under the Treaty of Rome.

On February 6, 1962, pursuant to Treaty Article 87, the Council of Ministers enacted Regulation 17/62.[8] This regulation represents a remarkable achievement in the legislative history of the EC for several reasons. First, under the terms of Regulation 17, the Commission is given wide powers of investigation in competition matters: it may act on its own initiative whenever facts come to its knowledge that may constitute a breach of Article 85 or 86. Similarly, individuals have a direct right of access to the Commission and may lodge a complaint in which they inform the Commission of potential breaches of Article 85 or 86, although this is subject to the limitation that individuals must be able to show a legitimate interest.[9] Member states are given similar rights to complain to the Commission.

The result of these provisions in Regulation 17 is that where an enterprise or association of enterprises believes that it is suffering as a result of a restrictive agreement or abusive conduct, it may lodge a complaint before the Commission and thus initiate antitrust investigations. A second and more frequently exercised power given to the Commission by Regulation 17 is its right to commence proceedings under Article 85 or 86 as a result of its systematic supervision of markets in different economic sectors.[10] The Commission may initiate such an investigation into individual economic sectors (Article 12 [1]) whether or not proceedings have been commenced under Article 3(2). Such wide powers are further amplified by Article 2 of Regulation 17, which provides that any undertaking or association may request the Commission for a ruling that Article 85 does not apply to a particular agreement, or that, although Article 85(1) applies to the agreement, it is exempt from this prohibition pursuant to Article 85(3). This system, whereby undertakings can submit an agreement to the Commission to discover whether or not it violates community competition rules, is known as "notification of agreements."

The supreme importance of notification of agreements to the Commission as part of the jurisdictional balance established in the application of EC competition rules needs to be stressed. If an agreement or practice is not notified and it is subsequently found by the Commission to be contrary to Article 85 or 86, the undertakings involved in the agreement or practice can be fined by the Commission a sum between 1,000 and 1 million units of account, or up to 10 percent of the turnover of the preceding year of each of the undertakings that are party to the infringement. If, however, the agreement is notified after November 1, 1962, and was in force on March 12, 1962,[11] no fine can be imposed for the period between notification and the Commission's decision.

A further important consequence of notification is that, pursuant to Article 9(1) of Regulation 17, the Commission has exclusive jurisdiction in the application of Article 85(3) of the Treaty, subject to review by the Court. Thus a national court adjudicating upon an agreement cannot grant it the benefit of an exemption under Article 85(3), whereas the same agreement being adjudicated upon by the Commission may benefit from such an exemption. In giving the Commission such wide jurisdictional competence, the aim behind Regulation 17 was clearly to establish a European antitrust authority with effective powers to pursue the objectives laid down by Article 3(F) of the Treaty. Although member states were still competent to apply Articles 85 and 86 by virtue of their direct effect and pursuant to Article 9(3) of Regulation 17, the tenor of Regulation 17 is clear. Member states are to enjoy only a subsidiary role in the application of Articles 85 and 86.

This new balance between state authorities and the Commission is reflected in a number of provisions of Regulation 17. Article 13 of Regulation 17 entitles the Commission to request the relevant authorities of a member state to carry out investigations on its behalf if the Commission considers such investigations necessary. The only limitation is that the Commission itself must enjoy the powers of investigation under Article 14 of Regulation 17 which it is requesting the member state to exercise. Similarly, in the Commission's internal procedure as established by Regulation 17,[12] the member states enjoy only a consultative role. National representatives are normally present at the oral hearing of a case pending before the Commission. These representatives are normally delegates from the national cartel authorities. However, pursuant to Regulation 17, there is only one occasion when they are expressly required to present their views to the Commission on the merits of the case: after the Commission has prepared a draft of its decision,[13] it submits the draft to the Consultative Committee on Restrictive Practices and Monopolies.

This committee consists of the representatives from the national cartel authorities, and it discusses the draft with the Commission and gives its opinion. This opinion prepared by the committee is not binding in any way upon the Commission, and it is not uncommon for the Commission to decline to follow the recommendations. The influence that the committee can exert is further diminished by the fact that its opinion is neither published generally nor brought to the notice of the undertakings concerned.

The provisions of Regulation 17 represented a drastic reversal in the traditional relationship between the Commission and the member states. Its enactment was one of the rare occasions after 1957 when member states agreed within the Council of Ministers to limit their own competence by giving wide ranging powers to the Commission. Despite this clear general balance established by the Regulation, and notwithstanding its detailed provisions, there are several questions which the Regulation left unanswered and which remain unanswered today. As a result of the provisions of Regulation 17, the same agreement is potentially subject to three different interpretations by Community authorities. For example, the Commission may publish a decision on a particular agreement or practice pursuant to an inquiry under Article 3(2) of Regulation 17. At the same time, the national court may be considering the same agreement. A further possibility is that the European Court may be giving an interpretation of the law within the context of the agreement as a result of a reference made to it by a national authority under Article 177 of the Treaty.

Article 177 represents a means of collaboration between domestic judicial authorities and the European Court of Justice. The wide powers given to the domestic courts in the application of Community laws is tempered by the requirement that national courts must seek questions of interpretation of the law from the European Court of Justice. The role of this Article has been described in the following terms:

Article 177 thus provides for an organic check point between the judicial authorities of the Member States and of the Community. Significantly, these relations are not established on a hierarchical basis which would have implied the subordination of national courts and tribunals to the European Court. Rather, they rest upon a mode of collaboration in the pursuit of common goals.[14]

The potential conflicts of resolution that may occur when three different jurisdictions are jurisdictionally competent to adjudicate upon the same agreement or practice pose very real legal problems. A national court may prohibit an agreement as being contrary to Article 85 while the Commission may exempt the same agreement from the provisions of 85(1) pursuant to Article 85(3). Such a problem was considered by the Court in the *Sabam Case* that was referred to the Court by the Tribunal de Première Instance (inferior court) of Brussels.

Litigation had been taking place before the Belgian tribunal to determine whether SABAM's[15] title to certain copyright rights was in breach of Article 86 of the Treaty. The Commission had already initiated an investigation into SABAM's activities. SABAM argued that the proceedings in the Belgian courts should be stayed, pending the Commission's decision pursuant to Article 9(3) of Regulation 17, which provides:

As long as the Commission has not initiated any action pursuant to Articles 2, 3, or 6, the authorities of the Member States shall remain competent to enforce Article 85(1) and Article 86 in accordance with Article 88 of the Treaty, even if the time limits for notification laid down in Article 5(1) and Article 7 have expired.

The Belgian tribunal referred the question to the Court under Article 177.

The previous case law of the Commission provided strong evidence that the national courts should suspend proceedings in such circumstances in order to avoid the legal insecurity of two jurisdictions reaching different conclusions on the same question of law. In its judgment in the SABAM case, the Court stated that the national courts and authorities entrusted with the execution of national antitrust laws were competent to apply Articles 85 and 86 of the Treaty. The Court stated that the national authorities *may* for the sake of legal security and consistency postpone its decision pending the outcome of the Commission's proceedings, but in clear-cut cases the national court should decide whether or not Article 85(1) had been infringed.

It thus appears to have been made clear, after several years of confusion,[16] that the European Court attributes great importance to the direct effect of Community law, to such an extent that it is willing to accept both the national and the Community authorities having parallel competence. Hence, although the Court stated in SABAM that the national court may suspend proceedings when the Commission is seized, there is no reason why the national court should not adjudicate upon the matter where there is a prima facie breach of Article 85(1).

This tripartite jurisdictional relationship between the national courts, the Commission, and the European Court has created a number of other unresolved difficulties. One of the most serious problems that has to be decided by the European Court is whether by allowing national courts to apply Article 85(1) when there is no doubt that an agreement is incompatible with it, even when the same agreement is the subject of Commission proceedings, national courts will in fact be implicitly taking a decision on the nonapplicability of Article 85(3) to the agreement in question. It can be argued that as part of a definite judgment that an agreement is incompatible with Article 85(1) it is necessary to discount the possibility that Article 85(3) could apply and hence exempt the agreement from Article 85(1). If the national judge implicitly applies Article 85(3) in this way he would be acting *ultra vires* the powers bestowed upon him by virtue of Regulation 17.

Equally, the Commission may subsequently exempt the agreement pursuant to Article 85(3) and thus raise doubts to the true interpretation of the national court's judgment. In its submissions in a recent case before the European Court,[17] the Commission stated that the national court must be free to decide whether Article 85(3) applied. In contrast, Advocate-General Mayras took a much stricter approach to the problem and stated that national courts were incompetent to apply Article 85(3) under all circumstances. Unfortunately, for procedural reasons, the Court itself did not deal with this question. The problem must accordingly remain.

Another incertitude within this context is when one national court has to reconcile two different and contradictory interpretations of the law with regard to a particular agreement, notably an interpretation given or about to be given by the Commission and a different statement by the European Court in reply to questions posed by another national court pursuant to a reference under Article 177. In such circumstances, much remains with the discretion of the national judge who is of course bound by the supremacy of Community law and the normative hierarchy existing between Community law and national law. If the Commission has been seized of the case but has not yet given its decision, we have seen that the first problem upon which the national judge has to exercise his discretion is whether to stay proceedings. Not only will he have to deal with the delicate problems of the relationship between Article 85(1) and 85(3) already referred to, but he may, as a preliminary issue, have to decide what constitutes seizure by the Commission. For example, does the mere fact that a complaint has been made to the Commission suffice for the Commission to be "seized," or must there be some stronger evidence to show that decision is going to be made? Unfortunately, the Court failed to set any firm criteria in the SABAM case as to what constitutes seizure; hence further uncertainties are created for the national judge when exercising his discretion.

A good example of the discretion that may be left to the national judge is to be found in a recent case considered by the English high court. Judge Graham was confronted with a situation where an appeal was pending before the European Court of Justice from a Commission decision on the same agreement which was now the subject of the high court proceedings.[18] Faced with a Commission decision which was subject to being overruled by the European Court, Judge Graham exercised the discretion which the authorities permit him in a sensible and pragmatic manner. He stayed the high court proceedings and stated that as the Commission's decision was being considered by the European Court it "would be much better that the EEC Court should decide."

Such a decision to stay proceedings was based on two fundamentally correct assumptions which are at the base of an effective equilibrium in the jurisdictional balance in competition matters within the EC. First, as a matter of convenience,[19] since only the Commission at first instance or the European Court are entitled to interpret Articles 85 and 86, the national judge should yield wherever possible to allow one or other or both of these institutions such an opportunity. Second, if the Commission has an opportunity to apply Article 85(3) to an agreement, the national judge should permit it to do so wherever possible in view of the doubtful competence of the national judge to apply exemption. Judge Graham thus states, "I should however say that as at present advised I find it difficult to think that the view of the Commission, whether this decision is technically faulty or not, that this agreement is contrary to Article 85(1) is not correct."

Such problems of the jurisdictional relationship between the Community system and the legal system of member states have still to be resolved. What is clear is that the European Commission has been given the primary *administrative* task in the application of the EC rules, although of course in all matters of interpretation the Commission and the member states are subject to the appellate jurisdiction of the European Court of Justice. In the application and interpretation of EC antitrust rules, the unity of the Community legal order is dependent upon a close collaboration between domestic courts and tribunals, the European Court, and Commission. By giving the Commission such wide jurisdictional competence, Regulation 17 has ensured that the national cartel authorities' competence is subordinate to the Commission with the European Court of Justice remaining the supreme judge in all matters of interpretation of the law.

Conflicts of Law

It has already been suggested that the integrating role of the national judge in competition matters is not limited to reconciling conflicts of resolution between parallel legal orders but equally towards dealing with conflicts of the substantial rules of these parallel legal orders. When national and Community antitrust rules are applicable to the same factual situation, there exists a potential conflict between the two, in particular since the appropriate directives or regulations pursuant to Article 87 (e) of the Treaty have not been enacted. In the absence of such express legislative enactment, the Community only shares competence with the member states in antitrust matters and does not enjoy exclusive competence.

To a certain degree, Articles 85 and 86 are limited in extent, and, by their very nature as provisions to ensure competition within the Common Market, they leave room for national laws to apply. For example, the requirement that interstate trade must be affected for Article 85 to apply is itself strong evidence that national laws have a field of application within the individual member states. Yet, although in many cases an agreement operating solely within the territory of one member state will not affect interstate trade, there may be circumstances when this is not the case. In such instances the same agreement will be subject to two sets of laws and may fall foul of both.

The Commission ruled on this question in the *Cementregling Voor Nederland* decision,[20] which concerned a purely national trade association accounting for some two-thirds of the national trade in cement in the Netherlands. The Association operated a concerted pricing policy and following notification of the agreements relating to it as an association, the Commission had to decide whether an association, such as this operating solely within one member state, could nonetheless affect interstate trade. In its decision the Commission decided unreservedly that such an association could affect interstate trade:

The restrictions on competition . . . contrary to the opinion of those making the notification, do not apply only to Holland but are capable of affecting trade between the Member States. It is true that the decisions taken by the VCH bind only the undertakings situated in Holland, but these rules are when taken as a whole capable of compromising in a way which is *directly or indirectly prejudicial to the setting up of a single market*, the freedom of trade between Holland on the one hand, and Belgium and West Germany on the other, and even France which is a potential supplier.[21]

Accordingly, the fact that national rules and community rules may have different objectives in no way prevents the parallel application of the two systems. This was clearly stated by the Court in its judgment in the Walt-Wilhelm case, which dealt with the relationship between Community competition rules and the competition rules of member states. The Court stated:

Community restrictive practices law and national restrictive practice laws consider cartels from different points of view. . . . It is true that as the economic phenomena and legal situations under consideration may in individual cases be interdependent the distinction between Community and national aspects could not serve in all cases as the decisive criterion for the delimitation of jurisdiction.[22]

When dealing with any question of the relationship between Community law and the national laws of member states, one must always start from the basic proposition that, in the event of conflict, Community law *must* prevail. In one of its most celebrated judgments, that of *Costa* v. *ENEL,* the Court made the following proclamation:

The integration into the laws of each Member State of provisions which derive from the Community, and more generally the terms and spirit of the Treaty, makes it impossible for the States, as a corollary to accord precedence to a unilateral and subsequent measure over a legal system accepted by them on the basis of reciprocity. Such a measure cannot therefore be inconsistent with that legal system. The executive force of Community law cannot vary from one State to another in defense to subsequent domestic laws, without jeopardizing the attainment of the objectives of the Treaty set out in Article 5(2) and giving rise to the discrimination prohibited by Article 7. . . . It follows from all these observations that the law stemming from the Treaty, an independent source of law, could not, because of its special and original nature be overriden by domestic legal provisions however framed without being deprived of its character as Community law and without the legal basis of the Community itself being called into question.[23]

In general terms, a potential conflict may exist wherever, by applying municipal laws, the full and uniform application of Community law would be impeded. Thus, within the context of antitrust rules, although individual member states are entitled to retain their own national rules with the Community rules existing side by side, the states must abstain from measures which may jeopardize directly or indirectly the full, uniform, and effective application of Articles 85 and 86 or measures implementing these Articles. This aspect of the supremacy of Community law was clearly stated by the Court in 1972 in the following terms:

The attainment of the aims of the Community requires that the norms of Community law contained in the Treaty itself and enacted under it should apply unconditionally at the same instant and with identical efficacy in the whole territory of the Community without the Member States being able to thwart it in any way.[24]

It is generally accepted that if national laws are *less* severe than EC rules, no conflict exists. Both EC rules and national laws can be applied since the application of national law reinforces the effects of the application of Community law. This so-called double impediment theory[25] is restricted only by the general equitable principle that the same offense ought not to be penalized twice. The possibility of a double sanction does not prevent parallel sets of proceedings: one set by the Commission pursuant to Community law and the other by national authorities under domestic laws. This was clearly established by the Court in the Walt-Wilhelm judgment. In this case, the German Federal Cartel Office had imposed fines on a number of manufacturers of dyestuffs in Germany. The Commission had already commenced proceedings for breach of Article 85 against four of these undertakings and, in its decision of July 24, 1969,[26] had imposed fines against them. The German court that deals with competition matters, the Kammergericht of Berlin, referred several questions to the European Court under Article 177, including one concerning the desirability of both national and Community authorities imposing fines in respect of the same agreement. After ruling in principle that a single agreement can be the subject of two parallel proceedings before Community and national courts, the Court stated that, as a general principle of equity, the authority taking the later decision should take account of the penalty imposed in the first when deciding the penalty to impose. It added, however, that until such time as a regulation has been issued under Article 87, Paragraph 2 (e) there was nothing in the general principles of law to prevent the imposition of two sets of fines.

Thus, subject to this general equitable principle of double jeopardy, and providing there is nothing in the existence or exercise of national cartel law to affect the full and uniform application of Community competition laws, national competition laws can be applied simultaneously with the Community laws. The practical consequence is that the same agreement or practice may have to overcome a number of barriers of municipal competition laws as well as the Community barrier before it can safely be construed as not constituting an antitrust violation.

There are, however, a number of situations where municipal antitrust laws and Community antitrust laws do not work in harmony, and in such situations several important legal questions are raised. There is, of course, the problem of supremacy in the event of conflict between two systems. At first glance, the answer to this problem seems to be relatively straightforward, since as a basic principle of Community law we have seen that Community law must prevail. However, in competition matters, because of the complicated jurisdictional relationship of the European Court, the Commission, and the national courts, the principle of supremacy of Community law encounters several complicating factors. If one accepts a strict interpretation of the double impediment theory, whereby an agreement has to clear the barriers of both national and EC antitrust laws before it is valid, a danger clearly exists that national laws that are more severe than Community laws or that approach competition theory from a different point of view to Community laws may prohibit an agreement or practice which is not incompatible with Article 85 or Article 86.

It is interesting to note that until the Court had confirmed that there was a conflict of laws in this situation, many had argued that the situation was not one of conflict since the application of national laws did not prevent the full application of Community laws. On this question Advocate General Roemer stated in the Walt-Wilhelm case that there was no contradiction between the two systems where the national cartel law applies stricter rules: "For that implies that the national cartel law operates to the same effect as Article 85(1) in keeping with the meaning of that Article, that is, that it *perfects* the conditions of competition."[27]

In fact, in such circumstances one must distinguish three different situations. The agreement may enjoy negative clearance by the Commission as not being contrary to Community competition rules. Such a negative clearance does not raise any question of the supremacy of Community law; indeed, the significance of the negative clearance is that there is no relevant violation of Community law. In effect, there is no conflict between Community competition laws and national competition laws because the former do not apply to the agreement. Similarly, if the Commission makes no intervention at all with regard to an agreement or practice which has come before it because the facts in no way justify such an inference, the matter ceases to be of Community concern. In both these instances, since the EC competition rules are inapplicable, the antitrust authorities in individual member states remain free to apply their own laws as they see fit. In short, since Community law is inapplicable, no conflict exists.

A far more complicated problem is posed when an agreement or practice is found by the Commission to be contrary to Article 85(1) but escapes prohibition because the Commission finds that it meets the conditions for exemption under Article 85(3). On the one hand, the Commission has found that the agreement or practice is of Community concern and constitutes a breach of Article 85, and yet despite this the Commission exempts the application of Article 85(1) pursuant to Article 85(3). Those who support the double impediment theory would argue in such circumstances that municipal competition rules may still prohibit the agreement or practice, since it has only cleared the Community barrier but not the national barrier. However, contrary to such a view it must be argued that by permitting municipal courts or tribunals to prohibit the agreement which has been cleared by the Commission pursuant to Article 85(3), the *full* and *uniform* application of Community law is impaired. The Court has taken a somewhat ambivalent approach to this problem, although it would appear that it favors the latter view rather than the double impediment theory. In several of its judgments, the Court has stressed that Article 85 must be considered as whole and should thus be applied in a uniform way.

Similarly, in the *Walt-Wilhelm judgment*, the Court stated:

The EEC Treaty has established its own system of law integrated into the legal system of Member States, and which must be applied by their own courts. It would be contrary to the nature of such a system to allow Member States to introduce or to retain measures capable of prejudicing the potential effectiveness of the Treaty: *The binding force of the Treaty and of measures taken in application of it must not differ from one state to another as a result of internal measures*, lest the functioning of the Community system should be impeded and the achievement of the aims of the Treaty placed in peril. Consequently, conflicts between the rule of the Community and national rules in the matter of the law on cartels must be resolved in applying the principle that Community law takes precedence.[28]

The emphasized words would, within their context, provide strong evidence that the Court considers that, if an agreement or decision were exempted pursuant to Article 85(3), the very aims of the Community competition rules and the uniform application thereof would be placed in peril should each member state be free to prohibit the same agreement by virtue of their own municipal rules. However, at a later stage in the same judgment, the Court raises doubts on such an interpretation and seems to grant a less positive role to Article 85(3) than to Article 85(1). Thus it describes Article 85(3) as permitting "the Community authorities to carry out certain positive though indirect action with a view to promoting a harmonious development of economic activities within the whole Community in accordance with Article 1 of the Treaty."

It is difficult to see how the words "full and uniform" application of Community law are to have any significance unless national courts are prevented from prohibiting agreements which have been exempted by the Commission from the application of Community competition rules pursuant to Article 85(3). Otherwise, there is a danger that an agreement which operates in several member states but which is exempted in Community law will later be declared invalid according to the competition laws of some of the states where it operates but not in other states where the same agreement operates. Nothing could prevent the attainment of the objectives established in Article 2 of the Treaty more than permitting individual member states such discretionary powers following the application of Community laws to a particular agreement.

It is suggested that there are only two occasions upon which the cumulative application of municipal and Community antitrust laws does not impede the full and uniform application of EC law. When the agreement is prohibited by both systems of law there is clearly no conflict since both systems produce the same result. The second is when the agreement or practice does not concern Community law. In both these cases the application of municipal law is totally consistent with the situation resulting from the application of Community law; in the latter case, because Community law is inapplicable and, in the former case, because the two systems reach the same conclusion. In any other case the full and uniform application of Community law must take precedence over the application of municipal law.

A problem which is associated with the application of the two sets of competition rules is that of the *status* of national rules which are in conflict with the Community rules. There are two possible solutions to the problem. Either those rules that conflict with the Community rules are void and thus implicitly repealed, or those provisions of national law are inapplicable without being implicitly repealed. Certain writers have preferred the former view and consider that directly applicable Community law results in contrary national law being by implication repealed. For example, R. Korvar writes that directly applicable rules have the effect of annulling state norms contrary to them.[29] However, the Court has declared on several occasions that national legislation that conflicts with Community legislation would not be repealed but rather become inapplicable. Hence in the Lück case, the Court declared that the national provisions were not void; rather, the Court left the question of the status of the national law to the discretion of the national judge. It states:

Although Article 95 of the Treaty has the effect of excluding the application of any national measures incompatible with it, the Article does not restrict the powers of the competent national courts to apply, from among the various procedures available under national law, those which are appropriate for the purpose of protecting the individual rights conferred by Community law.[30]

When considering these various problems of the relationship between Community competition rules and the national rules within each member state, the vital harmonizing role of the national judge in attempting to avert a conflict between the two systems is constantly being raised. In the Walt-Wilhelm case, the Court seemed to place the responsibility of avoiding a conflict upon the national judge taking appropriate measures to avoid a conflict of laws. The Court stated in this case:

Should it prove that a decision of a national authority regarding an agreement would be incompatible with a decision adopted by the Commission at the culmination of the procedure initiated by it, the national authority is required to take proper account of the effects of the latter decision. Where, during national proceedings, it appears possible that the decision to be taken by the Commission at the culmination of a procedure still in progress concerning the same agreement may conflict with the effects of decisions of the national authorities, it is for the latter to take the appropriate measures.[31]

Although such dicta make it clear that the national judge should act before a conflict arises, they give no clear indication of what form such action should take. There would appear to be two approaches open to the national judge. Since the Commission is obliged by Article 10 of Regulation 17 to provide the national authorities with information on the content and scope of its decisions or projected decisions, there is nothing to prevent the national authority that is dealing with a case (which is also the subject of Commission proceedings) from making inquiries of the Commission to discover its views before a decision has been formally adopted. The corollary of this is that the national authority's attention should be brought immediately to any proceedings before the Commission relating to the same agreement, decision, or practice it is considering.

Alternatively, the national judge may adopt the "SABAM" solution and suspend national court proceedings pending the Commission's decision. This would enable the national judge subsequently to align his interpretation of national law and indeed Community law so as to avoid a conflict with the decision taken under Community law. This may, of course, involve a declaration that the relevant national law is inapplicable. Clearly, once the national authority has actually taken a decision little can be done to avoid a subsequent conflict with a later and contrary Commission decision unless of course the national proceedings have not reached a final conclusion. Any other conclusion, once all national proceedings have terminated, would endanger the legal security for the enforcement of both sets of rules. Thus a close collaboration between the Commission and national antitrust authorities would seem to offer the most effective tool in harmonizing Community and municipal rules.

Conclusions

If one looks at the development of EC competition policy by the European Court of Justice and by the European Commission, one sees in the substantive principles attempts to harmonize the objectives of Article 3(f) while permitting member states sufficient flexibility to retain the special character of their own rules. Hence, many aspects of substantive Community competition rules constitute an evolving process in which the objectives of the Common Market and in particular Article 3(f), as expressed in Articles 85 and 86, are constantly being balanced against the existence in member states of a separate set of laws, only some of which may be compatible with these Community objectives. For example, in a series of very important decisions and judgments, the Commission and the Court have developed a regime for the existence and exercise of national trademark and patent rights in the EC.[32]

For the purposes of this essay, the interest in this jurisprudence is the conflict between the essentially monopolistic and exclusive nature of trademarks and patents within each individual member state and the requirements of the uniform application of Articles 85 and 86 together with the free circulation of goods within the EC as protected by Treaty Articles 30–36. Since patent and trademarks grant monopolistic rights, and since separate rules exist in each member state to protect such rights, a serious danger exists that the unity of the Common Market might be endangered by the exercise of such rights according to the rules of municipal law. The exercise of such national trademark and patent rights thus presents a serious potential threat to the full and uniform application of the Community competition rules and the rules on the free circulation of goods. Treaty Article 36 provides a narrow exception from the provisions on the free movement of goods for industrial property rights. Article 36 states: "The provisions of Articles 30–34 shall not preclude prohibitions or restrictions on imports, exports, or goods in transit justified on grounds of . . . the protection of industrial and commercial property."

The problem that the Commission and Court have considered is the relationship between such national industrial property as protected in Article 36 and the requirements of Articles 30–36 and 85–86. In resolving this problem, one finds an approach similar to that used when defining the general relationship between Community and national competition laws. Just as Community law permits the *existence* of municipal competition rules as long as their exercise does not interfere with the uniform application of Community rules, so the Commission and the Court have stressed in the case of national patent and trademark rights that their existence is compatible with Community law; however, their exercise may be contrary to the provisions relating to the free circulation of goods or Articles 85 and 86. If this is the case, the patent and trademark rights must give way to Community rules since in a conflict between Community rules and national rules the Community rules must prevail.

Thus, in the Sirena judgment, the Court made the following statement with regard to the relationship between Article 85 and national trademark rights:

A trademark right, as a legal entity, does not in itself possess those elements of contract or concerted practice referred to in Article 85(1). Nevertheless, the exercise of that right might fall within the ambit of the prohibitions contained in the Treaty each time it manifests itself as the subject, the means or the result of a restrictive practice. When a trademark right is exercised by virtue of assignments to users in one or more Member States, it is thus necessary to establish in each case whether such use leads to a situation falling under the prohibitions of Article 85. . . . If the combination of assignments to different users of national trademarks protecting the same product has the result of re-enacting impeachable impenetrable frontiers between Member States such practice may well affect trade between States and distort competition in the Common Market. The matter would be different if, in order to avoid any partitioning of the Market, the agreement concerning the use of national rights in respect of the same trademark were to be effected in such conditions as to make the general use of trademark rights at Community level compatible with the observance of the conditions of competition and unity of the market which are so essential to the Common Market that for failure to observe them is penalized by Article 85 by a declaration that they are automatically void.[33]

It is possible to look at virtually any aspect of the substantive EC competition rules and find a similar general development in Community jurisprudence concerning the relationship with the appropriate national rules. In creating the new legal order, as first described in *Costa* v. *ENEL*, it is always necessary to keep in perspective the legal orders of member states and define the Community rules accordingly. From Articles 85 and 86 there has emerged a uniform body of antitrust rules within the EC which has had an enormous degree of penetration within both the general Community legal order and the national laws of member states. The substantive rules that have emerged represent a delicate balance between national legislation and the overriding Community objectives of Article 3(f) of the Treaty. At the very basis of the development of such substantive rules was the establishment of solid jurisdictional base from which the Community organs and national jurisdictions could harmoniously develop the new European antitrust system.

An attempt has been made in this essay to discuss how this relationship between Community and municipal jurisdictions has developed from the basic provisions of Treaty Article 87 and Regulation 17. There is no doubt that divergences have occurred and will continue to occur between Community jurisprudence and the national jurisprudence of member states in competition matters. However, as we have seen, the national judge has been left a certain margin of discretion which, while allowing a necessary but limited flexibility, renders minor divergences inevitable. However, such divergences can *only* exist to the extent to which they are acceptable to the Commission or another member state, since either of these jurisdictions may bring proceedings under Treaty Article 169 or Article 170 against a state that abuses the discretion.

Similarly, the development of substantive rules was dependent upon the creation of a general policy to determine how the competition rules existing in member states related to the new Community rules and how conflicts of law should be resolved. We have seen that, although uncertainties still exist in this regard, the general relationship has been established sufficiently well to allow for the development of substantive Community rules implementing Articles 85 and 86. In his opinion in the *Walt-Wilhelm* case, Advocate-General Roemer described the relationship between Community rules on competition and national laws as being based "on an idea of *an overlapping* of two legal systems." In both conflicts of resolution and conflicts of law, the problems encountered as a result of this overlapping have been resolved by making the Commission and European law prevail over their respective national counterparts. The result has been a competition policy in which the Commission can act without fear of its work being diluted or interfered with by national antitrust authorities, although the latter may themselves enforce the Community rules, subject to the supervision of the European Court of Justice in their interpretation of Community law. Equally, the national antitrust jurisdictions may enforce their own national rules even where they overlap with the Community rules, providing they do not prevent the Community rules from being applied accurately and in their entirety. There has thus developed a harmony between these overlapping jurisdictions which has to help make the effective realization of the objectives set out in Article 3(f) of the Treaty of Rome a reality.

Notes

1. *Walt-Wilhelm Judgment*, European Court Reports [ECR] (1969), p. 14.

2. *Van Gend en Loos Judgment*, ECR (1963), p. 12.

3. *Italy* v. *Council*, ECR (1966), p. 504.

4. *Costa* v. *ENEL*, ECR (1964), p. 585.

5. Space does not permit a detailed examination of the substantive rules, which have in any case been dealt with elsewhere in a number of leading works. *See* , for example, Michel Waelbrook, *Le Droit de la Concurrence* (Brussels: Université Libre de Bruxelles, 1972) and Berthold Goldman, *European Commercial Law* (London: Stevens, 1973).

6. Robert Lecourt, *Le Juge Devant le Marché Commun*, Etudes et Travaux de l'Institut de Hautes Etudes Internationales, no. 10, (Geneva: Institute of Advanced International Studies, 1970), pp. 20-21. Translated by the author.

7. *See* the *Sabam Case*, ECR (1973), p. 313.

8. *Journal Officiel des Communautés Européennes* [JO] (1962), p. 204.

9. For a recent example of a complaint leading to a major Commission decision, *see Re The United Brands Company*, Common Market Law Reports [CMLR] (1976), p. D28.

10. *See*, for example, *Re Cartel in Aniline Dyes*, CMLR (1961), p. D23.

11. A distinction was made in Regulation 17 between agreements entered into before the entry into force of Regulation 17 and agreements entered into after its entry into force. The so-called old, pre-existing agreements were not open to fines for the period prior to notification provided that they were notified by November 1, 1962. There has been a long dispute, resulting from a series of conflicting dicta of the European Court of Justice, as to the *validity* of agreements during the period between notification of the agreement and the Commission decision. Some relevant cases are: *Bilger* v. *Jehle*, ECR (1970), p. 127; *Brasserie de Haecht* [no. 2], ECR (1973), p. 77; and *De Bloos* v. *Bouyer*, ECR (1977), p. 2359. The position would now appear to be, following the de Haecht decision, that between notification and the Commission decision, agreements are provisionally invalid.

12. The Commission's internal procedure here is also governed by later regulations, notably Regulations 27/1962, *Official Journal of the European Communities* (May 10, 1962), p. 118 and 99/1963, *Official Journal of the European Communities* (August 20, 1963), p. 2268.

13. The Commission is required to prepare and send each national cartel authority a summary of the case together with the most important documents and the draft decision. The national authorities may, although they are not required to, express their views on the conduct of a case by the Commission at any time.

14. A. Barav, "Aspects of the Preliminary Rulings Procedure in EEC Law," *European Law Review* 1 (1977): 3.

15. SABAM is a Belgian association of authors, composers, and music publishers.

16. *See* the Court's decisions in the de Haecht (no. 2) and the *Bilger* v. *Jehle* cases. In the latter case, the Court had taken the opposite view in stating that the national courts should suspend its own proceedings.

17. *The Concordia Judgment*, ECR (1977), p. 65.

18. *Sirdar* v. *Le Fils de Louis Mullier Torsay Knitting Wools Ltd.*, 1 CMLR (1975), p. 378.

19. Ibid., p. 382.

20. CMLR (1973), part 2, p. D16.

21. Ibid., p. D29.

22. ECR (1969), p. 13.

23. ECR (1964), pp. 593–94.

24. *European Commission* v. *Italy*, CMLR (1972), p. 708.

25. See E. Steindorff, "Le Droit des communautés en matière de concurrence et les droits nationaux," Report of the International Conference on the Law of Cartels (Frankfurt, 1960), p. 157.

26. CMLR (1969), p. D23.

27. ECR (1969), p. 23.

28. ECR (1969), p. 14 [author's emphasis].

29. R. Kovar, "L'Applicabilité directe du droit communautaire," *Journal de Droit International* [Clunet] 99 (1973): 279. See also J.V. Louis, "Les Réglements de la Communauté economique Européenne." (Brussels: Presses Universitaires de Bruxelles, 1969), p. 293, who writes "Le Réglement a toujours une efficacité directe par laquelle les lois contraires sont automatiquement abrogrées."

30. *Lück* v. *Hauptzollant Köln*, ECR (1968), p. 251.

31. ECR (1969), p. 13.

32. It must be stressed that no attempt is made to discuss in any depth the Community rules on patents and trademarks. Such a discussion would require a separate essay. The following are some of the leading judgments in patents and trademarks: *Parke-Davis Judgment*, ECR (1968), p. 55; *Sirena Judgment*, ECR (1971), p. 69; *Van Zuylen Freres* v. *Hag*, ECR (1974), p. 731; *Centrafarm Judgment*, ECR (1974), p. 1183; and *EMI* v. *CBS*, ECR (1976), p. 873.

33. ECR (1971), p. 82.

ROGER VAISSIÈRE
AND
JEAN-MARC MASCARO*

8

Health Policies in the EC: Attempts at Harmonization

Although the Treaty of Rome gave a firm legal foundation to a European health community, the idea of such a community predates 1957. Free circulation of physicians was quite common during the Middle Ages, and one physician, Théophraste Paracelse, was well known for practicing his art without hinderance throughout Europe. Later, the French Revolution recognized the idea of free circulation of individuals and trade,[1] and, although these revolutionary principles were eroded later by nationalistic and restrictive measures, there did exist nonetheless a "community." There were no restrictive measures preventing physicians from one country to travel and exchange opinions with their colleagues in neighboring countries, and it was a common and well-accepted practice—even as it was at the time of Paracelse—to observe some medical team and then return home with the knowledge gained.

This state of affairs reflects the "community of ideas" that existed prior to 1957. It was an altogether different matter, however, when the issue no longer concerned only the exchange of scientific information but the actual practice of

*Translated from the original French by Marc Millius and Leon Hurwitz.

Authors' Note: We would like to acknowledge the intellectual assistance and gracious cooperation given us in the preparation of this essay by M. Jean Mignon, Docteur en Droit, Directeur du *Concours Médical*, and Conseiller Juridique de la Confédération des Syndicats Médicaux en France.

medicine itself. It was at this stage that the Treaty of Rome marked an important turning point: European doctors could now seriously consider the possibility of being able to move from their observation posts in the back rows of their neighbor's teaching auditoriums down to the arena of daily practice. This possibility, first stated in 1957, became a reality on December 20, 1976, when the free circulation of EC physicians (giving physicians "European" status) came into force.

The 1976 decision on free circulation contains a major limitation, however. It is only applicable to those in private practice and does not include "public" employees. Thus, all public hospital physicians (and the majority of the European medical profession falls within this category) are deprived of whatever benefits the decision may have, but with the inexorable trend toward greater integration it would appear that this restriction is only temporary. Its repeal would represent a significant step toward the attainment of a truly *European* health community.

After the Treaty of Rome established the principle of free circulation, four important documents refined the framework of the European health care system, two of them being 1975 Directives dealings with the free circulation of physicians.[2] The first concerned the mutual recognition of diplomas, certificates, and other medical titles and contained measures aimed at facilitating the right of establishing a practice; the second dealt with the regulatory and administrative oversight of the physician's activities.

The third document is the well-known Nuremberg Charter,[3] which reaffirms the major principles of European medical ethics: freedom of the patient to choose a physician, respect for human life and for the human personality in its physical and spiritual wholeness, and medical care to be provided in accordance with sound and acceptable procedures. But the Nuremberg Charter also says that "economic expansion finds its major human justification in the improvement of the resources allocated to health care" and that the medical profession "should do its best to improve medicine's human and social effectiveness." Never before was the medical profession so concerned about including such economic and social considerations in a medical ethics statement. This is, indeed, a clear sign of the European medical profession's increased awareness of its social responsibilities, and it is a new—and welcomed—direction for the ancient art of medicine.

The fourth is the Charter of Hospital Physicians,[4] which, in the event free circulation of hospital physicians becomes effective, spells out certain guarantees that hospital physicians have the right to expect from their status, guarantees on professional, economic, political, and social independence. This Charter clearly defines the terms by which service heads are to be chosen so as to guarantee their professional qualifications and also maintains that hospital physicians should have an effective role in the management and decision-making process of the hospital.

The Health Care Systems

The health care systems in all the EC countries have the state as a principal actor through their health insurance schemes. But this government intervention has different forms in each country, and this diversity creates a major problem for the eventual integration of European health care systems. Two polar types of systems exist: (1) "private" medicine—medical practice takes place without governmental intervention (neither in terms of the financing and structures of health care nor of the actual delivery of medical care itself); and (2) "nationalized" medicine—medical personnel are "public" employees (the *fonction publique*) paid by the state, and all equipment and facilities are state property. These are polar types for, in reality, a compromise position exists in most European countries in the form of a health insurance fund (the caisse).

The triangular relationships among the patient, the physician, and the caisse may take two forms in terms of its financing component. In the case of direct payments, the patient, after the consultation, pays the physician the amount due (fee for service), and then the caisse reimburses the patient, in whole or in part. The second form is termed capitation payments: the caisse pays a predetermined amount per registered patient directly to the physician (some systems have a sliding scale which varies according to the services rendered), and the patient makes no direct payments to the attending physician.

The Federal Republic of Germany

In 1977, there were some 130,000 physicians in the Federal Republic (some comparative figures on numbers of physicians, projected rate of growth, and distribution of physicians in the EC are contained in Table 8.1). Although half of these had some "private" patients, a full 98 percent take part as "caisse physicians" in the health insurance system. Thus, there are only 2 percent (or some 2,600 doctors) with a purely private practice. These physicians do not receive any funds from the caisse, and the patient pays all fees directly without reimbursement by the caisse.

All physicians who request to participate are usually accomodated, provided they have met an eighteen-month waiting period. This eighteen-month period does not represent a training or education stage but, rather, is a legally required time period before the physician can treat insured patients. It is the physician's responsibility to secure a position in a hospital for this period, although three of the eighteen months may be spent at another physician's practice. This waiting period was considered to present some problems with the free circulation decision. The German government has since been directed to reduce this period to six months and to eliminate it totally within five years.[5]

There are approximately 57,000 salaried physicians on hospital staffs. The vast majority of German hospitals are either public or run by nonprofit institutions. Only 5 percent of German hospitals are "profit-making" institutions.

Table 8.1   Some Comparative Figures on Density, Number, and Rate of Increase of Physicians in the EC

	Density[a] (per 100,000)	Number of Physicians[b]	Projected % Increase[c] in Number of Physicians
Italy	199	145,000	106.0
Germany	194	129,146	47.0
Belgium	176	19,872	47.5
Denmark	165	11,000	22.0
Netherlands	149	22,913	34.5
France	147	86,306	56.0
United Kingdom	134	85,000	46.0
Ireland	119	3,900	21.0
Luxembourg	108	400	43.0

Source: World Health Organization *L'Annuaire des Statistiques Sanitaires Mondiales, 1973–1976, volume 3, 1976. (*Also published in English as *Yearbook of World Health Statistics, 1973–1976.)*

[a]Figures are for 1974.
[b]Figures are for 1977.
[c]For the period 1970–85. The effect of the projected percentage increase on density cannot be calculated without taking into account projected population increases for the same period.

The health insurance fund is financed by premiums: employers and employees each pay 50 percent. All salaried workers are covered, and numerous "self-employed" people are also covered—a total of 95 percent of the population. The insured have access to free medical treatment and hospitalization. Prescription drugs are also subsidized, with the patient paying the modest fixed fee of 2.50 deutschmark ($1.25) per prescription.

France

When considering the medical profession in France, one must distinguish between the practice of medicine in hospitals (the public sector) and medicine in the private sector.

Ten years ago, hospital physicians maintained a dual practice: one would teach courses at the hospital and medical school, treat patients in the hospital, *and* have certain hours for private consultations. In 1968, however, a fundamental reform under the leadership of Professor Robert Debré transformed the public sector physician. The "full-time" system was introduced whereby the public sector physician's time was entirely devoted to service in the hospital and university teaching. Private practice for the public sector physician has been progressively disappearing since 1968.

The private sector has also undergone change in the past fifty years. In 1933, a "social insurance" law was passed applying to sixty percent of the population. This law entitled the patient (it was the patient who paid the entire fee directly to the physician) to have approximately 50-60 percent (depending on geographical region) of the fee reimbursed by the caisse. This reform was modeled after the system then in existence in Alsace-Lorraine, which had been created by Bismarck after the Franco-Prussian war. In 1945, the obligation to join the health insurance system was extended to all salaried employees. In 1945, the relationships between the caisse and the physician were administered by department agreements between the local medical associations and the health insurance funds, and since these agreements were at the departmental level, they varied from one region to the next.

Popularly known as the "*loi Bacon*," a 1968 piece of legislation established a single type of agreement guaranteeing an 80 percent rate of reimbursement. Physicians had the option of not joining the system, and those who did not could set whatever fees they desired. The difference between the two types of private sector practices lay in the allowable fees and amount of reimbursement. Fees for those physicians in the system were fixed by the annual negotiations between the medical associations and the caisse, and their patients were reimbursed between 80 and 100 percent; physicians outside the system could charge whatever fee desired, and their patients were reimbursed only 35 to 40 percent.

A new system—the National Convention—was established in 1971, and was negotiated at the highest level between the government and the medical associations. It applies to all physicians but, as was the situation with the 1968 Bacon law, physicians are not required to participate. Nevertheless, the Convention has become vital, both in daily medical practice and for the economic protection of the patient, and by 1978 approximately 98 percent of all French physicians had joined the National Convention.

The rate of reimbursement for medical fees ranges from 80 to 100 percent and from 75 to 100 percent for prescription drugs. Physicians cannot exceed the fees set by the Convention, although, in order to "facilitate" the medical profession's adherence to the Convention, certain physicians are authorized to charge higher fees. These physicians are those with "established scientific reputations"; approximately 12 percent of all French physicians are in this category.

In conclusion, medicine in the private sector operates under a contract system which provides a set of guarantees to both the physician and the patient while at the same time allowing freedom of choice. The insured patient has the freedom to choose his GP (General Practitioner), specialist, and hospital; the physician is free to treat according to his judgment, prescribe whatever drug may be necessary, and practice anywhere in France. The patient pays the physician directly for whatever service rendered and then is reimbursed by the caisse. While the French system thus insures freedom for both the physician and the patient, its costs are high (although less than in the Federal Republic of Germany).

Italy

Prior to 1977, there were numerous insurance schemes in Italy covering, in various ways, approximately 90 percent of the population. These schemes were of two basic types: "indirect" and "direct." A patient with "indirect" insurance could see any physician listed by the local caisse, and the patient would pay the fees directly to the physician. The patient would then have part of the fee reimbursed, the amount varying according to the specific type of insurance. Only 0.2 percent of the insured population, however, was in this "indirect" system.

Under the "direct" insurance system, the patient did not pay any fees provided he was on the list of a physician in the locality. The patient could change lists, and, therefore, changing physicians was not too difficult. Consultation by a specialist or treatment in a hospital were also without direct charge to the patient if recommended by a GP (General Practitioner) and, of course, in emergency situations. With "direct" insurance, the physicians receive their fees directly from the caisse, and fees were based on a combination of the number of people on their lists (capitation fees) and on set fees for specific services rendered.

In 1977, Italy made a major effort to establish a coherent and uniform health care system. The current reform is intended to replace the hundreds of existing caisses with a single national health insurance system to cover the entire population. The delivery of health care would also be nationalized through a National Health Service. The existing insurances are financed by heavy employers' contributions and relatively low employee contributions, the large deficits being made up by government payments. These caisses will be replaced progressively by an insurance system financed entirely by taxes. One advantage of a single nationalized health insurance system will be the considerable simplification of the physician's administrative (and time-consuming) tasks. Under the old system, a physician had to make different agreements with the various caisses; he was considered a GP by some and a specialist by others; and he was paid by a variety of procedures (the patient, the caisse; by services rendered and/or capitation fees). All physicians within the service would be paid by capitation fees.

The second goal of the 1977 reform is seen to be the improvement in the availability of medical care in certain geographical regions in Italy. While Italy has a high physician density per 100,000 people (see Table 8.1 above), Italian physicians are distributed very unevenly over the country, and certain measures are being considered to persuade younger physicians to set up practice in the areas with a shortage of physicians.

This system resembles the British NHS (National Health Service) although the Italian scheme gives the patient more freedom to change physicians than does the British NHS. Physicians opting to join the Italian NHS would be government employees, and thus, for at least the time being, the free circulation decision would not be applicable. There has been some concern that, for those Italian physicians not joining NHS, a temptation will exist to look to another country (particularly France) where medical practice is more liberal. The large growth of Italy's medical population along with the progressive institution of NHS and the free circulation decision has made the French wary of a *"marée blanche."*[6] Some early figures since free circulation began, however, do not indicate a *marée* at all; rather, the figures indicate a mere migratory flow.

United Kingdom

Great Britain's health care system presents the perfect picture the European physician has of nationalized medicine, and one is usually more aware of the system's shortcomings (long waiting lists for non-emergency hospitalization, overcrowding at many GP practices) than of its unique characteristics and the benefits it has brought to the British population since its creation in 1948.

The British National Health Service is financed mainly (90 percent) by tax revenues, and 80 percent of the population has access to free medical care. There is, however, a nominal charge for each prescription (20p/40¢) as well as a modest charge for eyeglasses and dentures. There exists side by side with the NHS a private practice, but this fact is often ignored by the system's opponents. This private practice, however, represents a small portion of the GP's activities, and only one-half of the British GP's who joined the NHS (approximately 99 percent) maintain some private practice outside the NHS framework.

Patients are free to choose their own GP, but their main difficulty lies in changing physicians; that considerably limits freedom of choice. The request to change physicians can be made only if the patient changes his place ;of residence (or if the physician moves his practice) or if the patient has written permission from the physician he wishes to leave. The request is then submitted for the approval of the local medical council, and, although such requests are usually granted, the ever-present bureaucratic and administrative process delays the decision, and this often discourages people from making such requests. As in other European systems (Italy, the Netherlands, Denmark), the NHS covers the cost of a specialist but only when the GP recommended such a consultation.

Hospitalization appears to be the NHS's weakest point. The British may be generally satisfied with their GPs but not with their hospitals. The waiting period for nonemergency hospitalization can last up to several months in some areas and, consequently, patients resort more and more frequently to private consultations and private beds within the NHS' hospitals. But a 1976 law is progressively eliminating such private beds in all public hospitals, and the few private hospitals simply do not have enough space to handle the expected demand.

The density of physicians in Great Britain ranked seventh among the EC countries (only Ireland and Luxembourg are below the UK). This was due to the combined effects of three factors: (1) a limitation of the number of students admitted to medical school each year; (2) the emigration of several hundred physicians each year; and (3) a decrease in the number of foreign physicians immigrating to Great Britain (examinations were instituted in 1975 in order to guarantee a more even level of training). As is the case in Italy, there were also serious regional disparities in Great Britain where the government was attempting, through bonuses and other incentives, to encourage physicians to set up practice in areas with a physician shortage.

Different arrangements regarding the GP's training entered into force in 1980. These arrangements require a three-year "formation" period before they can treat insured patients. Two of these three years are to be spent at a hospital and the third as a GP's assistant or "trainee." A fixed annual salary is envisaged for these three years. This new obligation is also applicable to any European physician who wishes to migrate to Britain and enter the NHS. There is, of course, the possibility of not joining the NHS, and thus the immigrating physician need not spend the three years as a "trainee" but, instead, open a private practice. In any case, the new arrangements present an obstacle to free circulation. The British NHS physician, although paid by the NHS, is not considered a "public employee" and thus is not excluded from the free circulation decision.[7]

Instruments of Community Action

The previous section briefly described health care policies in the EC and highlighted their diversity. This section examines the instruments available to the EC for achieving the goals of Community action in terms of health care and for harmonizing the different aspects of health care policies. The Council of Ministers and the Commission constitute the essential decision-making institutions: Article 145 of the Rome Treaty gives the Council major decision-making responsibility,[8] and Article 155 gives to the Commission the authority to enforce Council decisions. But most of the real work in health care policies, including the free circulation decision, is performed by three advisory bodies: the Permanent Committee of Physicians of the EC, the Consultative Committee for Medical Education, and the Committee of Public Health Officials.

The Permanent Committee of Physicians of the EC

The Permanent Committee of Physicians of the EC was established in Amsterdam on October 23–24, 1959. It is a European group composed of recognized national medical delegations from each of the countries in the EC.[9] This committee is organized into several working subcommittees, and it dealt with several matters that eventually led to the 1975 free circulation directives. The major areas the committee dealt with were: a study of continuing medical education and medical practice in the EC; a study of the social security systems and particularly the health insurance systems; a study of the free circulation of physicians; and the constant representation of the medical profession's interest with the EC institutions.

In 1969, ten years after its creation, the Permanent Committee published several propositions which eventually formed the basis of the 1975 Directives. The committee's work did not end with the 1975 Directives, however; it is currently examining the very important questions of industrial medicine within the EC and the specific educational requirements for a European GP.

The Consultative Committee for Medical Education

The Consultative Committee for Medical Education was created in 1975 by a Council of Ministers decision.[10] The Consultative Committee is charged with maintaining the highest possible standards within the EC for all physicians (GPs and specialists). This committee forwards its opinions, recommendations, and suggestions (concerning proposed amendments to medical educational requirements) to the Commission and to the nine member states. This committee is composed, in equal strength, of representatives from the medical profession, the universities, and the national administrations.

The Committee of Public Health Officials

The Committee of Public Health Officials was also established by the Council's 1975 Directive,[11] and its major functions are as follows: (1) to anticipate and analyze the possible difficulties that the implementation of various Directives may face; (2) to gather and disseminate information on how general and specialized health care is delivered in the EC; and (3) to formulate proposals for submission to the Commission for the latter's use in amendments to the various Directives. This (consultative) committee is composed of high-level administrative officials in the nine countries who have direct responsibilities in the area of public health care.

Some Current Problems and Possible Solutions

The Language Barrier

The first obstacle that usually comes to mind when dealing with the idea of a European Community is that of language. Except for Ireland and the United Kingdom, and for France and parts of Belgium and Luxembourg, none of the nine EC countries have language in common with their neighbors. But the 1975 Council Directive states that "the member countries will see that the beneficiaries [of the free circulation decision] acquire, in their own interest and in the interest of their patients, sufficient language ability that may be necessary to practice in the receiving country."[12]

The text of the Directive is vague, however, and the words "sufficient language ability" are not seen as a formal legal obligation on the part of a migrating physician. In fact, it is not even accepted that a physician could be refused entry into a member country for not having a "sufficient" knowledge of the host country's language. Such a denial would probably be considered an illegal restriction of the right of establishment (guaranteed by Article 52 of the Rome Treaty) or, perhaps, discrimination based on citizenship (also prohibited by Article 20) or, as a last resort, a violation under the European Convention of Human Rights. Indeed, the assumed language barrier is a false problem. As Rolf Wägenbaur (a legal advisor to the EC Commission) writes, it is simply inconceivable that a physician—whose civil and criminal liabilities are tremendous—would treat patients without being able to understand their complaints and thus risk severe malpractice suits.[13] Although the language barrier is not a barrier in the formal legal sense, it should be obvious that the physician contemplating migration will take language into account.

Harmonization of Medical Education and the Mutual Recognition of Diplomas

The diversity of GP and specialist training across the EC and the resulting diversity in diplomas, certificates, titles, and so on illustrate several difficulties which must be overcome in the eventual harmonization of policies.

The medical curriculum and the required length of training in the different countries have created some problems. Certain specialties are recognized in all nine EC countries and, for these specialties, there is a fixed period (three to five years) which facilitates the overall mutual recognition of diplomas. For nonspecialists, four conditions have been listed concerning basic medical studies:[14] six years of study,[15] clinical training, service in a teaching hospital, and some responsibility in the organization and administration of hospital services. It is within the third cycle (the last two years) of the six years of study and within the period spent as an intern in the hospital that policies can be harmonized most easily on the European level.

It should be noted here, however, that not all the EC countries—and Italy is a good example—have a rigorous and/or limited selection process for admission to medical school. Italy's projected increase in number of physicians is seen to be over 100 percent from 1970 to 1985. Italy is quite likely to have some 350,000 physicians by 1985 and, of these, some 250,000 GPs. In addition, several EC countries (notably Denmark, Germany, the Netherlands, and the United Kingdom) have or plan to have some additional period after the receipt of the Medical Degree before the individual is allowed to practice. France is currently the only EC country to permit direct access to patients immediately after receipt of the M.D.

In reference to the mutual recognition of diplomas, it is stated (Article 2 of the June 16, 1975 Directive) that "each Member State recognizes diplomas, certificates, and other titles issued by, and held by citizens of, Member States." The recognized equivalents are specified in the Directive for both the GP level (Article 3) and the specialist (Article 5).[16]

The specific educational requirements for the GP will also affect the future of medicine in Europe. These requirements have been studied in depth by both the Permanent Committee of Physicians and by the European Union of GPs (UEMO). At issue is the question of the timing of a proposed additional "formation" period for the GP. The options are to have it as some sort of postgraduate training after the degree or require it before obtaining the degree. If one's goal is the coordination and harmonization of policies within the EC, the first option—the postgraduate option—seems to be the better choice (especially with the free circulation decision). To require this period *before* obtaining the degree would make medical studies more complex, would upset the previously agreed upon standards (the six years with a minimum of 5,500 hours), and would represent a real change for the medical profession (and changes are not always welcomed by the European medical profession).

Modes of Remuneration of Physicians in the EC

The different methods for physician remuneration and the wide variation in incomes existing in the EC present some difficult obstacles. We are not suggesting that incomes be standardized throughout the EC; nor are we suggesting that a uniform remuneration policy be adopted. The current variation is such, however, that some reform is needed. Space does not permit a full discussion of the income levels or the intricacies of how the European physician is paid; the following remarks serve only to illustrate the problems.

As Table 8.2 indicates, there exists a wide variation in physician incomes in the EC. The cost of living (and taxes) also vary, but the latter's variation is much less than the observed differences in Table 8.2. The lure of a (substantially) higher income may possibly become an important factor in the free circulation of physicians, and certain areas may have their medical shortages exacerbated.

The actual modes of payment also present some difficulties. Depending upon the physician's country and his type of position, remuneration can be based upon fee for service paid directly to the physician by the patient (as in France), capitation payments (a certain fixed amount per patient on the physician's list as in the United Kingdom), an annual salary, or a combination of any two or all three modes. The different health insurance funds also treat professional expenses differently, and such expenses are reimbursed at different rates. Capitation payments also vary, concerning both the maximum number of patients allowed on an individual physician's list and the amount of compensation paid per patient.

The Netherlands present a good illustration of sliding capitation payments. For the first 1,800 people on the list, a Dutch physician receives approxi-

Table 8.2   Approximate Annual Income of Physicians in the European Community
(dollars)

	GPs		Specialists	
	Gross	*Net*	*Gross*	*Net*
Netherlands	76–87,000	44–55,000	66–83,000	46–63,400
Germany	66,000	44,600	85,000	53,400
Denmark	48–72,000	48–58,000	—	—
France	—	27–28,600	62–64,000	42–44,000
Luxembourg	34,000	24–28,600	44,000	28–30,000
Belgium	—	18–28,000	56–66,200	—
Italy	—	20,000	—	—
Ireland	24,000	14–16,000	—	—
United Kingdom	19,400	12–13,000	—	—

Source: Mme. Deliege-Rott, *Medical Doctors in the Nine Countries of the Common Market* (Brussels: 1975), cited in *Concours Médical* (March 19, 1977), pp. 1921–1923.

mately $39 per patient; for patients 1,801-2,000, it is approximately $28 per patient; and for patients 2,001 and above, the physician receives approximately $24 per patient from the caisse. The caisse also makes a contribution to the physician's pension fund, but the capitation payments represent almost all the physician's income. For this gross amount, the physician then must meet his professional expenses (rent, equipment, travel, receptionist/medical assistant's salary, and so on).

Such capitation payments involve some benefits. By having a fixed amount and knowing the average size of the lists, the Government can facilitate the use of public monies and, by changing the fixed amounts, the caisse can adapt itself to economic and political realities present in the budgeting process. But fixed capitation payments may also influence the amount and type of medical care dispensed by the physician. Since the Dutch physician's income is based on the number of people on the list and *not* on fee for service, the physician has a financial interest in reducing his expenses (it costs the physician less, say, to, prescribe by telephone than in the office; it is less costly to have an office visit than to pay a house call). We are by no means suggesting that the quality of health care in the Netherlands is determined by such financial considerations, but it is a factor that cannot be ignored.[17]

Taxation policies also differ among the countries as well as within the same country (some tax the physician in private practice at a different rate than the salaried physician or one within a capitation system). Finally, there is quite a variation in policies concerning physician pensions, additional education, disability payments, and other "fringe" benefits normally associated with a sala-ried (or capitation) position. Policies in all these areas need to be more con-sistent throughout the EC, but since they are a result of specific historical, sociological, political, economic, and demographic factors, harmonization of these policies appears to be more distant than, for example, the standardi-zation of a European GP's education.

Physician Access to Insured Patients

In every country of the EC, the physician finds himself at the center of a more or less complex network linking the population and the insurance funds. We have noted above that the financial links (different in each system) between the physician and the various caisses, on one hand, and the diverse (and often incomparable) methods of remuneration, on the other hand, may eventually create a one-way migratory flow. In addition, the specific adminis-trative relationships between the caisses and the physician also affect the migrant physician's access to insured patients within the health care system.

Some examples of the different administrative relationships defining access will illustrate this problem. In France, the physician is entitled automatically to treat insured patients and deal directly with the caisse (if the physician opts to join the system). Access to insured patients in France is direct without any condition other than the right to practice medicine. The German system, on the other hand, introduces a fourth participant to the usual triangular relationship among patient, physician, and caisse: the Medical Association. The German physician—and the immigrant physician—also must be a "member in good standing" of the association before having access to insured patients, and just having the legal right to practice will not bestow the right of access. In ad-dition, the German requirement of the waiting period (mentioned above and scheduled to be eliminated in 1980) represented a truly protectionist measure with respect to potential migrant physicians and most certainly made a move to Germany less desirable than to France.

The harmonization of the different social security and health care systems would do much to alleviate the problems of access, and, fortunately, there are some signs that the systems are converging. First of all, the vast majority of the EC's population is in some way covered by the relevant social security legis-lation, and here it is a matter of coordinating existing policies already in place rather than legislating for the first time. Also, all nine EC countries are allo-cating an increasingly larger part of national income for health care costs, and the differences in health care expenditures are decreasing.

But there are also major areas of divergence across the EC. The contri-butions that each participant (the employee, the employer, the government) pays in the process vary widely. Some systems have equal contributions while others have employees (or employers) providing most of the funds. Still other systems have the entire system financed by public tax monies.[18] The complexities of the financial and adminstrative relationships between the physician and the social security organizations have a direct and immediate impact on access to insured patients, and such relationships need to be made more consistent throughout the EC.

There must be a uniform and standard access policy throughout the EC before the free circulation decision can have any real meaning. The migrating physician, of course, has, the option of not joining the host country's health insurance system (participation is not required in any country, including Great Britain and Italy). But what possible clientele could a migrating physician expect to have if he chose not to join or was denied access to the insurance system? In 1958, approximately 75 percent of the European population were within the insured system; in 1980, the figure is between 90–100 percent. Private practice may be a risky venture for the migrating physician, and access to insured patients is a necessity in any future European health care system. To allow a physician to establish a practice in the host country but then deny or delay his access to 95 percent of the population does very little for the integrative process.

Free Circulation of Physicians: Some Problems and Early Results

The Treaty of Rome established the principle of free circulation in two different places: (1) the right of establishment [Article 52], whereby the migrant can establish himself in the host country under the same conditions that apply to the host country's nationals; and (2) the right of actual practice [Article 60], whereby the migrant is entitled to practice his profession under the same conditions that apply to the host country's nationals.

Most of the EC countries have no laws restricting or regulating the implantation of physicians. None of the nine regulates the establishment of a physician engaged in *private* practice, although four countries (Great Britain, Denmark, Ireland and, since 1976, Italy within the framework of its National Health Service) have channeled the establishment of new physicians into areas with a shortage of physicians in order to achieve a more rational and equitable distribution. Such measures are not discriminatory toward the migrating physician, however, since they also apply to the host country's nationals. But since in Italy, for example, a physician has to be "designated" before being allowed to treat insured patients, the foreign migrating physician is at a disadvantage compared to his host country's colleagues. The migrating physician is not "in place" and thus may have to satisfy a waiting period before having access to the Italian NHS.

The effects of the free circulation decision became evident in 1978, and some analysis of the preliminary figures could be made. There has been no *marée blanche* whatsoever, even in countries such as France where there are no obstacles to migrant physicians and, moreover, relatively immediate access to insured patients is provided. Compared to the total physician population of the EC, the migrants represent only a minute fraction: from December 20,

1976, to late 1978, 449 or 0.1 percent of the 503,500 EC physicians took advantage of the free circulation decision. These 449 are, of course, the first, and any observable trends may not hold in the future. Yet is appears that the level of physician remuneration, as well as the level of physician density, have had very little influence in determining the choice of host country. This may change in the future, but physicians are not yet chasing the money or the patients.

The principal obstacle to free circulation appears to be language, and it should not come as a surprise that the choice of the host country is affected by language. Denmark and the Netherlands received very few migrant physicians (Danish and Dutch not being very popular), but over one-third of the sixty-two migrating Italian physicians went to France (French being closest to Italian).

Table 8.3 presents some figures on these migrating physicians, but only for France vis-à-vis the rest of the EC. It appears that physicians who completed their medical studies in a country other than their own have found it easier to migrate to (or remain in) the country from which they received the diploma, whose language, presumably, has already been mastered. In fact, of the eight British physicians who have established themselves in France, three possess a French diploma, and of the twenty-two Italians practicing in France, eight graduated from a French medical school.[19] Marriage between people of different nationalities also seems to be a relevant variable in the decision to migrate.

It is also possible that in the future, especially with the eventual admission of Spain, Portugal, and Greece into the EC, another variable will enter the physician's decision to migrate—climate. The EC might well have its own equivalent of the American "Sunbelt," with a one-way flow from the harsher climate in northern Europe to the more benign southern regions. Figures to date on free circulation do not support this, but its possible influence cannot be overlooked.

The free circulation decision only concerned those physicians who wish to

Table 8.3   Effect of Free Circulation of Physicians in France, 1978

From France to		To France from	
United Kingdom	13	Belgium	32
Belgium	11	Germany	24
Luxembourg	8	Italy	22
Ireland	2	Ireland	7
Denmark	1	Luxembourg	7
Netherlands	1	United Kingdom	7
Germany	n.a.	Denmark	3
Italy	n.a.	Netherlands	3

Source: Extracted from figures contained in the Supplement to the *Bulletin de l'Orde des Médecins* No. 1–78 (March 1978).

migrate formally and establish a practice in the host country. There is a different set of regulations, however, governing the activities of a physician who happens to be in another country on a temporary basis (vacation, research, education, and so on). A physician on such status who provides medical care during his stay receives "special permission" from the host country and, if it were medical aid given in an emergency situation, the "permission" can be as much as fifteen days retroactive (that is, the physician giving emergency aid will have legally received the right to practice prior to such aid even though such permission was not "in force" at that specific time).

A physician present in another country on a temporary basis usually has all the rights accorded to a "legally" established physician. In France, for example, such a physician has access to the health insurance system and can treat insured patients without any preliminary formalities. The caisse will regard his fees and prescriptions as if they were from a fully established physician, and the usual reimbursement policies would apply. It is possible, however that such a situation might be abused: there is no definition on what constitutes a "temporary" stay, and, therefore, a temporary stay could be the equivalent of a de facto established practice. It has been suggested that the EC attempt to standardize conditions and definitions for physicians on a "temporary" visit, and it appears that such standardization will be achieved shortly.[20]

A specific (and nonabused) example of visiting physicians can be found in border regions. Ever since the Brussels Convention of 1910, there has existed an agreement between France and Belgium allowing a physician in border areas to cross the frontier and treat patients on the other side if there is no host country physician in the area. Each country annually establishes a list of frontier localities qualifying for these border crossings. The Brussels Convention has worked quite well since 1910, and similar agreements should be extended to France's other EC neighbors as well as between the other EC countries.

Conclusions

Although there exists a basic framework for a unified health care system in Europe, we have attempted to show in this brief essay some of the real problems that make the actual harmonization of the different European health care systems difficult to achieve. In future years, the various decisions, directives, recommendations, and policies will undoubtedly be modified in response to changing medical practices and to the sociopolitical changes within the EC countries themselves. The creation of the EC—an act of creation which is still in progress—is not a revolutionary act. It is an evolutionary process consisting of the progressive adaptation of legislative and regulatory decisions to the real political environment. The EC will allow the countries of Europe to survive as economic units, and it will allow us to maintain our cultural and political identity with respect to the two superpowers.

Some specific problems were not mentioned in this essay, but they, too, will present future difficulties in a unified and integrated European health care system. These problems involve medical practice as well as medical and professional ethics. The countries of the EC have different legislation concerning areas such as organ transplants, the use (and disuse) of life-sustaining machines, definitions of "legal" and "clinical" death, abortion, "informed" consent of the patient, artificial insemination, medical experiments, and even the question of professional confidentiality between the physician and patient. These questions are as important as the ones we have discussed, and their resolution is also necessary before a real European health care system can exist.

But the European integrative process, while at times slow, is irreversible. The questions raised in this essay will eventually be answered, and the obstacles will eventually be overcome. The harmonization of health care policies will inevitably take place and then, at least for the medical profession, one will be able to talk about a *European* system rather than the nine different systems, and the authors will be described as *European* rather than as French physicians.

Notes

1. Article 2 of the Law of March 2 and 17, 1791, stated that "each person is free to engage in trade or practice any profession or art he chooses." Cited by Bernard Bonnici, *Condition de Circulation et d'Etablissement des Médecines dans la CEE* (Paris: Editions Médicales et Universitaires, 1978), p. 105.

2. EC Directives 75–362 and 75–363 (June 16, 1975).

3. Unanimously adopted at the Permanent Committee of Physicians of the EC Meeting, Nuremberg (November 24–25, 1967).

4. Unanimously adopted at the Permanent Committee of Physicians of the EC Meeting, Berlin (April 21–22, 1967).

5. Denmark has a five-year "formation" period after successfully passing the medical examinations before Danish physicians can establish a practice (the time can be spent in a hospital and/or with a GP). For large numbers of recent Danish medical school graduates, however, this period constitutes a serious bottleneck because there are insufficient numbers of positions available in Denmark. Time spent in a foreign hospital can, however, be applied toward this five-year period, and many young Danish graduates are looking beyond their own borders for a position. Sweden has been the traditional choice, but with Denmark's entry into the EC and the free circulation decision, there are now additional opportunities. This process does add to the integrative process, but since many EC countries are also short of such "formation" positions, the problem seems difficult to solve even at the European level.

6. Editor's note: Drs. Vaissière and Mascaro are making an analogy to a "*marée noire*" (a "black tide" literally but meaning an "oil spill"). The "*marée noire*" which inundated Brittany on March 16, 1978, from the Amoco Cadiz' 68 million gallons of crude oil gave visions of a "white tide" ("*marée blanche*") of physicians inundating France.

7. G.P. Cabanel, *Médecine Libérale ou Nationalisée?* (Paris: Editeur Dunod, 1977), p. 121.

8. It was the Council that passed the two Directives in 1975 (see note 2 above) providing for the free circulation of physicians in the EC.

9. In 1959, the Permanent Committee was composed of the six orginal EC members' delegations, and this was expanded to nine in 1973. The national groups or delegations are as follows:

Germany—Bundesärztekammer; Belgium—at first the Fédération Médicale Belge and then the Fédération Belge des Chambres Syndicales des Médecins; France—the Confédération des Syndicats Médicaux Français until 1961, and, since that date, joined by the Ordre National des Médecins; Italy—the Federazione Nazionale degli Ordini dei Medici d'Italia; Luxembourg—at first by the Syndicat des Médecins du Grand Duché de Luxembourg and then by the Association des Médecins et des Médecins-Dentistes du Grand Duché de Luxembourg; Netherlands—Koninlijke Nederlandsche Maatschappij tot Bevordering der Geneeskunst; Denmark—Den Almindelige Danske Laegeforening; Ireland—the Irish Medical Association; and Great Britain—the British Medical Association.

10. EC, Directive 167 of June 16, 1975, *Official Journal of the European Communities* (June 30, 1975): 17.

11. Ibid., p. 19.

12. Ibid., Article 20, paragraph 3, Directive 75–362 (June 16, 1975).

13. Rolf Wägenbaur, cited in *Concours Médical* (March 5, 1977): 1533.

14. EC, Directive 75–362 (June 16, 1975), *Journal Officiel des Communautés Européennes* (Official Journal of the European Communities) (June 30, 1975).

15. Editor's note: The six years of medical studies in Europe begin immediately at the university; one does not first earn the B.A. or B.S. as in the US.

16. The recognized equivalents are as follows: Belgium—the M.D. degree (in medicine, surgery, and obstetrics); Denmark—the M.D. as well as the certificate of the training stage obtained from the Health Service; France—the M.D. from a medical school or from schools combining medicine and pharmacy; Germany—the state certificate of M.D. (signalling the end of the preparatory period); Ireland and the United Kingdom—a certificate sanctioning the individual's knowledge and clinical experience (awarded upon passing a series of exams); Italy—the M.D. issued following the state examination by the Education Ministry) and a certificate issued by the Health Ministry; and the Netherlands—a university M.D. The equivalents for specialists are also listed, and they all entail, in one form or another, a certificate issued by the relevant authorities attesting to the individual's knowledge and experience in the specific field.

17. Of course, capitation payments can lead one to just the opposite conclusion. Since the Dutch physician is not paid on fee for service but, rather, his income is the same whether he treats or doesn't treat, the patient can be assured that any treatment prescribed is for sound medical reasons and *not* for possible additional fees.

18. In Great Britain and the Netherlands, no direct financial participation of the insured is required. In Belgium, the insured patient pays less than 25 percent of the cost of the GP, and consultation with a specialist is without additional charge. In Italy (until NHS is fully organized), the patient contributes only in the "indirect" medical insurance schemes. In France, the insured patient pays for some of the costs (*ticket modérateur*), but the amount is reduced in case of hospitalization and entirely eliminated for "costly" or prolonged illness. Some specific groups in France, the miners for example, have a totally free medical and prescription drug coverage.

19. B. de Casson and D. Levy, "Médecine Européenne," *Concours Médical* (September 16, 1978); 5285.

20. Jean Mignon, "Actualité Professionnelle: La Libre Circulation en France des Médecins de l'Europe des Neuf," *Concours Médical* (April 2, 1977): 2245.

ROBERT J. LIEBER *

9

Energy, Political Economy, and the Western European Left: Problems of Constraint

Energy has become a subject of pressing concern within the European Community since the October 1973 Mideast War provided a catalyst for the international energy crisis. Unlike much of the Community's previous experience with energy matters, the crisis put Europe to the kind of test that might have been expected to engender substantial progress toward greater unity. Earlier shocks, particularly the Second World War and the Cold War, had broken old ways of looking at the world and made European governing elites, as well as public opinion, far more willing to consider major innovations. Instead, however, the energy crisis led to serious failures of response within the European Community. Further, its impact has affected the member states in ways that continue to burden their internal politics, economics, and industrial structures, as well as their ability to cooperate among themselves.

*Author's Note: This essay builds upon, in very substantially revised and expanded form, a paper initially prepared for the 1977 Annual Meeting of the American Political Science Association Joint Country Groups Panel. For comments on earlier drafts of this essay, I am pleased to thank Fabio Basagni, Shai Feldman, Pierre Hassner, Nancy Lieber, Edward Morse, and Pierre Uri. Research support is also acknowledged, with appreciation, from a University of California research grant and from a Rockefeller Foundation International Relations Fellowship. In addition, I have benefited from the use of facilities at the Atlantic Institute for International Affairs in Paris.

It is first useful to review the main elements of the energy crisis as these impinged on the EC.[1] Shortly after the October 6, 1973, Arab attack on Israeli forces, Arab oil producers in OAPEC (Organization of Arab Petroleum Exporting Countries) began a boycott on delivery of oil aimed at forcing the U.S., Western Europe, and Japan to bring pressure to bear upon Israel. In this effort, OAPEC placed the nine member states of the EC in three different categories: states to be totally embargoed because of their sympathy for Israel (the Netherlands); "friendly" states to receive normal supplies (France and Britain); and those to be squeezed by proportional cuts of 5 percent per month (the remaining members of the EC).

In response to this treatment, the Community failed to coalesce; while paying lip service to common policy, most governments of the Nine reacted in ways that reemphasized national priorities or else moved beyond the EC level toward multilateral cooperation with the Americans, Japanese, and other OECD countries. In the former case, France in particular, but also Britain and Italy, sought to placate the Arabs by adopting more or less pro-Arab positions on the Middle East conflict. They then sought to ensure the security of their imported oil supplies by negotiating bilateral deals with individual oil-producing states, often via the sale of massive amounts of industrial goods, weapons, or development projects. Other EC member states sought, unsuccessfully, to rally the Nine to common energy policies or to cooperate at the OECD level with hopes of avoiding destructive competitive bidding for oil and of coping with the effects of what would become both a resource and an economic crisis.

Treatment of the Netherlands was a particular symptom of EC disarray. Under terms of the Rome Treaty providing for circulation of commodities freely within the EC, oil imported into any member state of the Nine should also have been available to other member countries. Thus, a boycott on delivery of oil to Dutch ports would not necessarily have precluded the Netherlands from receiving oil imports. However, both France and Britain rejected an October 1973 Dutch request that the Nine prepare to share oil supplies if this were to become necessary. Most members of the EC were heavily dependent upon oil imports, and, although European public opinion would have supported solidarity with the Dutch, many European governments feared to antagonize Arab oil suppliers. As Table 9.1 indicates, oil had become a matter of national security among states who depended upon petroleum imports for anywhere from 44 percent (Britain) to 70 percent (Italy) of their total energy needs. The atmosphere engendered was thus very much one of *sauve qui peut* (everyone for himself).

In this environment, the Dutch were not without certain means of protecting themselves. In addition to strong support from the Americans, Holland also benefited from the fact that it produced large amounts of natural gas, much of which was exported to its European neighbors. In mid-November the Dutch government warned its EC partners that if the supply crisis worsened, these exports could be jeopardized (not least to France, which received 40 per-

Table 9.1 Energy Sources, 1975
(percentages in terms of metric tons of coal equivalent)

	Domestic					Imported				
	Total Domestic	Coal	Natural Gas	Crude Oil	Hydro and Nuclear	Total Imported	Coal	Arab Oil	Non-Arab Oil	Other
U.S.	80.7	18.8	27.0	28.1	6.8	19.3	0	5.3	12.7	1.3
Japan	12.0	3.7	0.2	0.6	7.5	88.0	11.9	37.6	36.6	1.8
European Community	44.6	22.3	15.5	1.4	5.4	55.4	0.4	35.1	18.6	1.3
U.K.	59.9	39.9	15.3	0.5	4.2	40.1	-4.2	24.3	19.6	0.4
France	24.9	9.4	3.8	1.1	10.6	75.1	6.3	47.7	15.1	6.0
West Germany	49.1	37.2	6.0	2.4	3.5	50.9	-7.1	24.2	24.6	9.2
Italy	18.6	0.5	9.4	.8	7.9	81.4	6.1	54.5	15.5	5.3

Source: International Economic Report of the President, Transmitted to the U.S. Congress, January 1977, p. 173.

cent of its natural gas from Dutch fields). This had its effect, and by the end of November, behind-the-scenes agreements had been reached among the Nine to ensure that Holland would not in fact suffer any serious oil shortage. The situation was thus resolved, but only after the Community's lack of cooperation had been underscored.

Concern over security of oil supply characterized the first phase of the energy crisis. The second phase began as these fears gave way to worries over oil prices. By the beginning of 1974, it had become apparent that there would be no grave shortage of petroleum, but the price of this commodity was in the process of increasing some 400 percent over its pre-October levels. Here, too, the Community tended to be bypassed, this time at a multilateral rather than bilateral level, as states sought means of coping with balance-of-payments problems and petrodollar recycling. Mechanisms such as those of the OECD, IMF, IEA (International Energy Association), and other multilateral forums—all of which transcended the EC's regional boundaries—seemed more effective. In particular, cooperation with the United States (as well as recognition of a more explicit American leadership position) became a vital necessity. Only the U.S. possessed the size, continental scope, energy and monetary resources, lesser degree of dependence on the international economy, and even military strength, that could provide the basis for such a position. The Europeans, who had tended to distance themselves from American policies and positions but who were also extremely vulnerable because of their enormous dependence on international trade and imported oil, found themselves moving closer to the United States. This relationship was most explicit at the February 1974 Washington Energy Conference, at which only France persisted in refusing to join the American-conceived organization of what would become the IEA.

Prior to 1973, the EC lacked a coherent energy policy. In essence there had been scarcely more than the stating of (contradictory) objectives for both secure and inexpensive supplies of energy. During the dramatic events of 1973–74, the search for a common energy policy had been characterized by disarray and overwhelmed by the pursuit of other national and international means and priorities. Yet, more than half a decade after the onset of the crisis, the EC's own energy policy continued to have only limited scope. From 1973 to 1978, the Community had reduced its energy import dependence from 63 percent to 56 percent, but much of this reduction had been due more to the steep increase in oil prices coupled with a serious recession and lagging rates of economic growth rather than to planned conservation or concerted policies. Indeed, the Community's Commissioner responsible for energy, Guido Brunner, conceded that there could be no question of a centralized Community energy policy run from Brussels.[2]

While there has been general consensus on the need for adequate, secure and diversified supplies of energy, lesser import dependence, the development of new energy sources, and a foreign policy to promote these objectives, there is only limited agreement on the means to achieve them. The Commission tends to support maintenance of European coal production, a strongly increased nuclear program, and cooperation with the IEA, but its commitment to energy conservation has been largely one of lip service—if for no other reason than derisory amounts of funding: 16 million European Units of Account [about $22 million] in a 1979 energy budget of 262 million EUA and an overall EC budget of 14, 869 million EUA.[3] This relative neglect of conservation is all the more damaging in that a more "rational" use of energy could reduce consumption by at least 15 percent—an amount equivalent to North Sea energy production.[4]

In fact, the Commission has been candid in noting the obstacles to progress on a common energy policy. These include the very different energy situations of member states (some, the UK, for example, being net energy exporters, while others such as France and Italy remain desperately dependent upon energy imports); a general reluctance to increase the Community's energy budget, and differing views about the limits of common Community action as compared with the retention ("sometimes illusory") of national sovereignty.[5] In short, "nothing is coordinated nor communitaire."[6]

The EC remains heavily dependent on extremely costly petroleum, and its degree of dependence is lessening only slowly. In retrospect, Western Europe's shift in the late 1950s and the 1960s from a domestically supplied, coal-based energy economy to an imported, oil-based energy supply marks a transition that has not been readily reversible. Indeed, even the ambitious nuclear programs of member countries such as France and Germany have the effect of continuing some degree of foreign dependence, though in this case upon the U.S., for technology, licenses, and (particularly until French reprocessing and enrichment facilities are completed or expanded) enriched uranium. Further, as shown in Table 9.2, although EC Commission energy targets for 1985 indicate that domestic nuclear power can supply 9.5 percent of total energy needs, the Community will remain dependent on oil for 50 percent of its energy consumption, and imports will be necessary to meet between 48 and 53 percent of EC energy consumption, in comparison with a 1977 import dependence of 56 percent.

The consequences of the EC's inability to create a significant energy policy or achieve a major reduction in dependence on imported energy (especially oil) are profound, particularly as they affect the internal politics and economics of the Nine. These effects include balance-of-payments problems, inflation, economic stagnation, and increased unemployment. In substantial measure, these problems stem from the impact of increased energy prices and from the deflationary measures taken as one means of seeking balance-of-payments equilibrium. To be sure, energy alone was not the sole cause of the crisis; increased industrial development in the Third World, serious overcapacity in major in-

Table 9.2   European Community Energy Consumption:
Estimates and Targets

	1977		1985 targets	
	*Mtoe**	%	*Mtoe*	%
Solid fuel	201	21	240	18.5
Oil	529	55	640	50
Natural gas	162	17	245	19
Nuclear energy	26	3	120	9.5
Hydraulic, gothermal, etc.	40	4	35	3
Total gross consumption	958	100	1280	100
Import dependence		56		48 – 53

Sources: Commission of the European Communities, "The Community's Energy Policy," (1)
SEC (78) 4054, *Information Memo P-110*, October 1978; Guido Brunner, "Europe's
Energy Policy and the Task Ahead," *Inter-Economics* 12, no. 11–12 (1977): 308; and
Europe (Brussels, Agence intérnationale d'information pour la presse, no. 2421, April 5,
1978).

*Mtoe = million tons oil equivalent.

dustrial sectors, lagging international demand, and perhaps more basic structural problems all contributed to significant international and domestic
economic difficulties. But energy remained both the catalyst and perhaps the
most important single factor among an extremely complex series of causes.

All these elements not only made cooperation more difficult within the EC
but also created enhanced pressures toward increasingly strident competition
and potentially toward more protectionism. Thus, for example, President Giscard d'Estaing could offer televised exhortations to the French people that
France must "win" the international competition and that a 1 billion-franc
($225 million) monthly balance-of-payments surplus (in October 1978) was
worth 130,000 jobs to France.[7] The specter of exported unemployment was
implicit in this conception, since one country's payments surplus must ultimately be reflected in others' deficits. In addition, however, the energy-related
economic effects also have a significant bearing on the possibilities for
domestic change, political stability, and the choices and constraints facing
parties of the European Left. It is this latter set of concerns which provides the
primary focus for the remainder of this essay.

Implications for the European Left

The discussion is particularly applicable to the experiences of past, present,
or future left-of-center governments or political parties in Western and
southern Europe, and the most interesting cases are those where a European

state is both heavily energy dependent and has powerful left-wing political parties committed to programs of significant domestic change. This situation occurs when two conditions are met. First, when high dependence on imported energy makes a country particularly dependent on multilateral international organizations (IMF, GATT, OECD, IEA), especially in helping to manage balance-of-payments deficits and monetary problems. The nature of an asymmetrical interdependence (despite interdependence, some are much more dependent than others, giving rise to greater power for those who are less dependent)[8] tends to give countries such as the U.S. (and to a lesser extent Japan and Germany) a particularly influential role. Second, the priorities of an electorally successful left-wing party or coalition may be such as to commit it to policies of increased social spending, full employment, and nationalization. Since a country such as France already bears an enormously increased balance-of-payments burden to pay the costs of imported oil, there may be little room for enactment of socialist domestic programs without exacerbating balance-of-payments problems and inflation.[9] These consequences are likely to bring about a tension between a government's international involvements and its priorities.

To be sure, not every European country fits neatly into this general pattern. In Italy, parties of the Left, including the Socialists (PSI) as well as the large and powerful Communist party (PCI), have tended not to put dominant emphasis on policies aimed at the expansion of public spending or of demand. These, they fear, may create inflation and balance-of-payments deficits and yet—due to Italy's problems of regional and industrial structure, as well as bureaucratic inefficiency—may not produce the intended effects. Instead they are inclined to place more weight upon sectoral and microeconomic policies aimed at overcoming structural rigidities. For example, they support changes in management, investment, personnel, and marketing; efforts to make firms more dynamic; and measures for retraining and mobility of labor. In the public sector, they do advocate some expansion and rationalization, for example, in health care, where expanded and improved services are needed. In theory, all these policies are meant to facilitate growth while holding down inflation. Yet such policies open up divergences between left-wing parties and trade unions (or even between trade union leaders and workers), who can become impatient with austerity (whose price *their* members are paying) and increasingly skeptical about the achievement of beneficial economic results.

Further, full employment can occur without necessarily causing inflation and balance-of-payments problems. Until the early 1970s, many of the advanced industrial economies had enjoyed two decades of rarely interrupted full employment, strong economic growth, and low inflation. The conventional wisdom of the mid-to-late 1970s that claims to recognize a clear tradeoff between full employment and inflation is by no means always confirmed by experience. Not only are there the contrary examples in the 1960s, but many countries have (following the 1973–74 energy crisis) suffered from both relatively high unemployment and high inflation, thereby experiencing the worst of both worlds. Indeed, full employment can occur without the supposedly baneful consequences recently attributed to it.

Domestic Constraints on Governments

Since the Second World War, most of the governments of Western Europe have been held responsible for successful operation of both the managed economy and the welfare state. Conservative governments have generally seen their responsibility as one of consolidation or efficient operation, while social democratic or socialist governments have often sought to innovate or expand these areas of governmental activity. Popular expectations of governmental responsibility have grown accordingly, and voter opinion often tends to hold governments electorally to account for their performance, although in the post 1973–74 crisis environment electorates have tolerated weaker economic performance (France, Italy, Britain) than would previously have been supportable.

In recent years, the domestic demands on governments have sometimes threatened to run ahead of ability to respond. Thus in coping not only with energy but also with unemployment, inflation, social services, trade and payments problems, pollution, depressed regions, agriculture, education, investment, and even defense, governments have been increasingly constrained in their freedom of movement. These constraints stem from limited resources, competing or conflicting political demands, and the fact that governments do not fully control the factors determining some of the most important problems. Many of these significant factors (particularly the economic ones) lie out of reach, beyond a nation's borders; others are internal and involve fiscal limitations.

The impact of rising energy prices has sharply tightened all these constraints. Except for those states with substantial oil or natural gas reserves (the UK, Norway, the Netherlands), many of the others have tended to find themselves in some degree of financial difficulty.[10] Much of Western Europe thus faces a shaky balance-of-payments situation, inflation, lagging economic growth, and persistent unemployment. Partial exceptions are Germany and the Netherlands, both of which are favored by robust industrial economies and less acute dependence on imported energy. The problems of coping with supply and price consequences of the energy crisis are difficult enough for conservative and centrist regimes, or even a status quo–oriented social democratic government. But for a leftist government wishing to enact ambitious and costly programs of domestic change these constraints would likely be particularly troublesome. Thus, the 40 billion franc "foreign tax" on oil consumption which Giscard lamented[11] would plague a Socialist-Communist French government as much or more than it does a Conservative-Gaullist one.

How, then, may a leftist government cope with the supply and price aspects of the energy problem? Will it follow existing patterns or find it necessary to move in the direction of physical controls in order to meet its other priorities? These questions are variants on a larger and particularly important problem of political economy: can a socialist but democratic government achieve its aims within the existing domestic and international paradigms? If such governments are to avoid the successive perils of abandoning their programmatic aspirations and opting instead for essentially status quo policies; adopting a repressive Leninist socialism-in-one-country formula; economic chaos; or political collapse, they may need to walk several tightropes. In all these instances, the question of the international setting looms large.

International Constraints on Governments: The Left and the International Economy

As a result of interdependence, governments control within their national borders only some of the levers that shape key domestic outcomes of economic growth, inflation, unemployment, trade, investment, energy supply and price, and military security. Thus, a leftist government that seeks to carry out significant changes in domestic policy is likely to face troublesome restraints. In addition, even the mere prospect of a possible leftist election victory can precipitate capital outflows by individuals and businesses. Capital inflows from outsiders and emigrant workers may also lessen.

Specific reformist or leftist programs in many cases are likely to involve reflation in order to combat unemployment. This tends to be a high priority item since it particularly affects the economic well-being of working-class voters. However, in the absence of an incomes policy or other wage and price restraint, some forms of reflation may have the effect of causing upward pressure on wages. This in turn contributes to inflation and ultimately to decreased competitiveness of exported goods. In addition, increased purchasing power often causes increased imports. Ultimately, the balance of trade and payments is adversely affected. Spending on social services is another common programmatic commitment of left-of-center parties; however, this can increase budgetary deficits and contribute to inflation. Finally, nationalization proposals also may provide a claim on governmental resources (although means may be found to lessen or avoid such an effect).

To be sure, there are important qualifications here. Left governments often follow more conservative programs in office than they advocate while in opposition, and means may be found to reduce the costs of certain proposals. Further, left-wing governments may be more willing and able to consider assorted incentives, disincentives, and controls in order to achieve specific economic objectives while avoiding more harmful inflation and balance of payments consequences. (This is the objective of some French Socialist economists.) Finally, the successful attainment of full employment would bring about increased tax revenues and lower government expenditures for certain welfare programs, such as unemployment compensation. Both of these consequences are counter-inflationary and could be characteristic of a more optimal economic equilibrium than that experienced by the European and American economies with their "stagflation" in the early and mid-1970s.

Nonetheless, the overall effect of the domestic actions of leftist governments may yet be to heighten the serious balance-of-payments problems already caused by the high cost of imported energy. This makes them particularly vulnerable to international constraints, such as the austerity policies which the IMF effectively demanded of successive Labour governments in Britain[12] and of the Soares Socialists in Portugal. The policies of international bodies such as the IMF tend to reflect a conservative policy consensus in which tradeoffs between employment and social services on the one hand, and inflation and balance-of-payments deficits on the other, are assumed to be automatic. The conservative and deflationary thrust of IMF policies also inheres in the fact that no pressures comparable to those on deficit states are brought to bear on surplus states—which otherwise might be considered to have a reflationary obligation. In 1978, for example, OECD statistics indicated that Japan and Germany alone ran a combined balance-of-trade surplus of approximately \$50 billion (and a balance on current account of \$26 billion). Inherently, their surpluses were other countries' deficits.

The consensual policy choices, in effect, foster unemployment and limit social spending as what are considered to be lesser evils. There is no question that the choices favored by the IMF and other lending authorities reflect priorities which contravene many socialist or left-of-center ideals and preferences. IMF policies also have a way of making themselves felt. Thus, in the candid words of the IMF President, Jacques de Larosière, "we can go very hard" against countries that do not play the monetary game by the accepted rules.[13]

Both OPEC (Organization of Petroleum Exporting Countries) and OAPEC have also found that the Europeans' immense reliance on imported oil, amounting to 47.7 percent of the Nine's primary energy consumption in 1978,[14] makes them subject to major international bargaining constraints. Thus, the Nine have tended to put some distance between themselves and the United States on policy toward the Middle East and Israel, not because domestic opinion has become pro-Arab (indeed, it appears to be moderately sympathetic to Israel, even in France), but because of governmental concerns about energy supply and price, sales of goods and services to the Arab oil producers, and a desire to attract investments as a means of petrodollar recycling.[15] Leftist governments do or would find themselves face-to-face with the same constraints affecting conservative and centrist regimes; thus there is unlikely to be *significant* change in Middle East policy. Finally, some European policy makers take the view that the U.S. will protect Israel's survival, and they thus can afford the luxury, even irresponsibility, of tailoring their Middle East policies to fit their energy concerns.

Although Left-wing governments could experience improved relations with LDCs on energy and broader north-south issues, any change is likely to be limited for the reason that the domestic and international constraints on European governments sharply curtail their room to maneuver. The Euro-Arab dialogue has produced little in the way of tangible results, and there is not likely to be major change. The EC's own energy policy is also moribund. On the other hand, the EC has successfully negotiated on some north-south trade issues (the STABEX scheme with the fifty-two ACP [African, Caribbean and Pacific] states under the Lomé Convention and the even broader [Generalized System of Tariff Preferences] GSP arrangements). Commitment to these policies does not seem to differ markedly among the major governing parties and opposition groups of Western Europe.

Even the area of nuclear reactor exports is unlikely to experience major policy shifts. A Socialist-dominated government of France, no less than a Gaullist-conservative one, would have had compelling reasons to maintain nuclear export sales, despite the risks of proliferation. The presumed benefits of expertise in nuclear energy technology, export competitiveness, and the substantial balance-of-payments effects would probably have been too compelling to abandon.

In the realm of domestic nuclear power, any French government would have strong incentives to continue policies for expanded use of nuclear-generated electricity, including the breeder reactor program. Despite demands from ecologists and from some within the Left, and problems of mounting costs and technological uncertainty, the enormous balance-of-payments dependency resulting from imported oil and gas would create pressures for a leftist government to continue this nuclear program. Further, the considerable bureaucratic momentum and the limited means of policy access for alternative ideas (including more substantial conservation and alternative energy source programs) impose major obstacles to policy change. Potentially, however, left-wing governments in Europe could have significant motivation for major conservation efforts due to their favorable balance-of-payments impact and possible job-creating effects.

Overall, in energy, as in related economic and political areas, the governments of Western Europe, whether rightist or leftist, are increasingly preoccupied with the difficult tasks of meeting their national responsibilities. Because of international constraints and the fact that key economic problems extend far beyond their national boundaries, they have not yet resorted to sweeping protectionist devices of the sort prevalent in the 1930s, although nontariff barriers, subsidies, quotas, "voluntary" agreements, and other less overtly protectionist devices have multiplied. Nevertheless, international involvements are evaluated increasingly in terms of how these serve to facilitate the achievement of national goals. The orientation of regional or multinational bodies is thus instrumental rather than affective. In addition, at least some increased propensity toward mercantilism or a degree of greater protectionism seems conceivable[16]—perhaps slightly more so for governments and parties of the Left as they seek to make at least tentative steps toward implementing policy goals within the myriad international constraints binding them.

Energy, the European Community, and the United States

The increasing politicization of international economic relations has helped the Left by facilitating and further legitimizing a more direct governmental role in economic matters, including the affairs of transnational actors such as multinational corporations (MNCs) and oil companies.[17] However, the lessons of the 1973–74 energy crisis also convey a less comforting message for the Left: the same politicization tends to push the consideration of issues from a regional level to an international one.[18] Because of a de facto national veto power on questions of major national importance, and because the Left has the possibility of majority or plurality status among many countries of the Nine, individual left-of-center governments within the EC can look forward to exercising major influence at the European Community level in shaping policies which affect their countries and their region. This remains true despite emotional opposition to the Community on the left of the British Labour party and a more ideological antagonism on the left of the *Parti Socialiste*, which tends to see the Community as a protector of capitalist interest. Ironically, while French Communists are the most intransigent opponents of the EC, on narrowly nationalist grounds, the Spanish and particularly Italian Communist parties are among the very strongest proponents of expanded European unity.

The management of interdependence, not least in coping with the financial consequences of the energy problem, tends to shift important issues to an international framework involving the IMF, OECD, IEA, GATT, and other bodies. Here, individual parties and governments of the European Left find themselves with significantly less influence over policies, not least because the number of important actors is substantially wider and the orientations of countries such as the U.S., Japan, and Germany (even under Social Democratic auspices) are less favorable. In addition, the role of the United States is particularly enhanced by its somewhat lesser dependence on international trade and monetary transactions, its considerable domestic supplies of energy, its continental size, resources, and autonomy, and its stature as the only military superpower among the industrial democracies. Hence it benefits from asymmetrical interdependence and, as in the establishment of the IEA, has at times been able to exert successful linkage among issue areas. Thus, to the extent that treatment of energy and other related issues moves from a regional to an international organization level, governments of the European Left are also likely to experience increasing constraints.

In addition to increased politicization and a tendency for the management of the lessons of the 1973–74 energy crisis also suggest a number of other points.

In the several years prior to the crisis, particularly after August 1971, the nature of trade and monetary issues prominent in U.S.-European relations had obscured somewhat the asymmetrical nature of these relations. However, the crisis and its aftermath tended to illuminate the previously latent power implications. The first phase of the crisis, with compelling concerns about energy supplies, made energy a virtual security issue in itself. This allowed the U.S. to activate the linkages between economic issues and American political leadership. Indeed, at the Washington Energy Conference in February 1974, Secretary Kissinger explicitly made clear to the European governments that they could not go their own route on political and energy issues (that is, in the direction of special Euro-Arab relations, which the U.S. regarded as unwelcome) while continuing to rely on the U.S. for military security.[19] This position proved particularly effective in stimulating German support of U.S. initiatives and in getting eight of the nine EC countries effectively to reverse policy positions agreed upon at their Copenhagen summit meeting of December 1973 (where they had given an unprecedented opportunity of access to several Arab foreign ministers, an opportunity long sought by the U.S. but never attained) and at an EC Foreign Ministers session in January 1974.

In the face of increased national and transnational pressures, particularly (but not exclusively) those surrounding energy, governments tend to employ whatever means are available to them. As a result, during the supply phase of the crisis, national efforts (particularly attempts at bilateral deals with oil-producing states) tended to find favor. Subsequently, during the price concern phase of the energy crisis, efforts shifted to an international level. In both instances, however, the European Community and its regional institutions tended to be bypassed or at least were treated as of lesser importance.[20]

Policy Options for the Left

How might policies of Western European states differ with changes in government? At a basic level, domestic policies may involve either continuation of the status quo in some form or efforts at substantial reform or even radical change. Internationally, the choices may be represented as openness to continued participation in a liberal economic order or a move toward protectionism and a more closed orientation. Crudely, but perhaps usefully for heuristic purposes, these choices can be represented in a two-by-two diagram, as in Figure 9.1.

In domestic terms, the salience of a leftist party's commitment to radical change will vary from country to country. In France, the distribution of wealth and income is one of the most inegalitarian in Europe and is indeed worse than that of Spain.[21] In response, a hypothetical Socialist government in the 1980s, under a Mitterrand or a Rocard, would be likely to pursue both moderate and occasionally radical reform. One of the most important questions, therefore, is to what extent domestic policies may bring a leftist government into conflict

Figure 9.1   Schematic Diagram of Policy Choices for a Leftist Government: Some Past, Present, and Future Choices

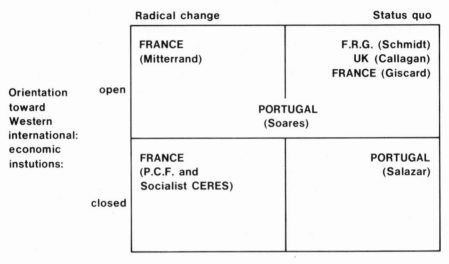

Domestic Policy:

	Radical change	Status quo
	FRANCE (Mitterrand)	F.R.G. (Schmidt) UK (Callagan) FRANCE (Giscard)
Orientation toward Western international: economic instutions: open	PORTUGAL (Soares)	
	FRANCE (P.C.F. and Socialist CERES)	PORTUGAL (Salazar)
closed		

with international economic organizations. For example, will a government choose to abandon its domestic aims in the face of international constraints? Or, will it seek to preserve its political equilibrium by pursuing a policy of greater controls or protectionism, or even one involving substantial closure? Or, is some compromise possible which would allow, for example, a French leftist government to follow a democratic socialist path at home while remaining an active participant in a relatively liberal and open Western economic order? In short, under what circumstances are policy options favoring either open or closed economic systems chosen? Clearly, the salience of a government's commitment to domestic change is one such determinant, just as the feasibility of open and closed international alternatives will also affect domestic choices.

Policy Options: The British Case

In the British case, international considerations and priorities have largely overridden domestic ones. In 1964–67, even without the pressures engendered by enormous energy import costs, the Wilson government tended to give priority to international factors, and, although the government did increase social spending, it made few other changes. In the 1974–78 period, particularly from 1975 onward, the more radical wing of the Labour and Trade Union Congress (TUC) leadership (Tony Benn, Michael Foot, Jack Jones, Hugh Scanlon) was either isolated or co-opted. Despite Labour's explicit October 1974 election manifesto commitment ("We are a democratic socialist party and our objective is to bring about *a fundamental and irreversible shift in the balance of wealth and power* in favor of working people and their families"),[22] few real domestic steps were taken, Instead, at a time when enormous energy costs (the supply of North Sea oil not yet having made a major impact) and inflation caused huge balance-of-payment deficits and pressure on the pound, the Labour government gave priority to international considerations. In part this reflected the desperate need to obtain the means to pay for the food and natural resources the country needed to survive.

It also reflected priorities which had long existed within the Labour leadership. Thus, such measures as deflation, acceptance of record postwar unemployment, and a cut in real living standards during the post-1974 period were carried out or tolerated as international priorities proved dominant. Indeed, in the year from mid-1976 to mid-1977, real living standards of British workers declined approximately 7 percent.

As a question for the late 1970s and early 1980s, the impact of North Sea oil and gas on the British situation is an intriguing one. In 1977, half of the UK's demand for oil was provided from the North Sea, and net self-sufficiency in oil will be achieved by 1980. Balance-of-payments benefits in 1976 amounted to £2 billion from gas and £1 billion from oil. Indeed, Britain had moved into a balance-of-payments surplus in 1977 and 1978, and by the end of the 1970s the potential balance-of-payments impact from this production would be about 5 percent of her total GNP.[23] Conceivably, the greater international room to maneuver afforded by a balance-of-payments surplus and self-sufficiency in oil could make available wider options to some future left-Labour government.

The particular importance of North Sea energy resources to Britain thus lay in the potential easing of balance-of-payments constraints which had bedeviled previous governments. This created the opportunity to pursue a greater degree of sustained national economic growth without being forced to lurch into the deflationary phase of a "stop-go" cycle each time a modest degree of domestic expansion began to pull in increased imports and thus throw the balance of payments into disequilibrium. However, it was by no means certain that a Labour government—or a Conservative one—would necessarily succeed in using the room for maneuver afforded by North Sea oil and gas to restructure and modernize successfully the British economy. Enough other obstacles, including problems of business competence and innovative skills, political culture, attitudes, and trade union resistance, all remained to be faced. The importance of energy resources to Britain and her position as a producer also made her a difficult partner for cooperative energy policy efforts among the other members of the EC—all of whom were major energy importers.

Policy Options: The French Case

The case of France is one of the most absorbing and important in Europe. On the one hand, the country is highly dependent (75.1 percent of primary energy sources) on imported energy, burdened by a large oil import bill (approximately 100 billion francs, or $24 billion in 1980) and deeply involved as a major actor in numerous regional and international groupings. On the other hand, a vigorous and powerful, though very seriously divided, leftist coalition only narrowly missed electoral victory in March 1978 and remains a long-term contender for political power within France. Would a Socialist-dominated government, which included Communists in some posts, be able to carry out major domestic policy changes, including the nationalization of nine of France's largest private corporations, while remaining an active participant in an open Western international economic order, or would it choose to be forced to seek closure in order to carry out its aims while maintaining internal equilibrium? Alternatively, might international constraints force the modification or even abandonment of domestic changes? A majority group within the PS leadership, around François Mitterrand, has favored an international posture of openness. Noting the baneful experiences elsewhere of "socialism in one country," it rejects closure on the grounds that democratic socialist policies have to be achieved in an open environment and with cooperation at the EC level.

Another Socialist faction, particularly the Centre d'Etudes, de Recherche, et d'Education Socialistes (CERES) under Jean-Pierre Chevenement, as well as a smaller number of those belonging to the Mitterrand majority (and the Communists), seem to lean toward a policy of relative closure. Their argument is based on the assumption that international hostility could obstruct or even sabotage implementation of the Left's Common Program and that a variety of protectionist economic, monetary and trade measures must be available for use.

A dominant commitment to avoid closure was reflected in the official manifesto of the PS for the June 1979 direct elections to the European Parliament, and which spoke of the "impossibility of autarchy":

In this universe of tensions and tempests, the policy of France cannot be that of return to new isolation. We depend today on the outside world for the greater part of our primary materials, in particular our energy, and this obliges us to export a growing part of our production. Also, failure of the industrial policy of grandeur, established at the beginning of the Fifth Republic, and the return which followed, under Giscard, to an uncontrolled laissez faire, have caused entire sectors of our industry to pass under the control of multinational firms, in conditions hard to reverse. Finally, technological progress, especially in the most modern sectors. . .leads us to growing cooperation with our neighbors. In these conditions, a rupture of our relations with the outside world, especially the EEC, would produce only a formidable economic and social recession, in which workers would bear the first costs.[24]

Given their sense of the inescapable involvement of France in the international (particularly European) economy and polity, French Socialist leaders have been aware of the programmatic limits this imposes. Thus Jacques

Attali, the PS's leading economic advisor in the period before the 1978 elections, noted that there was a very definite optimal limit to the reflation a leftist government could sustain. He cautioned that, in the existing condition of the French economy, to do more would be to do less, and he criticized the silence of the PCF (Parti Communiste Français) on the inflation problem associated with their demands for higher stimulus. Attali concluded, "An excessive reflation would produce inflation and the closing of frontiers. It fits only an autarchic vision of socialism. This is not ours."[25]

In the event that a leftist government did come face to face with drastic international financial or economic problems, what options would a Mitterrand—or a Michel Rocard—and his colleagues choose (or have forced upon them)?[26] In other words, might a French leftist government have to seek closure in order to carry out or consolidate change in France, or would the coalition collapse (perhaps in response to international pressures as well as differences among the PS, PCF, and trade unionists), with its prime minister forced to resign or, less likely, forced to turn to his right for allies?

The Manipulation of Weakness

While present and future left-wing governments find themselves deeply constrained by international factors, they are not without bargaining resources with which to defend their domestic priorities. This is so despite the asymmetrical nature of interdependence and the fact that some countries within Europe (Germany) are far more powerful economically and politically than others (Italy). Economic collapse and reversion to a 1930s type of protectionism or autarchy by a major country, such as the UK, France, or Italy, would have harmful consequences for all its European and even OECD partners. Thus, other countries as well as bodies such as the EC or GATT have an interest in seeking accommodation even when they may not sympathize with the policies of a particular government. In addition, de Gaulle's example of skillful maneuver illustrates how a determined player is sometimes able to obtain payoffs or compromises more favorable than his size and importance would seem to warrant. As another example, German and EC loans to Italy in recent years and GATT's willingness to turn a blind eye to Italian trade barriers reflect an awareness that all will suffer if one state goes bust.

To take the case of France, again, because of that country's enormous economic importance within the EC and the interdependence of trading and financial relationships among the Nine, governments of the other eight member states would find it necessary to cooperate with France despite their lack of sympathy for policies followed by some future government of the Left. This appears to apply particularly to Germany, for whom France is the largest single trading partner. By the same logic, however, the lesser degree of interdependence between France and the U.S. implies the lesser likelihood of a favorable American response.

The uses of weakness also apply to bargaining relationships between European governments and major oil-producing states. Energy dependence, payments deficits, petrodollar recycling, and investment patterns would appear to leave much of Europe in a position of serious vulnerability. However, were they to be pushed into economic chaos (and thus probably into grave political upheaval), the effects could also harm major producers such as Saudi Arabia. The Saudi government has shown itself not unaware of the dangers to itself of such instability, although Saudi ideological hostility to a European leftist government remains a possibility.

Policy Options for the United States

The lessons of the 1973–74 energy crisis reflect the fact of an inherent leadership position for the U.S. in its Atlantic relationships. Yet, the growing importance of U.S. energy imports, the size of European economies, and the fact that the Europeans possess certain bargaining tools do place some limits on the exercise of this influence. The extreme case of U.S. policy choice in dealing with an elected leftist government is that of Chile. This, as well as less dramatic policies toward Italy, Greece, Spain, and Portugal had a baneful effect on relationships between America and the European Left. For a time, it seemed to suggest an orientation of "Better Papadopoulos than Mitterrand."

With the onset of the Carter administration, however, the specter of crudely interventionist and antileftist policies in Europe receded. President Carter's Notre Dame speech of May 22, 1977, reflected this change:

Our [America's] rise to world eminence . . . dates from 1945, when Europe and the old international order both lay in ruins. . . . We helped to build solid testaments to our faith and purpose—the UN, NATO, the World Bank, the International Monetary Fund, and other institutions. This international system has endured and worked well for a quarter of a century. Our policy during this period was guided by two principles: a belief that Soviet expansion must be contained and the corresponding belief in the importance of an almost exclusive alliance among non-Communist nations on both sides of the Atlantic. That system could not last forever unchanged. Historical trends have weakened its foundation.

Yet, the sources of American policy toward Europe included not only a political idealism (implying a willingness to let others determine their own internal politics without outside interference). They also included a security realism, which dictated considerable concern for maintaining a coherent deterrent and defense capability versus the Soviet Union, in Europe as well as globally. Along with the fundamental American commitment to an open, that is, liberal international economic order, this suggested U.S. policies could oscillate depending upon which policy consideration seemed uppermost at the time and also to what extent domestic pressures within the U.S. impinged on administration conduct of foreign policy.[27]

By virtue of its continuing role in a Western institutional framework, the United States remains inescapably involved in European affairs. Through the IMF, IEA, GATT, and other relationships, U.S. policy makers will be faced with important decisions involving loans, investments, balance-of-payments problems, and energy questions affecting individual European governments, some of which may be leftist. There are certain to be irritants in these relationships, for example, in policy toward the Middle East, bilateral dealings between European governments and OPEC and OAPEC states, exports of nuclear reactors to countries such as Pakistan or Brazil, balance-of-payments problems, foreign arms sales, and the status of American investments abroad. Nonetheless, the facts of European energy and security dependence, and the nature of interdependence, confine the degree to which any Western European governments are likely to drift apart from the United States unless they are left with no other choice. A flexible American policy recognizing these factors should be able to maintain relationships in a way which minimizes tendencies toward mutually harmful economic chaos or political collapse and which is of long-term benefit to both sides.

Notes

1. For a comprehensive analysis of the impact of the energy crisis on the European Community, see Robert J. Lieber, *Oil and the Middle East War: Europe in the Energy Crisis* (Cambridge Mass: Harvard Center for International Affairs, 1976).

2. Commission of the European Communities (EC), "The Community's Energy Policy," (1) Sec (78) 4054, Information Memo P–110, (October 1978), p. 1.

3. EC, *Bulletin of the European Communities*, Supplement 6/78, preliminary draft General Budget of the European Communities for fiscal year 1979, pp. 27–29.

4. Ibid., p. 3.

5. EC, "The Community's Energy Policy," p. 3.

6. Marion Bywater, "La politique énérgetique commune: des performances satisfaisantes mais peu de stratégie," *Revue du Marché Commun*, 209 (August-September 1977): 333–36.

7. Televised interview, Paris, September 20, and November 21, 1978; *see* also *Le Monde* (November 23, 1978).

8. Personal relationships can also reflect these asymmetries. As Robert Keohane and Joseph Nye observe, power derives from asymmetrical interdependence because one side is more vulnerable to changes in a mutual relationship. *See* "World Politics and the International Economic System," in *The Future of the International Economic Order*, ed. D. Fred Bergsten (Lexington, Mass; D.C. Heath, 1973), pp. 118–22.

9. In 1978, France's balance of payments wasroughly in equilibirum, but the country had an inflation rate of 10 percent. In 1980, France's oil import bill may be 100 billion francs, according to Minister of Industry, André Giraud, *La Monde* (December 22, 1979).

10. The UK has had its own serious economic problems, but these are likely to be substantially ameliorated as the country becomes self-sufficient in oil around 1980. The Netherlands and Norway have also faced certain problems created by their energy resources. In the Dutch case, balance-of-payments effects have kept the value of the guilder higher than would otherwise have been the case and have thus made some exports less competitive internationally.

11. "This year we are going to pay a kind of foreign tax amounting to 40 billion francs on our oil consumption. If we could use this money for other things, we would really be well off." President

Valery Giscard d'Estaing, interview in *Le Figaro*, May 27, 1977. France's oil import bill in 1978 amounted to 54 billion francs.

12. By some accounts, British Labour governments actually welcomed IMF measures as a means of making possible politically what they preferred to do in any case. Leo Panitch argues persuasively that the essentially conservative economic policies followed by successive Labour governments were not so much forced upon them by the IMF as they represented a basic underlying consensus shared by leading governmental economic policy makers and businessmen. *Social Democracy and Industrial Militancy: The Labour Party, the Trade Unions and Incomes Policy, 1945–1974* (Cambridge, England: Cambridge University Press, 1976), p. 243.

13. Quoted, *International Herald Tribune* (Paris), September 30, 1978.

14. Calculated from 1978 forecasts of 953.5 mtoe consumption of primary energy and net oil imports of 455 million tons. See Commission of the European Communities, "Energy Situation in the Community and in the World" (1), Information Memorandum, COM (78) 101 (March 1978).

15. Conversely, the nature of Europe's ties to the United States helps to set certain limits against policy drifting to any completely pro-Arab orientation. Note that the share of the overall OPEC export market obtained by France actually fell from a 1972–73 figure of 10.3 percent to 8.4 percent in 1978 (in terms of France's share of total OECD exports to OPEC, including non-Arab states). See *OECD Economic Outlook*, 24 (December 1978): 118.

16. Note French efforts to protect shipbuilding and steel industries, as well as British and other European (and American) efforts, to restrain Japanese penetration of certain domestic markets.

17. Louis Turner makes the related point that, as the world economy becomes more dependent on oil flows, the need for consumer governments to encroach on oil company autonomy has grown. "The Oil Majors in World Politics," *International Affairs* (London) 52, 3 (July 1976): 378–80.

18. This theme is developed in Lieber, *Oil and the Middle East War*, especially pp. 53–59.

19. Ibid., pp. 48–59.

20. Ibid., particularly "Proposition 4," p. 59. In addition, Donald Puchala's study of the politics of rule enforcement in the EC, involving earlier issues, comes to similar conclusions regarding the tendency for the EC to be seen more as a means for coping with national problems than as an end in itself. "Domestic Politics and Regional Harmonization in the European Communities," *World Politics* 27, no. 4 (July 1975): 496–520.

21. Malcolm Sawyer, "Income Distribution in OECD Countries," *OECD Economic Outlook* (July 1976).

22. *Labour Party Manifesto* (London), October 1974, pp. 29–30. Italics added.

23. British Information Service, *Survey of Current Affairs* 7, no. 5 (May 1977): 194–97.

24. "Manifeste Socialiste pour l'Election Européenne, Adopté à la Majorité par le Comité Directeur du 21 octobre 1978," (Parti Socialiste), p. 2.

25. Jacques Attali, "Socialisme ou Capitalisme d'Etat," *l'Unité* (Paris) 261 (September 9–15, 1977): 8.

26. Serious financial problems may be no monopoly of a leftist government. Based on figures and assumptions set out in the official Seventh Plan, economists of the *Parti Socialiste* projected that a reelected government of the Right would face budget deficits of 55 billion francs ($11 billion) in 1978, 117 billion francs ($24 billion) in 1980, and 154 billion francs ($32 billion) in 1982. See Laurent Fabius and Jossette Alia, "Si la droite gagne.... Le coût des promesses," *Le Nouvel observateur*, 659 (June 27, 1977): 22–25.

27. See Robert J. Lieber and Nancy I. Lieber, "Eurocommunism, Eurosocialism and US Foreign Policy," in *Eagle Entangled: US Foreign Policy in a Complex World*, ed. Kenneth Oye; D. Rothchild; and R. Lieber, (New York: Longman, 1979).

DONALD J. PUCHALA

10

European Fiscal Harmonization: Politics During the Dutch Interlude

In contrast to some of the other contributions to this volume, this essay contains neither a broad analysis of Western European integration nor any overview and conclusions about the two decades since the signing of the Rome Treaty. Rather, what I shall do here is conduct a rather narrowly focused case study of Dutch behavior during the European Community's institution of the tax on value added (VAT), the first step toward community-wide fiscal harmonization. The essential events in this case happened during three years, 1964–967, and they occurred partly in The Hague and partly in Brussels. By hindsight, they had only marginal impacts on the progress of European integration. But, as I shall attempt to show, they are of great significance to those of us who make a profession out of trying to understand European integration better because they reflect some of the fundamental dynamics of the integration process.

Domestic Politics and Transnational Harmonization

How far and how fast can the Nine move toward economic union? Can they move beyond economic union, to monetary union, and perhaps beyond this to political union? These remain central among the concerns of scholars and policy makers attentive to the affairs of the European Community. Or, to put it slightly differently, these certainly are among the questions that policy makers most frequently put to scholars. Confronting them, moreover, has been the persistent goal of integration theorists, and the essence of existing theories is in their answers to "how far," "how fast," and "why."

The theoretical aim of this chapter is to tackle once again the "how far," "how fast," and "why" of European integration. Conceptually central to the analysis here is the notion of *political reverberation*. Simply stated, political reverberation means the transfer of issues and outcomes among the ten (or conceivably more) political arenas that compose the political system of the European Community. There is in the EC a "European" political arena played in by national governments, appointed delegations at various levels, the Commission and other Community institutions, transnational interest groups, and sundry others, including third-country governments. This arena, let us also call it "Brussels," has been the focus of attention of eminent contributors to the study of European integration, such as Lindberg, Scheingold, Caporaso, and Sidjanski; its structure and functioning are rather well understood.[1] But, there are nine national political arenas in the EC system as well. They vary considerably in structure and functioning—federations, unitary states, highly pluralistic Italy, preeminently corporatist Holland, planned France, liberal Germany, and so forth. Some aspects of political play in these domestic arenas have little to do with the European Community. Yet, others are directly linked to the Community and these linkages make the domestic arenas of the member states integral parts of the political system of the European Community. Analysis of national politics and European integration as well as the domestic politics of European integration probably began in Haas's *Uniting of Europe*; it has recently been furthered in works by Wallace, Rosenthal, and Busch.[2]

To study political reverberation in the European Community is to observe and explain how, when, why, and with what result issues are transferred between the national arenas and the European one. As I hope the analysis in this essay will demonstrate, studying political reverberation contributes in several ways to enhance understanding of European integration. First, it helps to dispel the image or notion that Community activities are discontinuous. To conceive of EC processes as moving in "fits and starts," with short periods of feverish activity interspersed among long lapses into immobility, is usually inaccurate. Once started by the Commission, Community activity in particular issue areas is normally continuous, from initiation to decision, to implementation, and *what appear to be intervals of inaction are really transfers of activity among arenas*. For example, when it appears that the Brussels institutions are deadlocked on a particular issue and it disappears from the agendas of Council, Commission, and COREPER for months or years, this often signals that the issue has been passed into the bureaucratic or pluralist politics of one or more member states, from whence it is likely ultimately to reemerge as a reformulated national position. The new national stance is then reinjected into the European arena to stimulate a new round of political play in Brussels.

Second, political reverberation explains *delay* in the deliberative processes of the European Community. Delay is obviously endemic to European integration, as almost everything having to do with transnational harmonization is either slower in starting or slower in reaching fruition than planned or expected. Some have interpreted the EC's propensities for delay as indicators of the fragility of the system, as signs of incapacity for collective action. Yet, what delay in decision or implementation generally means is that an issue has been transferred from the "European" arena to one or more national ones, where political avenues are being cleared so that internationally cooperative action can be taken at a later stage. When an EC member government refuses to cooperate in the European arena, hence causing delay in Community processes, it often means that politically significant forces or factions within the member state are blocking their government's ability to take internationally cooperative stances. Once such forces or factions have been pacified or otherwise overcome at the national level, the way is cleared for new progress at the European level. All of this invokes delays in European deliberations, but because the EC system so easily and readily tolerates such interludes "whilst problems are sorted out nationally" delay is an index not of its fragility but of its great strength. Member governments are rarely compelled to choose between Community objectives and national ones since the EC's benign attitude toward delay tends to afford all ample time to articulate diverse interests. Delays, then, are symptoms of political reverberation, and their occurrence alerts us to the transfer of issues among arenas.

Third, tracing political reverberations begins to reveal the true complexity of the politics of European integration. The striving for parsimony evident in the "models" phase of theoretical thinking about international integration considerably sharpened our image of the integration phenomenon. Yet, with regard to Europe at least, these classic theoretical efforts relegated to "exogenous" categories much of what is actually integral to the politics of European integration. As to the case in point, interconnectedness of policy inputs and outcomes and hence the interdependence of politics at national and "European" levels gets less attention in the integration models than its importance warrants. This is probably because the complexity of such interlinkages and interdependence defies easy modeling. Just imagine: ten arenas active intermittently in patterned fashion or sometimes simultaneously, most with both intrabureaucratic and pluralistic political processes active simultaneously, with nine linked to the tenth via formal mechanisms, delegated authority, and interpersonal networks, with nine also linked to each other via similar channels, and with dialogue and debate concerning international commitment and cooperation bouncing back and forth among arenas in pinball-like fashion. How are we to model this complexity, especially as the relevance of various arenas and processes within them, and the pattern of transfers changes from issue to issue and from time to time? To capture the complexity of the politics of European integration and to render them analyzable and their outcomes predictable, are among the important challenges to integration theory today. From this undertaking are bound to emerge better answers to "how far," "how fast," and "why." Looking at political reverberation, then, is one step toward intellectually mastering the complexity of the politics of European integration.

Fiscal Harmonization and Political Reverberation in the European Community

Matters of taxation are intensely political because they involve organizations', groups', and individuals' control over resources and relative power and autonomy associated with controlling more or fewer of these. No tax is neutral with respect to economic sectors or social classes, and every existing tax represents past political contests won or lost and legislative outcomes bargained or imposed. This being the case, attempts at fiscal reform invariably generate political controversy because to propose to change a tax system is to opt for changing patterns of benefit and cost imposed upon elements of society by the existing system. When the Six committed themselves to cooperate in implementing Articles 95–99 of the Treaty of Rome, each member government accordingly committed itself to domestic fiscal reform with the ultimate aim of harmonizing taxation policies throughout the Common Market. Knowingly or unknowingly, in 1958 each member government (save France) had also opened itself to several years of domestic political furor.[3]

This essay will not deal with the full range of the EC's experience in fiscal harmonization. Important elements of the story have been told elsewhere.[4] In addition, processes that will ultimately lead to the complete abolition of fiscal frontiers in the EC are still operating so that the story is not yet finished. Nevertheless, some overview is essential so that readers will be able to place the events dwelt upon below in appropriate context.

The relationship between fiscal harmonization and economic union is uncomplicated. A common market is less than "common" to the extent that different participants maintain differing fiscal regimes, since national taxes imposed upon imports, rebated on exports, or both can raise barriers to trade or otherwise distort international competition, sometimes to the extent of cancelling liberalizations gained through the elimination of tariffs. The drafters of the Rome Treaty understood that movement toward fiscal harmonization had to accompany tariff reduction as Europe's customs union evolved toward fuller economic union. Articles 95–99 of the Treaty set the stage for fiscal harmonization, and Article 99 specifically committed signatories to the standardization of national legislation with regard to indirect or turnover taxes.[5] It was from this threshold that the Commission stepped off in 1959 to begin to create the Community Tax on Value Added— the VAT.

The chronology of events surrounding the design, promulgation, and implementation of the VAT is crucially important to this analysis because their flow and tempo reveal patterns of political reverberation. It took the member states of the European Community fourteen years to move from treaty commitment to community-wide implementation of the VAT: three years of expert study and analysis (1959–62), five years of national and international deliberation (1962–67), and six years to complete implementation (1967–73). This span of time was somewhat longer than the five-to-seven-year average for policy making on major issues in the European Community, though in comparison with national experiences in fiscal reform, fourteen years is not a very long time to change tax regimes.[6]

What is most revealing about the fourteen years of the VAT episode is that activity toward bringing the new regime into existence was continuous, but it shifted several times ("reverberated," in effect) between the "European" arena and various national ones. To the observer stationed in Brussels and unprepared to look beyond, it would have appeared that action concerning the VAT occurred at irregularly spaced intervals, as for example in the autumn of 1962 when the Commission laid proposals for the VAT before the Council, in the spring of 1964 when revised proposals were tabled, in the spring of 1965 when the first two directives on the VAT were debated by the Council, and in the winter of 1967 when the Council agreed to establish the new tax throughout the Community. However, the observer stationed in Bonn might have had a very different interpretation of when the crucial action on the Community VAT took place because the significant and politically intense period for Germany was between 1962 and 1964, when interests in the German business community and the Ministry of Finance relaxed their opposition to fiscal reform and opted for a new turnover tax of the value-added variety.[7] This turn of events in Germany then opened the way for German leadership in the "European" arena in 1964 and 1965. In similar fashion, the observer stationed in The Hague would again have a different interpretation of important events during the evolution of the Community VAT. From the perspective of the Netherlands, the crucial period of political contact and controversy about the proposed new tax occurred between 1964 and 1967, during which time the Dutch abandoned their outspoken opposition to both the principle and the intended practice of the Community VAT. Dropping opposition meant changing policy, and the change of policy resulted from the intensely played intra-bureaucratic politics in The Hague. Finally, from the Italian perspective, the period of intense political activity surrounding the VAT occurred between 1970 and 1973, after the Council of Ministers had agreed to institute the Community tax.[8] Italy's apparent delinquency in implementation between 1970 and 1973 stemmed from the intense political opposition aroused as a result of the government's announced intention to go ahead with the tax. Until quelled by assurances, bargaining, solemn promises, side payments, and patronage distributions over a period of three years, Italian domestic opposition effectively held up the Italian VAT and, by implication, European integration as well.

Clearly, the sum of the politics of fiscal harmonization regarding the VAT between 1959 and 1973 was considerably different from and more complex than any of its parts. Politically tranquil periods in Brussels were very active periods within the member states, and political resolution or pacification within the member states opened the way for new periods of intense activity in Brussels. The issue of the community tax on value-added therefore reverberated among arenas. To complicate this already complex picture further, it must also be pointed out that during the entire fourteen-year period technical discussions about the VAT continued at several levels, and even countries politically opposed to the Community tax at various times remained technically involved in designing it.[9]

The Dutch Interlude, 1964–67

Both the transfer of the VAT issue from Brussels to Bonn in 1962, and the transfer from Brussels to Rome in 1970, have already been examined in detail elsewhere.[10] Belgian and British wrestlings with the VAT in 1969 and 1973, respectively, were relatively short-lived episodes of no major consequence to the overall EC experience.[11] France avoided a domestic interlude of VAT politics largely because the notion of a tax on value-added was a French one from the beginning, and instituting the tax in France was not really a measure of fiscal reform. But there was a Dutch interlude in the political chronology of the VAT that was of significance and that heretofore has not been examined in depth. Examining it casts further interesting light on political reverberation in the European Community.

Anyone looking over the chronology of events leading to the Council's adoption of the First and Second Directives on fiscal harmonization (those instituting the VAT) is struck by the apparent stagnation in the European arena between 1964 and 1967. As noted, the Commission presented its revised version of the First Directive on Fiscal Harmonization to the Council in June 1964. This established that the new Community-wide tax would be of the value-added variety. The Commission then prepared a Second Directive that contained detailed prescriptions for implementation, and this was presented to the Council in April 1965. However, the Council did not act conclusively on either of these directives until February 1967. There was, therefore, stagnation in the European arena between 1964 and 1967, and the source of it was no mystery: the Dutch government would not accept the Directives on the new VAT, and this opposition from The Hague was preventing closure in the Council of Ministers, where unanimity was required.

A Smokescreen of Principled Argument

The Dutch government's announced objection to the proposed value-added tax was one of principle. Dutch officials indicated that they could not evaluate the impacts of the new tax on the Netherlands or decide upon its acceptability unless they could be shown the blueprint for the Commission's ultimate scheme of Community-wide fiscal harmonization.[12] Was the EC moving toward the standardization of VAT rates, or was it not? Was it moving toward the abolition of fiscal frontiers, or was it not? Did it have a supplemental plan for the harmonization of direct taxes, or did it not? In short, where was the VAT to fit within the broader context of the EC's fiscal evolution?

Moreover, Dutch officials went on to explain, these concerns about overall designs were not merely demands for intellectual neatness since they had practical bearing upon the fate of the existing cascade-type turnover tax already in force in the Netherlands. If the VAT were to be introduced the existing tax would have to be dismantled, and this was not to be taken lightly since most Dutch financial authorities (and apparently a good many Dutchmen, too) believed that the existing tax ideally served a variety of Dutch fiscal and sociopolitical purposes.[13] As a matter of fact, ever since the European Community struck upon the idea of a value-added tax in 1960, Dutch fiscal specialists had been singing a chorus of condemnation.[14] The experts' conclusions were usually that the Netherlands had the best system of indirect taxation in the world, and there was no reason to reform it. In light of this, the Dutch government officially contended that it could not exchange a fiscal instrument of known efficacy for an untried one unless it could be persuaded that moving to the VAT was genuinely a major step toward European integration, and the Dutch would not be thus persuaded until they had examined the full blueprint for fiscal harmonization in the Community.

The official Dutch case against the principle of an isolated VAT was written into a memorandum to the European Commission sent in the early summer of 1964, wherein the Commission was asked

to pass an opinion, indicating the pros and cons, as to whether the undertakings to be made in the proposed Directive should be based on the broad concept of suppressing fiscal barriers, or on the more confined principle of neutrality of turnover taxes when it comes to the origin of goods and services rendered."[15]

To this the Commission quickly responded in August 1964, with a lengthy memorandum to the Council of Ministers arguing that "within the Commission there has never been any doubt about the scope and objectives to be fulfilled by the harmonization of turnover taxes, as called for in Article 99 of the Treaty."[16] The scope, the Commission indicated, included the total abolition of fiscal frontiers, and the objective was fiscal harmonization as an element of complete economic and monetary union. Despite the Commission's reasoned and apparently convincing answers to the Dutch questions and the assurances they embodied, there was no outward evidence of any change in the Dutch position. For example, as late as November 1966, *Agence Europe* could still report that "all delegations have confirmed the agreement of the member states with the adoption of a joint tax on value-added, except the Dutch delegation, which maintained a general reservation."[17]

Whether the Netherlands' principled objections to the VAT were facades, intended only for the media and for debates in Brussels and never taken seriously in The Hague, remains unclear. Some Dutchmen undoubtedly attributed significance to the principled argument, though most of those interviewed in the Foreign Ministry, the Economics Ministry, and Finance Ministry in January 1977 recalled that the official objections were voiced primarily as a smokescreen to cover over more fundamental reasons for coolness toward the proposed VAT.[18] These had to do with the implacable opposition to the VAT among an elite corps of Dutch fiscal officers in the Ministry of Finance, whose position was neatly reinforced by the intrabureaucratic structure of "European" policy making in The Hague.

In essence, the Dutch reluctance to endorse the principle of the Community VAT—and the three-year delay this created in EC deliberations—stemmed from the fact that Dutch fiscal officers did not like the new tax. Specifically, State Secretary of Finance W. L. G. M. Hoefnagels and Fiscal Director C. P. Tuk did not like it, and because these senior civil servants did not like it, Finance Minister A. Vondeling would not clear the way for Dutch cooperation in Brussels. The Finance officials offered several reasons for their strong stand, all of them genuine. First, there was a concern over the revenue potentials of the new regime, as compared with the existing one. There was also a question about the likely inflationary impact of the VAT, and there was a strong feeling that the new tax could not be employed to serve the social functions that the existing one was serving through its intricate pattern of differential rates and exemptions. In addition, there was fear that the VAT would discriminate against small business by imposing unreasonable bookkeeping obligations on shopkeepers, artisans, and the like, a fear much amplified by the Dutch Council for Middle and Small Business.[19] Also, there was concern over disrupting the Netherlands' orchestrated balance between revenue raised by way of direct and indirect taxation. These summed up to a rather formidable case against fiscal reform.

But the intensity of the Dutch taxmen's opposition to the Community tax had deeper roots still: the proposed VAT was rubbing up against professional pride and creative satisfaction. On the one hand, there was the feeling widely shared within the corps of Dutch taxmen that national fiscal systems were "forbidden domains" as far as Brussels was concerned, and, as one Dutch official explained, "this European integration business is probably something that is all right for Agriculture, but certainly not for Treasury."[20] Revenue collection was perceived as the essence of national sovereignty; revenue collectors saw themselves as custodians of sovereignty, and they were not prepared to relinquish their trust out of deference to "theoretical ideas thought up by others in Brussels."[21] Along with this reaction against outside interference went the universally endorsed notion that the existing turnover tax system in the Netherlands was in fact the best in the world, and something much more appealing than the VAT would have to emerge before the Dutch tax would be willingly scrapped. Then, finally, at the foundations of the Finance Ministry's adamance were the personal positions of two men, Hoefnagels and Tuk. The former was steadfastly convinced that the VAT could never be the vehicle for abolishing European fiscal frontiers, and the latter could not abandon the Dutch cascade tax because he himself had designed it, perfected it, and made a career out of overseeing its application.

An extensive analysis of the way that the Dutch organize bureaucratically for "European" policy making is beyond the scope of this essay. Nonetheless, some features of this structure are important for both explaining the intrabureaucratic strength of the Finance Ministry's position and the consequent tenacity of the Dutch holdout in Brussels. The apex of the "European" policy-making apparatus in The Hague is the Subcommittee on European Integration Affairs of the Dutch Council of Ministers, which regularly consists of the Prime Minister, the Foreign Minister and his State Secretary, the Finance Minister, the Economics Minister, the Minister of Social Affairs, and the Minister of Agriculture. This group prepares Dutch position papers for meetings of the European Council of Ministers. Immediately subordinate to this group is the Interministerial Coordinating Committee, composed of senior civil servants from the various ministries, which prepares Dutch positions for the weekly meetings of the COREPER (or CPR, Committee of Permanent Representatives). What is noteworthy in the standard operating procedures of both of these bodies is that they tend almost always to defer to and acquiesce in the positions of the ministries within whose jurisdictions particular issues most nearly lie. This was precisely the case with regard to the Ministry of Finance and the VAT. Intrabureaucratic debate was forceful and continuous over the three years that the politics of the VAT were centered in the Dutch arena. The Foreign Ministry pressed for accepting the VAT for "European" reasons; Agriculture did likewise; Economics joined after their econometric studies showed only marginal impacts on the cost of living from the new tax.[22] Still, the Treasury remained firm in opposition, and adherence to the rules of bureaucratic deference led repeatedly to obstructionist instructions for COREPER and ministerial delegations. Delegates were instructed to say "no" in Brussels because this was the position of the Ministry of Finance in The Hague.

Pressures from Brussels and the Dutch Shift

All during the interlude of stalemate in the European Council of Ministers, while the Dutch held out and held up movement on the VAT, international discussions and technical work continued at various levels, including the COREPER and the Standing Committee of Heads of National Revenue Departments. The aim of the Commission, and increasingly of member state delegates as well, was to bring pressure to bear upon the Netherlands in these forums. This was done by isolating the Dutch delegates and emphasizing the unreasonableness of their position in light of the consensus of the Five in the opposite direction. In the language of EC politics, applying pressure by isolation and unanimous opposition is called "flushing down the W.C." As a Community official described it:

Here is a case of placing a man in a group of peers and demonstrating to him that his peers stand uniformly against him. In a national government a single man can hold up legislation indefinitely if he happens to be the man in authority in a particular area. Nobody can overrule him because he is the top man. However, when set against men from other governments that are his counterparts or peers he cannot argue from a position of unapproachable authority; he has to argue a case strictly on its merits and to make his position carry he has to persuade others of its rectitude. If after trying, and failing, he must back off or lose credibility. This is called 'flushing him down the W.C.'[23]

Pressure on the Dutch within the EC committees mounted during 1966, as the Five let it be known that they intended to go ahead with the VAT even in face of The Hague's opposition. But, while the Commission takes credit for ultimately turning the Dutch taxmen around, the evidence of the case does not substantiate this. Hoefnagels and Tuk were never "flushed" in Brussels.

What actually happened was that the Finance officials eventually lost in the intrabureaucratic contest in The Hague. Decisive encounters in the Interministerial Coordinating Committee and the Subcommittee on European Integration Affairs apparently occurred between November 1966 and January 1967. In October 1966, the government of Dutch Prime Minister Cals fell, and after a few weeks of maneuvering, Jelle Zijlstra formed a new coalition in mid-November. This was to be a caretaker regime that would remain in office only until the general elections scheduled for February 1967. Zijlstra, a professor of economics and former finance minister, assumed the obligations of both Prime Minister and Minister of Finance in the new government. Hoefnagels was not retained as State Secretary in the Finance Ministry, and his departure greatly reduced the political clout of the anti-VAT faction. No new State Secretary was appointed. Tuk maintained his resistance, but his technical position in the Ministry carried relatively little political weight. During December 1966, Prime Minister Zijlstra was persuaded by his own analysis of the fiscal implications of the proposed VAT, by the arguments of his colleagues in the Foreign Ministry, and by hints that the Five might actually be prepared to move without the Netherlands, that the Dutch government should relax its opposition in Brussels. The anti-VAT faction in the Finance Ministry was finally overruled at cabinet level by the new Prime Minister (who was also the Finance Minister), and the long play of VAT politics in the Dutch arena drew to a close.

Zijlstra arrived at the February 9, 1967 meeting of the European Council of

Ministers prepared to compromise on the issue of the Community VAT. But, it was imperative for him that the outcome appear a genuine compromise. He had overruled his senior civil servants in The Hague and undoubtedly exhausted a considerable measure of domestic political capital in so doing. Therefore, as an official of the Community phrased it, Zijlstra "had to take something home with him" from Brussels.[24] It had to appear that the Netherlands had won deference to a number of its positions. At the Council meeting, Zijlstra made a stand on the need for national autonomy and flexibility in the applications of the VAT, including the prerogative to list "zero" rates for particular goods. The French objected to the Dutch demands largely on the grounds that a leaning to Zijlstra's position would upset the logic of the whole VAT enterprise.[25] Yet, ultimately a compromise was reached, and this was subsequently concretized into the marvellously ambiguous wording of Article 17 of the Second Directive on Fiscal Harmonization.[26] Both the First and Second Directives were adopted by the Council on February 9. A Community VAT was officially established, and member states committed themselves to implement it by 1970. The Dutch interlude was over.

Conclusions

What is to be learned about European integration from the politics of fiscal harmonization during the Dutch interlude? First and obviously, political reverberation occurred: the VAT issue and its political sorting out between 1964 and 1967 were transferred from the "European" arena to the Dutch arena and then back again to the "European." Moreover, in broader context, those political transfers specifically concerning the Netherlands took place immediately after similar rounds of reverberation involving the German and "European" arenas, and immediately before subsequent rounds involving Belgium and Italy.

As noted earlier, the analytical importance of the concept of political reverberation is that it alerts the student of European integration to focus his attentions and investigations on the internal workings of the member states. The value in this, beyond underlining that the nation states remain vital elements of the EC system, is that it opens intellectual pathways to improving answers to the central questions of integration theory as applied to Western Europe—how far? how fast? and why?

For example, observing and analyzing political reverberation, as during the Dutch interlude, leads to the conclusion that accomplishments in European unity can ultimately be as far-reaching as statesmen's visions and government's political wills permit. Moreover, much suggests that this might be very far indeed. While this conclusion may sound inconsistent with the case study, especially as it appeared that the Dutch were rather successful in resisting movement in a "European" direction for some time, it nonetheless follows from two observations. First, and most important, the episode ended with an agreement in Brussels that represented a major step forward in European integration. After the smokescreen was blown away, the stalling had been eliminated, and the politicking had run its course, the final political transfer was back to the "European" arena, and the final outcome there was integrative. Community-wide fiscal harmonization was launched, and Community institutions were assigned new tasks. Of course, the Dutch interlude was but one case, but a great deal of research suggests that, as it regards ultimate integrative outcomes, this was neither an isolated nor extraordinary case.[27] Patient observers can accurately conclude that when looked at in longer-run perspective most of the EC's integrative aims are in fact ultimately achieved.[28]

Second, save for the grumbling of some Dutch taxmen about "foreigners' " infringements upon national prerogatives, the Dutch government never raised questions about the integrative aims of fiscal harmonization in the European Community, and never did anyone involved in the case deny the ultimate value of European unity or the Dutch commitment to it. As intense as debate sometimes became, it still took place within an official, and personal, political-ideological atmosphere of dedication to further European integration. It is true that, even at the time of the Dutch interlude in the mid-1960s, relatively few believed that full political unity would be achieved for a very long time, and many already suspected that such full unity as envisioned by the early "Europeans" might not be the ultimate form of European integration. Yet, much that occurred during this episode leads an observer to conclude that the debate about the virtue and value of European unity was already long over by 1964, and that the Dutch answer to the question of "how far?" was *ever farther*.

In fact, the more significant question had become "how fast," and conclusions about answers to this also emerge from analyzing political reverberation during the Dutch interlude. While the attainments of European integration are determined by governments' political will, as indicated above, the pace of integration is largely determined by governments' *political capacity*. Particularly relevant here is their capacity to make decisions that establish or implement policies of international cooperation within the EC framework. It is obvious from the case study that fiscal movement at the "European" level was stalled between 1964 and 1967 because the Dutch government was incapable of changing its position on the proposed VAT. The incapacity stemmed from both the opposition of the Finance Ministry and its fiscal experts and the political-structural difficulty of circumventing or overriding these elements of resistance. Therefore, "Europe" could not move until the Dutch government moved, and the Dutch government would not move until its Finance Ministry moved. Whatever the degree of anyone's good will toward European unity in this situation, the fact was that the system was politically stalled because the Dutch could not change their policy.

What this suggests is that the pace of European integration is likely to be painfully slow, indeed, often so slow as to provoke rumors that movement toward unity has ceased altogether and that Monnet's noble experiment has finally failed. If the Dutch case explored here is not unique, we might expect that each major future initiative toward greater unity will generate widespread political reverberation, as member states sort out the implications and ride out the domestic political contests that calls for change will invariably foment. Moreover, it is unlikely that member governments' political capacities for international cooperation will increase in the future. Rather the reverse will likely be the case as integration issues raise increasingly poignant questions about national sovereignty and domestic prerogatives and as opposition to change consequently becomes more intense. Therefore, we can expect longer delays and more political interludes in national arenas, all compounded by an increased number of national arenas after the next enlargement. Yet, after domestic sortings out, the final outcomes are still likely to be integrative.

Political reverberation, then, is itself the answer to the theoretician's question "why?" It conditions both "how far" and "how fast." As in the Dutch case examined in this essay, political reverberation has been functional to progress toward greater European unity because it has been the EC's circuitous but ultimately dependable pathway to international consensus, but, the very indirection of the pathway has determined that progress along it must be at snail's pace.

Notes

1. Leon M. Lindberg, *The Political Dynamics of European Economic Integration* (Stanford, Calif: Stanford University Press, 1963); Leon N. Lindberg and Stuart A. Scheingold, *Europe's Would-Be Polity* (Englewood Cliffs, N.J.: Prentice-Hall, 1970); James A. Caporaso, *The Structure and Function of European Integration* (Pacific Palisades, Calif.: Goodyear, 1974); Jean Meynaud and Dusan Sidjanski, *Les Groupes de Pression Dans La Communauté Européenne* (Brussels: Editions de l'Institut de Sociologie de L'Université Libre de Bruxelles, 1971)

2. Ernst B. Haas, *The Uniting of Europe* (Stanford, Calif: Stanford University Press, 1958); Helen Wallace, *National Governments and the European Communities (London: Chatham House/PEP, 1973); Helen Wallace, "The Impact of the European Communities on National Policy-Making," *Government and Opposition* 6 (Autumn 1971): 520–38; Glenda G. Rosenthal, *The Men Behind the Decisions* (Lexington, Mass.: D. C. Health, 1975); Peter Busch and Donald Puchala, "Interests, Influence and Integration: Political Structure in the European Communities," *Comparative Political Studies* 9, no. 3 (October 1976): 235–54.

3. Donald J. Puchala, "Worm Cans and Worth Taxes: Fiscal Harmonization and the European Policy Process," in *Policy-Making in the European Communities,* ed. Helen Wallace, William Wallace, and Carole Webb (Chichester, England: John Wiley & Sons, 1977), pp. 249–71.

4. Donald J. Puchala, "Worm Cans and Worth Taxes;" Donald J. Puchala and Carl F. Lankowski, "The Politics of Fiscal Harmonization in the European Communities," *Journal of Common Market Studies* 15, 3 (March 1977): 155–79; Andrew J. Taussig, "The Impact of the European Communities upon German Ministries (Ph.D. Diss., Harvard University, 1971).

5. *Treaty Establishing the European Economic Community, Rome, 25 March 1957* (London: HMSO, 1973), p. 46.

6. Puchala and Lankowski, "The Politics of Fiscal Harmonization in the European Communities." pp. 159–64.

7. Ibid., pp. 164–71.

8. Ibid., pp. 171–77; see also Donald J. Puchala, "Domestic Politics and Regional Harmonization in the European Communities," *World Politics* 27, 4 (July 1975): 504–06.

9. For chronology and commentary on technical negotiations concerning the Community Tax on Value Added, see Executive Secretariat of the Commission of the European Economic Community, *Bulletin of the European Economic Community* vol. 7–10, January 1964–April 1967.

10. Taussig, "The Impact of the European Communities upon German Ministries"; Puchala and Lankowski, "The Politics of Fiscal Harmonization in the European Communities."

11. Puchala, "Worm Cans and Worth Taxes," pp. 263–65; T. M. Rybczynski, ed., *The Value Added Tax: The U.K. Position and the European Experience* (Oxford: Basil Blackwell, 1969).

12. *Agence Europe*, 2549 (November 8, 1966): 5.

13. K. V. Antal, "Harmonisation of Turnover Taxes in the Common Market," *Common Market Law Review* 1, 1 (June 1963): 41–57.

14. C. P. Tuk, "Onze verbruiksbelastingen bij internationale samenwerking," *Weekblad voor fiscaal recht* (May 1960); 399 ff.; C. P. Tuk, "Verleden, heden en toekomst van de omzetbelasting," *Weekblad voor fiscaal recht* (February 1961): 30ff.

15. *Agence Europe*, "Europe Documents" 335, September 9, 1965.

16. Ibid., p. 1.

17. *Agence Europe*, 2549 (November 8, 1966): 1.

18. Interviews conducted in The Hague, January 6, 10, 11, 1977.

19. Raad Voor Het Midden-en Kleinbedrijf, *E.E.G. en emzetbelasting* ('s-Gravenhage, 1963); Raad Voor Het Midden-en Kleinbedrijf, *E.E.G. en emzetbelasing II* ('s-Gravenhage, 1965). The large business community in the Netherlands was also opposed to the VAT, but, according to Dutch officials, their campaign was mounted too late to affect the policy debate within the government (Interviews at Ministry of Finance, January 11, 1977, Ministry of Economics, January 11, 1977, Verbond Van Nederlandse Ondernemingen, January 6, 1977).

20. Interview, Dutch Foreign Ministry, January 10, 1977.

21. Ibid.

22. Interview, Dutch Economics Ministry, January 12, 1977.

23. Interview, Secretariat of the European Council of Ministers, January 17, 1977.

24. Ibid., and *Agence Europe*, 2618 (February 9, 1967): 4–5.

25. *Agence Europe*, 2618 (February 9, 1967): 4.

26. EC, "Deuxième Directive Du Conseil du 11 avril 1967," *Journal Officiel Des Communautés Européennes* (April 14, 1967): 1303/67–1312/67.

27. Puchala, "Domestic Politics and Regional Harmonization."

28. Glenda G. Rosenthal and Donald J. Puchala, "Decisional Systems, Adaptiveness, and European Decision-Making," *The Annals of the American Academy of Political and Social Science* 440 (November 1978): 54–66.

EXTERNAL EC COLLECTIVE DECISION MAKING AND ITS INTERNATIONAL REALITIES

Part IV

CORRADO PIRZIO-BIROLI *

11

Foreign Policy Formation within the European Community with Special Regard to the Developing Countries

The Treaty of Rome does not explicitly give the European Community any overall mandate in the field of development cooperation. This is because development cooperation had a much lower profile in the 1950s than it has had since, and, until the late 1960s, the slow rate of progress in this area was due to the EC member states' reluctance to coordinate their foreign policies. This reluctance was overcome with the European Summit in The Hague (1969) and the establishment of the European Political Cooperation Effort (1970), which was based on the Davignon Report.[1] A growing sense of awareness within Community institutions, and most notably within the Commission, of the need for a renewed approach to development cooperation opened a new phase in Community relations with the Third World and in international relations in general. The reevaluation of the Community's development policy was not a consequence of, but rather preceded, the oil crisis, the rise of raw material prices, and the threat of shortages in basic foodstuffs. It preceded the LDCs' request for a "new deal" by offering one.

This new phase began in July 1971, when the Commission issued a "Memorandum on a Community Cooperation and Development Policy."[2] In February 1972, the Commission produced a "Program for Initial Action."[3]

*Author's Note: The views expressed in this essay are those of the author and do not necessarily represent the views of the European Commission.

These documents initiated a debate within Community institutions and the member states on an overall development cooperation policy. This debate reached its peak at the Paris Summit Conference of EC leaders in October 1972, where it was decided to "progressively adopt an overall policy of development cooperation on a worldwide scale." It is from this Summit that the Community obtained a clear mandate on cooperation and development. In September 1972, the European Council of Ministers met for the first time at the level of the Nine's cooperation ministers. Its aim was to attempt to coordinate development policies of the member states. An ad hoc group, the Development Cooperation Group, was set up to pursue this aim. Consequently, it was possible to extend the variety of cooperation instruments at the disposal of the Community, coordinate member states' positions in international forums (in particular at the UN), and adopt a number of common Council resolutions, such as on aid volumes and terms and on the principle of Community aid to nonassociated developing countries.[4] Moreover, in 1974, the Community proposed an "international action in favor of the developing countries hit by the recent trends in international prices" (Cheysson Plan), which was undertaken in line with the recommendations of the sixth special session of the UN General Assembly.

In the same year, the European Commission was invited by the European Council to give its thoughts on Community cooperation with the Third World. The Commission drew up the so-called Fresco,[5] establishing priorities and guidelines of Community development cooperation policy and action on a worldwide scale. The Fresco stressed: coordination between the aid of member states and that of the Community proper; diversification of aid means and instruments according to need; the need to establish priority objectives for Community aid to non-associates; and support for schemes encouraging regional integration among LDCs. After negotiations that had continued throughout 1974, the Lomé Convention was signed in early 1975. The year 1976 saw the conclusion of global cooperation agreements with the Maghreb countries (Algeria, Morocco, and Tunisia) and Mashrek countries (Egypt, Jordan, Syria, Lebanon) and the start of the Euro-Arab Dialogue. Since 1976, the EC and its member states have acted as a single unit in the context of the Conference on International Economic Cooperation (North-South Dialogue in Paris) and have taken a common stand on all problems of development cooperation in that forum.

It is commonly agreed that the Community's achievements in the area of global development cooperation agreements and complex international north-south negotiations are impressive, in particular when compared with the limited competence the Community derives from the Rome Treaty. There are five major reasons for these achievements:

1. The historical coincidence that, at the time the Treaty was signed, most of the orginal members of the Community still had colonial responsibilities;

2. The initiative of, as well as hard work by, the Commission;
3. External pressures arising from the Community's dominant position in world trade as well as from its military weakness and from its ideological flexibility, which made it a more acceptable partner for the LDCs than the superpowers;
4. Trade dependence on the developing countries, which constitute the Community's largest export market and provide close to one-half of the Community's import supplies; and
5. The member states' aspiration to recapture some of the sovereignty they had lost since the Second World War.

As all foreign policies, the Community's is a policy of defense of interests. The Community's interest is to promote a world system in which it can prove its independence from superpower politics by securing a fair share of influence in world affairs. This depends on its success in helping to build a world where it can assert and maintain its character as a civilian society. The way the Community shapes its international economic relations is therefore a highly political issue. In this context, the Community was capable of demonstrating an ability to innovate in the field of north-south relations, and the relationship of mutual support with the LDCs became a cornerstone of its foreign policy. The positive response the Community found to its offers of development cooperation was due not only to the LDCs' perceived interest but also to the belief that the socialist inclination of most European countries allowed them to understand better than other powers the LDCs' requests that the principles of resource allocation and income distribution presently applied in progessive Western democracies be applied to the international economy as well.

The EC's Global Approach to Development Cooperation

The main guideline of the Community's policy as outlined in the Commission's "Fresco," and the point of departure of such a policy, is the Community's recognition of diversity of the underdevelopment situations, of which four types were distinguished: poor countries with a small exportable surplus; countries whose economies are dependent on the export of commodities; countries which are in the process of becoming industrialized or are already semi-industrialized; and oil-producing countries with low absorption capacity.

The diversity of situations is matched by a diversity of needs and hence of forms of actions or combinations thereof: trade measures, stabilization of export earnings, commodity agreements, industrial cooperation, technical and financial assistance, food aid. Thus, for the poorest LDCs, it is financial and food aid that have the greatest meaning today. For those countries that depend heavily on commodity export earnings, it is the stabilization of the relevant export earnings. For medium and high-income countries, the grand design is to engage in technical and industrial cooperation by combining the wealth of the developing countries in raw materials, population, and area with the capital, technology, and the vast markets of the industrialized countries as well as with the capital derived from the sale of certain raw materials such as oil (OPEC).

The Community believes that the most effective external contribution to the satisfaction of such diverse needs can best be made in the framework of global cooperation agreements in which the different means of action described above are applied jointly and on an overall basis and equality between partners is fostered. This approach, which combines all instruments of development cooperation available, is geographically limited to member states of the Organization for African Unity, the Arab League, the Caribbean Community, and the South Pacific Forum.

Progress in the direction of the policy outlined above has been necessarily slow because it demands so much in terms of agricultural and industrial adjustment or money for aid or commodity stabilization. There is consequently a case for selecting certain countries with which there are strong political arguments for giving some priority to their particular problems. The choice of partners took into consideration historical, political, and economic factors.[6] In particular, these partners are part of the center of gravity of the Community's trade, which is a European monetary area with which the member states of the Community conduct some three-quarters of their foreign trade. It includes all European associates and other industrialized Western European countries, the African countries, and the Arab world. The Community's partnership conventions are the result of contractual acts. Once they are signed, the partners are assured of Community aid in all its forms: the Community has the right neither to revoke nor to modify its undertakings for the duration of the contract, and this is a valuable stabilizing factor for development. In this club, priorities and programs are mutually set around the same table; mutual aid is "de rigueur"; consultations and meetings, whether institutionalized or not, are frequent; not only the executive bodies, but also members of parliament, manufacturers, businessmen, and trade unionists get together, get to know each other, and exchange views. In this fashion it is easier to appreciate the real needs and consequently to adjust the means available and gain invaluable experience for adaptations and improvements within the region as well as worldwide.

Such an approach, which is essentially regional in nature, has world relevance insofar as it acts as a pilot scheme for the extension of new cooperation policies worldwide and insofar as it remains outward-looking. No LDCs are excluded per se from joint Community action, and partners do not inhibit the EC from making improvements in its policies towards the Third World. "Multilaterization" of EC action placing all LDCs on the same footing does not exclude the modulation of action to meet the special needs of individual LDCs. Moreover, the privileged position of the closest partners can always be reestablished through additional concessions. Despite its internal divisions, the EC has become the only place where there is a promise of dynamism and cooperation with the Third World. The EC's policy formulation process will be described below in three separate case studies: the Lomé Convention, the agreements with the Southern Mediterranean, and the Euro-Arab dialogue.

The Formulation of the Lomé Convention

The Lomé Convention is a political event of international significance which shows that the enlarged EC is capable of undertaking action in the sphere of foreign policy. Neither the Six nor the individual member states of the EC would have had the political and economic strength to conclude such a comprehensive agreement. The latter is additional proof that the Community has seized the opportunity to develop a policy in relation to the Third World which, as Commissioner Cheysson, in a press conference, has said, "differs from that of member countries, more complete, bolder and less linked with the past."

The Lomé Convention owes its existence to three related positions:

(1) The French *sine qua non* condition for signing the Rome Treaty to associate its colonies and overseas departments to the Community;[7]
(2) Later, the view of several member states that the associates should not be penalized for achieving their independence and that Part IV of the Rome Treaty, which referred to countries which were not yet subjects of international law, should be replaced by an international agreement with the newly independent countries;[8] and
(3) More recently, the British insistence that the Commonwealth developing countries not be discriminated against with respect to the Community's early associates.[9]

The Yaoundé Conventions, which preceded Lomé, were concluded despite the growing distaste of several EC member states, in particular Germany[10] and the Netherlands, which could not see why they should accept what was in essence a French backyard and favored a world approach to development cooperation on a nondiscriminatory basis. The Dutch reluctance to sign the Yaoundé I agreement was so great that they made their agreement conditional upon the other five member states issuing a Declaration of Intent entitling countries "similar" to the EC associates to ask the Community for equivalent arrangements. Although the immediate effect of this declaration was very limited (Arusha Convention with the three member states of the East African Community [1969–75], and the accession of Mauritius to the Yaoundé II Convention), it was important in that it facilitated the enlargement of the EC partnership arrangements to include the twenty Commonwealth as well as some other countries which were judged to be in a "similar" position to the original associates.

According to Protocol 22, the EC offered twenty independent Commonwealth developing countries a choice of three formulas of relations with it: to participate in the Yaoundé Convention of Association; to conclude a less global Convention of Association (with the Arusha Convention in mind); or to conclude a simple trade agreement. The formulation of this offer was simply taken from the Declaration of Intent adopted by the Council in 1963, and was thus not submitted to the careful screening it would have deserved nearly ten years later. A differently worded offer would probably have required weeks of negotiations among the Nine. As a consequence, the so-called associable countries reacted very unfavorably to the offer, which they found to be drafted in a neocolonial style, as it gave the impression that Europe encouraged the disunity of its potential partners by offering to negotiate several types of agreements with them. Moreover, the most attractive offer, full association, was too clearly linked to the Yaoundé Convention (which many Commonwealth quarters viewed as a French neocolonial enterprise) and lacked flexibility. In particular, the associables were suspicious about the meaning of the Yaoundé institutional set-up which Portocol 22 wanted renewed. Finally, the very word "association," which in French also means "partnership," designated the status of those Commonwealth countries which still depended on Britain for their defense and foreign policies.

Nearly one year went by following the Community's offer before the Africans were able to surmount deeply rooted psychological difficulties to meet and discuss whether a joint answer to the Community was feasible. One of the major stumbling blocks was the "reverse preferences" issue. The Secretary-General of the Commonwealth, Mr. Arnold Smith, took the inappropriate initiative to stir up the associables' feelings on this issue and virtually proposed a negotiating function for the Commonwealth Secretariat.[11] Senegal's President, L. Senghor, added dry wood to the fire by staunchly supporting the reverse preferences as the best guarantee of Europe's long-term engagement with Africa. The U.S. added to the confusion by exerting pressure on EC member states to drop the reverse preferences from any new agreement with their developing partners. All this fuss was about an issue which no member state had strong feelings about except France, as benefits accruing to European exporters from past and potential reverse preferences were estimated as insignificant.

Eventually, under the guidance of UN Economic Commission for Africa (ECA) Secretary-General, Robert Gardiner, a serious attempt was made to discuss the EC's offer at the Ministerial ECA meeting, which took place in Accra in February 1973. Despite careful preparation by an expert group,[12] the item was deleted from the agenda immediately after the opening statements on request of several "associables,"[13] although it remained a major subject of discussion in the corridors.[14]

During the period prior to the Accra Conference, the Council's action was conspicuous for its absence. The same can be said for the COREPER. The

Commission decided not to make use of its right of initiative before it had a clear picture about the best line to take for successful negotiations. Disagreements among the Commission officials, none of whom had experience with Commonwealth countries, increased the amount of shuffling which could be normally expected in such a situation. But if some of the senior officials found it difficult to change long-established habits within the Yaoundé framework, including the working language, others favored change.

Thus, as far back as 1971, a high Commission official circulated a personal note on the enlargement of the Association. His main points were as follows:

(1) The "associable" countries would all opt for full "association," provided the EC took a sufficiently open attitude;

(2) The Community should encourage all attempts by potential partners to negotiate on the basis of the first formula so as to achieve the "great design" of cooperation with all independent black African countries;

(3) No valid economic reasons could justify differential treatment between Anglophone and Francophone countries in Africa, and consequently one single agreement with all of them should be favored;

(4) Europe should not miss the historic opportunity to contribute to overcome the divisions in Africa—divisions which Europe had contributed to and strengthened—thus showing a capacity for innovation with respect to single member states and enhancing the political and economic impact of the arrangements to be negotiated;

(5) The reverse preferences should be dropped, despite the reservations to be expected within GATT. The high official could not see how the GATT, faced with a choice between reciprocal and unilateral preferences in relations between developed and developing countries, could opt for the former; and

(6) The volume of financial aid should reach 3 to 3.3 billion EUA (European Unit of Account, equivalent to about $1.40), and part of it should be earmarked for regional cooperation; the most disadvantaged partners should be favored both under the trade and aid provisions: trade among the developing partners themselves should be encouraged; and special provisions for industrial cooperation promotion and export promotion should be added.

The Commission's preparations for the enlargement of the Association continued in 1972 through extended consultations with ECA officials, in particular with Secretary-General Gardiner, a staunch and early supporter of a great negotiation between Europe and Africa. Two Commission staff members[15] participated in the work of the expert group convened by the ECA and met in Accra during the two weeks preceding the 1973 ECA ministerial meeting. The same two officials were joined for the latter meeting by the Director-General and the Deputy Director-General of the Commission Development Department.[16] Their presence was instrumental in discussing (in the corridors) the EC's offer with a large number of Africans, notably Anglophone ministers. Two member states, France and Britain, participated in the conference as associated ECA members, and most other member states participated as observers. They also did their share of lobbying, in particular the French and British delegates.

The group of experts[17] consisted of over a dozen people invited in their personal capacity and of representatives of a number of international organizations. It was, however, joined by representatives of about ten African countries (uninvited) who were anxious about the outcome of the discussions. Discussions were centered around the so-called Philip Report on intra-African cooperation and relations with the EC.[18] Despite the active lobbying by some African participants, including several Yaoundé associates, in favor of a recommendation stressing the dangers of association, the final document on this issue implied that Africa would negotiate in a concerted fashion with Europe. This was also the major conclusion which Commission participants drew from the Accra Conference: all independent black African countries would join in a united front to negotiate with Europe, including those not referred to in Protocol 22. Commission officials had made it clear to Ethiopia, Liberia, Sudan, and Guinea that, if not Protocol 22, the Declaration of Intent of 1963 concerned them as well. The Conference had also shown that neither the ECA nor a fortiori the Commonwealth Secretariat would play a major role in the negotiations and that the OAU (Organization for African Unity), for political reasons, would be the body in charge on the African side.

The key question was whether the Community would accept the "great negotiation" without preconditions. On April 4, 1973, just over one month after the Accra Conference, the Commission produced a "Memorandum to the Council on the Future Relations between the Community, the present Associated States and the Countries in Africa, the Caribbean, the Indian and Pacific Oceans (ACP) referred to in Protocol 22 to the Act of Accession."[19] It may be interesting to give here an excerpt of the Commission's Memorandum, not only because of its importance, as it was instrumental in convincing the doubt-ridden Anglophone ACP to negotiate with the EC, but also because it gives a good impression of the way the Commission exerts its right of initiative:

In order to enable all the countries concerned to prepare their position with the best possible knowledge of the facts, the Commission considers that it is the Community's responsibility to set out what might in its view be the main characteristics of a "model" for association, capable of meeting the preoccupations of the countries involved as a whole. In outlining this "model," there can be no question of limiting the scope of the negotiations by setting up any prior conditions; what the Commission is seeking to do is to provide a concrete point of departure to enable negotiations to get under way.

The Commission stresses that it is clearly in the light of the course of the negotiation that each country, which initially chooses to participate, will make its final decision....

All participating countries retain the right to request the Community to negotiate and conclude an agreement on a different basis. If necessary, and at the appropriate moment, other forms of relations, also provided for in Protocol 22, could be negotiated. It is clear that these forms of relations would involve different methods and a different balance, characterized in general by undertakings of a more limited nature.[20]

The stand the Commmission took with this memorandum was in line with the conclusions some of its officials had drawn previously. It spoke of the need for a "genuine renovation of the Association"; stressed the "constructive and open frame of mind in which it intends to hold discussions"; opened the door to black African countries not referred to in Protocol 22 but "with comparable products and structure"; supported the principle of a free trade area, but made clear that it did not "entail any obligation to grant preferences to the Community"; proposed "new additional mechanism capable of providing effective solutions within a regional framework to the crucial problem of instability of export earnings from primary products," greater support to industrial as well as regional cooperation, a substantial increase in the Community's financial and technical cooperation, and a greater say for the Community's partners in its execution.

The Commission's most revolutionary suggestions (the Commodity Export Earnings Stabilization Scheme-STABEX[21] and the sugar agreement, the latter in a separate memorandum) were rooted in Protocol 22 where is was stated that "the Community will have as its firm purpose the safeguarding of the interests of all countries (concerned) whose economies depend to a considerable extent on the export of primary commodities, and in particular of sugar." Similar legal texts are an invaluable support to the Commission's right of initiative and capability to make policy.

In May 1973, one month after the publication of the Commission Memorandum, the OAU Summit in Addis Ababa produced an "eight-Point Charter" for negotiations with the European Community. Nigerian President Gowon's election as OAU Chairman made the direct involvement of the until then most reluctant African country in these negotiations inevitable. Nigeria, the most populous ACP country and a major oil producer, became the natural spokesman for the ACP. Many agree in attributing much of the merit of keeping the ACP united all throught the Lomé negotiations to the skill of the Nigerian Ambassador, Olu Sanu. This unity was enhanced by the common stand that the OPEC countries took on oil the very month in which these negotiations truly started (October 1973). It was equally enhanced by the Africans overcoming the weakness they had shown during the Yaoundé negotiations in the mastery of economic details. Whereas in the Yaoundé negotiations the Africans mostly posed problems, during the Lomé negotiations they often proposed the working hypothesis. An example of this was the ACP's successful insistence that the European Development Fund (EDF) delegates in the ACP countries enlarge their function from administration of the fund to trade, training, and economic relations in general and that they be responsible to the commissioner in charge of development rather than to the head of the EDF.

The Commission acted as negotiator for the "Nine" except during the few ministerial meetings. This was an innovation with respect to the Yaoundé negotiations, which were conducted under the direct responsibility of the Council (and COREPER). It was due to the fact that COREPER felt that it would have otherwise been overcommitted in work that appeared from the outset too difficult and complex not to be a full-time job. Most of the negotiations were conducted at the ambassadorial level. Very technical subjects were discussed first in "expert groups." The EC member states were present as observers and available for consultations on the Commission's request. The decision-making process in the Community was stimulated by the ACP's unity throughout, which the Commission supported as far as it could. Such a process was furthermore facilitated by mater-of-fact negotiations, a far cry from the aggressiveness which plagues UN meetings.

The Commission's stakes in these negotiations were very high. A successful enlargement of the association was bound to lead the Nine progressively to cooperate in their development policies (as part of their foreign policies), thus enhancing European political unity and Europe's outward-looking image. In fact, a new regional agreement was bound to make the political link work which the 1972 Paris Summit had established between improvements in Europe's regional approach to development cooperation and an "overall European policy of development cooperation on a worldwide scale."[22]

The European Council of Ministers let the negotiations get started without formal approval of the Commission's memoranda. Several of the relevant proposals met with more or less strong reservations from one or more member states. For instance, France was reluctant to "give away" the reverse preferences, strongly opposed any sugar agreement (which was largely relevant to the Commonwealth partners), but supported the STABEX. The latter was strongly opposed by Germany, which saw it as a danger for an untrammelled free-market system, and by the Netherlands, which supported negotiating world commodity agreements. The latter two countries were at best lukewarm about strengthening the regional approach to development cooperation. The British (and within Britain the multinational Tate and Lyle) lobbied intensively for a generous sugar agreement, but they had mixed feelings about these negotiations in general because they exluded the Asian Commonwealth members. Italy and the smaller member states mostly supported the Commission's views. In particular, Ireland played a very active role in the final marathon sessions when Foreign Minister G. Fitzgerald was in the Council's chair, and this allowed Ireland to play the first major direct foreign policy role in its history. In addition, the European Parliament supported the Commission. It played a role in the preparation stage when the European Parliament Committee on Cooperation and Development undertook a useful fact-finding visit to Africa, as well as during the negotiations leading to the resolutions it adopted on December 10, 1974.[23]

But it is fair to conclude that probably none of the most innovative aspects of the Lomé Convention would have been successfully negotiated without the Commission's ideas and initiative as well as the ACP's Committee of Ambassadors and Plenipotentiaries' unity and strong stance. This was recognized by the European Parliament in its reports on the Lomé Convention.[24]

Negotiations for the renewal of the Lomé Convention were formally opened in July 1978. Like the first negotiations, they were preceded by several Commission memoranda to the Council, and the latter has provided the former with a limited mandate to start negotiations, not having been in a position to agree on all the Commission's proposals. As during the 1973–74 talks, those proposals were controversial both within the EC and the ACPs. According to the Europeans, the new talks were not to deal with sweeping changes but with adjustments and improvements so as to consolidate the present convention. The ACPs disagreed with this view as being too minimalistic, though no counterproposals surfaced immediately. But soon the dialogue assumed a businesslike character (with some political overtones). Agreement was officially reached on October 31, 1979 for a new five-year period (March 1, 1980–February 28, 1985).

The Lomé II Convention is a global contractual agreement between the nine EC members and 58 ACP countries representing altogether more than 500 million people. One of the main features of Lomé II is free market access, without reciprocity, to the EC for 99.5 percent of the goods exported from the ACP and originating in these countries. Lomé II also contains the right to financial compensation (mostly on a grant basis) when any of 43 agricultural exports (plus iron ore, temporarily) of the ACP to the EC providing foreign exchange earnings fall below prescribed reference levels. The relevant system, called STABEX, differs from a compensatory financing mechanism in so far as it is a trade mechanism on a product-by-product basis and not on a balance-of-payments basis.

There are several other main features to Lomé II. There is an accident insurance scheme for six minerals (or groups thereof), called SYSMIN, whose aim is the safeguarding of the existing mining potential. When natural disasters, grave political events, or economic factors (a price collapse) cause a substantial (> 10 percent) fall in the production or export capacity of any of the six minerals by the ACP country, the EC is committed to make a special loan (10 years of grace with a 40 year amortization at 1 percent interest) to re-establish the original mining conditions. There is also a commodity agreement on raw sugar, according to which the ACP and the EC commit themselves to respectively sell and buy 1.4 million tons of sugar at prices close to the Community's domestic sugar prices (quasi-indexation).

Lomé II calls for industrial and technological cooperation that can benefit from a jointly-managed Center for Industrial Development. This is aimed at promoting a better international division of labor on lines advantageous to the

ACP. A reinforced trade consultation mechanism aims at providing mutually greater transparance of market prospects, notably on sensitive or product groups. Also present are investment promotion and protection provisions, according to which any investment agreements entered into by an EC member with an ACP country must be extended to other ACP countries asking for it and ready to subscribe to the same obligations. Moreover, specific agreements with rights and obligations may be sought by governments and firms concerning energy or mining projects.

A jointly-managed Technical Center for Agricultural and Rural Cooperation has been established to strengthen cooperation in the area of agriculture. There is also a framework for bilateral fishery agreements in which the EC provides concessions in exhange for fishing rights—three such agreements have already been signed—and increased coordination regarding conservation and utilization of fishery resources. There is also increased cooperation in sea transport. Lomé II also contains reciprocal undertakings to guarantee to the nationals of any one of the signatories of the convention legally residing in any signatory state the same working conditions, pay, and job-related social security benefits as nationals of that state.

The convention also calls for financial and technical assistance amounting to EUA 5,227 million (about US $7,500 million) for the duration of the convention, of which some 80 percent is in the form of grants and the rest is concessional assistance. This includes EUA 600 million for regional aid, EUA 200 million for emergency aid, EUA 550 million for the STABEX, EUA 280 million for the SYSMIN, and EUA 685 million in loans from the European Investment Bank. It excludes up to EUA 200 million that the EIB is committed to make available for projects of mutual interest in mining and energy in the ACP.

Finally, Lomé II has some common institutions. The administration of the Convention is the responsibility of the ACP-EC Council of Ministers assisted by a Joint Committee of Ambassadors. An ACP-EC Consultative Assembly, composed on a basis of parity of members of the European Parliament and of representatives designated by the ACP, holds periodical meetings with the aim to provide political impulse and advice to the ACP-EC Council.

The Formulation of the Community's Overall Mediterranean Policy[25]

The Mediterranean region was no doubt in the minds of the Mediterranean community legislators (France and Italy) who helped draft Article 238 of the Rome Treaty, which permits "new associations characterized by reciprocal rights and obligations."[26] This is confirmed by the combined reading Articles 133 and 134 (which are the basis of the preferential policy) and of Article 227, which refers to Algeria, as well as two declarations of intent[27] and one of protocol[28] that are annexed to the Treaty.

However, nowhere does the Rome Treaty mention the Mediterranean region as such, and, in essence, the subsequent formulation of the Community's Mediterranean policy relies on political considerations. It appears at least two Community member states, Italy and France, as well as the European Commission, were conscious from the very outset of the need to work out a global cooperation approach with the whole Mediterranean region. The first full-fledged proposal was the "Moro Memorandum," which the Italian Government submitted to the Council as far back as 1964. The Moro Memorandum supported the creation of a Mediterranean free-trade area for industrial goods, aid to be provided by the richer Community members to the less developed countries in the region, and limited concessions in the agricultural sector. The latter would be granted only on condition that the interests of the Community's Southern regions be properly dealt with through the necessary trade incentives, structural aids, and the establishment of a EC regional policy.[29] The Moro Memorandum was never seriously discussed in the Council, but it did play an important role in the Community's foreign policy formulation process. Two years later, in 1966, the Commission proposed to the Council a global cooperation approach to the Maghreb countries and asked for a mandate for exploratory talks. But this initiative also failed to get off the ground. The Commission then decided to go ahead on a more limited scale by exploiting fully the only instrument of development cooperation the Rome Treaty had given it, namely trade.

The Commission's action could be justified as follows: The preferential trade relations inherited by some EC member states[30] not only derogated to the most-favored nation GATT clause, but were also in contradiction with the unity of the European Common Market. As it was politically difficult to abolish such preferences, it appeared easier to extend them progressively to all Community member states until free-trade areas could eventually be established. Other convincing arguments for the Council were provided by the political pressures exerted by the non-Community Mediterranean countries themselves in favor of such arrangments. Thus, the Community became involved in a number of nonpreferential as well as preferential[31] trade agreements with Mediterranean countries for want of a global strategy.

The Commission was, however, aware that these trade agreements constituted no more than a first step and that the pressure of events would make it necessary to improve them later on. This was due to the disparity between the growing number of Mediterranean agreements, which would become increasingly difficult to justify and was politically unacceptable; the demonstration effect of the Yaoundé (later Lomé) model; and the increasing capacity the Community desired for foreign policy formulation and implementation. Hence, despite the failure of its proposal for a Maghreb policy in 1966, the Commission in its 1971 Memorandum on Development Cooperation struck out in favor of an even bolder initiative: a more homogeneous and effective policy in the whole Mediterranean basin.[32] This time, the Council responded favorably by inviting the Commission, in June 1972, to examine the overall pattern of relations between the Community and the Mediterranean countries.

Three months later, the Commission submitted its proposal for an overall cooperation policy with the Mediterranean basin covering trade, economic, technical, and social cooperation which recalled in many respects the Moro Memorandum of eight years earlier.[33] In October 1972, the Paris Summit of European Heads of State and Government (which included the three new members) took a stand in favor of an overall Mediterranean approach. The Council accepted the Commission proposal as a "working hypothesis" (notably the geographical spread as well as the free-trade area concept) in November, and issued its first negotiation directives to the Commission for the Maghreb countries and Israel (plus Spain) in June 1973. These were complemented by additional directives in July 1974 on the Commission's request.

In February 1973, the European Parliament somewhat belatedly blamed the Council, as well as the Commission, for having concluded an ill-defined set of agreements in the Mediterranean and demanded that they be made more consistent.[34] That the Community's Mediterranean policy suddenly gained momentum was not only due to an increased perception of the Community's economic and political interests in the region but also to the fact that the association agreements of Morocco and Tunisia expired in September 1972, which required some quick decision as to what to do next. Regarding the positions taken and the influence exerted by individual member states on the formulation of the Community's Mediterranean policy,[35] three groups may be distinguished: the Mediterranean coastline Community members (France and Italy), the "Atlanticists", and the other Northern European members.

The Italian position is the most complex and interesting one. Italy can benefit enormously from the Mediterranean policy, which allows it to move from the periphery of the present Community to the center of a larger integrated region. Moveover, such a policy is more fundamental to Italy's own security than to that of its northern partners. But Italy's economic vulnerability, and in particular the structural weakness of its "Mezzogiorno," does not allow her to undertake alone the structural adjustments called for by the increased competition it faces through the lowering of tariffs in the Mediterranean area. This explains why Italy fluctuated between bold initiatives (Moro Memorandum) and reluctance and why it was ready to compromise provided it could obtain some compensation for the sectors most affected by the Mediterranean policy. Hence, in April 1975 Italy refused to accept the additional concessions for Maghreb agricultural products proposed by the Commission unless compensation was provided by the Community for its southern farmers.[36] Equally, Italy favored granting better terms to migrant labor from the Maghreb, but on condition that Community preference for migrant workers from within the Community (mostly Italy) was clearly established.

Why has France, which had always been particularly reluctant to entrust the Community with foreign policy-making responsibilities, done so in the case of the Mediterranean? In essence, it found that it lacked the minimum economic and political dimension needed for a Mediterranean policy which was independent of that of the two superpowers and it felt that the Community instrument appeared the most appropriate for that purpose. However, in France's case, government action was hampered by the opposition of its farmers to concessions on agricultural imports as well as that of those manufacturing industries which had found it hard to compete with an increasing flow of cheaper goods exported from Mediterranean countries. The stiffest competition came from countries such as Spain, but more recently the argument had held also for some North African countries, such as Tunisia.

The Federal Republic of Germany, Great Britain, the Netherlands, and Denmark, despite their acceptance of the idea of an overall Mediterranean policy at the Paris Summit, clearly lacked enthusiasm and attempted more than once to remind their partners that any futher progress in cooperation with neighboring countries was linked with new Community initiatives in development cooperation worldwide. In addition, these countries wanted to avoid increasing the tensions that existed with the U.S.—displeased with, if not opposed to the Community's Mediterranean policy—which they feared might endanger the Atlantic Alliance. On the other hand, after the bankruptcy of the Hallstein doctrine, the FRG, felt that the Community's Mediterranean policy was well suited to facilitate contacts with the Arab states on a new basis. Belgium, Ireland, and Luxembourg all proved strong supporters of the Commission's Mediterranean initiatives.

It can be concluded that the divergent positions of the Community governments, as well as those of different economic lobbies and interest groups within single member states, tended to neutralize each other as to their effect on Mediterranean policy formulation. The result, until the early 1970s, was a zero-sum game. The situation changed later, but only because all the member states concluded that their general perception of their own interests had changed. The enlargement of the EC to Greece, Spain, and Portugal and the increase in weight of European pressure groups related to agriculture may to some extent reduce the prospects for further concessions to the Southern Mediterranean partners. On the other hand, politically as well as economically, the governments of Southern Europe will remain deeply interested in the Community's Mediterranean policy, from which they particularly expect to be able to derive benefits (if the appropriate safeguards are taken) for reasons which include geographical location and cultural similarity.

Negotiations were successfully completed in 1976 with the Maghreb countries on one side and with the Mashrek countries on the other, as well as with Israel and, in early 1977, with Lebanon. These Community's Southern Mediterranean partners now have free access to the European Common Market for an unlimited period for all primary commodities and all industrial products originating in their countries. The fundamental importance of such a guaranteed access for investors should be emphasized. Most now enjoy privileged access to the European Common Market regarding agricultural products, although there are several precautions (quotas, import timetables).

The Maghreb and Mashrek agreements do not involve obligations of reciprocity, but the Israeli agreement does. However, the liberalization of trade remains their ultimate objective once the gap between the partners' development levels has been reduced. Meanwhile, the Maghreb and Mashrek partners will grant the Community most-favored-nation status, though provisions allow them to discriminate in favor of other developing countries, as well as in the context of regional economic integration. The financial protocols, expiring in 1981, involve a total amount of 639 million EUA (equivalent to over U.S. $750 million), of which 339 million EUA is for the Maghreb, 270 million for the Mashrek, and 30 million for Israel. A considerable proportion of this is in the form of concessional flows, except in the case of Israel.

The Mediterranean agreements are global cooperation agreements of the Lomé type. The differences are related to the EC Mediterranean partners' greater geographic proximity, greater economic strength and greater competitiveness with European production and to political considerations. These differences include the lack of a STABEX or a SYSMIN system or of any arrangement along the lines of the Lomé sugar arrangement, smaller amounts of aid (relatively speaking), more limited access to the European Common Market, and the final goal of setting up a free-trade area (with "reverse preferences"). On the other hand, the Mediterranean agreements, unlike Lomé, are concluded for an unlimited duration. (Specific dates, the next is 1983, have been set for the examination of the results and possible improvements, within the framework of an ongoing institutionalized dialogue.) Clauses on social equality for migrant workers moving to the Community are included. Moreover, provisions are made for cooperation in relation to energy, encouraging participation by EC firms in prospecting, production, and conversion programs and the good management of long-term delivery contracts for oil products (for Algeria and Tunisia).

The European Community is not in a position, nor is it willing, to employ power politics in the Mediterranean. Its fundamental aim is to create a new Mediterranean order so that it can develop into an area of peace and prosperity. The Community believes that stable overall cooperation with all countries in the region on a nondiscriminatory basis will be of mutual advantage to all the countries concerned. Economically, their degree of interdependence is unequalled anywhere and can be futher enhanced. Politically, a Mediterranean "grand design" appears the best means for the partners involved to achieve a greater degree of control over foreign policy implementation with respect to their own region. This would obviously reduce the risks of war in the area and hence reduce the influence of the two superpowers. In 1975, Israeli Foreign Minister Allon in a press conference said: "In the Middle East, like in Europe, economic integration could represent an important factor of pacific coexistence. The EC's close links with both Israel and its neighbors should contribute to the establishment of the economic structure which is required in the region."

By contrast, the superpowers—which have been in essence hostile to the Community's Mediterranean policy—do not seem to be in a position to pursue a similar "grand design," as they have little chance of being able to establish the minimum of truly nondiscriminatory economic cooperation needed.[37] The overriding preoccupation of both the U.S. and the USSR is, quite understandably, their mutual relationship, in which the military balance plays a major role. But detente has had virtually no effect on peripheral conflicts where the superpowers face each other through their respective client states. These conflicts are stimulated and/or supported by the superpowers in particular in those areas where the sharing of zones of influence has not yet been made or fully accepted, such as the Middle East.

The prospects for Mediterranean cooperation would be greatly improved if the complementary nature of agricultural production between the northern and the southern coastline countries, which for "Mediterranean" products such as fruits and vegetables is at present limited to the winter season, could be increased. This would require the intermediate aim of a certain amount of planning of production and supply on the basis of a better agreed division of labor in the area. This could in turn involve long-term supply contracts, a measure repeatedly advocated by European Commissioner Claude Cheysson, providing purchase as well as supply guarantees to Mediterranean partners.

The study of the interactions existing between the Community's external and internal policies, which the Commission had devoted increasing attention in the context of the Mediterranean area, is leading to a greater awareness of the problems which affect the Community's southern regions, and may point the way towards their solution. The Community's external policy over the Mediterranean basin must eventually be internalized, and the signing of the cooperation agreements with its less-developed Mediterranean partners was therefore not only an important step toward assuming a greater responsibility in the area but also a bold initiative which implies the speeding up of structural change within the Community itself.

The Formulation of the Euro-Arab Dialogue

The Euro-Arab Diaglogue (EAD) supplements the Community's global agreements with eleven out of twenty-one member countries of the Arab League,[38] with which it has run in parallel despite its different character. The European Parliament's Committee on Development and Cooperation rightly pointed out that the expansion of the Yom Kippur War and its influence on Arab oil policy made it essential for the EC to define its attitude. On November 6, 1973, the Community foreign ministers published a declaration on the Middle East in which the EC summarized its position on the Middle East question.[39] If reaffirmed its commitment on UN Security Council Resolutions 238 and 242, stressed its opposition to Israel's territorial expansion in the wake of the 1967 June War, and stated that a just and lasting peace would have to take into account the legitimate rights of the Palestinians.

This declaration attracted immediate attention in the Arab world. Only two weeks later, the Arab Summit Conference in Algiers (November 26–28 1973) stressed the affinities between Arabs and Western Europeans and the importance of mutually beneficial cooperation. On December 14–15, 1973, the European heads of state and government, meeting for a summit in Copenhagen, received the unexpected visit of four Arab ministers, including two oil ministers (Algeria and Saudi Arabia). At the height of the oil embargo, the latter submitted a proposal on behalf of "the twenty" to enter into a dialogue with Europe. The Community's Copenhagen Declaration confirmed the importance of entering negotiations with oil-producing countries on comprehensive arrangements comprising cooperation on a wide scale for the economic and industrial development of these countries' industrial investments and stable energy supplies to the EC Member countries at reasonable prices. In January 1974, France presented a concrete plan for the initiation of an EAD, and in subsequent weeks a consensus formula was worked out. It expressed the view that the initiative should not hamper international efforts in the oil and raw material sectors nor interfere with the diplomatic efforts for a peaceful settlement in the Middle East.[40] On March 4, 1974, the governments of the Nine called for a meeting with the Arabs aimed at establishing the machinery necessary to start the Dialogue.

The latter was formally opened at a ministerial level meeting in Paris on July 31, 1974,[41] when the General Committee, the Dialogue's managing body, was instituted. Political difficulties delayed the start of formal talks with the result that the General Committee met for the first time only in May 1976. This did not prevent the EAD from gathering momentum in the course of three joint meetings—Cairo (June 10–14, 1975), Rome (July 22–24, 1975), and Abu Dhabi (November 22–27, 1975)—which helped define the general principles and the instruments of the Dialogue as well as discuss certain promising areas for cooperation in some detail.

The General Committee held its first session (at ambassadorial level) in Luxembourg on May 18–20, 1976, when it "established the organizational framework for the Dialogue so as to provide an institutionalized structure for the relations between the European Communities and the Arab World."[42] The General Committee's second session was held in Tunis, February 10–13, 1977; the third session was held in Brussels, October 26–28, 1977; and the fourth in the fall of 1978.[43]

The EAD idea is rooted in the perception on both sides that rapidly increasing economic interdependence and the growing importance of political relations between the two regions require greater coordination in defining common interests and priority objectives. But the EAD is not an easy dialogue. First, its genesis, in a climate of tension and confrontation, was hardly conducive to constructive cooperation. Second, "one of its difficulties," as Ismail Khelil has pointed out, is "that it takes place between two very different Communities. On the one hand an economic community, which has achieved its economic integration, to a large extent, and is embarking on political union; on the other hand, an Arab part which has not even started its economic coordination process." "The Arab World," Khelil adds, "is in the process of establishing a common foreign policy with Europe within the framework of the EAD and with Africa within the framework of the Afro-Arab Dialogue. However, it still lacks an inter-Arab policy."[44]

Similarly, the interests of the individual members of the Nine, who are commercial competitors in the important Arab market, are also different; and since the Community has no common foreign policy and the views of the member states on the Arab-Israel dispute vary, they cannot meet Arab desires for real political negotiations. Hence, it is likely that cooperation between Western Europe and the Arab world will initially have more positive results in the economic field. As the Schuijt Report says, "the long-term aim of this dialogue (EAD) should be economic interdependence between the two areas and the creation of a large single area around the Mediterranean." It adds that "this dialogue is not a question of exclusive relations between one side and the other, but involves close cooperation finding its natural basis in the geographical, historical, cultural and human circumstances."[45]

In the economic sphere, the mutual interests of Arabs and Europeans are very real. Europe's concerns relate to its lack of energy sources[46] and of space, its need for petrodollar investments in European industry, and its payments deficit with the oil producers. Europe needs to tap all the marketing possibilities in the area which the sudden increase in Arab wealth has created. On the other hand, the Arabs require Europe's technology and know-how and market, since their own markets do not provide a broad enough base for diversified industrial expansion. "The Arabs can purchase an industrial plant anywhere in the world, but only Europe is a real partner for what comes afterwards, and ultimately determines success or failure, namely, maintaining skilled production and selling their products in the long-term on markets which are within reach."[47] Moreover, reduced emigration prospects for their unemployed need to be counteracted with greater employment at home as well as with greater job stability for their migrant labor in Europe,[48] which Europe's cooperation could help bring about. Finally, they need the tourist income which provides a large proportion of foreign exchange.

Europe is a far more important trade partner for the Arabs than either the U.S. or the USSR. The Community is not only the principal client of the Arab

League, buying 40 percent of the latter's exports in 1975 (one and a half times as much as the U.S., Eastern Europe, and Japan together) but is also their foremost supplier providing close to one-half of the Arab League's total imports (half as much again as the U.S., Eastern Europe, and Japan together). Similarly, for the Community, the Arab countries represent its major export market outside the Community itself. They purchase over 14 percent of total Community exports, which compares with about 11 percent and 10 percent for the U.S. and Eastern Europe, respectively, 7 percent for the ACP countries, and 2 percent for Japan. Moreover, the Arabs are a key supplier of Community imports (over 20 percent of the total), in particular for oil and oil products (70 percent of the EC's relevant imports).

The organs of the Euro-Arab Dialogue are:

(1) The general committee (ambassadorial level), which establishes general guidelines for the Dialogue and meets about twice a year, mainly in restricted sessions (without minutes). Chairmanship is held jointly by the heads of the Arab and European delegations; and

(2) The working committee (expert level), which may submit specific proposals and recommendations to the general committee before embarking on their execution. They are equally cochaired by the two sides. Seven have been set up so far: Agriculture and Rural Development; Industrialization; Infrastructure; Financial Cooperation; Culture Labor and Social Affairs; Trade; and Scientific and Technological Cooperation. They may meet at any agreed time, alternatively in Europe and an Arab country. They are entitled to form specialized groups to carry out specific tasks (eighteen to date).

The first meeting of the General Committee also proposed the creation of a coordinating committee to deal with topics of a practical and administrative nature and to coordinate the business of the working committees under the supervision of the general committee. But so far there has been no need for it to meet. The chairmanship of each side rotates every six months; but for the Arab side these are lunar, not calendar months. In theory the two sides are each homogeneous, and national labels are not used. This device allowed the EC to accept a Palestinian presence among the Arab negotiators, and PLO representative Ahmed Sidki was the Arab spokesman in the political committee in Tunis. A meeting at the foreign ministerial level is a possibility for the future, despite initial European reluctance.[49]

For the Community, the EAD is a hybrid. Part falls within Community competence, and part is the responsibility of the machinery for political cooperation. The distinction between economic cooperation questions, which fall within the Community framework, and political questions, which fall within the national responsibilities, has been maintained so far in deference to what appears an increasingly old-fashioned concept of national sovereignty. The elimination of this distinction, which would be in line with the increasing difficulty of separating the political from the economic, would have created undesirable frictions with the larger EC countries (in particular France). European coordination is therefore carried out in parallel. The following remarks describe these parallel routes:

Some subjects (such as those affecting the Community budget, trade, Community scientific research, and labor matters) are considered by an ad hoc group which reports to COREPER. But the whole EAD package is considered by the European Coordinating Group consisting of the 9 Member States represented at Ambassador level (and presided over by whichever country is currently in the chair) plus the Commission, assisted as necessary by European co-chairmen of Working Committees. This coordinating group (which meets about monthly) may seek general orientations on political matters from the regular meetings of the European Political Directors in the political cooperation framework.

These two parallel routes for European coordination might theoretically be considered not to meet: COREPER reports to the Council of Ministers while the Political Directors report to the meetings of Ministers of Foreign Affairs for political cooperation. Since, however, these are in fact the same Ministers wearing different labels, there is no difficulty in practice.[50]

The first meeting of the General Committee put the Dialogue on a proper structural footing. The most important agreements reached so far, and passed on through directives to the group concerned, were on the following matters: financing of joint actions in the Dialogue, creation of a Euro-Arab center for the transfer of technology, multilateral Euro-Arab agreement on the protection of investments, general terms of industrial model contracts, launching of studies for agricultural projects, and trade relations.

This agreement on certain aspects of economic cooperation went in parallel with declarations of the two sides on *political matters*. In the joint communiqué following the Tunis Conference, the two sides stated their support for the establishment of a "just and lasting peace" in the Middle East, and for a solution to the Palestinian problem based on the recognition of the legitimate rights of the Palestinian people, which is essential for the conclusion of this peace. The European side reaffirmed the principles of the declaration of November 6, 1973, recognizing in particular the legitimate right of the Palestinian people to give effective expression to their national identity; its "anxieties" over the continued occupation by Israel of Arab territory, and that Europe oppose any policy directed at establishing "colonies" there, a policy "which could only result in endangering the prospects of peace"; its opposition to any attempt to change unilaterally the status of Jerusalem. (Which is why the EC Commission has refused to yield to repeated Israeli requests to open its delegation in Jerusalem instead of Tel Aviv.) The EC countries also declared themselves to be in favor of the independence, unity and territorial integrity of Lebanon. They also undertook to create a "committee for political consultation."

However, disagreements persist for the time being. In particular, the Arab side still demands a new overall preferential trade convention with the EC without reciprocity, aimed especially at the free entry of refined oil and derivatives. The EC has pointed to the existence of preferential agreements with eleven Arab League countries within the framework of Lomé and of its "overall" Mediterranean policy (which leaves only the two Yemens, among the poor Arab League members, out in the cold) and believes the General Scheme of Preferences offers sufficient export opportunities for the richer Arab countries. Europe's reluctance may be explained partly by its fear of a serious competive threat to its industry (in the future) if the Arabs were given free access. More seriously, it would be hard to justify the extension of preferential concessions made for poor developing countries to countries which are rich. In addition, any further expansion of the Community's preferential area would make it increasingly difficult to resist requests of other countries to negotiate similar agreements. Finally, the Community may be inhibited by U.S. pressures aimed at preventing the extension of its preferential area beyond the Mediterranean.

To the Arabs, the Dialogue is a means of confirming their hope that between the two superpowers, who are involved in a dangerous international game, there is a peaceful source of support: the European Community. The great hope the Arabs pin on the EAD hinges on their belief that the Community's political role, in the long term, will be important enough to keep them out of the rivalry between the superpowers. In addition, the oil producers expect that direct Euro-Arab producer consumer cooperation could help them reduce the influence of foreign (mostly American) multinational companies in the area (whose role has not always been confined to economics) in what is essentially a sellers' market. They feel, particularly Algeria and Libya, that the Italian and French oil policies point to the possibility that the Europeans might be able to disengage themselves from the control of oil distribution of the "seven sisters."[51]

Europe was quick to recognize with its Middle East declaration in 1973 that the economic dimension of its regional cooperation in the Mediterranean and beyond could not be safeguarded unless set in a political framework. Its reluctance to act on this belief was overcome more by instinct than reason, despite the clear political stake which it had from the security point of view in a resolution of the Palestinian imbroglio. Some Europeans, in particular in the south, even believe that the EAD could allow Europe to regain its traditional influence in the Mediterranean area and to use it to support the equality of rights and duties of all the countries in the region and the attainment of a truly peaceful coexistence and cooperation. But politics has proved an important source of disagreement in the context of the EAD stemming marginally from disagreements between those members of the Arab League that want to emphasize politics and the EC which is reluctant to do so, possibly in part as a result of U.S. influence. Europe's ineffectiveness in curing this situation so far lies, of course, in the continuing weakness of its political coordination process, which may sometimes be aggravated in this case by fears of displeasing the U.S.

The Nixon-Ford administration (in particular Dr. Kissinger) was apparently suspicious of the EAD because members preferred the (Kissinger) plan of setting up a bloc of industrialized oil importers and engaging in confrontation tactics in order to bring the prices of oil to "more reasonable" levels. They also preferred the political role of Europe in the region to remain limited and feared that the Dialogue might disturb the politico-economic balance the superpowers had established in the Mediterranean area. For this reason, the U.S. asked the EC not to publish their foreign minister's statement on the Middle East of December 1976, even after the U.S. had published its own statement (April 1977). The Community, however, resolved to do so on June 20, 1977 after Egypt had stepped up Arab pressures to this effect (June 22, 1977).[52]

After the Camp David Agreement, the EAD was temporarily interrupted because of disagreements within the Arab League. But at the end of 1979, it was decided to resume the talks although this would not be easy if Egypt were to be kept in the picture, as the Community wished. It appears that Europe will move increasingly toward supporting true self-determination for the Palestinian people. This is likely to help the EAD. At the same time, the West Germans have advocated the negotiation of a nonpreferential trade and cooperation agreement with the Gulf states. It is not clear whether this will have any effect on the EAD.

Conclusions and Prospects

The European Community has gone a long way toward achieving its first foreign policy objective as spelled out in the 1972 European Summit Conference in Paris: a more favorable response to the expectations of the LDCs through the policy of association, an overall and balanced approach in the Mediterranean basin, and the progressive adoption of an overall policy of development cooperation on a worldwide scale. In this context the Community's foreign policy decision-making procedure has proved cumbersome but effective.

This procedure, which assigns a pivotal role to the Commission, has allowed the latter not only to give the Europeans a new perception of their dependence on the LDCs and of changing economic power relationships but also to work out and implement, piece by piece, a new approach of external relations in line with this perception. In this process, the Commission has proved able to take advantage of external factors calling for Community reaction; to channel the support existing within the member states or organizations, as well as mobilize that of undecided European actors for its proposals, which represent what the

Commission perceives as the European interest; and to work out together with the other major Community institutions the compromises necessary to make the Community system work and play a greater role in international affairs. In this area, to use Gerhard Mally's term, events do confirm the Commission's role as an "internal federator."

In the area of north-south relations, it has proved particularly difficult to maintain the traditional distinction between economic cooperation questions (which may fall within the Community framework) and political questions (which fall within the national responsibilities of the member states) in view of the increasing difficulty of separating the political from the economic. Recent Community coordination and development cooperation with regard to the Horn of Africa have clearly taken into account political considerations. The same holds true for the Community's Mediterranean policy. "As to the procedure adopted by the Community in the EAD," Commissioner Cheysson has stated that "the Commission has every possibility to exert its right of initiative and will not refrain from using its rights to give its opinion also on subjects which are not strictly speaking included in the Rome Treaty." The EAD might well help speed up the process of Community integration by dropping the artificial (juridical) screen separating Community economic from political issues. The Community's development policy ought to be seen more and more in the context of nonalignment, although it would be very far-fetched to say that this is not in all European minds, for nonalignment is not only ideological, it is also a politico-economic concept. The Lomé policy—said Claude Cheysson— exists only insofar as no one is "aligned."

If one or the other side makes attempts or pressures in favour of any political alignment, the Lomé policy is dead. . . . The Africans are aware of the fact that, among their foreign relations, there exists only one which is completely nonaligned, because it is based on a contract and is a fact of all of them: the Lomé agreements with Europe.[53]

The nonaligned countries—three of whose five founders came from the Euro-Afro-Arab Grouping[54]—tend to look toward the Community as a reasonable guarantee against neocolonial practices of some of the major powers. Why? First, "Europe" lacks hegemonic aspirations, which disagreements among member states' government policy goals would make impossible anyway. Moreover, Europe appears a more neutral and, why not, a more "nonaligned" entity than the two superpowers, since it is more flexible ideologically and therefore more inclined to accept the partners' full right to choose their own development models, be they Arab socialism (which is nonmaterialistic), Yugoslav self-management, Marxism-Leninism, or capitalism.

This essay may convey the impression that the Community's development policy achievements were obtained fairly smoothly; it may also lead to the conclusion that the Community's future prospects in this policy area are as bright as its past performance appears to justify. But this is not so. The Community's foreign policy formation process is particularly complex because it is based on multi-factor linkages of the tenth order (the number of member states plus the Community) and notably those between historical circumstances, legal texts, interactions between internal and external policies, perceptions of national, Community, and institutional interests, and personality factors. All of those factors have been described in this essay except the last, which might well be the most important.

The Community's development policy formation process has proved that coordination among, as well as within national bureaucracies, is an antagonistic process, particularly when it involves a perceived transfer of power which may in fact be a net addition of power. This may be aggravated by lack of flexibility of individual negotiators who may fight to one ditch beyond what their respective country or institution would have been ready to accept. Member states' reluctance to extend Community responsibility to new areas has often resulted—as in the examples given here—in refined legal debates on the Commission's international negotiating capacity and on Community representation on specific issues.

Both inter and intra-bureaucracy coordination are to a good extent a matter of personalities. This is obviously true within the Commission as well. Differences in ideological positions or approaches at the top, as well as of key lower staff drafting or commenting on Commission proposals, have inevitably led to internal tensions (for example, on STABEX). This has been particularly true since Claude Cheysson (a French Socialist) became Commissioner for Development in 1973. On the other hand, those tensions have proved constructive. Much is due to the remarkable vision and skill shown by Cheysson, a forceful personality who proved ready to take unorthodox initiatives and to fight them through, if development cooperation became the Community's success story in a period of crisis as the early 1970s.

Future prospects are uncertain and very much depend on urgent progress in the Community's domestic policies. This is because the Community's foreign policies increasingly impinge on the Community's own economy. In particular, the growing linkages between the Community's trade and development cooperation policies sometimes have grave repercussions on the European Common Market and in particular on employment in its poorer regions. As Commissioner Cheysson has said, "When a development aid policy ceases to be marginal, when it goes beyond financial aid, it becomes a domestic policy in the industrial countries."[55]

A fundamental contradiction has indeed surfaced within the Community between an external laissez faire policy and the internal mixed policies of the member states. In particular, the liberalization of the EC's external trade, which has been a goal of its development cooperation policy, has created pressures for the structural adjustment of the Community's production system with the related social costs, which must be borne by the member states. In order to reduce these social costs, the member states are tempted to resort to the use of national instruments of protection, which are still in their own hands (subsidies, taxes, credits) and to do so in an uncoordinated way and in contradiction to the Community's (or indeed their own) foreign policies. Since these social costs are the product of Community policies (in this instance, the cooperation policy—notably trade and financial assistance—with the developing countries) and are not necessarily distributed among the member states in the same way as the benefits, there are real grounds for a closer link between the Community's progress towards the liberalization of its trade and the implementation at the Community level of policies which provide for both the social cost to be borne and the process of internal adjustment to be accelerated.[56]

If there is to be further liberalization of trade, particularly with the developing countries, it is necessary, first, to adapt the means available to the Community for conducting a policy of structural adjustment (social fund, regional fund, European Agricultural Guidance Fund, European Investment Bank, European Coal and Steel Community, industrial policy); second, to take into account the interactions between these aspects of external policy and relevant aspects of the internal policies (industrial, employment, regional, energy); and third, to establish regular consultations with country groupings enjoying free access to the EC, such as the Lomé and Mediterranean partners. Insofar as these internal policies actively promote redeployment toward more competitive productions within the Community, time-limited import controls might be justified. The alternative could be the replacement of a liberal Community by autarchic member states. In fact, the free-trade option is increasingly difficult to maintain in the absence of a rapid return to full employment in the Community countries. Trade liberalization remains an overriding Community interest since it is largely geared to international trade and is finding in the developing countries a growing market for its exports (36 percent of the 1976 total). But without a greater coherence between the Community's internal and external policies the latter, and particularly the trade and development cooperation policies, could soon be approaching their ceiling.

The study of the interactions between the Community's external, notably development, and internal policies is one of the Commission's major tasks today. It is in line with a request of the European Council of Development Ministers of November 8, 1976, and it implies substantial progess in the coordination of the economic policies of the EC member states. This coherence exercise, which started in the spring of 1977, is possibly the greatest challenge the Community has faced so far. If it succeeds, it will mean the extension of Community competence over existing and/or new common policy areas. If it fails, it could mean a plunge back into autarchy and the disintegration of the Community or, at best, a very painful and dangerous standstill at a time when progress is called for by the difficulties of enlargement to Greece, Spain, and Portugal.

Notes

1. The 1970 Davignon Report contributed to national officials' gradual acceptance of the need to "think European," and it was a modest but practical step in creating a Europe "capable of speaking with one voice." The Davignon Report led to the Political Cooperation Effort, which is an essentially intergovernmental effort based on two diplomatic protocols (but without legal treaty foundations) involving coordination of viewpoints on those fields of foreign relations not covered by the Treaties through regular consultations three times a year for heads of government, more frequently for foreign ministers and political directors. The latter constitutes what is called the "Davignon Committee" (or European Political Committee).

2. Commission of the European Communities (EC), *Memorandum de la Commission sur une Politique Communautaire de Coopération au Développement* (SEC[71] 2700 Final).

3. EC, *Memorandum de la Commission sur une Politique Communautaire de Coopération au Développement: Programme pour une Première Série d'Actions* (SEC[72] 320 Final).

4. EC, "Development Cooperation: Towards Community Policy on a Worldwide Scale," *EC Bulletin* 7/8 (1974). Nonassociated countries are developing countries not party to the Community's global contractual agreements.

5. EC, "Development Aid: Fresco of Community Action Tomorrow" (Communication of the Commission to the Council on November 5, 1974), *EC Bulletin*, Supplement 8/74.

6. Since Community action needs to be based on legal grounds, the legal services of the Community are entrusted to find (or "fabricate") the legal arguments of a decision which is usually based on reasons of a different nature.

7. The official reason given by France was that its colonies and overseas departments would have otherwise lost the preferences they enjoyed on the French market. The French request led to Part IV of the Rome Treaty.

8. This led to the Yaoundé I (1963–68) and Yaoundé II (1969–75) conventions with eighteen, later nineteen, African countries. It is safe to assume that without Yaoundé I, the Community would probably not have a policy of development cooperation at present.

9. This led to Protocol 22 to the Act of Accession of the UK, Denmark, and Ireland to the EC (1972).

10. If the need for a decision as vital as that of Yaoundé I had arisen ten years later, instead of in 1963, it is possible that a more assertive Germany would have vetoed it.

11. Arnold Smith convened a series of preparatory meetings for the Commonwealth countries concerned in London in order to consider the options open to them regarding their future relations with the EC. Moreover, he envisaged a meeting of Commonwealth associates to take place after the Accra Conference.

12. Economic Commission for Africa, *Report of the Panel of Experts on Intra-African Economic Cooperation and Africa's Relations with the EEC* (Accra, 10–15 February 1973), Conference of Ministers Second Meeting, Accra, February 19–23, 1973, E/CN.14/584.

13. This had been agreed at a last-minute meeting, organized on request of an East African delegation, of all Commonwealth African countries which took place in Lagos during the preceding weekend. It was meant to avoid a split before agreement could be found among such countries on a common approach to the EC.

14. Only the Kenyan Minister, Mr. Kibaki, took the liberty to state at the Conference that all cliches be forgotten (Yaoundé, Arusha, and so on) and that a new single formula be worked out, to be named later.

15. Mr. D. Frisch and the author of this essay.

16. Mr. H.-B. Krohn and Mr. M. Foley. The latter was the first British national appointed to the Development Department of the Commission, which he joined after having relinquished a Parliament seat in Britain; as a former junior minister for Commonwealth affairs, he had many friends and acquaintances among the African ministers. The former became the day-to-day negotiator of the agreement and may well be called its "father."

17. This group met in Accra between February 10–15, 1973, with Mr. Asante, Principal Secretary, Foreign Affairs, Ghana, in the chair.

18. Economic Commission for Africa, *Intra-African Economic Cooperation and Africa's Relations with the European Community* (Report prepared by a team led by Professor Kjeld Philip), E/CN.14/L.409, 1973.

19. EC, Doc. COM 500 final. Reprinted in *EC Bulletin*, Supplement 1/73 (January-1973).

20. Memorandum, paragraph 4, p. 4, and paragraph 6, p. 6.

21. The Commission worked out the STABEX proposal as a necessary compensation for the dilution caused by the association's enlargement of the preferences previously enjoyed by the Yaoundé associates and for the effects of the forthcoming multilateral trade negotiations under GATT on the preferences to be granted to the ACPs.

22. See D. Frisch, "Perspektiven der Assozierung aus der Sicht der Europäischen Gemeinschaft", IFO, Forschungsbericht der Afrika Studienstelle (Research Report by The African Department), no. 49, Weltforum Verlag, Dok. 722 C 2 B/DT/4-1973.

23. More important is the role the European Parliament has been able to play in supporting the Commission's request for funds needed to implement the worldwide development policy that it had been advocating and had formulated for some time. For instance, during the procedure for the 1976 budget, the Parliament in its draft budget reinstated 20 million EUA (U.S. $28 million) of aid to non-associates of the 100 million EUA provided for in the Commission's original proposal but dropped in the Council's draft. For the 1977 budget, the Commission proposed 120 million EUA, the Council reduced this figure to 30 million EUA, and the Parliament raised it again to 45 million EUA. The same happened with the 1978 budget, where it raised the relevant figure to 70 million, and the 1979 budget where it raised it to 110 million. An increase to 150 million is expected in the 1980 budget.

24. European Parliament, "Flesch Report," PE 41.182, October 10, 1975, Document 283/75.

25. Though this policy concerns in principle all Mediterranean coastline countries (except Yugoslavia and Albania) plus Jordan, the following analysis will not refer to forthcoming or other potential new members of the EC in that area (Greece, Spain, Portugal, Turkey).

26. France had the Maghreb (as well as Indochina) in mind; and Italy, Libya. The latter has been unwilling to negotiate with the Community so far, but there are signs that their attitude may be changing.

27. Declaration of Intent on the association of the independent countries of the Franc Area with the EC (Morocco and Tunisia), and Declaration of Intent on the association of the Kingdom of Lybia with the EC.

28. Protocol on goods originating and coming from certain countries and enjoying special treatment when imported into a member state.

29. Ph. Petit-Laurent, *Les fondements politiques des engagements de la Communauté Européenne en Méditerranée* (Paris: Presses Universitaires de France, 1976), p. 87.

30. The Maghreb countries within the Franc Zone; Malta and Cyprus within the Commonwealth.

31. The 1969 agreements with Morocco and Tunisia were confusingly called "association agreements," though they are strictly speaking preferential trade agreements.

32. "La Commission estime qu'il est de l'intérêt de la Communauté de rechercher les moyens de donner aux engagements actuels, d'une part, plus d'homogénéité et, d'autre part, plus d'efficacité en complétant progressivement les dispositions commerciales des accords par un volet de

coopération technique et financière englobant certains aspects sociaux. Ainsi confère-t-on à la politique communautaire à l'égard des pays du Bassin Méditerranéen les instruments nécessaires à une cooperération équilibrée et reciproque au sens large du terme." EC, *Memorandum de la Commission sur une Politique Communautaire de Coopération au Développement* (SEC[71] 2700 Final).

33. It is not clear what role the Algerian request for an association agreement including financial and technical assistance played in the Commission's proposal and/or the Council's decision.

34. See the Rossi Report by the European Parliament's Commission of External Relations.

35. Petit-Laurent, *Les Fondements Politiques*, pp. 83–89, 118–20.

36. In this case, the uproar caused in the Arab world by the early signing of the EC-Israel agreement in 1975—which seemed for a moment to jeopardize the Euro-Arab Dialogue—helped to break the deadlock, as the Community agreed unanimously to reestablish the usual parallelism between its relations with Israel, on the one hand, and with the Arabs on the other by speeding up the conclusion of the Maghreb agreements. It seems that several Community officials pushed for the signature of the agreement with Israel, which had been ready for some time, as the best way to break the Maghreb deadlock (ibid., p. 116).

37. Petit-Laurent points to an "incompatibility" between the Mediterranean countries and the two superpowers, which leads him to believe that any nonmilitary aid provided by the latter within the Mediterranean region would be tantamount to financing the "rapprochement" of the recipient countries and the EC, their irreplaceable partner.

38. Mauritania, Somalia, Sudan, and Djibouti under the Lomé agreement; Algeria, Morocco, and Tunisia under the Maghreb agreements; and Egypt, Jordan, Lebanon, and Syria under the Mashrek agreements. These countries represent 75 percent of the total population of the Arab League. Community aid commitments to these countries total 800 million EUA in 1977–81 (not counting bilateral aid from EC member states), or about one-fifth of total commitments of Community financial and technical assistance proper, excluding food and emergency aids, to the Afro-Arab region.

39. European Parliament, *Draft Report on Trade Relations between the European Community and the Countries of the African Continent* (Rapporteur, Mr. W. J. Schuijt), PE 45.547, September 14, 1976.

40. Ibid., paragraph 32.

Galley 108 pg 504-1

41. Participating in this meeting on the European side, Mr. Sauvagnargues, French Foreign Minister and President-in-Office of the European Council of Ministers, and EC Commision President, Mr. Ortoli; on the Arab side, Kuwaiti Foreign Minister, Sheikh Sabbah, President-in-Office of the Arab League at the time, and Arab League Secretary-General Mr. Mahmoud Riad.

42. Paragraph 11 of the EAD Luxembourg Final Communiqué.

43. The Arab cochairmen are usually the Secretary-General of the Arab League and the Arab Ambassador in Brussels of the country chairing the Arab League. The European cochairmen are the Commission Director-General for Development (at present Mr. Klaus Meyer) and the undersecretary of the country holding the presidency of the EC.

44. Khelil believes that the Tunisian recommendation to the Arab League for the creation of a permanent secretariat in Brussels could fill this gap, as "This secretariat could be the necessay coordinating body." Interview by H. Arafa for *Dialogue* review, no. 129, February 21, 1977, Tunis. Translated by the author.

45. Schuijt, *Draft Report*, paragraph 37.

46. Europe imports 80 percent of its oil consumption, 70 percent of which is supplied by the Arab producers. It depends on oil for about half of its total energy supplies. Security of oil supplies clearly appears the ideal Arab bargaining tool for obtaining free access to the EC.

47. Schuijt, *Draft Report*, paragraph 35.

48. The relevant remittances are their third most important source of foreign exchange revenue after oil and tourism.

49. The EAD Luxembourg Final Communiqué (final paragraph) says, "Both sides expressed their expectation that a Euro-Arab Dialogue meeting on the level of Foreign Ministers be held at an appropriate date. They agreed to consider practical steps for the preparation of this meeting."

50. These remarks are from an internal note on the structure of the EAD by Christopher MacRae, February 24, 1977, EC Commission. The European Parliament follows the EAD through its Foreign Affairs Committee rather than through its Committee on Development and Cooperation, as is the case for the Lomé and Mediterranean cooperation agreements.

51. Petit-Laurent, *Les Fondements Politiques*, p. 48.

52. This might explain the "blitz" visit of U.S. Treasury Undersecretary Mr. Gerald Parsky to Abu Dhabi in 1975 which coincided with the third Euro-Arab joint meeting (November 22–27). Parsky spoke of a new deal between the Arabs and the U.S.—a theme very similar in scope and content to the EAD, which was meeting next door. U.S. officials claimed that the timing of Parsky's visit was not intentional. It may only be a coincidence, but the Arab request to exclude energy (other than oil refining and petrochemicals) from the EAD coincided exactly with Parsky's visit.

53. Quoted in an interview in the *Nouvel Observateur*, "Expliquer les Drames de l'Afrique par la Seule Rivalité Est-Ouest Est une Tromperie" (August 5, 1978).

54. Tito (Yugoslavia), Nasser (Egypt), and Nkrumah (Ghana); the other two being Nehru (India) and Sukarno (Indonesia).

55. At a symposium on a NIEO (New International Economic Order) held in The Hague (May 22–24, 1975), Ministry of Foreign Affairs, the Netherlands.

56. EC, *Reciprocal Implications of the Community's Development Cooperation Policy and its Other Policies: The General Issues*, Staff Paper, R.I.P., no. 1, SEC (77) 2060. This report led to the creation of a study group under the chairmanship of Paul-Marc Henry, which reported to the Commission in 1978 under the title "The European Economic Community and Changes in the International Division of Labor." (Brussels, January, 1979).

12

EC-US Relations in the Post-Kissinger Era

In the immediate postwar era, the United States saw its role as the benevolent defender of democracies. The bipolar structure of the balance of power at that time placed several countries and groupings of countries under U.S. protection with the latter's nuclear umbrella and, in some cases, with the presence of ground forces. Several treaties and alliances were signed NATO (North Atlantic Treaty Organization), SEATO (Southeast Asian Treaty Organization), ANZUS (Australia, New Zealand and U.S. Treaty Organization), and its relationship with Western Europe was conceived as a partnership in the context of an Atlantic Alliance within which the United States would remain *primus inter pares*, or the senior partner. The United States linked its own security with that of Western Europe, and the U.S. assumed the primary initiative for organizing and funding this defense.

These perspectives were guided by an image of the global system where there were clear centers of power, the basis of which was military with nuclear capability at the core. An East-West axis dictated an American system of alliances, shaped and guided by the United States. Zbigniew Brzezinski, currently Special Assistant to the President for National Affairs, during an address at Blacksburg, Virginia, in April 1974, indicated that out of the Second World War there had emerged a new international system, shaped largely by the United States on the basis of an Atlantic connection. In contrast to its predecessor, the system became Atlantic-centered, American-protected, and New York-financed.[1] He went on to state that the system was based on several optimistic assumptions, including the notion that Atlantic cooperation would parallel European unity and that the latter itself would not be incompatible with the notion of Atlantic cooperation.

The European Community was a byproduct of United States support for European recovery based on the Marshall Plan. Assistance was conditioned on the understanding that European countries reach an agreement concerning their economic requirements and the part that they would take in giving effect to U.S. support. Within less than a year the Organization for European Economic Cooperation (OEEC) was established to assist in the administration of the program.

The several distinct efforts and phases of European Community evolution— ECSC (European Coal and Steel Community), EDC (European Defense Community), EPC (European Political Community), Euratom (European Atomic Energy Agency), and EEC (European Economic Community)— were met with formal U.S. diplomatic support. Developments in Europe during the 1960s were viewed as supporting basic U.S. interests. A spokesman on U.S. policy in 1963, J. Robert Schartzel, then Deputy Assistant Secretary of State for European Affairs, who later served from 1966–72 as Head of the U.S. Mission to the EC, stated that the Atlantic partnership was to serve American security, the vitality and growth of her economy, and the ability of the United States with its Western European allies to meet the growing requirements of the less developed countries for capital and markets.[2]

The Nixon Years

In addressing the course of American foreign policy for the 1970s, the Nixon Doctrine called into question the traditional U.S. hegemonial role. The President maintained the United States to be in a period of transition toward that time when it would exert its power and leadership less directly, as the self-reliance of the allies increased and the pattern of international politics became more multipolar. Robert Osgood in 1973 summarized this revised outlook:

The United States will support its existing commitments but will be very reluctant to undertake new ones. It will remain politically engaged in behalf of Japan and the NATO allies and continue to manage their regional security, but it will continue moderate retrenchment of its military presence as the allies take up a larger share of their security burden and as the achievement of negotiated mutual balanced force reductions in Europe may permit.[3]

In 1973, the Nixon administration proclaimed the "Year of Europe." With U.S. involvement terminated in Vietnam and the President's visits to Peking and Moscow on record, Washington turned its attention to Western Europe and Japan. In April, in an address to the Associated Press, Henry Kissinger put forward a series of proposals for Western stabilization. His call for a "New Atlantic Charter" was an appeal for a revived Atlantic Alliance, which was interpreted by the Europeans as an implication that they were to manage their own local affairs with global affairs left to the United States with its "global interests and responsibilities." Kissinger indicated in his address that "for us, European unity is what it always has been—not an end in itself but a means of strengthening of the West."

As the 1970s unfolded, the United States became increasingly aware of a shift in global issues from military to economic. While the United States had expected to lead the Western world militarily, it was questionable whether it could lead the developed world economically. Ralf Dahrendorf underscored this shift in the context of a basic change in the world power structure, reaching its first climax with the Yom Kippur War of 1973: "Whatever this war is remembered for in the Middle East, the rest of the world is more likely to think of the oil embargo, the rise in the price of energy, and the consequent aggravation of the impending recession."[4]

In evaluating its policies toward Western Europe during the Nixon administration, the United States became faced with the necessity of reassessing its political and economic strength. Its military strength dictated commitments, suggestive of leadership priorities, in response to which the United States became overcommitted economically. It perceived a major challenge to its international economic and monetary position, particularly evident in its dealings with Western Europe and later Japan. President Nixon's New Economic Policy, initiated in August 1971, underscored his concern for the deteriorating state of the U.S. balance of payments. In his efforts to provide redress, he imposed a surcharge of 10 percent on all imports not already subject to quota restriction; provided temporary export subsidies for American corporations; called for a 10 percent reduction in foreign aid; and introduced, in the spring of 1973, a proposal for new trade legislation, which became known as the Trade Reform Act. Whereas its predecessor, the Trade Expansion Act of 1962, had emphasized the liberalization of world trade, the new act was viewed as protectionist. Its main feature gave the President the authority to raise, lower, or eliminate American tariffs, plus a simplification of the authority to raise import barriers against countries which unreasonably restricted U.S. exports. It contained a general provision allowing the raising or lowering of import restrictions in order to keep the balance of payments in equilibrium and combat inflation.

Nixon had aimed toward a reform of the international monetary system and wished to realign Western currencies in order to limit U.S. imports and boost its exports. Paralleling these efforts was the desire further to remove trade barriers alleged to curtail American exports to Western Europe, particularly relating to agricultural commodities. Although the United States had a consistent surplus in its balance of trade with EC, the latter's Common Agricultural Policy was viewed as protectionist. The American efforts, particularly following the passage of the Trade Reform Act, were viewed by the Europeans as protectionist. European critics argued that the New Economic Policy was an attempt to unload a purely American problem on the shoulders of other nations.

Early in 1972, the United States and the EC concluded an "agreement in principle" on interim arrangements to ease trade difficulties between them pending a general settlement, with negotiations in (GATT) General Agreement on Tariffs and Trade scheduled the following year. The agenda was to have included talks regarding nontariff trade barriers and national agricultural policies. A ministerial meeting of GATT was held in Tokyo in September 1973. It has subsequently been called the "Tokyo Round," a name which the continuing negotiations have maintained, although the meetings have been shifted to Geneva. The initial Tokyo Declaration underscored the economic competition between the U.S. and the EC and its reconciliation became basic to the foreign policy projected when Jimmy Carter entered office. The president-elect announced as his first foreign policy task the repairing of American relations with the Western European allies. This was in part based on an assumption that these relations had been neglected by Henry Kissinger, an assumption two years out of date. As Secretary of State, following the termination of hostilities in Southeast Asia, Kissinger had become a frequent visitor in European capitals, to the point that European leaders were known to favor a Ford victory, partly to extend these renewed collaborations.

The Post-Kissinger Era

The Post-Kissinger Era gave immediate emphasis to economic issues, viewed in the context of relations among the developed nations. The cornerstone of the Carter administration's new foreign policy was subsumed under the label "Trilateralism," prescribing primarily the relationship between the United States and the principle democratic, industrialized, market-economy countries. The term was generated by the Trilateral Commission, an organization of influential private citizens from these countries and whose membership included Zbigniew Brzezinski and Richard Cooper, the future Assistant Secretary of State for Economic Affairs. Among the objectives outlined by the Trilateral Commission were the formation of joint policymaking institutions among the allied nations of Western Europe, Japan, and North America (anticipating coordination on foreign policy and economic planning); a need for the allied industrial countries of Western Europe, Japan, and the United States to act as a unit in coordinating economic and political relations with the Third World and the Communist bloc nations; and a restructuring of international economic institutions through the reform of the International Monetary Fund by making the latter a federal reserve bank for the world economy.[5]

The ultimate result, according to Brzezinski, would be "a community of the developed nations."[6] The three points of the triangle were the United States, Western Europe, and Japan—the loci of the bulk of the world's productive capacity. Trilateralism was intended as a reaction to the former Treasury Secretary John Connally-dominated economic policy of the Nixon administration, a policy based upon the assumption that Western Europe and Japan had prospered at American expense and that the dynamism of their economies had come because of U.S. leadership.

Trilateralism was an uncertain basis upon which to restructure relations, particularly with Western Europe. Could it represent a shared leadership role for the developed states or would it be styled more as a means to recapture status as the first among equals? Various U.S. administrations have referred to a partnership, but without guarantees as to its nature. When during the 1950s the United States supported European unification movements, partly as a basis for focusing Western European initiative, it was the hegemonic power. The geopolitical map has drastically changed, and now Western Europe and the United States bargain from positions of varying strengths. While the balance in security matters still weighs in favor of the United States, the balance in economic relations is shifting to Western Europe.

In focusing on relations with Western Europe there remains the question, What is Western Europe? In commenting on a European perspective relative to international power, Ralf Dahrendorf asks whether Europe is the participants in the Conference on Security and Cooperation, the members of the Council of Europe, or the European Community.[7] He responds that "the ambiguities of Europe, and the European Community in particular, have given rise to two conclusions which have influenced the foreign policy of powers, including the United States." The conclusions are that there is and is not a European Community, yet he indicates both to be wrong. Although the latter may not be regarded as a natural partner, neither do its members act as unguided by similar attitudes.

In an analysis of the Western Alliance in the 1970s, William Diebold focused directly on the Community of Nine, as institutionalized in the EEC. Yet U.S. policy in general relates to those countries which are included in the (OECD) Organization for Economic Cooperation and Development, whose membership overlaps with the EC, (EFTA) European Free Trade Association, and the Council of Europe. The EC itself is not a single entity but an evolving relationship where participants retain individual initiative in various international political, economic, and monetary matters. Since 1973, the expansion from six to nine; the affiliation and possible membership of Greece, Spain, and Portugal; the associate status of Turkey and Malta; the special concessions to the remaining members of EFTA; and the signing of the Lomé Convention have clouded the character of the Europe to which the United States is to relate.

Before the election in 1976 some European diplomats were saying a Carter victory would be the EC's best hope. As a candidate, Carter had offered both a promise and a challenge by saying, "I believe that we should deal with Brussels on economic issues to the extent that the Europeans themselves make Brussels the focus of their decisions."[8] In the first week of the Carter administration, Vice President Walter Mondale paid a visit to the EC's headquarters. He expressed the new administrations's desire to improve consultations between the EC Commission and the U.S. government. In April, the new President of the Commission, Roy Jenkins, was second only to the British Prime Minister as a major European figure to meet the new U.S. President. At these meetings President Carter gave support for the Commission President to be present in his own right at the scheduled economic summit in London. Carter himself visited the EC Commission during his European tour in January 1978. During his meeting with the Commission President, he emphasized that his administration was more committed to backing European integration than those of his predecessors. He also suggested that he and Jenkins should meet every six months in the future.

Relations with Western Europe, the OECD, and the EC are in part determined by the role that the latter is itself permitted to play in European affairs. The EC is not a political union. There are at present three European Communities: ECSC, EEC, and Euratom. All have shared one Commission since 1965, but each have separate legal personalities. The activities of the EEC have received more attention as its objectives focus on the establishment of a basis for a closer union among the European nations. Since 1968, the Community has been governed by a complete Customs Union, with freedom of movement of workers in the Community. In 1969, work began on an economic and monetary union, a common commercial policy toward third countries, and the establishment of procedures whereby the economic policies of the member states could be coordinated and disequilibria in their balances of payments remedied. At a Paris "summit" in October 1972, the Nine affirmed the aim of "Economic Union" by the end of 1980. While work progressed on common external trade policies and the coordination of financial commercial, economic, and social policies, the economic recession that followed the 1973 OPEC oil price increase delayed further efforts for achieving economic union by the target date.

Since 1970, the foreign ministers of the members have met at least twice yearly to consult on foreign policy. At their December 1974 "summit," Leo Tindemans, Prime Minister of Belgium, was invited to submit a "comprehensive report on an overall concept of European Union." His report, published on January 7, 1976, stressed that member states should accept an obligation to reach a common foreign policy on major issues, if necessary by majority rather than unanimous voting. It was suggested that such a policy could begin with the less developed countries, the United States, defense, and non-EC European countries.

While the report was meant to restore some sense of purpose to the Community, the economic conditions within the EC during the succeeding year reflected a split between the economically stronger and weaker member states, evidenced by different inflation rates, growth rates, and living standards. The economic gaps within the EC were reflected in a series of monetary crises in the member states. The economic disunity within the Community was exacerbated by the difficulties within the wider world economic situation. By 1976 the Community had become decreasingly relevant as a forum where global problems of recession, inflation, or monetary crisis could be thrashed out. The EC suffered a loss of economic competence to wider international bodies like the IMF, the OECD, and the institution of regular summits of the industrialized countries.

The status of the Community was questioned during the Rome meetings in March 1977. In a difficult compromise it was agreed that Roy Jenkins could be their representative at the economic summit to be held in London in May. The smaller countries had not been invited to the two previous economic summits (Rambouillet in 1975 and Puerto Rico in 1976), and they desired to have their interests represented at London. The strongest opposition was offered by French President Giscard d' Estaing, who opposed measures that could enhance the powers of the EC Commission. He was persuaded to change his position whereby the Community would have a "technical presence" in Jenkins' participation. The Commission President became an ex officio participant in the areas which concerned the EC directly (north-south dialogue, multilateral GATT negotiations, and energy policy).

The status of the Community was also questioned by the slow progress toward a monetary union. Full economic integration requires that the member countries coordinate their monetary policies to avoid balance-of-payments difficulties and severe unemployment or inflation. Without coordination, the growth patterns within the Community will remain uneven. As the EC moves toward wider monetary control, there emerges the question of a single currency, with eventual development of an institution similar to the Federal Reserve System in the United States. Inflationary pressures during the late 1970s have suggested a need for currency reform on a European scale. Advocates have given the name "Europa" to a European currency proposed to parallel national money, convertible into national currencies at rates guaranteeing stability of purchasing power over goods and services.

In July 1972, various members of the EC, plus Norway and Sweden agreed to an exchange rate parity club referred to as the "snake." However, the United Kingdom and the Irish Republic remained out of the club, and both Italy (February 1973) and France (between January 1974, and July 1975, and again in March 1976) left. The agreement was that fluctuations of individual currencies would be limited so that the strongest and the weakest should not deviate from each other by more than 2.25 percent of the value of the strongest, the effect of which was to create a deutschmark currency bloc. The snake was seen by some supporters as a step toward economic and monetary union.

When the heads of governments of the EC met in Copenhagen in April 1978, interest was revived in development of a "European currency zone," partly to create a new basis for defining the U.S. dollar's relationship to European currencies and, by including the weaker currencies, to keep the stronger ones from floating too high. Three months later, at Bremen, the European Community Council (the name given to the regular meetings of the EC heads of government) agreed to establish within six months a European Currency Unit (ECU). The plan called for a gradual linking of Community currencies, beginning in 1979, to "float" against the U.S. dollar and a $50 billion reserve. Initially the proposed system would be run by the central banks of the member countries, but within two years control would pass to a new Community institution which would run the European Monetary Fund and police governments' observance of agreed policy guidelines. The intent of the Bremen framework is to stabilize European currencies and promote an inflation-free, market-oriented, European economic system, concentrating on making technologically sophisticated products. Under the leadership of German policy makers, there has been an effort to institute a development strategy as a complement to the broader monetary union. The vehicle for this would be the European Investment Bank, an institution which, like the wider European monetary union, would draw much of its funding from West Germany.

The Carter administration has indicated that it will monitor the European currency system to determine that it does not threaten international exchange rules or undermine the IMF. The United States, through Undersecretary Cooper, has indicated that it would oppose exchange market intervention of a kind that promoted European exchange rate stability but had an adverse "side effect" on the dollar market. European reserve holdings include "substantial" amounts of dollars, and it was the uncertainty of these dollar holdings that led the Western European governments, although not eager to undermine the dollar, to seek a substitute. EC members hope to achieve exchange stability by reestablishing among themselves a fixed-exchange-rate system similar to the Bretton Woods system that collapsed in 1971, when President Nixon suspended the convertibility of the dollar into gold. Under the Bretton Woods agreements, the international monetary system had been constructed in the form of a gold exchange standard based on the dollar, with the United States functioning as central banker. In practice this meant that the amount of new money placed in circulation depended mainly on the magnitude of the annual deficits in the United States' balance of payments. When the world's demand for new money exceeded the supply available, the United States ran deficits.

By 1958, however, the demand for new money no longer exceeded the supply. The United States foreign disbursements exceeded its earnings and it began to finance its international spending essentially on credit. Many countries, particularly in Western Europe, came to hold a larger proportion of their reserves in dollars; the holdings of which, in effect, extended credit to the United States.

With the emergence of the EC, the status of the dollar was challenged, particularly by the German deutschmark. The situation was further stimulated by the Eurodollar market, through which the credit pool of the dollar deposits was allowed to expand beyond the control of the U.S. Treasury. The combined bank deposits in external currencies, whether in Eurodollars or other Eurocurrencies, rose from $1 billion in 1961, to a total of $220 billion in 1974, doubling again by 1978. Huge international capital flows, especially during crises, placed considerable stress on the fixed-exchange-rate system.

During the 1970s, two factors emerged which further undermined the American balance of payments. While suffering periods of recession, the American economy, in balance, was growing faster than foreign economies, particularly those of Western Europe and Japan. This caused Americans to increase foreign purchases. In addition, the rise in oil prices meant an increasing proportion of the trade deficit was due to a single import. The result was an increase in the number of dollars, which if not held by American creditors, would be devalued. During the Nixon-Ford administrations, the United States had proposed that emerging payment imbalances be corrected quickly by small changes for the currencies, with the creditors taking as much of the adjustment burden as the debtors. The Europeans indicated that the United States was asking them to finance its monetary excesses by revaluating their currencies whenever the United States fell into deficit, as well as holding more dollars in their reserves. They desired that the dollar be made fully convertible, with the United States accepting more responsibility for the dollar balances the rest of the world held.

The context of continued U.S.-Western European dialogue became evident during the economic summits which unfolded between 1975 and 1978. The initial conference held at Rambouillet (November 1975) included six major industrial countries (the U.S., Britain, France, West Germany, Italy, and Japan). In June the following year, in Puerto Rico, Canada was added to the membership. Discussion has consistently focused on currencies, trade, economic growth, energy, and relations with developing countries. The five items are not separate but form the basis of an economic package. While most of these concerns received a place on the agenda during the summit in London (May 1977), the focus rested primarily on an effort to reach agreement with respect to tariff and nontariff barriers to trade pending in the multilateral negotiations within GATT. At Bonn (July 1978), emphasis shifted to the achievement of a more balanced pattern of growth among the industrial nations. Under discussion were a series of measures designed to create a more favorable climate for growth, energy conservation, stabilization of currency markets, trade liberalization, and expanded aid to developing countries.

As in past summits, the Europeans and Japanese focused on the American trade deficit, due in no small measure to the high oil imports. The Europeans and Americans lobbied the Japanese to reduce their trade surplus. The Europeans accused both Japan and the United States of protectionism. The Americans pressured the Japanese and the Germans to stimulate the growth of their economies. The U.S. economy had continued to grow faster than those of its trading partners. The result has been an inflation rate of over 8 percent averaged over the first two years of the Carter administration. The feeding of dollars into the world economy has continued with an annual U.S. trade deficit approaching $30 billion, four times a record set first in 1972. The U.S. position remains that Germany and Japan, as leaders, should attract more imports and reduce their trade surpluses. Among the seven industrial nations at the summits, the Germans had slowed their inflation to the lowest (2.4 percent).

To achieve long-term sustained growth, it has been important to free up trade. As the 1970s drew to a close, however, there was growing recourse to protectionism throughout the Western industrialized countries. In referring to the period since 1975, Fernard Spaak, head of the Washington delegation of the Commission of the European Communities, indicated that

with few exceptions trade deficits piled up, partly as a result of the ever increasing cost of imported oil. The response to all that has been a flurry of requests and demands for protection, both in the United States and Europe, that surpasses anything since the Depression of the 1930s.[9]

Trade liberalization, not restrictions, had been the agenda since the conclusion of the Kennedy Round in 1967. As a part of the Smithsonian Agreement on exchange rates in December 1971, they agreed to embark on a broad-based trade negotiation, which was approved in Tokyo. The Tokyo Declaration underscored the economic competition between the U.S. and the EC and its reconciliation came to be basic to the Carter administration.

A timetable for the trade negotiations was agreed to by the U.S. and the EC in July 1977, with January 15, 1978, designated as the ultimate date for putting all the trade issues on the table in Geneva. Although ninety-seven countries were to be involved in the negotiations, the real bargaining remained between these two giants who together account for two-thirds of world trade. Moreover, the relative positions between the two had shifted. By 1975 the total population in the Community was just short of 260 million, compared with 212 million for the United States. Its gross domestic product was $1,362 billion, within $200 billion of equaling the latter.[10] By 1978, the Community's volume of imports (excluding trade among its members) was $178 billion, against $130 billion for the United States; and the volume of exports (again excluding trade among members) was $158 billion, against $115 billion for the U.S. The EC had become both the world's largest importer and exporter, with its foreign trade accounting for 25 percent of its gross domestic product.[11] Most Western European countries, however, trade chiefly with one another: in 1976, of the exports of the European members of the OECD, 65.9 percent stayed within its borders and 59.8 percent of its imports came from the same area. The EC was the principal trading area for its nine members, with 51.3 percent of EC exports and 48.9 percent or EC imports staying in the area. West Germany was the most important single trading partner of the other eight: 12.7 percent of the exports of the eight went to West Germany, and 13.1 percent of their imports came from there. In addition, Western Europe, in 1976, was more important to the United States as a customer than the United States was to Western Europe. The United States had directed 27.9 percent of all its exports to Western Europe, with only 5.6 percent of the latter's exports going to the United States. The trade surplus with Western Europe for the United States was $9.4 billion, at a time when its worldwide trade deficit was $6.8 billion.

The United States remained a principal supporter of free trade, particularly regarding access to world markets for its own industrial and agricultural products. However, new competition, inflation, slowed economic growth, and unemployment on both sides of the Atlantic transformed relationships between individual economies and the international trade system. Trade liberalization was no longer viewed as working automatically in favor of American interests.

In the negotiations preceding the Tokyo Declaration some Europeans, influenced by the French president, stressed that a stable monetary system was a prerequisite for pursuing successful trade talks. The French were reluctant at the time to negotiate tariff concessions without knowing the advantage U.S. exports would gain through possible future dollar devaluations. Other European Community countries, especially West Germany, had preferred to keep trade and monetary negotiations separate. The then U.S. Secretary of the Treasury George Shultz had recognized the relationship between monetary matters and trade but warned that progress in one area of negotiation should not be "held hostage" to progress in another. At the same time, the United States pressed that negotiations toward trade liberalization include concessions on farm trade as part of any agreement on industrial products.

The Europeans have been less attached than the Americans to free trade in the farm sector. The CAP represents a common effort to sustain agricultural incomes at a fixed minimum. The result has been a protected market with the added feature of Community subsidies for farm exports to support the sale of agricultural surpluses at low prices on the world market. With the entry of the United Kingdom, the CAP system raised the level of protection of the British market and stimulated a higher level of Community production, thus encouraging the purchase of French and German products and threatening U.S. grains. An additional problem posed for the United States was competition in third country markets by those countries no longer having Commonwealth preferences with the British. The United States has repeatedly attacked the protectionism of the Common Agricultural Policy, urging a modification to permit increased American exports of agricultural commodities. American criticism is viewed in the Community as deceptive since for farm products of which the United States is an importer rather than an exporter it has had its own farm protection system through GATT waivers and through quotas on such items as dairy products.

The traditional goals of trade negotiations have been augmented to include new issues. The GATT agenda following the Toyko Declaration was extended beyond the traditional goal of lowering tariff barriers and included three issues for the advanced countries: domestic policies that distort international competition (such as nontariff barriers, export credits, and subsidies to industries); devising better safeguard clauses; and ensuring access to raw materials. Nontariff barriers relate to procedures which impair reductions in import duties, and these are particularly evident in the valued-added levies forming part of the CAP. Other barriers are evident in various labelling regulations, quantitative reductions, licensing controls, antidumping measures, and tax discrimination between domestic and foreign goods.

The main protagonists in the reactivated trade talks under the auspices of GATT have been the U.S. and the EC. While Japan has often been in the middle, it has appeared to go along with the agreements reached by the other two. The negotiations preceding and following the Bonn summit (July 1978) focused on basic arguments on codes aimed at curbing trade restrictions in five areas: (1) standards that served as barriers to trade (auto emission rules, packaging and labelling requirements, and food and drug regulations); (2) customs valuation systems deliberately designed to hold down imports (American "selling price" system); (3) safeguards that governments impose to protect industries against surges of imports (the "escape clause" restrictions); (4) subsidies that distort trade patterns (European government aids to steelmakers and regional development schemes); and (5) discrimination against foreign goods in purchasing by government agencies.

A priority for the United States has been the effort to open up purchasing by foreign governments with provision for open and nondiscriminatory bidding on government contracts, many of them often awarded solely to local suppliers with no public disclosure. U.S. and EC proposals have varied. The United States had desired governments to open up official purchasing of products worth an estimated $50 billion yearly to exporters signing the code. The EC has proposed to exclude most items of particular interest to the United States, such as railroad, telecommunications, and heavy electrical equipment. The proposed codes would require the United States to scrap its Buy American Act (1933). The United States claims, however, that concessions from the EC are insufficient to persuade the Congress to repeal the Act. The EC desires to keep selective restrictions against products of individual countries. In the negotiations on standards, the aim has been to ensure "transparency," with foreign suppliers retaining a say in the process via public hearings.

The toughest negotiations have involved government subsidies to industries where the purpose has been to achieve domestic goals, such as maintaining employment or helping depressed regions. A proposed code would attempt to set guidelines defining what types of subsidies are excessive. While willing to pledge not to use subsidies that distort trade, the EC has been unwilling to identify them specifically. The United States government itself has been cautious in accepting legally binding restrictions. An additional stumbling block remains in agricultural products. Officials in the Geneva discussion maintained that without an agreement on farm products a broader accord would remain in danger. Farm products are the biggest export item for the United States. As part of a package, the Europeans have insisted on commodity agreements for wheat and food grains. The EC wanted an international stockpile of wheat from which sales would automatically be made when the world price climbed to a specific level; conversely, stockpile accumulations would be made to boost sagging price levels. The United States held out against rigid maximum and minimum prices, favoring a flexible system spread over several levels, based on consultations rather than automatic actions. It also wanted wheat-producing countries to agree to reduce production during times of low prices, and consuming countries to agree to reduce purchases when prices were high.

U.S. industries and farms shipped $120 billion worth of goods in 1977, more than any other single country. But U.S. imports soared to $147 billion, creating a $27 billion trade deficit. At the same time, West Germany alone managed a surplus of $18 billion, partly through increased sales to the United States. This led some writers to conclude that U.S. industry was unable to compete in world markets, due in part to anti-export policies of both the Congress and successive administrations.[12] In addition, U.S. payments for oil imports alone constituted one-third of the total purchases ($45 billion in 1977), equal to almost double the trade deficit in the same period. Thus, there was a growing impatience in Western Europe with the United States to adopt an energy policy that would address the difficulty. Some U.S. policymakers have held that the trade gap would automatically be closed by an economic revival abroad and by depreciation of the dollar under a system of floating exchange rates. In part, the trade gap has reflected a slower economic recovery in Europe and Japan at a time when the United States was at the peak of a business expansion, resulting in a strengthening demand in the United States for foreign products and a weak demand in those countries for U.S. goods.

The Carter administration, both at London and again at Bonn, attempted to persuade Western Europe, particularly West Germany, and Japan to increase efforts to stimulate their economies. Adjustments in the value of the dollar, while reflecting a U.S. imbalance in trade, also reflected differences in inflation rates in respect to both Western Europe and Japan. The Western

European and Japanese economies had not kept pace with the United States. Some economists began to reflect that the differences were derived from a transformed relationship between the economies of the industrialized and the less developed countries. This is a reflection of an emerging new world economic system. The growing economic strength of the developing countries has compounded the difficulties of the European and Japanese more than the United States because they have been more dependent on exports. The rise in protectionism has been in large part a response to growing competition from the advanced developing countries, with a severe reaction occurring in Western Europe. In an effort to approach the competition from the developing counties, many economists have pressed for an increase in trade through a faster growth. The desire is for the United States, Western Europe, and Japan to reach agreement on a coordinated program of expansion. A catch has been a split between the Western Europeans and Japanese on the one hand and the United States on the other over the means for spurring growth with the high cost of energy. American actions—or lack of them—on energy policy appeared a power play to improve the U.S. position in world trade at the expense of the other developed countries.[13]

The huge oil imports have inflated the United States foreign trade deficit, weakening the dollar as an international basis of exchange. Some members of OPEC pressed to raise oil prices to recoup their loss in revenues while oil is priced in U.S. dollars. An American energy program is expected to reduce the U.S. trade deficit and relieve pressure on the dollar, restoring both American purchasing power and the value of dollar holdings. OPEC might then cut prices, to the benefit of all industrial countries. In the interim, some members of the thirteen-nation OPEC group began pegging oil prices to a basket of currencies instead of to U.S. dollars.

During the first eighteen months of the Carter administration, the dollar lost 10 percent of its value in the international monetary system. Western Europeans remained worried over the weak level against their currencies. They pressed the United States to fight inflation by slowing its economic growth rate in order to ease the flow of additional dollars into the international market. They were inclined to blame their own lack of investment and expansion on the decline of the dollar itself. The European monetary system was in part an effort to create a currency bloc as a complement, or even substitute, for the dollar. In the early stages of implementation the realignment of European currencies, however, put additional pressure on the dollar, moving the German mark, to which the European currencies were tied, toward being competitive with the dollar. The realization emerged that the German mark was increasingly undervalued, given West Germany's low inflation rate.

Conclusions and Prospects

The Carter administration initially focused on an awareness of an interdependency among the three developed areas: North America, Western Europe, and Japan. It hoped for a shared leadership suggesting concessions on all points of the triangle. The thrust of Trilateralism was that these areas would pump up their economies in order to expand their ability to buy foreign goods. Growing interdependency was viewed as requiring "positive" international coordination, moving beyond the reduction of barriers to trade, to monetary and fiscal plans. The latter did not evolve. Western Europe and Japan did not stimulate their economies. The Japanese surplus in trade was at the expense of both the United States and Western Europe. While the United States suffered a growing trade deficit, this was not with Western Europe but rather as a result of the unrestrained imports of oil forcing the price of the latter up at the expense of Western Europe, and the United States entered 1979 with continuing balance-of-payments deficits and pressures on the dollar.

Although the EC remains economic rather than political, the significance of economic issues in foreign policies has stimulated cooperation among the members. The economic differences between Western Europe and the United States have brought the leadership in the Community closer together. At both the London and Bonn summit meetings, West German Chancellor Schmidt and French President Giscard d'Estaing moved toward closer cooperation, most evident in their agreement to join with the President of the European Commission, Roy Jenkins, in support of a European Monetary Union. The proposed monetary system has the potential for creating a substitute for the U.S. dollar as an international reserve, freeing Western Europe from its dependency upon the latter. The development of a Community institution, paralleling the U.S. Federal Reserve Bank, will focus attention on common monetary policies and controls.

Until now the EC has not functioned as a single entity. Steps toward economic union in the early 1980s will alter relationships with third countries, particularly the United States. The U.S. is itself instrumental in these developments. Continued deficits undermining the status of the dollar in an evolving new world economic system, lack of an effective U.S. energy policy, and the increased emphasis on an achievement of a balanced pattern of growth among industrial nations places a significance on intra-European cooperation. The byproduct of Trilateralism has been increased cooperation within the EC, and its enlargement (Spain, Portugal, and Greece) will create an entity with a quarter of the world's trade.

Trade liberalization was for several decades following the Second World War the cornerstone of U.S. and Western European foreign economic policies. Competition, inflation, slowed economic growth, and unemployment within the industrialized nations have led to various forms of protectionism. Efforts to contain the latter through renewed trade negotiations have opened discussions concerning the nature of the international monetary system itself. Monetary union in Western Europe has the potential of placing Western Europe in a coordinate role with the United States in the international economic system. This is a change not evident until the summit conferences in 1977 and 1978.

It was not until the London summit meeting that the European Community was directly represented in the discussions among the Western industrialized countries. Prior negotiations had taken place among the heads of government. Presently, the European heads meet as a European Council prior to the summits. They arrive with agreement on priorities and options. Prospects for further economic union and an integrated European foreign economic policy rest with the stabilization of a European currency. Should the latter be successful, the European Community will henceforth negotiate with the United States as a unit.

Notes

1. As quoted in *European Community* (July 1974): 10.
2. As quoted by Livingston T. Merchant, "Evolving United States Relations with the Atlantic Community," in *The Atlantic Community*, ed. Francis O. Wilcox and H. Field Haviland, Jr., (London: Frederick A. Praeger, 1963), p. 96.
3. Robert E. Osgood, "How New Will the New American Foreign Policy Be?," in *The New Era in American Foreign Policy*, ed. John H. Gilbert, (New York: St. Martin's Press, 1973), p. 77.
4. Ralf Dahrendorf, "International Power: A European Perspective," *Foreign Affairs* Vol. 56, no. 1 (October 1977): 77.
5. See the *Christian Science Monitor*, February 14, 1977.
6. Zbigniew Brezezinski, "U.S. Foreign Policy: The Search for Focus," *Foreign Affairs* 51, 4 (July 1973): 727.
7. Dahrendorf, "International Power," p. 73.
8. As quoted in the *Christian Science Monitor*, November 10, 1976.
9. As quoted in *European Community* (July-August 1978): 6.
10. Ibid. (January-February 1977): 20.
11. Ibid. (January 1978): 8.
12. *Business Week* (April 10, 1978): 54–66.
13. Ibid. (July 24, 1978): 7.

Abbreviations

ACPs	African, Caribbean, Pacific
ANZUS	Australia, New Zealand and United States Treaty Organization
Association	Association of Cooperative Savings and Credit Institutions of the European Community
AUAs	Agricultural Units of Account
Benelux	Belgium, The Netherlands, and Luxembourg
BEUC	European Bureau of Consumer's Association
BFEC	Banking Federation of the European Community
CAP	Common Agricultural Policy
CCC	Consumer Consultative Committee
CCRPM	Consultative Committee on Restrictive Practices and Monopolies
CDU	Christian Democratic Union
CEA	European Insurance Committee
CEEP	European Center of Public Enterprises
CERES	Centre d'Etudes, de Recherche, et d'Education Socialistes
CET	Common external tariff
CIBE	Confederation of European Sugar Beet Producers
CIC	International Confederation of Executive Staffs
CIF	International Organization of National and International Public Service Unions

cif	Cost, insurance, and freight
CGIL	Confederazione Generale Italiana del Lavoro
CGT	Confédération Générale du Travail
CMLR	Common Market Law Reports
COCCEE	Committee of Commercial Organizations of the European Community
COFACE	Committee of Family Organizations in the European Community
COMEPRA	European Committee for Agricultural Progress
COPA	Committee of Professional Agricultural Organizations in the European Community
CPR/COREPER	Committee of Permanent Representatives
CSU	Christian Social Union
DBV	German Farmers' Union
DG	Directorate-General
DM	Deutschmark
EAD	Euro-Arab Dialogue
EAGGF	European Agriculture Guidance and Guarantee Fund
EC	European Community
ECA	(UN) Economic Commission for Africa
ECFTU	European Confederation of Free Trade Unions
ECR	European Court Reports
ECSC	European Coal and Steel Community
ECU	European Currency Unit
EDC	European Defense Community
EDF	European Development Fund
EEB	European Bureau of the Environment
EEC	European Economic Community
EFTA	European Free Trade Association
EIB	European Investment Bank
ELC	Employers' Liaison Committee
EMS	European Monetary System
EMU	European Monetary Union
EO/WCL	European Organization of the World Confederation of Labor
EP	European Parliament
EPC	European Political Community
ERP	European Recovery Program
ESC	Economic and Social Committee
ETUC	European Trade Union Confederation
EUAs	European Units of Account
EURATOM	European Atomic Energy Community
EUROCOOP	European Community of Consumer's Cooperatives
EUROPMI	Liaison Committee for Small and Medium-Sized Industrial Enterprises in the European Community
FB	Belgian franc
FDP	Free Democratic Party
FNPL	National Federation of Milk Producers
FOB	Free on board

FIPMEC	International Federation of Small and Medium-Sized Enterprises
FRG	Federal Republic of Germany
GATT	General Agreement on Tariffs and Trade
GCECEE	Savings Banks Group of the European Community
GDP	Gross domestic product
GNP	Gross national product
GP	General Practitioner
GSP	Generalized System of Tariff Preferences
ICFTU	International Confederation of Free Trade Unions
IEA	International Energy Agency
IfD	Institut für Demoskopie Allensbach
IMF	International Monetary Fund
LC/IRU	Liaison Committee of Professional Road Transport of the European Community
LDCs	Less developed countries
MCAs	Monetary Compensatory Amounts
MFN	Most favored nation
MNCs	Multinational corporations
MTOE	Million tons of oil equivalent
NATO	North Atlantic Treaty Organization
NHS	National Health Service
OAPEC	Organization of Arab Petroleum Exporting Countries
OAU	Organization for African Unity
OECD	Organization for Economic Cooperation and Development
OEEC	Organization for European Economic Cooperation
OPEC	Organization of Petroleum Exporting Countries
PC	Permanent Conference of Chambers of Commerce and Industry of the European Community
PCF	Parti communiste français
PCI	Italian Communist Party
PS	Parti socialiste
PSI	Italian Socialist Party
RA	Relative acceptance
SABAM	Belgian Association of Authors, Composers, and Music Publishers
SEATO	Southeast Asia Treaty Organization
SEPLIS	European Secretariat of the Liberal, Intellectual, and Social Professions
SOFRES	Société française d'Etudes pour Sondages
SPD	Social Democratic Party
STABEX	Commodity Export Earnings Stabilization Scheme
SYSMIN	Mineral Accident Insurance System
TUC	Trades Union Congress
UA	Unit of Account
UACEE	Union of Craft Industries and Trades of the European Community
UEMO	European Union of General Practitioners

UK	United Kingdom
UN	United Nations
UNICE	Union of Industries of the European Community
USA	United States of America
VAT	Tax on value added
VNO	Verbond van Nederlandse Ondernemingen
WC	Water closet
WCL	World Confederation of Labor
WEU	Western European Union

Bibliographical Essay

The literature on European integration has grown in quantity and sophistication just as EC integration itself has grown in the postwar period. This brief bibliographical essay traces the development of the European integrative process. The origins of the EC can be seen, of course, in events which far predate 1945—the Roman Empire, the Holy Roman Empire, Christiandom of the Middle Ages, the writings of various philosophers—but space does not allow a full recapitulation. One can perhaps say that the origins of the EC began in the interwar period when Benelux was established—a customs union among Belgium, the Netherlands, and Luxembourg (Alan Valentine, "Benelux: Pilot Plan of Economic Union," *The Yale Review* 44, no. 1 (September 1954)). In 1946, Winston S. Churchill, in a speech at Zurich, urged Franco-German reconciliation within "a kind of United States of Europe" (Winston S. Churchill, *The Sinews of Peace: Postwar Speeches*. London: Cassel and Co., 1948).

One year later, in 1947, U.S. Secretary of State George C. Marshall offered a massive injection of U.S. economic aid for a collective European Recovery Program (ERP) and in 1948, the Organization for European Economic Cooperation (OEEC, later called OECD) was established for the joint administration of Marshall Plan aid (Hans O. Schmitt, *The Path to European Union: From the Marshall Plan to the Common Market*. Baton Rouge: Louisiana State University Press, 1962). Cooperation in the military field increased with the 1948 Brussels Pact, a collective security agreement among France, the United Kingdom, and Benelux (Arnold J. Zurcher. *The Struggle to Unite Europe: 1940–1958*. New York: New York University Press, 1958) and in 1949 with the establishment of NATO (Lord Ismay; *NATO: The First Five Years, 1949–*

1954. Paris: NATO, 1955). The Council of Europe, strengthening European-wide cooperation in several areas and establishing some intergovernmental bodies, was also created in 1949 (A. H. Robertson; *The Council of Europe: Its Structure, Functions and Achievement*. London: Stevens and Sons, 1961).

In May 1950, French Foreign Minister Robert Schuman proposed placing Europe's coal and steel economies under a common European authority. In April 1951, the treaty establishing the European Coal and Steel Community (ECSC) was signed in Paris by France, Germany, Italy, and the Benelux countries. The ECSC's executive body, the High Authority, began functioning in August 1952, with Jean Monnet as first President, and in 1953 the ECSC had established a common market for coal, iron ore, scrap, and steel (William Diebold, Jr. *The Schuman Plan: A Study in Economic Cooperation, 1950–1959*. New York: Praeger, 1959; Louis Lister; *Europe's Coal and Steel Community*. New York: Twentieth Century Fund, 1960).

A further attempt to integrate along military lines was the European Defense Community (EDC), but this failed in 1954 (Clarence C. Walton; "Background for the European Defense Community;" *Political Science Quarterly* 68, no. 1 (March 1953); Hamilton Fish Armstrong; "Postscript to the EDC;" *Foreign Affairs* 33, no. 1 (October 1954)). The Western European Union (WEU) was established in 1955, and the six countries of the ECSC began talks aimed at the possible enlargement of the functional areas of integration (Tibor Scitovsky. *Economic Theory and Western European Integration*. Stanford, Calif: Stanford University Press, 1958). The Messina Conference was held in 1955, with the foreign ministers of the six deciding on further economic integration as the basis for future political unity (Comité Intergouvernmental crée par la Conférence de Messine; *Rapport des chefs de délégations aux ministres des affaires étrangères*. Brussels: 1956). In 1956, at the Venice Conference, the six foreign ministers authorized a subsequent conference to draft a treaty expanding European integration (Ernst B. Haas; *The Uniting of Europe: Political, Social and Economic Forces, 1950–1957*. Stanford, Calif: Stanford University Press, 1961).

The Treaty of Rome, creating the European Economic Community (EEC) and the European Atomic Energy Commission (Euratom), was signed in Rome in March 1957 (*Treaty Establishing the European Economic Community, Rome, 25 March 1957*. London: HMSO, 1973). The treaties went into force on January 1, 1958: Euratom's first President was Etienne Hirsch, and EEC Commission's first President was Walter Hallstein (Walter Hallstein; *United Europe: Challenge and Opportunity*. Cambridge, Mass: Harvard University Press, 1962, and *Europe in the Making*. New York: W.W. Norton, 1972). The Rome treaties established the governing institutions and organizations of the EEC: the Council of Ministers, a Court of Justice, the Commission, and a Parliament which, until direct popular elections in June 1979, was chosen by and from the six national Parliaments (David Coombes: *Politics and Bureaucracy in the European Community: A Portrait of the Commission of the EEC*. London: George Allen and Unwin, 1970; Sir Barnett Cocks, *The European Parliament: Structure, Procedure and Practice*. London: HMSO n.d.).

Western Europe was now split into two main economic areas: the Six of the EEC and the Seven of the European Free Trade Association (EFTA), created in 1960 by the United Kingdom, Norway, Denmark, Sweden, Austria, Switzerland, and Portugal (Emile Benoit: *Europe at Sixes and Sevens: The Common Market, the Free Trade Association and the United States*. New York: Columbia University Press, 1961). In late

1961 and early 1962, Denmark, Ireland, Norway, and the United Kingdom opened negotiations aimed at joining the EEC, but on January 14, 1963, French President Charles de Gaulle declared that the UK was "not ready" for Community membership. De Gaulle thus exercised a de facto veto, and shortly thereafter negotiations between the UK—and the other three—and the Community were broken off (Miriam Camps. *Britain and the European Community, 1955–1963*. Princeton, N.J.: Princeton University Press, 1964).

In June 1964, the first Yaoundé Convention entered into force, associating seventeen African states and Madagascar with the Community. In July 1965, the Council of Ministers failed to reach an agreement on financing a common farm policy. The French boycott of the Council of Ministers began a seven-month crisis, but in January 1966, the foreign ministers agreed to resume full Community activity (John Newhouse; *Collision in Brussels: The Common Market Crisis of 30 June 1965*. New York: W. W. Norton, 1967). In February 1967, the Community agreed to introduce the VAT turnover tax in all six countries (K. V. Antal. "Harmonisation of Turnover Taxes in the Common Market;" *Common Market Law Review* 1, no. 1 (June 1963); T. M. Rybczynski. *The Value Added Tax: The UK Position and the European Experience*. Oxford: Basil Blackwell, 1969). In July 1967, all Community executive institutions were merged, and the organization became known as the European Communities (EC). For the second time, Britain, Ireland, and Denmark, opened negotiations for EC membership, but in November 1967, de Gaulle "objected" to Britain's entry, and in late 1967 negotiations broke off once again.

A common external tariff (CET) and a full customs union were achieved in July 1968, and the Community was able to remove the last remaining restrictions on the free movement of workers as well as the last remaining national obstacles to member states' workers in employment, pay, and other conditions. Yaoundé II was signed in 1969, and the December 1969 Hague Summit of the EC foreign ministers agreed to complete, enlarge, and strengthen the EC. The UK, Denmark, Norway, and Ireland opened negotiations to enter the EC for the third time, and, with the resignation of Charles de Gaulle, entry was assured. The Norwegians rejected by a national referendum their country's entry in 1972, but on January 1, 1973, the United Kingdom, Ireland, and Denmark entered, enlarging the EC to nine members (Uwe Kitzinger. *Diplomacy and Persuasion: How Britain Joined the Common Market*. London: Thames and Hudson, 1973).

The period 1973–79 saw the EC solidify the base of economic and political integration by formulating common policies in regard to EC functional areas as well as with external relations. Some of these policies, however, were not very successful (Robert J. Lieber. *Oil and the Middle East War: Europe in the Energy Crisis*. Cambridge: Harvard Center for International Affairs, 1976); some policies were reasonably more successful (William F. Averyt, Jr. *Agropolitics in the European Community*. New York: Praeger, 1977; Bernard Bonnici. *Condition de Circulation et d'Etablissement des Médecins dans la CEE*. Paris: Editions Médicales et Universitaires, 1978; Frans A. M. Alting von Geusau. *The External Relations of the European Community*. Westmead England: D.C. Heath/Saxon House, 1974; Ph. Petit-Laurent. *Les Fondements politiques des engagements de la Communauté Européenne dans la Méditerranée*. Paris: Presses Universitaires de France, 1976; James Caporaso. *The Structure and Function of European Integration*. Pacific Palisades, Calif: Goodyear, 1974;

Helene Wallace; William Wallace; and Carole Webb. *Policy-Making in the Euro-pean Communities*. London: John Wiley and Sons, 1973; and Roger Williams. *European Technology: The Politics of Collaboration*. New York: John Wiley and Sons, 1973).

Recent developments, especially in 1979, point toward an increased and strength-ened process of integration: the European Monetary System (EMS) was established in March; Greece signed the Accession Treaty with a five-year transition period before becoming the tenth EC member; direct popular elections for the enlarged European Parliament were held in June; and Spain and Portugal are negotiating their entry into the EC. For current literature, one is well advised to see the *Journal of Common Market Studies, West European Politics, International Organization, World Politics, International Studies Quarterly, Common Market Law Review*, and the Official Journal of the European Communities.

Index

Accra Conference (UN), 230, 231, 232
ACP (African, Caribbean and Pacific) states, 199, 232, 233–35. *See also* LDCs; Third World; *names of individual countries*
Action Committee of Walloon Peasants, 134
Africa. *See* ACP; East African Community; ECA; OAU
Age: of farm workers, and financial aid, 131; and opinion on United States of Europe, 67; and support of EC, 72–73
Agence Europe (publication), 215
Agricultural units of account. *See* AUAs
Agriculture: policy, 236 (*see also* CAP); prices (*see* Prices: agricultural)
Agrimonetary system, 129. *See also* Currency
Algeria, 226, 236, 240, 242, 246, 253 n.33. *See also* Maghreb countries
Allon, Yigal, 241
Almond's functional analysis, 10, 98, 99
Alsace-Lorraine, 175
Antitrust policy, 13–14, 151–68; and trademark and patent rights, 166–67. *See also* Trade flows

ANZUS (Australia, New Zealand and U.S. Treaty Organization), 255
Arabs: and Arab-Israeli conflict (*see* Middle East conflict); and Arab League, 228, 241, 243–44, 246–47; and EC energy policy, 16, 190, 198; Summit Conference of (1973), 242. *See also* EAD; Oil
Armington, P. S., 80
Arusha Convention, 229, 230
Association of Cooperative Savings and Credit, 104, 116
Atlantic Alliance, 20, 239, 255, 257; and "Atlanticists," 238
Attali, Jacques, 205
AUAs (Agricultural units of account), 128, 137
Australia, 87
Australia, New Zealand and U.S. Treaty Organization (ANZUS), 255
Austria, 54, 87
Averyt, William F., Jr., 10, 100, 119 n.35, 135, 137

Banking Federation of the EEC. *See* BFEC

Beer, Samuel, 10, 100
Belgian Association of Authors, Composers, and Music Publishers. *See* SABAM
Belgium, 179; agriculture in, 129; and European Parliament, 28, 42, 50 n.12; health care system in, 186, 188 nn.16, 18; and Mediterranean policy, 239; and trade flow, 87, 160; and VAT, 214, 219. *See also* Benelux countries
Benelux countries, 86, 128. *See also* Belgium; Luxembourg; Netherlands
Benn, Tony, 202
Bertram, Christoph, 70
BEUC (European Bureau of Consumers Association), 106, 112–13, 114, 116
BFEC (Banking Federation of the EEC), 113, 116, 119 n.34
Bismarck, Prince Otto von, 175
Bretton Woods agreements, 262
British National Farmers' Union, 134
Brunner, Guido, 63, 192
Brussels, demonstrations in, 136, 138
Brussels Convention (1910), 186
Brzezinski, Zbigniew, 255, 258–59
Busch, Peter, 210
Buy American Act (U.S., 1933), 266. *See also* United States of America

Callaghan, James, 17
Cals (Dutch P.M., 1966), 218
Camp David Agreement, 247. *See also* Middle East conflict
Canada, 87, 263
CAP (Common Agricultural Policy), 9, 11–13, 41, 93 n.18, 265, 266; budget for, 147; and community decision-making, 123–24, 132–37; domestic policies and, 137–40; evolution of, 124–32; and farm interest groups, 135–37; and financial aid, 130–32, 138; growth and problems of, 123–47; national civil servants and, 141–44, 145; and prices (*see* Prices); and Special Committee on Agriculture, 133; U.S. view of, 21, 257–58, 266
Caporaso, James A., 10, 96, 98–100, 112, 210
Caribbean Community, 228. *See also* ACP
Carter, Jimmy, and Carter Administration, 21, 206, 258, 260, 262, 264, 267, 268
CDU/CSU (Christian Democratic Union/Christian Social Union, Germany), 54, 137
CEA (European Insurance Committee), 108, 113, 116, 119 n.34

CEEP (European Center of Public Enterprises), 113, 116, 119 n.34
Cementregling Voor Nederland decision, 160
Center for Industrial Development, 235
CERES (Centre d'Etudes, de Recherche, et d'Education Socialistes), 204
CGIL (Confederazione Generale Italiana del Lavoro), 102 n, 105
CGT (Confédération Générale du Travail), 102 n, 105
Chevènement, Jean-Pierre, 204
Cheysson, Claude, and Cheysson Plan, 226, 229, 241, 248, 249
Chile: U.S. policy toward, 206
Chirac, Jacques, 44
Christian Democratic Union (CDU), 137
Christian Democrats, 45, 105
Christian Social Union (CSU), 137
CIBE (Confederation of European Sugar Beet Producers), 134
CIC (International Confederation of Executive Staff), 105, 109, 110, 116
CIF (International Organization of National and International Public Service Unions), 105, 110, 116
Civil servants, national. *See* Integration
Club of Rome, 106
COCCEE (Committee of Commercial Organizations of the EEC), 109, 113, 115, 116, 119 n.34
COFACE (Committee of Family Organizations in the European Community, 105–6, 113, 114, 116
COMEPRA (European Committee for Agricultural Progress), 134
Committee of Commercial Organizations of the EEC. *See* COCCEE
Committee of Family Organizations in the European Community. *See* COFACE
Committee of Permanent Representatives. *See* CPR/COREPER
Committee of Professional Agricultural Organizations in the European Community. *See* COPA
Committee of Public Health Officials, 15, 179
Committee on Cooperation and Development. *See* European Parliament
Commodity Export Earnings Stabilization Scheme. *See* STABEX
Common Agricultural Policy. *See* CAP
Communism and Communist party: and Communist bloc nations, 21, 258; and European unity, 200; in France, 29, 43, 196, 200, 204,

205; influence of, 7, 8, 65–66; in Italy (PCI), 29, 195, 200; policies of, 195; represented in European Parliament, 44, 48; coalition with Social Democrats feared, 8, 65; and trade unions, 105; turnout of, in election for European Parliament, 29–30, 42–43
Community Tax on Value Added. *See* VAT
Competition. *See* Antitrust policy
Confédération Générale du Travail. *See* CGT
Confederation of European Sugar Beet Producers. *See* CIBE
Confederazione Generale Italiana del Lavoro. *See* CGIL
Conference on International Economic Cooperation, 226
Conference on Security and Cooperation, 259
Congress, U.S., 266, 267. *See also* United States of America
Connally, John, 21, 259
Conservatism: European attitude toward, 72–73; and "swing to Right," 5–7, 44–45, 47–48
Conservative government (France), 196, 199
Conservative party (Great Britain), 31, 38, 43, 44, 45, 51 n.16
Consultative Committee of the EC, 99
Consultative Committee for Medical Education, 15, 178, 179
Consultative Committee on Restrictive Practices and Monopolies, 156
Cooper, Richard, 258, 262
COPA (Committee of Professional Agricultural Organizations in the European Community), 11, 96, 108, 109, 110, 116, 135, 138–39; influence of, 100, 112–13, 115, 134
COREPER. *See* CPR/COREPER
Costa v. *ENEL*, 161, 167
Council of Europe, 259
Council of Ministers, 10, 11, 18, 210; and agricultural prices/policies, 126, 144, 146; and antitrust policies, 155, 156; as decision-making unit, 14–15, 132–36, 178; and developing countries, 226, 230, 234–38 passim, 245, 250; Directives of, 4, 14, 104, 179–81, 214, 219, 238; and health care policies, 15, 178–80; interest groups and, 99, 100–101, 110–16 passim; power shift to, 12, 132–33, 144; and VAT, 213–19 passim
Court of Justice, 110
CPR/COREPER (Committee of Permanent Representatives), 12, 133, 136, 142, 144–

45, 210, 217, 230, 234, 245
Currency: agrimonetary system and, 129; common European, 8; common European, "Europa," 261; common European, German attitude toward, 7, 56, 57, 65, 139; devaluation, 65, 128, 129, 138, 145–46; ECU (European Currency Unit), 139, 262; "green rates" and, 127–29, 138, 139, 145; reform considered, 261–62; revaluation, 128, 145–46; Smithsonian (exchange rate) Agreement, 264; U.S. dollar, 21, 128, 262–63, 268, 269; Western, Nixon and, 257, 262, 263. *See also* Inflation; Prices; Trade flows
Customs Union, 104, 105, 114, 151, 260

Dahrendorf, Ralf, 257, 259
Davignon Report, 225
DBV (Deutsche Bauern Verband), 134
Debré, Michel, 44
Debré, Robert, 174
Decision-making process, 4–5, 56, 96, 97; CAP and, 123–24, 132–37; on foreign policy, 247; interaction in, 135–37, 178; interest groups and, 106–9, 113, 116–17; national civil servants and, 124, 141–44, 145
De Gaulle, Charles, 205. *See also* France
de Larosière, Jacques, 198
Democratic Farmers' Action of Germany, 134
Denmark, 3, 87, 239; and agriculture, 131, 144; and currency value/prices, 128, 129; and European Parliament, 28, 34, 35, 40, 42, 45, 47; health care system in, 177, 180, 184, 185, 187 n.5
Deutsch, K. W., 4, 77
Deutsche Bauern Verband (DBV), 134
Developing countries. *See* Foreign policy; LDCs; Third World
Development Cooperation Group, 226
Diebold, William, 259
Dillon Round (tariff negotiations, 1962), 83, 88. *See also* Tariff(s)
Directives. *See* Council of Ministers

EAD (Euro-Arab Dialogue), 20, 199, 226, 229, 241–47, 253 n.36. *See also* Arabs
EAGGF (European Agricultural Guidance and Guarantee Fund), 12, 126–32 passim, 140, 144, 146–47, 250
East African Community, 229

Eastern Europe, 244; and rapprochement with West, 66–67, 69–70

EC (European Community), 260; enlargement of, 83, 104, 114, 239, 251, 259, 269 (*see also* Greece; Portugal; Spain); summit meetings of (*see* Summit meetings); U.S. Mission to, 256. *See also* Foreign policy; Integration

ECA (UN Economic Commission for Africa), 230, 231–32

EC Commission, 9, 10, 12, 20, 123 n, 210, 260, 261,264; and agricultural policies, 132 –38, 139, 144, 146 (*see also* CAP); and antitrust policies, 14, 153–68; as decision-making unit, 14–15, 132–36; and developing countries, 225, 226, 232–35, 237–38, 245, 247–48; and energy policies, 192–93, 261; and financing, 131; and health care policies, 15, 178–80; and interest groups, 97–101 passim, 104, 110–12, 116; and public-opinion surveys, 53 (*see also* Eurobarometers); U.S. and, 260; and VAT, 213, 214–15, 217–18

ECFTU (European Confederation of Free Trade Unions), 102 n, 105–6. *See also* ETUC

Economic and Monetary Union, 114

Economic and Social Committee, 8, 10, 99, 101, 110–11, 136

Economic Commission for Africa (UN). *See* ECA

ECSC (European Coal and Steel Community), 104, 250, 256, 260

ECU (European Currency Unit), 139, 262. *See also* Currency

EDC (European Defense Community), 256

EDF (European Development Fund), 233

EEB (European Bureau of the Environment), 106, 114, 115, 116

EEC (European Economic Community), 256; and EEC Treaty (*see* Treaty of Rome); as separte from ECSC and Euratom, 260

EFTA (European Free Trade Association), 81, 83, 85, 86–87, 88, 90, 92, 259

Egypt, 226, 247, 254 n.54. *See also* Mashrek countries

EIB (European Investment Bank), 236, 250, 262

Employment/unemployment: tradeoff with inflation, 195–96, 197–98. *See also* Inflation

EMS (European Monetary System), 4, 21

EMU (European Monetary Union), 139, 269

Energy and Research, EC Commissioner for, 63

Energy policy, 16–17, 189–207, 261; and EC energy consumption (table), 194; and energy crisis, 16–17, 189–90, 192, 196–97, 200, 201, 206; energy sources (table), 191; and IEA, 21, 192, 195, 200, 207; Middle East conflict and, 16, 189–90, 198; and nuclear power, 54, 193, 199, 207; U.S., 16, 17, 21, 190, 192, 198, 200–201, 206–7, 246, 267, 269. *See also* Oil

EO/WCL (European Organization of the World Confederation of Labor), 102 n, 105–6. *See also* ETUC

EP. *See* European Parliament

EPC (European Political Community), 256

Ertl, Joseph, 137

Ethiopia, 232

ETUC (European Trade Union Confederation), 96, 102 n, 105, 108, 109, 110, 113, 114, 115

EUA (European Units of Account), 193, 231, 236, 240, 252 n.23, 253 n.38

Euratom (European Atomic Energy Agency), 256, 260

Euro-Arab Dialogue. *See* EAD

Eurobarometers, 53; and European Parliament, 6, 29, 34, 48; and German attitude toward EC, 7, 71

Eurocommunism, 8, 65. *See also* Communism and Communist party

EUROCOOP (European Community of Consumer's Cooperatives), 113, 116

Eurocrats, 141, 145

"Europa" currency, 261. *See also* Currency

European Agricultural Guidance and Guarantee Fund. *See* EAGGF

European Atomic Energy Agency. *See* Euratom

European Bureau of Consumers Association. *See* BEUC

European Bureau of the Environment. *See* EEB

European Center of Public Enterprises. *See* CEEP

European Coal and Steel Community. *See* ECSC

European Committee for Agricultural Progress. *See* COMEPRA

European common currency. *See* Currency

European Community. *See* EC

European Community Council, 262

European Community of Consumer's Cooperatives. *See* EUROCOOP
European Confederation of Free Trade Unions. *See* ECFTU
European Conservative group, 44
European Convention of Human Rights, 180
European Council, meetings of. *See* Summit meetings
European Court of Justice, 13–14, 152–68
European Currency Unit. *See* ECU
European Defense Community (EDC), 256
European Development Fund (EDF), 233
European Economic Community. *See* EEC
European Free Trade Association. *See* EFTA
European Insurance Committee. *See* CEA
European Investment Bank. *See* EIB
European Monetary Fund, 262. *See also* EMS; EMU
European Organization of the World Confederation of Labor. *See* EO/WCL
European Parliament, 8, 10, 55, 101; Committee on Cooperation and Development, 234, 241; and decision-making, 136; and developing countries, 234, 235, 236, 238, 241; effect of direct elections to, 11, 112, 116; first direct election for (1979), 4, 6, 27–49; German attitude toward, 57 (*see also* Germany); interest groups and, 110, 111–12; limited powers of, 99, 112, 116; and "swing to Right," 5–7, 44–45, 47–48
European Political Community (EPC), 256
European Political Cooperation Effort (1970), 225
European Progressive Democrats, 44
European Secretariat of the Liberal, Intellectual, and Social Professions. *See* SEPLIS
European Social Fund, 119 n.36
European Trade Union Confederation. *See* ETUC
European Union of General Practitioners (UEMO), 181
European Units of Account. *See* EUA
EUROPMI (Liaison Committee for Small and Medium-Sized Industrial Enterprises in the EEC), 104, 116
Exchange rates. *See* Currency

FDP (Free Democratic party), 54, 137
Federal Republic of Germany. *See* Germany
Federal Reserve System (U.S.), 261, 269
Fédération Nationale des Producteurs de Lait (FNPL), 134

Feld, Werner, 11–13
Finland, 87
FIPMEC (International Federation of Small and Medium-Sized Enterprises), 108, 110, 116
Fiscal harmonization, 17–18, 209–21. *See also* Integration
Fitzgerald, G., 234
Flag, European, German attitude toward, 7, 56, 59, 61
FNPL (Fédération Nationale des Producteurs de Lait), 134
Foley, M., 252 n.16
Foot, Michael, 202
Ford, Gerald, and Ford Administration, 247, 258, 263
Foreign policy: and developing countries, 19–20, 225–51 (*see also* LDCs; Third World); Mediterranean area, 20, 236–41, 243, 246–48
France, 179, 210, 212, 263; agriculture in, 13, 129, 134, 140, 144, 146; attitude of, toward EC, 58; and colonies/developing countries, 229, 230, 231–32, 234, 236–37, 238, 239, 245; and currency/exchange rate, 128, 138, 139, 261; distribution of wealth in, 201; and EAD, 242; and EC energy policy, 16, 17, 190, 192–99 passim, 203–5, 246; and European Parliament, 29, 34, 42–43, 44, 50 n.15; "Gaullists" in, 42–43, 44, 196, 199; health care system in, 174–75, 177, 180–86 passim, 188 n.18; inflation in, 8, 65; leftist government/parties in, 29, 43, 196–200 passim, 202, 204–5; tariffs in, 86, 265; and trade flow, 86, 87, 140, 160, 195, 205, 265; and VAT, 214, 219
Free Democratic party (FDP), 54, 137
"Fresco," 226, 227
Frisch, D., 252 n.15

Gardiner, Robert, 230, 231
GATT (General Agreement on Tariffs and Trade), 21, 88, 195, 200, 205, 207, 231, 237, 258, 261, 263, 266. *See also* Tariff(s)
"Gaullists," 42–43, 44, 196, 199
GCECEE (Savings Bank Group of the European Community), 115–16
GDP (Gross Domestic Product), 81, 87–88, 264–65
General Agreement on Tariffs and Trade. *See* GATT
Generalized System of Tariff Preferences

(GSP), 199. *See also* Tariff(s)
German Farmers' Union (DBV, Deutsche Bauern Verband), 134
Germany (German Federal Republic), 210, 263; agricultural policies and, 123, 129, 131, 134, 137, 144; and currency value/inflation, 7–8, 65, 128, 139, 262, 263, 268; and developing countries, 229, 234, 239, 247; and EC energy policies, 193, 195, 196, 200, 205; and European currency, 56, 57, 65, 139; and European Parliament, 34, 41, 43, 50 n.15, 56–58, 60, 62, 65–66, 70; European stance of, 7–8, 54–73; Federal Cartel Office, 162; health care system in, 173–74, 175, 180, 183; inflation in, 7–8, 65, 128, 139, 262, 263, 268; intervention prices in, 129; and trade flow, 86, 87, 88, 146, 160, 198, 264, 265, 267; and U.S., 201, 267; and VAT, 213, 219
Ghana, 254 n.54
Giscard d'Estaing, Valery, 194, 196, 204, 261, 269; and Giscardians, 42–43
GNP (Gross National Product), 127, 203
Government, European: common, German attitude toward, 56, 58; domestic and international constraints on, 196–200; leftist, 17, 194–206; leftist, policy choices for (table), 202 (*see also* Communism and Communist party; Labour party; Socialist party and ideology)
Gowon, Yakubu, 233
Graham, Judge, 159
Great Britain, 87, 179, 196, 261, 263; agriculture in, 129; currency valuation of, 128, 138; and developing countries, 229, 230, 231–32, 234, 239; and EC energy policy, 16, 17, 190, 193, 196, 203; as EEC member, 3, 265; and "European Currency Unit," 139; and European Parliament, 28–31, 37–38, 40, 41, 43–44, 45, 47–48, 50 n.15; health care system in, 176, 177–78, 180, 181, 184, 188 n.18; and inflation, 147; interest groups of, 100; intervention prices in, 129; and "swing to Right," 6, 7, 44; and VAT, 214. *See also* Labour party
Greece: possible admission of, to EC, 4, 13, 16, 55, 140, 146, 185, 239, 251, 259, 269; U.S. policy toward, 206
"Green rates." *See* Currency
Gross Domestic Product. *See* GDP
Gross National Product. *See* GNP
GSP (Generalized System of Tariff Preferences), 199. *See also* Tariff(s)

Guinea, 232

Haas, Ernst B., 10, 95, 96, 106, 210
Hague, The: meetings at (*see* Summit meetings). *See also* Netherlands
Hallstein doctrine, 239
Health policies, 4, 14–16, 171–87; and health care systems, 173–78
Hoefnagels, W. L. G. M., 216, 217, 218
Hospital Physicians Charter (1967), 14, 172
Human Rights, European Convention of, 180

ICFTU (International Confederation of Free Trade Unions), 102 n, 105. *See also* ETUC
IEA (International Energy Agency/Association), 21, 192, 193, 195, 200, 207
IMF (International Monetary Fund), 192, 195, 198, 200, 206, 207, 258, 261, 262
Import levies. *See* Tariff(s)
Inflation, 261, 265, 267, 269; CAP and, 12, 147; in France, 204; in Germany, 7–8, 65, 139, 268; and "stagflation," 198; tradeoff with employment, 195–96, 197–98; in U.S., 198, 264, 268. *See also* Currency; Prices; Trade flows
Inglehart, Ronald, 6
Institut für Demoskopie, 70
Integration: CAP and, 123–24 (*see also* CAP); civil servants and, 12, 124, 141–44, 145; contemporary perspectives on, 3–22; definitions of, 98; delay in, 211; economic, 9–10, 77–92, 142, 209–21, 261 (*see also* Trade flows); German attitude toward, 55–72; interest groups and, 95–177; Subcommittee on European Integration Affairs, 218. *See also* EC; United States of Europe
Interest groups: aims and objectives of, 109–10; behavior of, at community level, 95–117; channels of influence of, 110–12, 134–35; definition of, 95–96; evolution of, 101–12; and farm strategies, 135, 136; impact of, 10–11, 112–15
Interministerial Coordinating Committee, 218
International Confederation of Executive Staff. *See* CIC
International Confederation of Free Trade Unions. *See* ICFTU
International Energy Agency/Association. *See* IEA
International Federation of Small and Medium-Sized Enterprises. *See* FIPMEC
International Institute for Strategic Studies (London), 70

International Monetary Fund. *See* IMF
International Organization of National and International Public Service Unions. *See* CIF
Ireland, 3, 128, 179, 261; agriculture in, 129, 134, 144; and developing countries, 234, 239; and European Parliament, 28, 39, 41, 43, 45; health care system in, 178, 184, 188 n.16
Israel: conflict with Arabs (*see* Middle East conflict, Palestinian people and issue); EC negotiations with, 238, 239–40, 241
Italy, 210, 263; agriculture in, 13, 129, 134, 140, 146; Communist party in (PCI), 29, 195, 200; and currency/exchange rate, 128, 139, 261; and developing countries, 234, 236–38; and EC energy policies, 16, 17, 190, 193, 195, 196, 246; and European Parliament, 29, 30, 35, 37, 42, 45; health care system in, 176–77, 180, 184, 185, 188 n.18; inflation in, 8, 65; Socialist party in (PSI), 195; tariffs in, 86; and trade flow, 87, 146, 205; U.S. policy toward, 206; and VAT, 213, 219

Japan, 263; and energy policy, 16, 21, 190, 200; and trade flow, 87, 88, 195, 198, 244, 264, 266, 267, 268, 269; Trilateral Commission, 258–59, 269; U.S. and, 256, 257
Jenkins, Roy, 260, 261, 269
Johnson, Harold, 19, 20–22
Jones, Jack, 202
Jordan, 226, 252 n.25. *See also* Mashrek countries

Kennedy Round (tariff negotiations, 1968–72), 83, 88, 264. *See also* Tariff(s)
Khelil, Ismail, 243
Kirschner, Emil, 8, 10–11
Kissinger, Henry, 20, 201, 247, 257, 258
Koester, Ulrich, 124
Kon, Stephen, 11, 13–14
Korvar, R., 165
Krohn, H.-B., 252 n.16

Labor unions. *See* Trade unions
Labour party (Great Britain), 198, 200, 202–3; and European Parliament, 6, 31, 37–38, 43, 44, 48, 51 n.16
Language: coefficients, and trade flow, 8, 90, 91, 92; differences, German attitude toward, 64; and language barrier in health care, 15, 179–80, 185

La Palombara, Joseph, 10, 100
Law: municipal and community, balance between, 151–68; patent and trademark rights, 166–67
LC/IRU (Liaison Committee of Professional Transport of the European Community), 105, 114, 116
LDCs (less developed countries), 104, 199; and EC development policies, 19, 225–51. *See also* Third World
Lebanon, 226, 239, 245. *See also* Mashrek countries
Lecourt, Robert, 154
Leftist governments. *See* Government, European
Less developed countries. *See* LDCs
Liaison Committee for Small and Medium-Sized Industrial Enterprises in the EEC. *See* EUROPMI
Liaison Committee of Professional Road Transport of the European Community. *See* LC/IRU
Liberal party (Great Britain), 38, 51 n.16
Liberia, 232
Libya, 246, 252 nn.26,27
Lieber, Robert J., 11, 16–17, 96
Lindberg, Leon, 4, 10, 95, 96, 210
Lomé Conventions/policy, 20, 199, 226, 229, 235–37, 240, 246, 248, 250, 253 n.38, 259
London Summit meeting (1977). *See* Summit meetings
Lück case, 165
Luxembourg, 129, 178, 179, 239, 242; and European Parliament, 42, 50 n.12. *See also* Benelux countries

Maghreb countries, 226, 237, 238, 239–40, 252 n.26, 253 n.38. *See also* Algeria; Morocco
Mally, Gerhard, 248
Malta, 259
Marshall Plan, 256
Mascaro, Jean-Marc, 11, 14–16
Mashrek countries, 226, 239–40, 253 n.38. *See also* Egypt; Jordan; Lebanon
Mauritius, 229
Mayras, Advocate-General, 158
MCAs (Monetary Compensatory Amounts), 127–29, 138–39, 140, 145–47. *See also* Currency; Prices
Medical policies. *See* Health policies
Mediterranean policy. *See* Foreign policy
Meyer, Klaus, 253 n.43

Meynaud, 96

Middle East conflict, 241, 242, 243; and Camp David Agreement, 247; and EC energy policy, 16, 189–90, 198; Palestinian people and issue, 244, 245, 246, 247; Yom Kippur War, 242, 257. *See also* EAD

Migration: and migrant labor, 238, 243; of physicians, 16, 185–86 (*see also* Health policies)

Mineral Accident Insurance System. *See* SYSMIN

Mitrany, David, 10, 96

Mitterrand, François, 17, 201, 204, 205, 206

MNCs (multi-national corporations), 200, 234, 246

Mondale, Walter, 260

Monnet, Jean, 221

Morocco, 226, 238, 252 nn.27,31. *See also* Maghreb countries

"Moro Memorandum," 237, 238

Multi-national corporations. *See* MNCs

National Alliance of Italian Farmers, 134

National Federation of Milk Producers in France (FNPL, Fédération Nationale des Producteurs de Lait), 134

Nationalism, 17, 170; German, 56, 61, 64, 65

Nationalization programs, 97, 114, 197, 204; and renationalization, 147

National League of Family Farmers of Ireland, 134

NATO (North Atlantic Treaty Organization), 70, 206, 255, 256

Nelson, Charles G., 4

Netherlands, 210; agriculture in, 129, 131, 144; and developing countries, 229, 234, 239; and EC energy policies, 190, 192, 196; health care system in, 177, 180, 181–82, 185, 188 n.18; and trade flow, 87, 160, 196; and VAT episode, 17–18, 209, 212–21. *See also* Benelux countries

New Zealand, 255

NHS (National Health Service). *See* Health policies

Nigeria, 233

Nixon, Richard, and Nixon Administration, 20–21, 247, 257, 259, 262, 263; "New Economic Policy" of, 21, 257, 258; Nixon Doctrine, 20, 256

Noelle-Neumann, Elisabeth, 6, 7–8

North Atlantic Treaty Organization. *See* NATO

Norway, 31, 87, 196, 261

Nuclear energy. *See* Energy policy

Nuremberg Charter (1967), 14, 172

OAPEC (Organization of Arab Petroleum Exporting Countries), 190, 198, 207

OAU (Organization for African Unity), 228, 232, 233

OECD (Organization for Economic Cooperation and Development), 8, 16–17, 259, 260, 261, 265; and energy crisis, 190, 192, 195, 198, 200, 205; trade flow among countries of, 77, 83–87, 92

OEEC (Organization for European Economic Cooperation), 256

Oil: boycott, 190; EAD control of, 246; and EC negotiations with oil-producing states, 16, 190, 205–6; European imports of, 190–98 passim, 204; "foreign tax" on, 196; North Sea, 193, 203; prices, 21, 192, 247, 260, 263, 268; U.S. imports of, 267, 268. *See also* Energy policy; OAPEC; OPEC

Olympic team, European, German attitude toward, 7, 56, 58, 60–61

OPEC (Organization of Petroleum Exporting Countries), 198, 207, 228, 233, 260, 268

Organization for African Unity. *See* OAU

Organization for Economic Cooperation and Development. *See* OECD

Organization for European Economic Cooperation (OEEC), 256

Organization of Arab Petroleum Exporting Countries. *See* OAPEC

Organization of Petroleum Exporting Countries. *See* OPEC

Osgood, Robert, 256

Pacific states. *See* ACP; SEATO; South Pacific Forum

Palestine Liberation Organization (PLO), 244

Palestinian people and issue. *See* Middle East conflict

Papadopoulos, George, 206

Paracelse, Théophraste, 171

"Paris-Berlin: 1900 to 1933" (Paris exhibition), 71

Paris meeting (1972). *See* Summit meetings

Parsky, Gerald, 254 n.52

Parti Communiste Francais. *See* PCF

Parti Socialiste. *See* PS

Patent rights, 166–67

PC (Permanent Conference of Chambers of Commerce and Industry of the EEC), 113, 115, 116, 119 n.34
PCF (Parti Communiste Francais), 205. *See also* Communism and Communist party
PCI (Italian Communist Party), 195. *See also* Italy
Permanent Committee of Physicians of the EC, 15, 178–79, 181
Permanent Conference of Chambers of Commerce and Industry of the EEC. *See* PC
"Philip" Report, 232
Physicians: comparative figures on, 174, 182, 185. *See also* Health policies
Pirzio-Biroli, Corrado, 19–20
PLO (Palestine Liberation Organization), 244
Portugal, 87, 198; possible admission of, to EC, 4, 13, 16, 55, 140, 146, 185, 239, 251, 259, 269; U.S. policy toward, 206
Pravda, 29, 39
Prewo, Wilfried, 8–10
Prices: agricultural, 12, 13, 112–14, 117, 125–26, 128, 137–38, 139, 267, (*see also* COPA); "common," 138–39; energy, 196 (*see also* Oil); food, 12, 124, 126, 129; intervention, 125–26, 129, 145. *See also* Currency; Inflation; Trade flows
Protectionism. *See* Tariff(s)
PS (Parti Socialiste), 200, 204–5. *See also* Socialist party and ideology
PSI (Italian Socialist Party), 195
Public-opinion surveys. *See* Eurobarometers
Puchala, Donald J., 4, 11, 17–18

RA (relative acceptance) model (Savage and Deutsch), 4, 77
Rabier, Jacques-René, 6
"Railway test," 69, 71
Relative acceptance model. *See* RA
Roemer, Advocate-General, 163, 168, 205
Rome Treaty. *See* Treaty of Rome
Rosenthal, Glenda G., 135, 137, 210

SABAM (Belgian Association of Authors, Composers, and Music Publishers) case, 157–59, 166
Sanu, Olu, 233
Saudi Arabia, 206, 242
Savage, I. R., 77; and Savage-Deutsch RA model, 4
Savings Bank Group of the European Community (GCECEE), 115–16

Scandinavia, 86. *See also* Denmark; Norway; Sweden
Scanlon, Hugh, 202
Schartzel, J. Robert, 256
Scheingold, Stuart A., 210
Schmidt, Helmut, 137, 269
Schmitter, Philippe C., 10, 96, 97–98
Schuijt Report, 243
SEATO (Southeast Asian Treaty Organization), 255
Senegal, 230
Senghor, L., 230
SEPLIS (European Secretariat of the Liberal, Intellectual, and Social Professions), 106, 109, 114, 116
Schultz, George, 265
Sidjanski, Dusan, 96–97, 210
Sidki, Ahmed, 244
Sirena case, 167
Smith, Arnold, 230
Smithsonian (exchange rate) Agreement, 264
Social Democratic party. *See* SPD
Socialist party and ideology, 105; Arab, 248; and European Parliament, 31, 42–43, 45, 48; in France, 196, 197, 199, 200, 204, 249; in Germany, 65; in Italy (PSI), 195; and Leninist socialism, 197; in Portugal, 198
Southeast Asian Treaty Organization (SEATO), 255
South Pacific Forum, 228. *See also* ACP
Soviet Union, 67, 206, 241
Spaak, Fernard, 264
Spain, 200, 201; EC negotiations with, 238; possible admission of, to EC, 4, 13, 16, 55, 140, 146, 185, 239, 251, 259, 269; and trade, 87, 239; U.S. policy toward, 206
SPD (Social Democratic party), 42, 54, 67, 97, 105, 200; coalition with Communists feared, 8, 65
Special Committee on Agriculture, 133. *See also* CAP
"Spillover" concept, 96, 142
STABEX (Commodity Export Earnings Stabilization Scheme), 199, 233, 234, 235, 236, 240, 249
Structure and Function of European Integration, The (Caporaso), 98
Subcommittee on European Integration Affairs, 218. *See also* Integration
Sudan, 232
Summit meetings, 136; Arab (1973, Algiers), 242; European Community (1969, Hague),

104, 225; European Community (1972, Paris), 104, 106, 226, 234, 238, 247, 260; European Community (1973, Copenhagen), 201, 242; European Community (1974), 260; European Community (1978, Bremen), 139; London (1977), EC represented at, 21, 261, 263–64, 270; OAU (1973, Addis Ababa), 233

Sweden, 87, 261

Switzerland, 86, 87

Syria, 226. *See also* Mashrek countries

SYSMIN (Mineral Accident Insurance System), 235, 236, 240

Tariff(s), 78, 80; changes in, 8, 82, 86–87, 91, 92, 257; elasticities, 88, 90, 91; GSP and, 199; and import levies, 126, 127–28; negotiations, 83, 88, 258, 264–65; and protectionism, 199–200, 257–58, 264, 266, 269; reductions/elimination of, 9, 83, 87, 88, 212, 238, 257. *See also* GATT

Tate and Lyle (British MNC), 234

Taxation policies, 212–14. *See also* VAT

Technical Center for Agricultural and Rural Cooperation, 236

Third World, 19, 20, 21, 193, 258; and EC development policies, 225–51. *See also* LDCs

Tindemans, Leo, 260

Tokyo Round/Declaration (tariff negotiations, 1973), 258, 264, 265, 266. *See also* Tariff(s)

Tönnies, Ferdinand, 54

Trade Expansion, Trade Reform Acts (U.S.), 257–58

Trade flows, 9; currency revaluation and, 146; diversion vs. creation, 83, 86–87, 90; elasticities of, 87–88; Europe-Arab world, 243–44; interdependence of, 77–92, 195–200, 205; interstate, 160; and LDCs, 104; and oil boycott, 192 (*see also* Energy policy; Oil); "Trilateralism" and, 21, 258, 259, 269; U.S. and, 87, 244, 264, 265–69. *See also* Antitrust policy; Currency; Tariff(s)

Trademark rights, 166–67

Trades Union Congress (TUC), 202

Trade unions, 117; agricultural, 134; and consumer/environmental issues, 114, 115; "international" character of, 105; left-wing divergences, 195

Transaction flow analyses, 5, 9, 77–79; "measurement without theory" in, 78

Treaty of Rome (EEC Treaty), 4, 87, 93 n.18, 105, 106, 110, 190, 209; and CAP, 124–25, 132, 146; and development cooperation, 225, 226, 229, 236, 237, 248; and fiscal harmonization, 212, 215; and health care, 171–72, 178, 180, 184; municipal-community law balance in application of, 151–68

Tribunal de Première Instance (inferior court) of Brussels, 157

Trilateral Commission, and "Trilateralism," 21, 258, 259, 269

Tripartite Conferences on Employment and Social Questions, 110

TUC (Trade Union Congress), 202

Tuk, C. P., 216, 217, 218

Tunisia, 226, 238, 239, 240, 252 nn.27,31. *See also* Maghreb countries

Turkey, 259

UACEE (Union of Craft Industries and Trades of the European Community), 116

UEMO (European Union of General Practitioners), 181

UN (United Nations), 206, 226, 230, 234, 242; Economic Commision for Africa (*see* ECA)

UNICE (Union of Industries of the European Community), 96, 109, 110, 113, 115–16, 119 n.34

Union of Craft Industries and Trades of the European Community (UACEE), 116

Union of Industries of the European Community. *See* UNICE

United States of America, 193; dollar, value of (*see* Currency); energy policy of (*see* Energy policy); interest groups of, 100; as oil importer, 267, 268; policy options for, 17, 206–7; position of, vis-à-vis EC, 17, 20–22, 192, 195, 198, 200–201, 206–7, 230, 239, 241, 246–47; position of, vis-à-vis EC, in post-Kissinger era, 255–70; and trade flow, 87, 244, 264, 265–69; trade legislation in, 257–58, 266

United States of Europe, 55–58, 65–70, 139, 141; German attitude toward, 56, 69, 72. *See also* Integration

Uniting of Europe, The (Haas), 210

Vaissière, Roger, 11, 14–16

VAT (value-added tax): agricultural prices and, 127; the Dutch and, 17–18, 209, 212–21

Veil, Simone, 27
Vondeling, A., 216

Wägenbaur, Rolf, 180
Wallace, Helen, 210
Walrasian theory, 79
Walt-Wilhelm case, 161–65, 168
Washington Energy Conference, 192, 201.
 See also United States of America
WCL (World Confederation of Labor), 102 n,
 105. *See also* ETUC

Wilson, Harold, and Wilson government, 17,
 202
World Bank, 206
World Confederation of Labor. *See* WCL

Yaoundé Conventions, 229–34, 237
Yemens, 246
Yom Kippur War. *See* Middle East conflict
Yugoslavia, 248, 252 n.25, 254 n.54

Zijlstra, Jelle, 218–19

About the Editor

LEON HURWITZ is associate professor of political science at Cleveland State University in Cleveland, Ohio. He is the author of *Introduction to Politics*, as well as articles in *Political Studies, Comparative Politics*, and other journals.

Contributors

WERNER J. FELD (Referendar [Law], University of Berlin; Ph.D., political science, Tulane University) is professor and chair, Department of Political Science, University of New Orleans.

LEON HURWITZ (Ph.D., political science, Syracuse University) is associate professor, Department of Political Science, Cleveland State University.

RONALD INGLEHART (Ph.D., political science, University of Chicago) is professor, Department of Political Science, and a faculty associate at the Institute for Social Research, Center for Political Studies, University of Michigan.

HAROLD S. JOHNSON (Ph.D., political Science, University of Michigan) is professor of political science, Justin Morrill InterCollege Programs and professor of racial and ethnic studies, Michigan State University.

EMIL J. KIRCHNER (Ph.D., political science, Case Western Reserve University) is lecturer, Department of Government, University of Essex (United Kingdom).

STEPHEN D. KON (B.A., University of Sussex; dipl. supérieur d'hautes études européennes, College of Europe, Bruges) is a Solicitor of the Supreme Court of England and Wales and lecturer in law, School of European Studies, University of Sussex (United Kingdom).

ROBERT J. LIEBER (Ph.D., political science, Harvard University) is professor and chair, Department of Political Science, University of California at Davis.

JEAN-MARC MASCARO (M.D., University of Strasbourg) is an anesthesiologist in private group practice in Grenoble (France).

ELISABETH NOELLE-NEUMANN (Ph.D., mass communications, University of Berlin) is professor of mass communications, Johannes Gutenberg University, Mainz, and director of the Institut für Demoskopie Allensbach, Allensbach am Bodensee (West Germany).

CORRADO PIRZIO-BIROLI (Ph.D., economics, Rome State University; dipl. economic planning and dipl. industrial development programming, Institute of Social Studies, The Hague) is currently an economic counselor at the Delegation of the European Commission to the United States (Washington, D.C.).

WILFRIED PREWO (Ph.D., political economy, Johns Hopkins University) is a research associate, Institut für Weltwirtschaft, University of Kiel (West Germany).

DONALD J. PUCHALA (Ph.D., political science, Yale University) is professor, Department of Government and director, Institute on Western Europe, Columbia University.

JACQUES-RENÉ RABIER (licencié en droit et en economie; dipl. de l'Ecole libre des Sciences politiques), a former EC Director-General, is currently a Special Advisor to the EC Commission for Public Opinion (Brussels).

ROGER VAISSIÈRE (M.D., University of Paris) is an anesthesiologist in private group practice in Grenoble (France) and is a director of the *caisse primaire* of the French national health insurance system.